MAKING SENSE
OF AMERICA

LEGACIES OF SOCIAL THOUGHT

Charles Lemert, Series Editor

Roads from Past to Future (1997), by Charles Tilly

The Voice of Anna Julia Cooper, including "A Voice from the South" and other essays, papers, and letters (1998), edited by Charles Lemert and Esme Bhan

Making Sense of America: Sociological Analyses and Essays (1999), by Herbert J. Gans

MAKING SENSE
OF AMERICA

Sociological Analyses and Essays

· Herbert J. Gans ·

ROWMAN & LITTLEFIELD PUBLISHERS, INC.
Lanham • Boulder • New York • Oxford

ROWMAN & LITTLEFIELD PUBLISHERS, INC.

Published in the United States of America
by Rowman & Littlefield Publishers, Inc.
4720 Boston Way, Lanham, Maryland 20706

12 Hid's Copse Road
Cumnor Hill, Oxford OX2 9JJ, England

British Library Cataloguing in Publication Information Available

Library of Congress Cataloging-in-Publication Data

Gans, Herbert J.
    Making sense of America : sociological analyses and essays /
Herbert J. Gans.
        p.   cm.
    Includes bibliographical references.
    ISBN 0-8476-9040-7 (alk. paper).—ISBN 0-8476-9041-5 (pbk. :
alk. paper)
        1. United States—Social conditions—1945–   2. Minorities—United
States.   3. Sociology—United States.   I. Title.
HN57.G23   1999
306′.0973—dc21   98-36860
                                                                        CIP

Printed in the United States of America

∞ ™ The paper used in this publication meets the minimum requirements of
American National Standard for Information Sciences—Permanence of Paper for
Printed Library Materials, ANSI Z39.48–1984.

For Louise and David, as Ever

Contents

Series Editor's Foreword

For social scientists, in 1969 in Boston, the only game in town was the Friday luncheon lecture at the Harvard-M.I.T. Joint Center for Urban Studies. Or, so it seemed to me. Bob Wood, one of the Kennedy-Johnson era's most brilliant urban policy makers, had just returned from Washington to become the Center's director. He presided elegantly over the confusion, his ever present worry beads well in hand. Barney Frank, now a United States congressman from Massachusetts, was then very young but still the most visible of Boston mayor Kevin White's administrative staffers. Frank, as I recall, moved about the room in stocking feet to seek and find any opportunity to proclaim his views in the rapid-fire, sure-sighted, but slightly lisped speech for which he is still famous.

Everyone and anyone who cared about urban politics made it his or her business to put in an appearance. We younger associates of the Joint Center vied with, among others of our lesser rank, the many followers of Boston's and M.I.T.'s Mel King for a place at the table—a chance to hear, perhaps get known by, any of the many notables who inhabited this wonderful, uncertain local moment in the afterglow of the Great Society.

Herb Gans was a regular at these weekly festivals. He had, if I remember well, accepted a position at M.I.T. (one that was, in any case, short-lived). I did not have the impression that the Cambridge circus was his cup of tea. Though my acquaintance with him, then and since, has been slight but thoroughly positive, I remember him most of all from those Friday afternoons in 1969. Somehow Herbert Gans was not like all those characters who, in the spirit of the times, were so full of themselves, perhaps in inverse relation to their sense that Nixon's election meant the end of their dreams to remake the world.

I do not remember when, exactly, I associated this youthful, passing encounter with Gans with a photograph of him that appears in *The Urban Villagers*. But that photograph has long since explained to me at least why he did not seem to enjoy the mix in Cambridge. In it, Herb Gans is seated amid one of the expanded families of the West End. They are gathered at the kitchen table, the domestic center of social life in their community. Food and wine fill the table. All are smiling. Gans is too. Indeed, he is among those in the picture who seem perfectly at ease with the camera they are facing. His smile and manner are relaxed. His hand holds, it would seem, a fork of food, poised in abeyance until the picture is taken. Herb Gans is, if not exactly at home, at least at ease among these people about whom he would write one of the most admired and important books in American sociology.

Herbert Gans's success as a sociologist has a great deal to do with his ability to distinguish between the values of local people living in neighborhood and the free form play of an academic circus. The point I take from the photo is that Herbert Gans seems always, and unfailingly, to have kept his sociological values straight, clear, and honest.

Making Sense of America offers the reader the supreme delight of reading the best work of a sociologist who, since his first published report in 1951 on field work in Park Forest, a Jewish community outside Chicago, has been taking to the field in order, quite simply, to understand. Yet, what Gans has come up with over the years is never quite simple. Always clearly conveyed, his ideas somehow reach with disciplined ease from the experience of those he studies to the experience of his readers. This, of course, is most true of his well-read ethnographies.

Plans for urban redevelopment are one thing to movers and shakers at boisterous luncheons in Cambridge. They were quite another to the folk of modest means who lost their homes just across the Charles River because, among other reasons, they had no idea, literally, just what destructive effects "redevelopment" meant for their community. That the men and women of Boston's West End in the 1950s, most of them second-generation Italian immigrants, were unable to resist the plans to take their homes is, when you think about it, a startlingly complex idea. How can it be that people cannot see the social evil about them? Gans was not the first to ask the question. But, in *The Urban Villagers,* he was a pioneer in answering it in a compelling way. With the one hand, he told the story of the men and women with whom he lived and ate for a year or so in order, with the other hand, to draw the lines from their experiences to some of sociology's most unsettling concepts. In the early chapters of that book (well before the selection in *this* book), Gans stops just short of saying that the West Enders, in effect, possess no self as we middle-class acculturated think of self. They were, instead, too dependent on their local peer group society, which demanded so much of the West Ender's personal energies that too little (or almost nothing) was left over for even trying to deal with the largely hostile world beyond their neighborhood (or city). This Gans said about the same time Erving Goffman, in a very different way, was saying much the same thing. But he said it more cleanly than Goffman, who always dealt a mysterious literary hand. In the process of accounting for the structure of group and self among the West Enders, Gans helped subsequent generations of students understand for the first time the meaning of George Herbert Mead's utterly abstract concept of the self-constituting dialogue of the "I" and the "Me." This is but one example.

It is entirely possible to use the early chapters of *The Urban Villagers* as a kind of introductory text for first year sociology studies. It would be hard to find a more lucid account of the basic concepts of self, family, community, and social structures displayed in all their empirical grandeur. This is not less true for Gans's work as a whole.

To read *Making Sense of America* is to take a basic course in sociology and to learn how basic topics like ethnicity, politics, and popular culture might be better understood. The reader will also see that, though Herbert Gans never waves and shouts, he is perfectly capable of surprising turns of the sociological imagination. Though, as he says, he wrote "The Positive Functions of Poverty" with dead seriousness, the reader cannot help but be disturbed to good effect by the counterintuitive adjective "positive"—and, thus, to be drawn even deeper into the sad mysteries of life in American society.

Making Sense of America is a title well chosen. American society, like most others but to an extreme degree, does not make a great deal of sense. What Herbert Gans has done over his distinguished career as one of his adopted country's most widely read and influential sociologists is, precisely, to make sense of it. Yet, notwithstanding the honors that have come his way, Herbert Gans has never lost touch with the simplest, first principles to which any sociologist who seeks to understand the world must adhere. The very act of "making sense" may not be all that difficult to practice, but it can only be practiced well and effectively when the sociologist keeps his language clear, his head unmuddled, and his heart patient unto the careful, slow work of living with, listening to, then thinking long and hard about the lives of people in communities—Jewish people in Park Forest, new suburbanites in Levittown, the men and women who run the newsrooms of the American media, and even the community of sociologists whom Gans has studied most recently.

Making Sense of America is a book that will instruct its readers about many of the senses of American life, as it will lead them to appreciate how the very process of making sociological sense might work. You won't find an academic circus here. There are no impossible to comprehend locutions and no overheated claims. Just plain and good sense. This collection is, in effect, a reminder to the many who have forgotten that, whatever its problems, sociology is a staple of life in the modern world. Herbert Gans lets us see once again just what good sociological sense is.

—Charles Lemert

PREFACE

I am a Jewish refugee from Nazi Germany who arrived on the shores of the United States in 1940, and, like many another immigrant to this country, I have spent a lifetime trying to make sense of America. So far, I cannot say that I have succeeded, but I have turned my curiosity into an exciting and productive career. Indeed, just about all my sociological work—as a teacher, researcher, and writer of sociology—has been about America.

Moreover, my immigrant origin has been my source of interest in several of the specific fields of sociology in which I have worked. For example, being a very poor immigrant influenced my later concern about poverty, and coming here as a Jewish refugee led to my subsequent interest in ethnicity. I think even my fascination with participant-observation—now sometimes called ethnography—as a sociological method is connected to my origins. Not having grown up among Americans may be partly responsible for my desire to be with the people I have studied rather than looking at them from the distance created by survey research or statistical analyses. (I describe other connections between my origins and my research in Appendix A.)

This book offers my favorite essays in some of the above-mentioned and other fields.★ It also has other aims to show—to the students and others who read it—that sociological research and writing can be put to a variety of uses. (Its alternative title might be *Varieties of Sociology.*)

One such use is the analysis and critique of public and private policy. Actually, the book begins with such an analysis—the destruction urban renewal wreaks upon poor people's neighborhoods—taken from my first book, *The Urban Villagers,* and it ends with a policy critique that appeared in, of all places, a review of a children's book. Sociology is also helpful

---

★Not all the fields in which I have published are represented here, and the essays on my work in urban planning, urban poverty, and related fields appear in another collection: *People, Plans and Policies: Essays on Poverty, Racism and Other National Urban Problems,* Columbia University Press, 1991.

xiii

in writing "op-eds," understanding movies, and for waxing satirical about phenomena that are too distressing, at least for this writer, to be analyzed solely with a social scientist's detachment. The discipline can even be employed for self-analysis, as is illustrated in an autobiographical essay framed as a sociological self-analysis. I put it in the first appendix of this book, although readers who want to know the author before his work may choose to read it first.

In demonstrating the many uses of sociology, I also want to show how many ways it can be written. Virtually all of these ways conflict with the monographic and research journal article format in which most sociology is packaged these days. Still, as many academics have discovered, tenure brings a freedom to publish in other formats, even light-hearted ones. Of course, there are limits; stand-up comics are often very good sociologists, but unfortunately sociologists are not often encouraged to pursue stand-up comedy. (I regret that I have so far never tried.)

Celebrating Sociology

Finally, the book seeks to be a celebration of what I have always thought to be the most lively and interesting of all the social sciences. I came into sociology just after World War II, when it was, or at least seemed to me, the most diverse and the freest of all social sciences. Its approaches, perspectives, and subjects were so eclectic that just about any social phenomenon was accessible to sociological analysis. Sociology was also on the verge of becoming well known outside the ivory tower, for just a few years after I began my graduate studies, David Riesman and his colleagues published *The Lonely Crowd*. (Even today it remains the best-selling sociological study of at least the last half century, as my analysis of sociological best-sellers in Chapter Thirteen reports.)

My celebration of sociology can also be read as a defense of the discipline because, for the last decade or so, sociology's reputation has declined. The reasons are many, including the fact that many of our best ideas and approaches have been borrowed freely by the other social sciences, the humanities and journalism. However, sociology also has its faults, including a needless oversupply of jargon, numbers, and findings that dwell too much on the obvious, a preoccupation with poorly explained theoretical issues, as well as an excessive enthusiasm for too many of the more dubious intellectual and cultural fads and fashions of the moment.

Most of the other social sciences are subject to the same foibles as sociology, but journalists and humanists have ignored theirs and highlighted ours, so that sociology has become a favorite intellectual whipping boy—and girl. (Undoubtedly, sociology and the other social sciences had similar and worse faults when I was a student, but then I was too innocent to see them.)

Be all that as it may, I continue to be excited by sociology. I am not out to sell sociology but only to suggest that I have learned much *from* it and *with* it, both about my adopted country and other matters in the half century since I first began to think of myself as a sociologist. I hope that others continue to be turned on by sociology in the future, because I also think it can contribute to our understanding and betterment of American society in ways that the other social sciences cannot. In addition, I think it can be more fun.

In all fairness to my fellow sociologists, what I mean by sociology reflects my own predilections and biases. It is predominantly empirical, based whenever possible on the ethnographic methods described and illustrated in Part One of this collection. Partly as a result, its theory is "grounded," a term Leonard Schatzman and Anselm Strauss invented to describe the theorizing that emerges as empirical researchers, starting with questions they want to answer and puzzles they want to solve, react to and make conceptual sense of their data. I like to think that this kind of theory is also grounded in common sense. It is what Robert K. Merton would call "middle range" rather than grandly abstract, although he, and an earlier middle-range theorist who was one of my teachers, Everett C. Hughes, came up with some pretty good abstract theory, too.

Not all of the research questions that intrigue me most are derived from the attempt to make sense of America. Others stem from my values, including a concern for the optimization of political democracy and economic equality, a faith in the possibilities of populism, and a variety of other economic and political values, which I have long called left-liberal. As a result, my sociological research is often as much policy-oriented as basic. The research puzzles come from everyday experiences and observations; here having been trained as an ethnographer gives me a head start.

The six parts of the book reflect the agenda I have just sketched. Each part has its own introduction, which explains some of the contexts of the individual pieces—and the reasons why I wrote them. Part One reprints chapters from my major ethnographic studies; Part Two includes analytic and policy articles that deal with my major intellectual preoccupation of the last three decades—poverty and inequality. Part Three deals with ethnicity and related topics. It includes some very old articles because this field was one of my first interests; and some new ones because that old interest was reawakened, thanks in part to several of my Columbia University graduate students who are members of the new, post–1965 immigration. Part Four reports on one of my newer interests, the sociology of American sociology, which I had a chance to develop while president of the American Sociological Association in 1988. Part Five offers some of my writings in less standard varieties of sociology. My sociological autobiography and a selected bibliography of my books, monographs, and articles appear in the two appendixes.

ACKNOWLEDGMENTS

This book owes its existence to Charles Lemert, the editor of the Legacy of Social Thought series, who proposed it, while Dean Birkenkamp, the guiding editorial light of Rowman & Littlefield, with backup by Lemert, helped me make my selections for this volume. Dean Birkenkamp also supplied the specialized advice that helped to make the pieces fit for a new audience, as well as other support that an anthology seems to require. Many other people deserve thanks for helping me write the original pieces or providing me the time to do so, and I have acknowledged them in individual chapters.

H.J.G.
New York, September 1998

· *Part One* ·

THE ETHNOGRAPHIES

The first three chapters of the book—Part One—come from my most intensive efforts to make sense of America, being abridged chapters from my three major participant-observation studies. The first reports the destruction of the West End of Boston, a poor and moderate-income neighborhood I studied from 1957 to 1958; the second describes how social life in Levittown, New Jersey, compared to the still-persisting stigmatizing myths about suburbia that were spawned in the late 1940s by the original Levittown in New York. The third chapter reports on the values of a journalistic community—the four national news organizations (two newsmagazines and two network TV news programs) that I studied during the 1960s and again in the mid-1970s.

Participant observation, or ethnography, involves being—and even living—with the people one studies: getting to know them and the community or institution under study because the participant observer is among them practically all the time. Until the 1960s, the method had always been most identified with sociology at the University of Chicago. After World War II, Everett C. Hughes—who trained a generation of such well-known field-workers as Howard Becker, Eliot Freidson, Erving Goffman, Joseph Gusfield, among others—practically personified participant observation.

Although many quantitative sociologists do not consider participant observation as capable of producing social *science,* I believe it the most scientific method because it puts you closest to the people you study. The researcher can see what they do and how they act, and can then talk to them about their acts, as well as their thoughts and feelings, and those of the people with or against whom they act. Because participant observers spend so much time with the people they study, they also learn to know them and the contexts in which they conduct their social lives. Other empirical methods are limited to a stranger learning what people say. In the most widely used sociological method, the survey, that stranger, now often on the telephone, forces the people under study to fit their reports of acts, thoughts, and feelings into the standardized questions made up by researchers who never meet them. The numbers that quantitative researchers analyze are usually obtained by similar strangers in similar ways.

I also like ethnographic research because it produces the kind of sociology most easily communicated to, and I assume read by, the general public. Well-written fieldwork studies sell more books than others in sociology; for example, *Tally's Corner,* the late Elliot Liebow's classic study of a ghetto street corner in Washington, D.C., has sold more than 700,000 copies since it was published in 1964. For what it is worth, participant observers also have a better chance of being elected presidents of the American Sociological Association than other sociologists.

3

No research method is perfect, however, and besides, the questions that drive the research must determine the method or methods. Partly as a result, my fieldwork studies have also used other methods. Only the study I report in Chapter One, about the West End of Boston, was conducted solely by fieldwork—in part because my assignment was to live in the area to conduct fieldwork before other members of the research team conducted a 500-person interview study.

I spent a year in the West End, observing and talking with people every day, to understand the life of the area and its Italian-American residents, who constituted the majority of the multiethnic area. *The Urban Villagers,* the book about my study, described the area's major institutions. It also focused around the question of whether Italian-American life was shaped more by the West Enders' moderate- and low-income jobs and class position or by their ethnicity—and my answer was class. The chapter reprinted here, however, is the most famous one, which reported how the West Enders reacted to the news of their area's forthcoming "clearance" as a "slum."

Chapter Two reports on the fieldwork I conducted immediately after I left the West End in the new suburban community of Levittown, New Jersey (later restored to its original name, Willingboro). Ever since I had written my master's thesis in a year-old suburban town near Chicago, Park Forest (see also Chapter Eight), I had planned to move to another new town at its very beginning and watch as the home buyers who moved in as strangers began to build that set of institutions, organizations, and other social bodies we call a community. (I was, as I remember, home buyer No. 25.)

As always, the reality turned out to be more complex than the research plan. The builder had his own ideas about the community he wanted to see, and the farmers and other residents of the county in which Levittown was being built had their ideas. So did a variety of professionals who were associated with the national headquarters of the churches, voluntary associations, political parties, and the like that moved into Levittown to establish local branches for their particular organizations in the new community. All of these had more power, money, and time than the new residents, who had jobs to commute to, children to raise, and families to grow—priorities that were more urgent than community building. Still, they also participated, sometimes by vetoing or simply ignoring the plans others made for them. Sometimes they even bent the big national organizations—who needed the Levittowners as much or more than the new residents needed them—to their will.

How it all came out is reported in my book, *The Levittowners.* The present chapter focuses mainly on how they lived in the community, what effects they thought it had on their lives, and how they felt about it, contrasting their reports with the myths about suburbanites as a homogeneous and conforming set of near-robots whose lives were ruined when they left the city's socially and culturally vibrant atmosphere. Cities have changed considerably since I was in Levittown and so have suburbs, but the myths remain alive and well.

Because I needed reports from a cross section of residents as well as from those new residents who had come from the city, I also used data from lengthy interviews I drafted that graduate students conducted for me while I lived in the community and studied it as a participant observer. As a result, the chapter is based both on what I learned during my fieldwork and what I analyzed from the interview questions about the same topic.

Chapter Three reports on a piece of my study of the journalists who put together *Newsweek, Time,* and the half-hour network news programs of NBC News and CBS News. I conducted my study during decades when these news media had larger audiences and more of a monopoly on the attention of the national news audience than is true today, although neither the TV news nor the magazines have changed as much as is often claimed by critics who argue that "infotainment" has replaced hard news.

The origin of that study goes back almost to 1940, the year I came to the United States as a refugee from Nazi Germany, for six weeks after I arrived, I was appointed the editor of my school newspaper. (Having studied English in Germany and then in England, I was the only one with sufficient knowledge of the rules of English grammar.) That began a lifelong infatuation with journalists, which continued when I worked as an unpaid stringer for a Chicago daily newspaper, edited the high school newspaper, and did the same for an army camp newspaper when I was in military service.

Living in Levittown I used to compare my study with the very different "study" of the community that local journalists conducted. I was still doing research in Levittown during the Bay of Pigs crisis, when the national news media were supplying jingoistic and war-loving stories, which seemed intended to help precipitate World War III. I thought to myself that, should we survive the potential exchange of nuclear bombs, I would like to study how national journalists decide what is news.

I could not undertake the study until several years later, and decided to focus on domestic news, although one of the major domestic stories of the time was the U.S. war in Vietnam. Thanks to a generous grant from a liberal news media owner, Stimson Bullitt, I was able to "hang out" at the four newsrooms as the journalists were doing their work, studying them much the same way as I had studied the West Enders and the Levittowners, albeit with very different questions.

In *Deciding What's News,* I reported on how journalists decide, but in the chapter abridged here, I focused on the values that, along with a number of other factors, went into their decision making. This chapter employs another mix of methods—content analysis and fieldwork. Before I studied the journalists, I undertook a complicated content analysis to determine what the news was about, which included a section on the values I saw emerging from the content analysis. However, I rewrote the section at the end of my fieldwork, adding what I had learned about the journalists' values as I "lived" and talked with them in their newsrooms.

National news organizations, and the world they cover, have changed considerably since I published my book in 1979, but the journalists' values have remained remarkably stable—one reason I chose the chapter for this collection.

· 1 ·

THE DESTRUCTION OF BOSTON'S WEST END

The idea for redeveloping Boston's West End dates back to the turn of the century, when the area was already known as a densely occupied low-income neighborhood. In the late 1930s, Nathan Straus, one of the founders of the public housing movement in America, visited the West End and suggested that the entire area be cleared and replaced with public housing. Although his advice was not heeded, the creation of the federal slum clearance program after World War II did lead the Boston Planning Board to suggest that the West End, together with the North and South Ends, were ripe for clearance. In 1950, the Boston Housing Authority applied to the federal government for preliminary planning funds to study the West End, but work proceeded slowly, and it was not until April 1953 that the decision to redevelop the West End was announced officially.

At about that time, the first stirrings of protest were heard from the West End. A small group of young West Enders organized the Save the West End Committee, and with the help of a Beacon Hill resident who had opposed other city modernization schemes in the past, they carried on several years of opposition to the project.

The Committee received little overt support from the rest of the West Enders, and its opposition did not significantly interrupt the city's planning. Soon after federal and local approval of the plan was obtained, the project was opened to bidders. The private developer chosen for the new West End proposed a 2400-unit complex of elevator apartment buildings—and a handful of townhouses—to be rented for about $45 a room, a figure that placed the project firmly in the luxury housing category. The plans were presented at a public hearing in April 1957 and approved by the City Council and the Mayor three months later.

This chapter is abridged from "The Redevelopment of the West End" in *The Urban Villagers: Group and Class in the Life of Italian Americans.* © 1962 by The Free Press. © 1982 by Herbert J. Gans. Reprinted with permission of the Free Press, a division of Simon & Schuster.

In October 1957, the Redevelopment Authority commissioners held an informal hearing in the West End regarding the scheme they were taking over from the Housing Authority. Two hundred people from the West End attended this hearing, most of them strongly opposed to the redevelopment. According to one of the commissioners with whom I later spoke, his group was impressed with the protest. But after "a lot of soul-searching," the commissioners concluded that the process had gone too far to be reversed. In January 1958, the city and the federal government signed the contract that would require the latter to pay two-thirds and the former, one-third of the cost of purchasing the land, relocating the present residents, and clearing the site for the redeveloper.

Surveyors started to come into the West End at that time, and in February 1958, a site office was set up to handle relocation surveys and other procedures for relocation and clearance. The city took official title to the land under the power of eminent domain during the last week in April, thus marking the beginning of actual redevelopment and relocation.

When schools closed for the year in June 1958—some of them never to reopen—West Enders began to move out in large numbers. The exodus continued throughout 1958, and by November of that year, 1200 of the 2700 households had departed. After a slowdown during the winter, the moveouts resumed in spring 1959; by the summer of 1959, the West End was emptying rapidly. As the Redevelopment Authority began to tear down buildings as soon as they had become vacant, this encouraged the departure of people in neighboring structures. Thus the relocation process, which had been expected to take three to four years, was completed after little more than eighteen months. By the summer of 1960, only rubble remained where two years ago had lived more than 7000 people. Meanwhile, foundations were being laid for the first of the new apartment buildings, and in January 1962, the initial residents of the new West End started to move in.

THE CITY'S REASONS FOR REDEVELOPMENT

There were many reasons for the city to redevelop the West End. Boston is a poor city, and the departure of middle-class residents and industry for the suburbs has left it with an oversupply of tax-exempt institutions and low-income areas that yield little for the municipal coffers. Through the federal redevelopment program, the city fathers hoped to replace some of the low-yield areas with high-rent buildings that would bring in additional municipal income. Moreover, they believed that a shiny new redevelopment project would cleanse its aged, tenement-dominated skyline, and increase the morale of private and public investors. This in turn would supposedly lead to a spiral of further private rebuilding in the city.

The West End was thought to be particularly suitable for redevelopment. Because of its central location adjacent to Beacon Hill and near the downtown shopping area, real estate men had long felt that the area was "ripe" for higher—and more profitable—uses. The long block fronting on the Charles River was considered attractive for luxury housing. Some businessmen believed that the decline of the downtown shopping district could be ended by housing "quality shoppers" on its fringes. Moreover, Massachusetts General Hospital was expanding rapidly, and its trustees had long been unhappy about being surrounded by low-income neighbors.

The business community and the city's newspapers were favorably inclined, as were the political leaders of the city outside the West End. And even the West End protest seemed muted. Some years earlier, when it had been proposed to clear the North End, the citizens and the political leaders of that area had raised such an outcry that the project was immediately shelved. But the local politicians in the West End were too few and too powerless for their protests to be heeded. Nor could the West Enders themselves make their voices heard. The Save the West End Committee's protest was noted, but as the group's membership was small, the Committee, in effect, had no political influence. Moreover, the local settlement houses and other caretaking agencies all approved of the redevelopment, partly because their lay leaders were drawn from the Boston business community, and partly because the staffs of these agencies felt that the fortunes of the West Enders would be thereby improved. The Catholic Archdiocese, whose local church was to be saved for architectural reasons, also gave its blessing.

Finally, all of Boston was convinced that the West End was a slum that ought to be torn down not only for the sake of the city but also for the good of its own residents. This belief was supported by the general appearance of the area, by studies that had been made in the West End by public and private agencies, and by stories that appeared in the press. In 1957, for example, a popular Boston columnist could wildly exaggerate both past and present conditions in the area to claim that:

> The West End is today definitely a slum area. In fact it has always been.
> . . . It gradually degenerated into a roominghouse section and then went
> from bad to worse. . . . Around the turn of the century . . . every conceivable sort of vice that makes for a slum flourished. . . . That was nearly
> sixty years ago. Any change since has slowly slid towards the worse.[1]

After calling the area a cesspool, the columnist urged his readers to "come back in ten years, and you won't know the reborn city."[2]

To the West Enders, the many years between the announcement that the area would be redeveloped and the actual clearing of their neighborhood appeared quite differently than it did to the city and its officials. No one with whom I talked was quite sure when the West Enders had first heard about the plans for redeveloping their neighborhood. The Planning Board's recommendation in 1949 had been made public, of course, and the press had also carried stories of the preliminary planning studies that had begun in 1951. At that time, the residents were opposed to the redevelopment, but did not feel themselves sufficiently threatened to be alarmed.

The initial announcement, however, did have some more important consequences. During the postwar era, the West End—like most other inner-city districts—had begun to lose some of its recently married couples to the suburbs. The announcement itself undoubtedly spurred additional moves, and it seems also to have discouraged other people from moving into the West End. Whatever the causes, the vacancy rate in the area began to climb, especially in buildings owned by absentee landlords, who then began to have a change of heart about the redevelopment. Eventually, in fact, they became its most fervent adherents, and in later years urged the city and federal government to hasten the process, because they were losing money on vacant apartments that they could no longer rent.

Tenants, and resident owners whose buildings were still occupied, were almost unanimously opposed to the redevelopment. Some of the tenants in the most dilapidated structures were hopeful that government action would provide them with better places to live. But the vast majority of West Enders had no desire to leave. They were content to live in the West End, and were willing to overlook some of its physical defects in comparison with its many social advantages. Those who had been born there cited the traditional belief that "the place you're born is where you want to die." Even criticism of the area would sometimes be stilled by the remark, "never disparage a place in which you've grown up." Many of the people who had left the West End at marriage would come back occasionally—if only to shop—and one man whose family had left the area shortly after his birth twenty years earlier insisted that "you always come back to the place of your childhood."

Most people were not very explicit at that time about their feelings toward the area. Because the West End still existed, and because they had never known anything else, they could not estimate how its disappearance might affect them.[3] "What's so good about the West End? We're used to it," was one quite typical comment. Subsequently, however, I heard more anguished remarks that indicated how important the area and its people were to the speaker. In December 1957, the day after the federal government gave the city the go-ahead, one young Italian man said:

> I wish the world would end tonight. . . . I wish they'd tear the whole damn town down, damn scab town. . . . I'm going to be lost without the West End. Where the hell can I go?

Another West Ender told me: "It isn't right to scatter the community to all four winds. It pulls the heart out of a guy to lose all his friends." Shortly before the taking, a barber in his early sixties ended a discussion of death that was going on in the shop with these comments:

> I'm not afraid to die, but I don't want to. But if they tear the West End down and we are all scattered from all the people I know and that know me, and they wouldn't know where I was, I wouldn't want to die and people not know it.

Perhaps because most people were opposed to the redevelopment, they could not quite believe that it would happen. Over the years, they began to realize that the redevelopment plans were in earnest, but they were—and remained—skeptical that the plans would ever be implemented. Even on the day of the taking, the person just quoted told me: "I don't believe it; I won't believe it till it happens. I'll wait till I get my notice. . . . You'll see, they'll start at the lower end, and they'll never come up here."

There were several reasons for the West Enders' skepticism. First, they had considerable difficulty in understanding the complicated parade of preliminary and final approvals, or the tortuous process by which the plans moved back and forth between the Housing Authority, the City Council, the Mayor, the State Housing Board, and the federal Housing and Home Finance Agency. Instead of realizing that each approval was one step in a tested and finite administrative procedure, the West Enders saw it as merely another decision in a seemingly purposeless, erratic, and infinite series. Thus, when the federal housing agency did give its final approval in the winter of 1957, most West Enders did not understand that this was the last step in the process. They recalled that the same agency had approved it several times before, without any visible result. Thus, they felt certain that there would be more meetings, and more decisions, and that twenty-five years later, the West End would still be there.

Their failure to understand the process can be traced back partly to the poor information that they received from the press and the city agencies. The latter, assuming that West Enders understood the nature of the process, did not attempt to describe it in sufficient detail. Moreover, city officials did not see that to West Enders, all government agencies were pretty much the same, and that notions of city-state-federal relationships were strange to them. The West Enders in turn paid little attention to the press releases, and were more receptive to distorted facts and the many rumors that they could hear from friends and neighbors.

Moreover, they noted that official announcements were vague about when things would begin to happen in the West End. If estimates were given, they were usually wrong.

Nor could West Enders really conceive of the possibility that the area would be torn down. They had watched the demolition of parts of the North End for the Central Artery—the city's expressway system—and while they disapproved, they realized that a highway was of public benefit and could not be opposed. But the idea that the city could clear the West End, and then turn the land over to a private builder for luxury apartments seemed unbelievable.

Their skepticism turned to incredulity when the city awarded the re-development. The idea that a private builder could build apartments then estimated to rent for $40 to $50 a room—more than they were paying for five- and six-room apartments—was hard to believe. And that the government could encourage this venture seemed imcomprehensible except as a result of political corruption, the exchange of bribes, and the cutting in of politicians on future profits.[4] As one West Ender among many pointed out:

> The whole thing is a steal, taking the area away from the people, and giving it to some guys who had paid off everyone else. . . . It is just someone making money at our expense. There are many areas lots worse than this one. Look at [the Mayor], a city clerk once, and now he's rich enough to buy up Boston itself. Yes, just a city clerk and look at him now.

Thereafter, all of the steps in the process were interpreted as attempts to scare the West Enders out of the area, so that the values of the buildings would be reduced and the private developers could buy them more cheaply. But even then, people were skeptical that this scheme would come to fruition, partially because it was so immoral. Many West Enders argued that only in Russia could the government deprive citizens of their property in such a dictatorial manner.

Also, West Enders found it hard to think far ahead. Even if they could admit to themselves that the area might eventually be "thrown down"—as they put it—it was still difficult to think about what might happen years hence, especially in the absence of incontrovertible evidence. As already noted, official announcements and newspaper stories generally were not accepted as evidence; people had to see more concrete examples of the city's plans before they would believe that the city was in earnest. For example, the registered letters, which the Redevelopment Authority sent to all West Enders indicating that it had taken over the area, were less persuasive than the announcement that, as of May 1958, rents were to be paid not to landlords but to the city's relocation office. Only when people saw their neighbors—and especially their landlords—going to that office to pay their rents did all of them realize that the end had come. Conversely, a few weeks earlier, when the announcement of the taking was imminent, West Enders were much cheered by the city's repaving of streets immediately outside the project area and by the gas company's installation of more modern gas meters in West End apartments. These were concrete actions that could be taken as evidence, especially since they seemed to prove what West Enders wanted to believe—that nothing was going to happen—and were considered much more reliable than official announcements or news stories.[5] And finally, of course, West Enders simply denied the possibility of redevelopment because they did not want it to happen. They were content to live in the West End, and could not imagine living elsewhere, or going about the city looking for "rooms."

As a result, life in the West End went on as always, with relatively little overt concern about the redevelopment and even less public discussion of it. On the days following the announcement of another decision in the process, people would talk about it heatedly, but then it would be forgotten again until the next announcement. There had been so many announcements, and so many meetings, and nothing ever seemed to happen afterward. Surely it would be safe—and easy—to assume that nothing would ever happen.

Social agencies knew, of course, that the area would be redeveloped, and were not in doubt over the outcome of the long process. This knowledge, the gradual reduction in the number of their clients, and the appearance of some of the lower-class newcomers, sapped their morale. Although most of the agencies and their staffs were in favor of the redevelopment, they were also sorry to see the neighborhood torn down and its residents dispersed. They did not voice their feelings in public, but at the annual board meeting of one of the settlement houses, the staff put on a skit about the redevelopment that reflected its ambivalence toward the destruction of the West End. The caretakers also tried, with little success, to prepare the West Enders for what was about to happen. Some of them urged the redevelopment agency to improve its relocation procedures, but by then it was too late.

The best illustration of the lack of impact of the redevelopment process on the West Enders was the failure of the Save the West End Committee to attract their overt support, and the absence of other forms of protest. As noted earlier, the Committee came into being in 1956, when a handful of West Enders met with a local civic and political leader who had long been interested in the West End. An upper-class Bostonian, he helped to build the park, pool, and boating area along the banks of the Charles River and had participated in other improvement projects since the 1930s.[6] He promised to support the group politically and financially, and, with his help, the Committee rented a vacant store in the area. Over the years, it held a number of meetings, spoke at public hearings, published pamphlets and leaflets, went to Washington to try to overturn the decision, and eventually took its case to the courts. The Committee sought, of course, to enroll the neighborhood in its work, but attracted only a small—although loyal—group of members, who kept up a steady barrage of protest over the years. Not until the very end, however, did they gain a wider audience.

One of the major obstacles to the Committee's effectiveness in its own neighborhood was its outside leadership. Although many West Enders had heard of the civic leader who helped to guide the Committee, they knew also that he lived outside the area, and, that however strong his sympathy, he was in class, ethnic background, and culture not one of their own. Nor was he at ease among the West Enders. While he identified with the neighborhood, he often seemed to feel more strongly about the facilities on the riverbank—which were of little interest to the West Enders—than about the tenement streets and their occupants.

Moreover, the other active members—and the people who originally asked for his guidance—were neither typical West Enders nor the kinds of people who could enroll them. Among the most active were an Italian writer and an artist, a young Jewish professional, a single Polish woman, and a number of elderly ladies who lived in the Charlesbank Homes. While some of them did have leadership ability, almost all of them were in one way or another marginal to their own ethnic groups in the West End. Thus, they could not attract these groups to their cause.

This inability had nothing to do with the Committee's point of view, for that was based on the beliefs shared widely by a majority of West Enders: That the redevelopment was motivated by political chicanery and individual greed; that government actions to scare the West Enders into leaving stemmed from sympathy or collusion with the builders; and that until definite proof was available, there was no reason to believe the West End would actually be torn down.

The Committee, however, did not develop a program that would require West Enders as a whole to take action. Its pamphlets and speeches expressed the same indignation and incredulity felt by all, but it did not ask them to act, other than to come to meetings, help the Committee in its mailings, and stay in the West End.

Yet all of these considerations for the Committee's lack of success in gaining active neighborhood support paled before the most important one: the inability of the West Enders to organize in their own behalf. Indeed, other causes were only effects of that basic inability. Had the West Enders flocked to meetings in larger numbers, the leadership would probably have gone to someone whom the residents would have followed. As it was, they watched the activities of the Committee with passive sympathy. Some were suspicious: they argued that the Committee consisted of people who had been left out when the graft was distributed; that the leadership was Communist; and that an officer of the Committee who was Jewish was related to one of the developers. The majority, however, did agree with all that the Committee claimed, and shared its anger. But even then, they could not break out of the peer group society and organize in common cause. It was impossible to fight city hall; this was a function of the local politician. If he failed, what else was there to do?

Action-seeking West Enders would have relished a march on City Hall to do violence to the officials principally associated with the redevelopment, but the act of joining with neighbors to work together for halting the redevelopment was inconceivable. At the meetings at which West Enders spoke, they spoke as individuals, about their own individual cases. The local politicians who appeared at these meetings spoke *to* the West Enders rather than *for* them; they convinced the audience of their own opposition to the redevelopment, and tried to display themselves as loyal representatives of the West End. But they too were unable—and perhaps unwilling—to organize an effective protest movement.

Even the resident leaders of the Committee—notably those of Italian background—were ill at ease about guiding a protest group that called for citizen participation. They realized that their Beacon Hill supporter could not attract the West Enders, but they were also skeptical as to their own ability to rally them. In addition, they were ambivalent about their personal involvement. They were able to make speeches and to share their anger with an audience, but other activities came less easily. Being a leader without any proof of results, spending time away from family and friends or from second jobs and other individual pursuits was difficult. When Committee members were asked to carry out the routine tasks of organization, and failed to come through—as was often the case—the leaders who gave the orders resented having to carry out these tasks themselves. They were hurt that they should give up their own free time, and extend themselves for the group if no one else did and if there was no reward for such self-deprivation. Thus, the Committee itself was constantly split by bickering, by people withdrawing from activity when no support was forthcoming, and by individuals offering new solutions and making speeches to each other when more prosaic activity was called for.

The leaders were also hampered by lack of information. The politicians claimed—with some justification—that since they were opposed to the project, they had not been kept properly informed by redevelopment officials. Also, they and the leaders of the Committee were unable to deal properly with what information was available. Like most other West Enders, they believed that the project's fate was in the hands of one individual, the Mayor, and that it could be overturned simply by persuading him of its immorality. As unable as the rest of the West Enders to follow the series of steps that led to the final taking of the land, some of them believed until the last moment that the redevelopment would never take place. They accepted the rumors that swept the area like everyone else, and could not detach themselves sufficiently from their neighbors to look objectively at the doings of the outside world. Thus, none of the prerequisites or minutiae of organizational activity came easily to the Committee leaders. Much of the time, only their anger at the outrage they felt was being perpetrated against themselves and their neighbors kept them going.

The truth was, that for a group unaccustomed to organizational activity, saving the West End was an overwhelming, and perhaps impossible, task. Indeed, there was relatively little the Committee could do. The decision to redevelop the West End had been made early in the decade, and it had received the blessings of the city's decisive business leaders and politicians. The West End's local politicians all opposed the redevelopment, but were powerless. Nor did the West End have other attributes of power, such as those displayed by the neighboring North End. This area had a larger population and a much larger business community—some of it politically influential. Most important, the North End was the center—and symbol—of Italian life in Boston. Its destruction thus would have been a threat—or at least an insult—to every Italian voter in Boston, and the city's politicians simply could not afford to alienate this increasingly influential vote. Conversely, although the Italians were also the largest group in the West End, they were not in the majority. And because they had attained a plurality only comparatively recently, the area had never really been considered an Italian neighborhood. Thus, it is doubtful whether even a unanimous turnout in opposition by the West Enders would have been sufficient to set in motion the difficult process of reversing years of work by local and federal agencies and giving up the large federal grant that financed the clearance of the area.

REDEVELOPMENT: THE LAST DAYS OF THE WEST END

With every decision, the more knowing West Enders began to realize that the days of the area were numbered. When the state gave its approval in October 1957, and the federal government signed the final contracts in January 1958, the die was cast. Even then, many West Enders were still not sure that these steps would lead to action. Conflicting signs appeared to confuse those who were looking for concrete evidence. Surveyors were sent by the city to map the area, but as noted before, the repaving of streets leading into the project area gave some people hope that another decision that would spare the neighborhood would soon be forthcoming. Other surveyors came to interview the residents, to find out where they wished to be relocated, and how much rent they could afford. Some people refused to answer; a few threw out the interviewers; but the majority answered, and then discounted the significance of the questionnaire.

Thus, in the spring of 1958, life went on pretty much as before. There were fewer businesses than had started the winter, and others were threatening to shut. A barber, who had closed his shop at the age of eighty-four, died shortly afterward, and many people felt his death had been caused by the redevelopment "scare." But otherwise, the routine prevailed. Housewives prepared for Passover or Easter, and gave their apartments the traditional spring cleaning.

On April 22, 1958, stories began to appear in the city papers that letters would be sent to the West Enders any day, announcing the taking of the land and the beginning of redevelopment. Only the week before, one of my neighbors had insisted, "They're still arguing about something; it might be five years yet." Another was thinking that nothing at all might happen, and that he would find a first-floor apartment in the area, and fix it up properly. Even the newspaper stories had relatively little impact. Many people did not read the papers regularly, and heard about it from neighbors.

"It's just another attempt to scare us," said one; "I'm not frightened by the article. We'll wait till we see something." One of the local politicians was among those not yet convinced.

On April 25, all West Enders received registered letters from the Redevelopment Authority announcing the taking, explaining that rent was to be paid to the city from now on, and pointing out the procedures involved in relocation. But as the letters were written in the traditionally formal language of official agencies, I doubt seriously that many West Enders read them through to the end. There could be no doubt now, however, that the West End was coming down. Even so, the real impact of the decision did not come until about a week later, when the May rent payments were due at the relocation office. The idea of no longer paying rent to the landlord and of taking it to a city office was the concrete evidence West Enders needed to accept the redevelopment of their neighborhood.

The first reaction was a feeling of relief that the suspense was over, and that hopes would no longer be raised or lowered by contradictory evidence. For some people, the news was a real shock. But most West Enders were not overly excited. They now accepted what they had known or suspected all along, and what they should have realized earlier. For many years, they had considered the possibility of the neighborhood's destruction, and even if they had rejected the idea each time, the periodic reappearance of the threat had left a residue of belief. What they had denied so fervently before, they could now accept more easily.

The shock was softened by other conditions. One was the inevitability of the event. "Underneath we are all upset, but what can we do?" asked one West Ender. Another mitigating factor was the traditional resignation toward the behavior of the outside world. Because West Enders had always expected the worst from this world, the redevelopment was just another in a long series of deprivations and outrages. Since the city had estimated that relocation would take three years, some felt they could remain in the West End for a considerable time yet.

Finally, there were many who still did not accept the facts, and looked for even more concrete evidence. As one lady put it, "We won't believe it until we see something; we'll find out when something happens." Others found solace in the belief that the taking was illegal because the city could not charge rent under eminent domain and they had not paid the landlords for their property when they took it. One of my neighbors argued that there had been no taking: "They didn't even give the landlords a dollar. I won't believe it until I see something come down." Another neighbor pointed out that the only people who had started to move were nurses and transient middle-class residents in the area; the real West Enders were staying put.

The notices also drew people closer together, and offered them some opportunity for feelings of revenge against the landlords. A Holy Name picnic, which took place as scheduled two days after the notices came, attracted an overflow crowd. A few days later, one of my neighbors remarked, "Everyone is more friendly, like old times: why couldn't it be like that before?" Tenants who felt that they had been mistreated by their landlords were glad that the latter would now be paying rent like everyone else. Some landlords raised the rents that relatives were paying at the last moment, in the hope of increasing the value of their buildings, and other tenants were pleased at the discomfort this caused. There was some feeling of relief that one no longer needed to be polite to landlords. As one neighbor said, "Now we can have some parties; we don't have to worry about the landlord anymore." But tenants also felt sorry for the "good" landlords and the resident owners, whose properties had been taken by the city without immediate payments.

Since the city had now become the landlord and had promised to keep the buildings in good condition, some West Enders thus made demands on the city to make those repairs the landlords had neglected. The people who were angriest sought more direct forms of revenge, and found it by withholding rent payments. After the first week in May, only half the people had paid their rent to the city. At the end of the year, however, the relocation office reported that only about 150 households had actually withheld rent monies for any length of time.

In the weeks immediately following the taking, the area's anger caused the Save the West End Committee to experience an energetic but short-lived renaissance. Right after the announcement, the Committee scheduled a mother's march on City Hall, a form of protest that had worked well for the West End some decades earlier when the neighborhood had still been predominantly Jewish. But, as no one except the leaders of the march appeared at the appointed time, it had to be cancelled. One of the Italian men explained that they would not allow their women to take part in such forms of public display.

Then, in the week after the taking, the Committee underwent a change of leadership. A young Jewish student, who had been an inactive member of the group, suddenly became interested following the announcement—spurred on considerably by the anger of his family that had now lost its store and livelihood. Since the Committee's original area leaders had lost hope, he was asked if he wanted to take over. Thereupon, he formulated an eleven-point program, which included an appeal not to pay rent and not to move out; a march on City Hall to see the Mayor; and a scheme for rehabilitating the area with the monies being paid to the city as

rents. A public meeting was called for May 5, about ten days after the taking, and over two hundred people—the largest crowd ever to attend a
Committee meeting—showed up. They listened enthusiastically to an area
politician urge the people not to move, and somewhat less so to the student's eleven-point program. But for some, the meeting restored the hope
that the area might still be spared.

This hope—fantastic as it seemed—was based on the previously mentioned assumption that the redevelopment had been planned and executed
by the Mayor, and that if he could be persuaded to change his mind, the
West End might be saved. Immediately after the meeting, however, plans
for implementing the program foundered over the question of how to persuade the Mayor. The philosophy student, a pacifist, and a follower of Gan-
dhi's principles of civil disobedience, urged people to be kind and loving
to their enemies, and to persuade the Mayor through nonviolent methods.
Even at the public meeting, this proposal had been received with grumbling. At a long strategy session afterward, the old leaders of the Committee, and some other West Enders who had stayed behind—all Italians—
disagreed strongly. "The Mayor is a thief," they said, "and how can you
trust a thief or respect him?" Some suggested a one-hundred-car caravan
to City Hall that would threaten the Mayor with violence if he did not call
off the redevelopment.

Because the student would not agree to demonstrations of violence
and the others refused to follow his approach, the Committee was virtually
stymied. Nevertheless, another meeting was called for the following week,
and notices were posted in the West End, proclaiming that there was still
hope:

> For five years, and once in every three months, they have been announc-
> ing, in big headlines, that the West End would fall and that we would be
> cast forth from our homes before the dawn of another season. These
> were lies, for we're still here, and we're not moving.

Again the meeting drew over two hundred people, but the local politician
who had been the main speaker the week before did not come as he had
promised, and the West Enders felt that they had been deserted. Again, they
did not respond to the student's appeal for a Gandhian approach, and by
now it was evident that he would not be accepted as a leader. Moreover,
the laws about incitement to riot made it impossible for any of the speakers
to urge nonpayment of rent, leaving West Enders no other way of expressing their anger. Although another meeting was held the subsequent week,
the audience was smaller, and by the end of the month, people began to
think about moving.

As buildings began to empty, the remaining tenants were loath to remain in them, and even those who had planned to stay to the bitter end began to leave. People were afraid of being alone, of being the last in the house and thus isolated from the group. Then, unknown teenagers began to roam through semideserted buildings, using them for nocturnal parties, setting fires, and vandalizing wherever they could. The families still remaining in these buildings became fearful and moved more quickly than they had intended. The empty structures were torn down as soon as the last tenant left, and the resulting noise and dirt encouraged people in adjacent buildings to move also. Consequently, the West End was emptied in little more than eighteen months after the official taking of the land.

I was told that before the West End was totally cleared—and even afterward—West Enders would come back on weekends to walk through the old neighborhood and the rubble-strewn streets.[7] The last time I saw the area, it had been completely leveled except for the buildings that had been marked for preservation. A museum of Yankee artifacts and the library—now closed—remained at one corner, the Hospital at another. The Catholic church—where services were still being held for parishioners living on the Back of Beacon Hill—stood in lonely isolation in the center of the cleared area. The Hospital had graded some of the adjacent property for temporary parking, and at a far corner, fronting on the river, the first of the new buildings were going up. The cleared area looked very tiny, and it was hard to imagine that more than 20,000 people had once lived there.

NOTES

1. Bill Cunningham, "Two Project to Alter Boston," *Boston Herald,* November 17, 1957.

2. *Ibid.*

3. For a more detailed discussion of the West Enders' reactions, see Marc Fried and Peggy Gleicher, "Some Sources of Residential Satisfaction in an Urban 'Slum,' " *Journal of the American Institute of Planners* 27 (1961): 305–15; and Marc Fried, "Grieving for a Lost Home," in *The Urban Condition,* ed. Leonard J. Duhl (New York: Basic Books, 1963), 151–71.

4. I heard from several disparate sources that one of the city councilors had asked for a sizable "campaign contribution" in exchange for a favorable vote on the redevelopment. Since his vote was not needed, he did not get the money. Eventually, he voted for it anyway.

5. These feelings even affected me. Although I knew enough about redevelopment procedures to realize that the process was moving toward its inevitable climax, I was opposed to the redevelopment, and hoped it would not take place. Since I

was not in touch with city officials, occasionally I would begin to share the West Enders' beliefs that "our children will still be here when they break it up," and wondered whether the rumors that the project had collapsed might not be true. It is thus understandable that West Enders, who knew much less about the process, and could not call city officials to get the facts, would hold these beliefs more stubbornly.

6. His father had been a founder of the public playground movement in the United States; and his relatives, who included all of the famous names of Boston's aristocracy, had helped to build the West End settlement houses. They also supported the charities and social welfare agencies that served the area and the larger community.

7. I left the West End in May 1958 to begin my already scheduled study of Levittown, New Jersey.

· 2 ·

SUBURBAN HOMOGENEITY AND CONFORMITY: MYTH AND REALITY

THE QUALITY OF SOCIAL LIFE

Perhaps the most frequent indictment of suburban life has been leveled against the quality of social relationships. The critics charge that the suburbs are socially hyperactive and have made people so outgoing that they have little time or inclination for the development of personal autonomy. The pervasive homogeneity of the population has depressed the vitality of social life, and the absence of more heterogeneous neighbors and friends has imposed a conformity that further reduces the suburbanite's individuality. Indeed, studies showing the importance of physical propinquity in the choice of friends have been interpreted to suggest that physical layout, rather than people, determines the choice of friends. Because many suburbanites are transients or mobile, they have been accused of wanting social companions only for the duration of their stay, disabling them for more intimate friendship.

Evidence from Levittown suggests quite the opposite.[1] People report an accelerated social life, and in fact looked forward to it before moving to Levittown. The major reason for the upswing is indeed homogeneity, but an equally appropriate term might be "compatibility." Propinquity may initiate social contact, but it does not determine friendship. Many relationships are indeed transient, but this is no reflection on their intensity. Finally, conformity prevails, although less as malicious or passive copying than as sharing of useful ideas. In short, many of the *phenomena* identified by the critics occur in Levittown but their alleged *consequences* do not follow. Lev-

This chapter is abridged from Chapter 8 of *The Levittowners: Ways of Life and Politics in a New Suburban Community.* © 1982 by Columbia University Press. © 1967 by Herbert J. Gans, Pantheon Books. Reprinted with permission of Pantheon Books, a division of Random House.

ittowners have not become outgoing, mindless conformers; they remain individuals, fulfilling the social aspirations with which they came. To be sure, social life in Levittown has its costs, but these seem minor compared to its rewards.

Neighboring[2]

About half the Levittowners interviewed said that they were visiting more with neighbors than in their former residence: about a quarter said less, and the remaining quarter reported no change.[3] The greatest increase was reported by the people who said they had wanted to do more visiting, particularly those who had had little opportunity for it in their previous residence. As one Philadelphian said, "We used to be with the in-laws and with my mother; we didn't bother with the neighbors before." Others had lacked compatible neighbors: people living in apartments had found few opportunities to get acquainted, and those in older or transitional areas had found their fellow residents unsuitable. This was as true of former suburbanites and small-town residents as of those from cities, and affected owners as well as renters. One homeowner explained, "Here in Levittown I have more in common; where we lived before, the neighbors were all my mother's age."

Another Levittowner, describing her next-door neighbor, said, "We see eye to eye on things, about raising kids, doing things together with your husband, living the same way; we have practically the same identical background." Conversely, the people who reported less neighboring were those who could not find compatible people on the block: older ones, some (but not all) people of highest and lowest status, and those who had difficulties in relating to neighbors, particularly second generation Jewish women from Philadelphia who were used to living among Jewish neighbors.[4] A handful wanted to continue spending their social life with relatives or preferred to have nothing to do with neighbors.

Of course, some friendliness was built into the neighbor relationship, for people needed each other for mutual aid. In a community far from the city, women are cut off from relatives and old friends—as well as from commuting husbands—so that readiness to provide mutual aid is the first criterion of being a good neighbor. This includes not only helping out in emergencies, but ameliorating periodic loneliness by being available for occasional coffee-klatsching and offering informal therapy by being willing to listen to another's troubles when necessary. Helping out also offers an opportunity—rare in everyday life—to practice the dictates of the Judeo-Christian ethic and brings appropriate emotional rewards. The reciprocity engendered by mutual aid encourages—and allows—neighbors to keep a constant watch on each other, as they do in established neighborhoods everywhere. The mutual observation that makes the block a goldfish bowl goes on mainly among adjacent neighbors, for with houses only ten feet apart, they see each other frequently and have to maintain friendly relations if that is at all possible. More distant neighbors could be ignored, however.

Even propinquity did not require visiting. Although a number of studies have shown that social relationships are influenced and even determined by the site plan, this was not the case in Levittown.[5] Since Levittown was laid out with curved blocks, houses facing each other across front and back, there were relatively few neighbors with whom one had constant and involuntary visual contact. Sometimes, even relationships with directly adjacent neighbors could be restricted to an exchange of hellos. For example, it took more than a year for me to meet the occupants of a house diagonally across the street from mine, even though we had been saying hello since the first weeks of occupancy. Another person told me he had never even met his next-door neighbor. Thus, despite a fairly high building density—five to six houses to the acre—there was no pressure to be sociable. Neighboring rarely extended more than three or four houses away in each direction, so that the "functional neighborhood" usually consisted of about ten to twelve houses at the most, although people did say hello to everyone on the block.

Fully 82 percent of the respondents mentioned compatibility as the reason for choosing the neighbor they visited most frequently. If the site plan had forced some neighbors into constant visual contact—as do court or cul-de-sac schemes—they might have reacted by increased visiting (or intense enmity if they were incompatible), but the block layout gave Levittowners the opportunity for choice.

Neighbor relations among adults were also affected by the children, for children are neighbors too, and their mingling was determined almost entirely by age and propinquity.[6] The relatively traffic-free streets and the large supply of young children enabled mothers to limit their supervision of the children's outdoor play and to give youngsters a free choice of playmates. But children were likely to quarrel, and when this led to fights and childish violence, their quarrels involved the parents. Adults quarreled most often when childish misbehavior required punishment and parents disagreed about methods. If the parents of fighting children agreed on discipline, each punished his child the same way and the incident was soon forgotten. If they disagreed, however, the parent who believed in harsh punishment often felt that the more permissive parent, not having punished "enough," was accusing the other child of having been at fault. A single parental disagreement might be forgiven, but if it happened repeatedly, an open break between neighbors could result.

Another type of adult quarrel involved physical disciplining of children by neighbors. Some people believe that only parents should spank their children; others, that neighbors have the right to do so if the child misbehaves out of sight of the parents. When a neighbor punishes another's child, he not only takes on a quasi-parental role but, by implication, accuses the parents of not raising and watching their children properly. In one such case, where a neighbor punished a little boy for sexual exhibitionism, the parent never spoke to him again.

Basically, differences over discipline reflect class differences in child-rearing. Middle-class parents tend to be somewhat more permissive than working-class ones, and when two children play together, the middle-class child may be allowed to act in ways not permitted to the working-class one. Also, working-class parents administer physical punishment more freely, since this is not interpreted as a withdrawal of affection, whereas middle-class families reserve spankings for extreme misbehavior. Then, as children get older, practices change. The working-class child is given more freedom, and by comparison, the middle-class child is given much less. He is expected to do his homework while his working-class peers may be playing on the streets. Middle-class people who observe this freedom, as well as the working-class parents' tolerance of childish profanity, interpret it as neglect.

In some cases, middle-class families even prohibit their children from playing with working-class children. Prohibition is feasible if children are old enough to respect it or if parents supervise the children's play. Younger children cannot be prevented from playing with each other, however, and parental quarrels may result. If the working-class children are older and in a minority, as they often are on the block, they may become outcasts, and since they are mobile, may look around for other, similarly discredited companions.

The repetition of parental conflict over children's quarrels can lead to increasing estrangement, because other values and behavior patterns also differ between the classes. For example, in one case, what began as a series of minor disagreements about child rearing was soon reinforced by critical comments on the part of the middle-class people about the working-class neighbor's laxity toward his lawn and his taste for expensive automobiles. All of these disagreements spiraled into considerable hostility over a year's time. Eventually, one of the feuding neighbors may move out—usually the middle-class family that has greater resources to go elsewhere.

If the overall social climate of the block is good, other neighbors will try to patch up conflicts between parents. On one block, a child hit another with a toy, drawing blood and requiring a doctor. The mother of the injured youngster admitted it was his fault and suggested to the other mother that the two children be kept apart for a few days. However, she did not punish her child at once, and this was resented by the other mother (of working-class background). She, in turn, forbade her child to see the guilty one, and both she and her husband broke off with his parents as well. After about a week, however, the feud ended. Each mother told other neighbors of what had happened, and the woman whose child had provoked the incident finally learned that the other mother thought he had not been properly punished. She thereupon let it be known among her neighbors that the child had in fact been punished on the day of the incident. In a few days the message reached its intended destination, whereupon the mother whose child had been hit invited her neighbor and another, neutral, neighbor to coffee. The coffee-klatsch resolved the differences, but only because the block's friendly climate had provided for the prior and circuitous communication that allowed the one mother to learn that the guilty child had indeed been punished. Had communication been poorer, other differences between the two neighbors might have been invoked to increase the conflict. Indeed, when the block's social climate is poor, the struggle will be limited to the involved parents, for no one wants to take sides. If a family becomes enmeshed in battles with a number of neighbors, however, that family is likely to be quickly ostracized, regardless of the social climate.

The importance of compatibility is extended also to relationships that do not involve children, and is underscored by the problems encountered by neighbors who differ significantly. One potential trouble spot was age. Although some elderly Levittowners were able to assume quasi-grandparental roles toward the street's children, others were lonely and uncomfortable among the young families, and enthusiastic gardeners were upset when children romped over flowerbeds and carefully tended lawns. The difficulty was exacerbated by the builder's prohibition of fences, a clause in the deed restriction that was later violated on a number of blocks and actually taken to court.

Class differences also expressed themselves in areas other than child rearing. Upper middle-class women—whose concept of after-housework activity did not include coffee-klatsching, conversation about husbands, homes, and children, or gossiping about the neighbors—rejected and were rejected by the neighbors. So were women who were especially active in organizational life. Perhaps the major problems were faced by working-class people who had been used to spending their free time with relatives or childhood friends and found it hard to become friendly with strangers (especially middle-class ones). The change was particularly distressing to those who had spent all their lives in the neighborhood in which they grew up. If, when they moved to Levittown, they were sufficiently "open" to respond to friendly neighbors and found others of working-class background nearby, they could adapt; if not, they were virtually isolated in their houses. For the latter, a small minority to be sure, life in Levittown was hard. Ethnic differences were also a barrier between neighbors. Groups without a strong subcommunity were isolated, notably a handful of Japanese, Chinese, and Greek families. Some neighbors came with ethnic and racial prejudice, and anti-Semitism, though rare, could be justified by the old charge of Jewish clannishness and by class differences resulting from generally higher incomes among Jews.[7]

A final barrier was sexual, and this affected the women whose husbands worked irregular schedules and might be home during the day. A woman neighbor did not visit another when her husband was home, partly because of the belief that a husband has first call on his wife's companionship, partly to prevent suspicion that her visit might be interpreted as a sexual interest in the husband. This practice is strongest among working-class women, reflecting the traditional class norm that people of the opposite sex come together only for sexual reasons, and becomes weaker at higher class levels; in the upper middle class there are enough shared interests between men and women to discourage suspicion.[8] The sexual barrier sometimes inhibited neighbor relations among women whose husbands traveled as salesmen, pilots, or seamen, forcing their wives to associate with each other.

Couple Visiting[9]

Although 40 percent of the Levittowners reported more couple visiting than in their former residences, the change was not quite as great as for neighboring, requiring as it does the compatibility of four rather than two or more of a commitment toward friendship as well.[10] Like neighboring, the increase in couple visiting resulted principally from the supply of compatible people, although it was also encouraged significantly by organizational activity; members of voluntary associations and of the highly organized Jewish subcommunity reported the greatest increase. Even the people who had not wanted to do more visiting before they moved to Levittown found themselves doing more if they were in organizations. Whether organizational membership encourages more visiting or vice versa is not clear; most likely, the same gregariousness that induces visiting also makes "joiners," for the latter have more friends in Levittown than the unaffiliated.

The patterns of couple visiting in Levittown question two features of the suburban critique—the superficiality of friendships and social hyperactivity. According to many critics of suburban life, the transience of the population induces transient relationships, which end with departure from the community. Transient relationships undoubtedly exist; one Levittowner, who had gone back to visit old friends in her former community, returned to report that she no longer had much in common with them and that they had been, as she put it, "development friends." Other transients established close friendships, however, and one family, temporarily transferred, returned to the block to be close to friends even though they would have preferred to move into one of Levitt's newer houses.

The criticism of "development" friendship harbors an implicit comparison with "bosom" friendship, assumed to have existed in the past, but there is no evidence that the comparison is emprically valid. Close friendships, I suspect, typically develop in childhood and adolescent peer groups, and can continue in a static society where people have as much in common in adulthood as in childhood. But in American society, and especially in the middle class, geographical and social mobility often separates people who have grown up together, so that shared interests among childhood friends are rare. Often, only nostalgia keeps the relationship going. Many Levittowners talk about close friends "at home," but they see them so rarely that the current strength of the friendship is never properly tested. Instead, they develop new friends at each stage of the life cycle or as they move up occupationally and develop new social and leisure interests. Closeness is not replaced by superficiality, but permanent friendships give way to new, and perhaps shorter, ones of similar closeness.

Whether or not this relationship is desirable depends on one's values. People today, particularly the middle classes, are more gregarious than those of the past. The working class, restricted in social skills or content to range within a smaller, perhaps closer, network of relatives and childhood friends, comes nearest to retaining the traditional "bosom" friendship. But these people, in my research as in many other studies, report difficulties in making new friends as their life conditions change.[11]

The critics' charge that the reason suburbanites indulge in hyperactive visiting is to counteract boredom and loneliness brought on by the lack of urbanity in their communities is equally mistaken. Coming from academia where the weekend brought parties, and having just lived in an Italian working-class neighborhood in Boston where people maintained an almost continual "open house," I was surprised at how little entertaining took place among Levittowners.[12] Although people often had visitors on Sunday afternoons, weekend evenings were not differentiated from the rest, a fact that should be obvious from the high ratings of television programs on the air at that time. I would guess that, on the average, Levittowners gathered informally not more than two or three times a month and gave formal parties about once a year, not counting those around Christmas and New Year's Eve. Social life in Levittown was not hyperactive by any stretch of the imagination, except perhaps in the first few months of putting out feelers. I suspect that the critics either confuse the early hyperactivity with the normal pattern once life had settled down, or they generalize from observations in upper middle-class suburbs, where partying is a major leisure activity.

Admittedly, the critics could question my assumption that an increase in social life is equivalent to an improvement in its quality, and argue that it represents instead an escape from pervasive boredom. If the Levittowners had found their social life boring, however, they would either have cut it down or complained about greater boredom. The data indicate just the opposite, for those visiting more were less bored (and vice versa). Besides, if social life had been as dull as the critics claim, why would the interview respondents have been so enthusiastic about the friendliness of their fellow residents?

THE PROS AND CONS OF POPULATION HOMOGENEITY

The suburban critique is quite emphatic on the subject of demographic homogeneity. For one thing, homogeneity violates the American Dream of a "balanced" community where people of diverse age, class, race, and religion live together. Allegedly, it creates dullness through sameness. In addition, age homogeneity deprives children—and adults—of the wisdom of their elders, while class, racial, and religious homogeneity prevent children from learning how to live in our pluralistic society. Homogeneity is said to make people callous to the poor, intolerant of Negroes, and scornful of the aged. Finally, heterogeneity is said to allow upward mobility, encouraging working- and lower-class people to learn middle-class ways from their more advantaged neighbors.

There is no question that Levittown is quite homogeneous in age and income as compared to established cities and small towns, but such comparisons are in many ways irrelevant. People do not live in the political units we call "cities" or "small towns"; often their social life takes place in areas even smaller than a census tract. Many such areas in the city are about as homogeneous in class as Levittown, and slum and high-income areas, whether urban or suburban, are even more so. Small towns are notoriously rigid in their separation of rich and poor, and only appear to be more heterogeneous because individual neighborhoods are so small. All these considerations effectively question the belief that before the advent of modern suburbs Americans of all classes lived together. Admittedly, statistics compiled for cities and suburbs as a whole show that residential segregation by class and by race are on the increase, but these trends also reflect the breakdown of rigid class and caste systems in which low-status people "knew their place," and which made residential segregation unnecessary.

By ethnic and religious criteria, Levittown is much less homogeneous than these other areas because people move in as individuals rather than as groups, and the enclaves found in some recently built urban neighborhoods, where 40 to 60 percent of the population comes from one ethnic or religious group, are absent. Nor is Levittown atypically homogeneous in age; new communities and subdivisions always attract young people, but over time, their populations "age" until the distribution resembles that of established communities.

Finally, even class homogeneity is not as great as community-wide statistics would indicate. Of three families earning $7000 a year, one might be a skilled worker at the peak of his earning power and dependent on union activity for further raises; another, a white-collar worker with some hope for a higher income; and a third, a young executive or professional at the start of his career. Their occupational and educational differences express themselves in many variations in lifestyle, and if they are neighbors, each is likely to look elsewhere for companionship. Perhaps the best way to demonstrate that Levittown's homogeneity is more statistical than real is to describe my own nearby neighbors. Two were Anglo Saxon Protestant couples from small towns. The breadwinners were employed as engineers—one an agnostic and a golf buff; the other a skeptical Methodist who wanted to be a teacher. Across the backyard lived a Baptist white-collar worker from Philadelphia and his Polish-American wife, who had brought her foreign-born mother with her to Levittown; and an Italian-American tractor operator (whose ambition was to own a junkyard) and his upwardly mobile wife, who restricted their social life to a brother who lived down the street and a host of relatives who came regularly every Sunday in a fleet of Cadillacs. One of my next-door neighbors was a religious fundamentalist couple from the Deep South whose life revolved around the church; another was an equally religious Catholic blue-collar worker and his wife—he originally a Viennese Jew, she a rural Protestant—who were politically liberal and as skeptical about middle-class ways as any intellectual. Across the street there was another Polish-American couple, highly mobile and conflicted over their obligations to the extended family; another engineer; and a retired Army officer. No wonder Levittowners were puzzled when a nationally known housing expert addressed them on the "pervasive homogeneity of suburban life."

Most Levittowners were pleased with the diversity they found among their neighbors, primarily because regional, ethnic, and religious differences are today almost innocuous, and provide variety to spice the flow of conversation and the exchange of ideas. For example, my Southern neighbors discovered pizza at the home of the Italian-American neighbor and developed a passion for it, and I learned much about the personal rewards of Catholicism from my Catholic convert neighbors. At the same time, however, Levittowners wanted homogeneity of age and income—or rather, they wanted neighbors and friends with common interests and sufficient consensus of values to make for informal and uninhibited relations. Their reasons were motivated neither by antidemocratic feelings nor by an interest in conformity. Children need playmates of the same age, and because child-rearing problems vary with age, mothers like to be near women who have children of similar age. And because these problems also fluctuate with class, they want some similarity of that factor—not homogeneity of occupation and education so much as agreement on the ends and means of caring for child, husband, and home.

Income similarly is valued by the less affluent, not as an end in itself, but because people who must watch every penny cannot long be comfortable with more affluent neighbors, particularly when children come home demanding toys or clothes they have seen next door. Indeed, objective measures of class are not taken into account in people's associations at all, partly because they do not identify each other in these terms, but also because class differences are not the only criterion for association. Sometimes neighbors of different backgrounds but with similar temperaments find themselves getting along nicely, especially if they learn to avoid activities and topics about which they disagree. For example, two women of diverse origins became good friends because they were both perfectionist housekeepers married to easygoing men, although they once quarreled bitterly over childrearing values.

But Levittowners also want some homogeneity for themselves. Cosmopolitans are impatient with locals, and vice versa; women who want to talk about cultural and civic matters are bored by conversations about home and family—and, again, vice versa; working-class women who are used to the informal flow of talk with relatives need to find substitutes among neighbors with similar experience. Likewise, young people have little in common with older ones, and unless they want surrogate parents, prefer to socialize with neighbors and friends of similar age. Some Levittowners sought ethnic and religious homogeneity as well. Aside from the Jews and some of the Greeks, Japanese, and the foreign-born women of other nations, observant Catholics and fundamentalist Protestants sought "their own"—the former because they were not entirely at ease with non-Catholic neighbors; the latter because their time-consuming church activity and their ascetic lifestyles set them apart from most other Levittowners. They mixed with their neighbors, of course, but their couple visiting was limited principally to the like-minded.

Most people had no difficulty finding the homogeneity they wanted in Levittown. Affluent and well-educated people could move into organizations or look for friends all over Levittown, but older people and people of lower income or poorly educated women were less able to move around either physically or socially. Women from these groups often did not have a car or did not know how to drive; many were reluctant to use baby-sitters for their children, only partly for financial reasons. Heterogeneity, then, may be a mixed blessing, particularly on the block, and something can be said for class and age homogeneity.

The alleged costs of homogeneity were also more unreal than the critics claim. It is probably true that Levittowners had less contact with old people than some urbanites (now rather rare) who still live in three-generation households. It is doubtful, however, that they had less contact with the older generation than urban and suburban residents of similar age and class, with the exception of the occupational transients, who are far from home and may return only once a year. Whether or not this lack of contact with grandparents affects children negatively can only be discovered by systematic studies among them. My observations of children's relations with grandparents suggest that the older generation is strange to them and vice versa, less as a result of lack of contact than of the vastness of generational change.

This is also more or less true of adult relationships with the older generation. Social change in America has been so rapid that the ideas and experiences of the elderly are often anachronistic, especially so for young mobile Levittowners whose parents are first- or second-generation Americans. Philadelphia women who lived with their parents before they moved to Levittown complained at length about the difficulties of raising children and running a household under those conditions, even though some missed their mothers sorely after moving to Levittown. A few found surrogate mothers among friends and neighbors, but chose women only slightly older than themselves and rarely consulted elderly neighbors. As for the husbands, they were, to a man, glad they had moved away from parents and in-laws.

That suburban homogeneity deprives children of contact with urban pluralism and "reality" is also dubious. Critics assume that urban children experience heterogeneity, but middle-class parents—and working-class ones, too—try hard to shield them from contact with conditions and people of lower status. Upper middle-class children may be taken on tours of the city, but to museums and shopping districts rather than to slums. Indeed, slum children, who are freer of parental supervision, probably see more of urban diversity than anyone else, although they do not often get into middle-class areas.

The homogenity of Levittown is not so pervasive that children are shielded from such unpleasant realities as alcoholism, mental illness, family strife, sexual aberration, or juvenile delinquency, which exist everywhere. The one element missing on most Levittown blocks—though, of course, in many city neighborhoods too—is the presence of Negro families. Although young Negro women came from nearby Burlington to work as maids, there were only two Negro families in the three neighborhoods built before Levittown's integration.

A generation of social research has demonstrated that racial and other forms of integration occur when diverse people can interact frequently in equal and noncompetitive situations. Here the suburbs are at an advantage when it comes to religious and ethnic integration, but at a disadvantage for racial and class integration, for aside from residential segregation, suburban high schools bring together students from a narrower variety of residential areas than do urban ones. Again, mere diversity does not ensure the kind of interaction that encourages integration, and a school with great diversity but sharp internal segregation may not be as desirable as one with less diversity but without internal segregation. Judging by life on the block in Levittown, maximal diversity and extreme heterogeneity encourage more conflict than integration, and while conflict can be desirable and even didactic, this is only true if it can be resolved in some way. People so different from each other in age or class that they cannot agree on anything are unlikely to derive much enrichment from heterogeneity.

A corollary of the belief in diversity as a stimulant to enrichment holds that working-class and lower-class people will benefit—and be improved—by living among middle-class neighbors. Even if one overlooks the patronizing class bias implicit in this view, it is not at all certain that residential propinquity will produce the intended cultural change. In Levittown, working-class families living alongside middle-class ones went their own way most of the time. For mobile ones, heterogeneity is obviously desirable, provided middle-class people are willing to teach them, but nonmobile ones will react negatively to force feedings of middle-class culture. Neighbors are expected to treat each other as equals, and working-class residents have enough difficulty paying the higher cost of living among middle-class people, without being viewed as culturally deprived. When working-class organizations used middle-class Levittowners for technical and administrative services, they rejected those who looked down on them and constantly tested the others to make sure they measured up to the norms of working-class culture. Children are not yet fully aware of class, so that they can be with (and learn from) peers of other classes, and there is some evidence that in schools with a majority of middle-class children, working-class children will adopt the former's standards of school performance, and vice versa.

Critics of the suburbs also inveigh against physical homogeneity and mass-produced housing. Like much of the rest of the critique, this charge is a thinly veiled attack on the culture of working- and lower middle-class people, implying that mass-produced housing leads to mass-produced lives. The critics seem to forget that the townhouses of the upper class in the nineteenth century were also physically homogeneous; that everyone, poor and rich alike, drives mass-produced, homogeneous cars without damage to their personalities; and that today, only the rich can afford custom-built housing. I heard no objection among the Levittowners about the similarity of their homes, nor the popular jokes about being unable to locate one's own house. Esthetic diversity is preferred, however, and people talked about moving to a custom-built house in the future when they could afford it. Meanwhile, they made internal and external alterations in their Levitt house to reduce sameness and to place a personal stamp on their property.[13]

CONFORMITY AND COMPETITION

The suburban critique is especially strident on the prevalence of conformity. It argues that relationships between neighbors and friends are regulated by the desire to copy each other to achieve uniformity. At the same time, the critics also see suburbanites as competitive, trying to keep up or down with the Joneses to satisfy the desire for status. Conforming (or copying) and competing are not the same—indeed, they are contradictory—but they are lumped together in the critique because they are based on the common assumption that, in the suburbs, behavior and opinion are determined by what the neighbors do and think, and individualism is found only in the city. Both competition and copying exist in Levittown, but not for the reasons suggested by the critics. They are ways of coping with heterogeneity and of retaining individuality while being part of the group. They exist in every group, but are more prevalent among homeowners and, because of the fascination with suburbia, more visible there. But this does not make them suburban phenomena.

Enough of the suburban critique has seeped into the reading matter of Levittowners to make "conformity" a pejorative term, and interview questions about it would have produced only denials. Competition is talked about in Levittown, however, and 60 percent of the random sample reported competition among their neighbors.[14] The examples they gave, however, not only included copying, but half the respondents described it positively. "I don't know what competition is," said one man. "Perhaps when we see the neighbors repairing the house, and we figure our own repairs would be a good idea." Another put it more enthusiastically: "Friends and neighbors ask me what I've done, and, by our visiting different neighbors, we get different ideas about fixing up the house—how we are going to paint. Instead of both of us buying an extension ladder, we go half and half."

In effect, diverging or deviant behavior can be seen as competition, conformity, or the chance to learn new ideas, depending on the observer. One who dislikes behavior common to several neighbors may accuse them of copying each other. If the behavior is dissimilar, it must be a result of competition: "keeping up with the Joneses" or "spending beyond one's means." When the behavior is approved, however, it is interpreted as sharing ideas. The observer's perspective is shaped principally by his relative class position, or by his estimate of his position. If the observer is of *higher* status than the observed, he will interpret the latter's attempt to share higher-status ideas as competing, and his sharing of lower status ways as copying. If the observer is of *lower* status than the observed, his ideas will not be shared, of course, but he will consider the more affluent lifestyle of the higher-status neighbor as motivated by status-striving or "keeping up with the Joneses."[15] As one blue-collar man put it, "There are some who act so darned important, as if they have so much, and I can't figure out what they are doing in Levittown when they have so much." Another blue-collar man who had taught his neighbors about lawn care, and felt himself to be their equal, was not threatened: "One or two try to keep up with the Joneses, but generally people are not worried. If one gets ahead and another copies him, we laugh. Our attitude is, all the more power to him. When we can afford it, we make improvements too." In other words, when the observer feels he is equal to the observed, he will see competing and copying either as sharing or as friendly games. And socially mobile people tend to judge the ways of higher-status people positively, for they can look to their neighbors for guidance about how to live in the suburbs. "Everyone has fixed up their houses, but not to compete," a former city dweller reported. "At first none of us had anything and maybe you saw what others did and you copied it." Needless to say, those who are copied may consider the mobile neighbor a competing upstart.

Status-striving is generally ascribed to people with more money, more education, and a different lifestyle by those who cannot afford the style or prefer a different one. The same motive is inferred about social relations. Lower-status observers see cliques of higher-status people as groups that coalesce for prestige reasons, and higher-status observers view lower-status cliques as groups that come together to conform. When relations among neighbors of unequal status deteriorate, the higher-status person explains it in terms of culturally or morally undesirable actions by the lower-status neighbor; the lower-status person ascribes the break to his neighbor's desire to be with more prestigious people. In reality, instances of overt status-striving, carried out to show up the lower status of neighbors, are rare. "Keeping up" takes place, but mainly out of the need to maintain self-respect, to "put the best face forward" or not to be considered inferior and "fall behind." Serious status-striving is usually a desperate attempt by a socially isolated neighbor to salvage self-respect through material or symbolic displays of status, and is dismissed or scorned. One such neighbor was described as "trying to be the Joneses, and hoping people will follow him, but we don't pay any attention to him." Indeed, the social control norms of block life encourage "keeping down with the Joneses," and criticize display of unusual affluence, so that people who can afford a higher standard of living than the rest and who show it publicly are unpopular and are sometimes ostracized.

Conforming and copying occur more frequently than competition, mostly to secure the proper appearance of the block to impress strangers. A pervasive system of social control develops to enforce standards of appearance on the block, mainly concerning lawn care. Copying and some competition take place in this process, but neither the Levittowners nor the suburban critics would describe it in these terms. Everyone knows it is social control and accepts the need for it, although one year some of my neighbors and I wished we could pave our front lawns with green concrete to eliminate the endless watering and mowing and to forestall criticism of poor lawns.

The primary technique for social control is humor. Wisecracks are made to show up deviant behavior, and overt criticism surfaces only when the message behind the wisecracks does not get across. Humor is used to keep relations friendly and because people feel that demands for conformity are not entirely proper; they realize that such demands sometimes require a difficult compromise between individual and group standards. When it comes to lawn care, however, most people either have no hard-and-fast personal standards, or they value friendly relations more. Since the block norms and the compromises they require are usually worked out soon after the block is occupied—when everyone is striving to prove he will be a good neighbor—they are taken for granted by the time the block has settled down.

The demand for compromise is also reduced by limiting block standards to the exterior appearance of the front of the house and the front yard, the back being less visible to outsiders. Interiors, which involve the owner's ego more, are not subjected to criticism. People are praised for a nice-looking home, but there are no wisecracks about deviant taste in furnishings—at least, not to the owner. The same limitation holds for cars and other consumer goods purchased. Although I drove a 1952 Chevrolet, by far the oldest car on the block, no one ever joked with me about it,[16] but Levittowners who used trucks in their work and parked them on their streets at night, giving the block the image of a working-class district, were criticized by middle-class neighbors. The criticism was made behind their backs, however, because it affected the neighbors' source of livelihood. In this case, as in some others, social control was passed on to the township government, and eventually, it voted an ordinance prohibiting truck-parking on residential streets.

Competition, Conformity, and Heterogeneity

Both competition and conformity are ways of coping with heterogeneity, principally of class. When lower-status people are accused of copying and higher-status ones of living beyond their means to impress the neighbors, disapproval is put in terms of negative motives rather than class differences, for accusations of deviant behavior that blame individuals make it more difficult for the deviant to appeal to his group norms. Such accusations also enable people to ignore the existence of class differences. Class is a taboo subject, and the taboo is so pervasive, and so unconscious, that people rarely think in class terms.

Competition and conformity exist also because people are dependent on their neighbors. In working-class or ethnic enclaves, where social life is concentrated among relatives, their criticism is feared more than the neighbors'. Upper middle-class people, having less to do with neighbors, conform most closely to the demands of their friends. In Levittown, neighbors are an important reference group, not only for lower middle-class people but for working-class ones cut off from relatives. Even so, the prime cause of both competition and conformity is home ownership and the mutual need to preserve property and status values. Only 11 percent of former renters but 70 percent of former homeowners reported noticing competition in their former residence, but both observed it equally in Levittown. Moreover, whether they came from urban or suburban neighborhoods, they reported no more competition in Levittown than in the former residence. Consequently, competition is not distinctive either to Levittown or to the suburbs.

What then accounts for the critics' preoccupation with suburban conformity, and their tendency to see status competition as a dominant theme in suburban life? For one thing, many of these critics live in city apartments, where the concern for block status preservation is minimal. Also, they are largely upper middle-class professionals, dedicated to cosmopolitan values and urban life and disdainful of the local and antiurban values of lower middle-class and working-class people. Believing in the universality of these values, the critics refuse to acknowledge the existence of lower middle-class or working-class ways of living. Instead, they describe people as mindless conformers who would be cosmopolitans if they were not weak and allowed themselves to be swayed by builders, the mass media, and their neighbors.

The ascription of competitive behavior to the suburbs stems from another source. The upper middle-class world, stressing as it does individuality, is a highly competitive one. In typically upper middle-class occupations such as advertising, publishing, university teaching, law, and the arts, individual achievement is the main key to success, status, and security. The upper middle class is for this reason more competitive and more status-conscious than the other classes. Popular writers studying upper middle-class suburbs have observed this competition, and some have mistakenly ascribed it to suburbia, rather than to the criteria for success in the professions held by these particular suburbanites. Those writing about lower-status suburbs have either drawn their information from upper middle-class friends who have moved to lower middle-class suburbs for financial reasons and found themselves a dissatisfied minority, or they have, like upper middle-class people generally, viewed the lower-status people about whom they were writing as trying to compete with their betters.

Finally, the new suburbs, being more visible than other lower middle- and working-class residential areas, have become newsworthy, and during the 1950s they replaced "mass culture" as the scapegoat and most convenient target for the fear and distaste that upper middle-class people feel for the rest of the population. Affluent suburbs have become false targets of dissatisfaction with the upper middle class's own status-consciousness and competition, the "rat-race" it experiences in career- and social-striving having been projected on life beyond the city limits.

The inaccuracy of the critique does not, of course, exclude the possibility that conforming and competing are undesirable or dangerous, or that too much of both take place in Levittown. I do not believe either to be the case. If one distinguishes between *wanted* conformity, as when neighbors learn from each other or share ideas; *tolerated* conformity, when they adjust their own standards in order to maintain friendly relations; and *unwanted* conformity, when they bow to pressure and give up their individuality, only the last is clearly undesirable, and in Levittown it is rare. Tolerated conformity requires some surrender of autonomy, but I can see why Levittowners feel it is more important to be friendly with one's neighbors than to insist on individual but unpopular ways of fixing up the outside of the house. The amount of copying and conformity is hardly excessive, considering the heterogeneity on the block. Indeed, given the random way in which Levittowners become neighbors, it is amazing that neighbor relations were so friendly and tolerant of individual differences. Of course, the working-class and upper middle-class minorities experience pressure for unwanted conformity, but the latter can get away from the block for social activities, and ultimately, only some of the former suffer. Ironically, their exposure to pressures for conformity is a result of the heterogeneity that the critics want to increase even further.

NOTES

1. Many of the findings on Levittown's impact are based on interviews with two sets of Levittowners, one a nearly random sample of 45 buyers in the first neighborhood to be settled and the second, of a Philadelphia sample of 55 others in the neighborhood who had moved there from the city.

2. Neighboring, or visiting with neighbors, was defined in the interview as "having coffee together, spending evenings together, or frequent conversations in or out of the house; anything more than saying hello or polite chatting about the weather." It was further defined as taking place among individuals rather than couples, and people were asked, "Are you yourself doing more visiting with neighbors than where you lived before, or less?"

3. Fifty-four percent of the random sample was neighboring more than in the previous residence; 16 percent, less; and 30 percent, the same. Among Philadelphians, the percentages were 48, 19, and 33, respectively.

4. Thus, one third of the least educated in the random sample, and two thirds of the college-educated in the Philadelphia sample reported less neighboring. Jews

from smaller towns who had already learned to live with non-Jewish neighbors, and third-generation Jewish Philadelphians did not report less neighboring.

5. The principal post-World War II studies are Merton; Caplow and Foreman; Festinger, Schachter, and Back; Dean; Whyte, Chap. 25; and Willmott, Chap. 7. Critical analyses of these studies can be found in Gans and Schorr, Chap. 1; of earlier ones, in Rosow.

6. This relationship varies with age, of course, and older children do not choose propinquitous playmates as often. Olsen's study of children's birthday parties reported in the Levittown newspaper showed that among three-year-olds, guests came from a median distance of 364 feet; 775 feet among four-year-olds, 1130 feet among seven-year-olds. The distance then remained fairly stable until it rose to about 2000 feet among twelve- and thirteen-year-olds.

7. Jews often move into communities where the median income is lower than their own, partly because some prefer to spend a lower share of their income on housing, partly because they fear rejection from non-Jewish neighbors of similar income and education.

8. The sexual overtones did not affect my interviewing because strangers were exempt. Women are permitted to have latent sexual interest in casual encounters—giving rise to jokes about the iceman and the milkman—and only neighbors' husbands are taboo.

9. People were asked about "the visiting you and your husband (wife) do with other couples, either among neighbors or anywhere else in Levittown."

10. Forty-four percent of the random sample reported more couple visiting; 21 percent, less; and 35 percent, no change. Among the Philadelphians, the percentages were almost the same: 39, 22, and 39, respectively. In a new working-class suburb, 38 percent said "they entertain friends at home" more often than before, but 27 percent reported less. See Berger, p. 65.

11. Low-status respondents have as many friends as middle- and high-status ones, but the former do less couple visiting than in the previous residence.

12. The neighbors I knew best in the West End of Boston had open house every Tuesday night, visited the open house of relatives every Friday night, and visited with yet other relatives and friends on Sundays.

13. It is illuminating to compare the early popular writing about Levittown, New York, to more recent reports. Initially, the Long Island community was widely described (and decried) as a hideous example of mass-produced housing that would soon turn into a slum; twenty years later, journalists report the diversity produced by the alternation of houses, and the charm created by the maturing of trees and shrubbery—and, of course, the demand for the houses, which now sell for about twice their original price.

14. People were asked, "What kind of competition have you noticed between the neighbors about such things as getting things for the house, fixing up the yard, or repainting the house?"

15. Forty-four percent of the blue-collar respondents reported "keeping up with the Joneses" among their neighbors, but only 31 percent of the white-collar and professional ones did so.

16. In fact, I was more often praised for having taken good care of the car, for my thrift, and for my good luck in possessing a better car than the more recent models.

REFERENCES

Berger, Bennett M. *Working Class Suburb.* Berkeley: University of California Press, 1960.

Caplow, T., and R. Foreman. "Neighborhood Interaction in a Homogeneous Community." *American Sociological Review* 15 (June 1950): 357–66.

Dean, John P. "Housing Design and Family Values." *Land Economics* 29 (May 1953): 128–41.

Festinger, L., S. Schachter, and K. Back. *Social Pressures in Informal Groups.* New York: Harper, 1950.

Gans, Herbert J. "Planning and Social Life." *Journal of the American Institute of Planners* 27 (May 1961): 134–40.

Merton, Robert K. "The Social Psychology of Housing." In *Current Trends in Social Psychology,* edited by Wayne Dennis, 304–12. Pittsburgh: University of Pittsburgh Press, 1947.

Olsen, William, "The Location of Children's Birthday Party Attendance in Levittown, New Jersey," Unpublished paper, Department of City Planning, University of Pennsylvania, 1960.

Rosow, Irving, "The Social Effects of the Physical Environment." *Journal of the American Institute of Planning* 27 (May 1961): 127–33.

Schorr, Alvin L. *Slums and Social Insecurity.* Washington, D.C.: Social Security Administration, 1961.

Whyte, William H. Jr. *The Organization Man.* New York: Simon and Schuster, 1956.

Willmott, Peter. *The Evolution of a Community.* London: Routledge and Kegan Paul, 1963.

· 3 ·

Values in the News

Journalism is, like sociology, an empirical discipline. As a result, the news consists not only of the findings of empirical inquiry but also of the concepts and methods that go into that inquiry, the assumptions that underlie concepts and methods, and a further set of assumptions that could be tested empirically if journalists had the time. These assumptions being mainly about the nature of external reality, I call them reality judgments.

Like other empirical disciplines, the news does not limit itself to reality judgments; it also contains values, or preference statements. This in turn makes it possible to suggest that there is, underlying the national news, a picture of nation and society as it ought to be. The values in the news are not necessarily those of the journalists, nor are they always distinctive to the news. Many are shared by or originate with the sources from whom the journalists obtain information and from other sectors of America.

The Analysis of Values

Journalists try hard to be objective, but neither they nor anyone else can in the end proceed without values. Furthermore, reality judgments are never altogether divorced from values. The judgment that the president and leading public officials represent the nation, for example, carries with it an acceptance of, if not a preference for, this state of affairs; otherwise, stories that investigate whether the president does, in fact, represent the nation would be more numerous.

The values in the national news are rarely explicit and must be found between the lines—in what actors and activities are reported or ignored, and in how they are described. If a news story deals with activities that are

---

This chapter is abridged from Chapter 2 of *Deciding What's News: A Study of CBS Evening News, NBC Nightly News, Newsweek and Time.* © 1979 by Herbert J. Gans. Reprinted with permission of Pantheon Books, a division of Random House.

generally considered undesirable and whose descriptions contain negative connotations, then the story implicitly expresses a value about what is desirable. In the process, the news also assumes a consensus about values that may not exist, for it reminds the audience of values that are being violated and assumes that the audience shares these values. When a story reports that a politician has been charged with corruption, it suggests, *sotto voce,* that corruption is bad and that politicians should be honest. Much news is about the violation of values, which is why so much of what journalists report is "bad news."

Nevertheless, because journalists do not, in most instances, deliberately insert values into the news, these values must be inferred. Since inference cannot take place without an inferrer, however, and different people come to the news with different preconceptions, they may infer many different values from what they see or read. Also, the analyst's own values make him or her more sensitive to some values in the news than to others; as a result, content analysis is often a comparison of the analyst's values with those that "exist" in the content.

Furthermore, even if the values *in* the news could be inferred unambiguously—that is, if all inferrers agreed about them—there are also values that stem *from* the news. There is a difference between the values in the news and the value implications of the news; but while the former may ultimately originate with the journalists, the latter do not. Journalists are sensitive to the difference between the news and its implications, but critics and content analysts are not always equally so, and the values they may see in the news and among journalists are actually implications. Conservative critics have attacked the news media for their coverage of the ghetto disturbances and the antiwar demonstrations, maintaining that these stories, by publicizing dissent, had negative implications for the status quo. Critics on the left do likewise, for they perceive stories that fail to report the faults of capitalism or that ignore the activities of radical activists as holding back drastic change. Although the dividing line between values and value implications is not always easy to maintain, my analysis will eschew the latter as much as possible.

Even so, identifying values in the news is a virtually impossible task because there are so many of them; indeed, every story expresses several values. Consequently, I shall employ a narrow definition of values, examining only preference statements about nation and society, and major national or societal issues. I also distinguish between two types of values, which I call topical and enduring, and I will analyze only the latter. Topical values are the opinions expressed about specific actors or activities of the moment, be they a presidential appointee or a new anti-inflation policy. These manifest themselves in the explicit opinions of newsmagazine stories and television commentary, as well as in the implicit judgments that enter into all stories. Enduring values, on the other hand, are values that can be found in many different types of news stories over a long period of time; often, they affect what events become news, for some are part and parcel of the definition of news. Enduring values are not timeless, and they may change somewhat over the years; moreover, they also help to shape journalists' opinions, and many times, opinions are only specifications of enduring values.

The list that follows is limited to the enduring values found in the national news in the 1960s and 1970s, although all are probably of far more venerable vintage; obviously, it includes those that this inferrer, bringing his own values to the task, has found most visible and important. The list does not claim to be complete; and because I undertook no quantitative analyses, it does not suggest which values appear most frequently.

The methods by which I identified the values were impressionistic; the values really emerged from continual scrutiny of the news over a long time. Some came from the ways actors and activities are described, the tones in which stories are written, told, or filmed, and the connotations that accrue to commonly used nouns and adjectives, especially if neutral terms are available but not used. When years ago the news reported that Stokely Carmichael had "turned up" somewhere, while the president had, on the same day, "arrived" somewhere else; or when another story pointed out that a city was "plagued by labor problems," the appropriate values were not difficult to discern, if only because neutral terms were available but were not used. However, sometimes neutral terms are simply not available. The news could have called the young men who refused to serve in the Vietnam War draft evaders, dodgers, or resisters, but it rarely used the last term. Of course, individual words only provide clues to values, not conclusions about them; also, newsmagazines are more easily analyzed by this method because they eschew neutral terms for stylistic reasons, although all of the above examples are from television.[1]

ENDURING VALUES IN THE NEWS

The enduring values I want to discuss can be grouped into eight clusters: ethnocentrism, altruistic democracy, responsible capitalism, small-town pastoralism, individualism, moderatism, social order, and national leadership. There are many others, of course, which I shall leave out either for reasons of space or because they are taken for granted, even though they are values. Among these, for example, are the desirability of economic prosperity; the undesirability of war *sui generis* (which does not always extend to specific wars); the virtues of family, love, and friendship; and the ugliness of hate and prejudice. The news often supports the kinds of values sometimes unfairly belittled as "motherhood values."

Ethnocentrism

Like the news of other countries. American news values its own nation above all, even though it sometimes disparages blatant patriotism. This ethnocentrism comes through most explicitly in foreign news, which judges other countries by the extent to which they live up to or imitate American practices and values, but it also underlies domestic news. Obviously, the news contains many stories that are critical of domestic conditions, but these conditions are almost always treated as deviant cases, with the implication that American ideals, at least, remain viable. The Watergate scandals were usually ascribed to a small group of power-hungry politicians, and beyond that, to the "Imperial Presidency"—but with the afterthought, particularly following Richard Nixon's resignation, that nothing was fundamentally wrong with American democracy, even if reforms were needed.

The clearest expression of ethnocentrism, in all countries, appears in war news. While reporting the Vietnam War, the news media described the North Vietnamese and the National Liberation Front as "the enemy," as if they were the enemy of the news media. Similarly, weekly casualty stories reported the number of Americans killed, wounded, or missing, and the number of South Vietnamese killed; but the casualties on the other side were impersonally described as "the Communist death toll" or the "body count."

Again, as in war reporting everywhere, the committing of atrocities, in this case by Americans, did not get into the news very often, and then only toward the end of the war. Seymour Hersh, the reporter credited with exposing the Mylai massacre, had considerable difficulty selling the story until the evidence was incontrovertible. The end of the war in Vietnam was typically headlined as "the Fall of South Vietnam," with scarcely a recognition that by other values, it could also be considered a liberation, or in neutral terminology, a change in governments.

Altruistic Democracy

While foreign news suggests quite explicitly that democracy is superior to dictatorship, and the more so if it follows American forms, domestic news is more specific, indicating how American democracy should perform by its frequent attention to deviations from an unstated ideal, evident in stories about corruption, conflict, protest, and bureaucratic malfunctioning. That ideal may be labeled altruistic democracy because, above all, the news implies that politics should follow a course based on the public interest and public service.

The news tends to treat politics per se as a contest, identifying winners and losers more than heroes and villains. Although the news has little patience for losers, it insists that both winners and losers should be scrupulously honest, efficient, and dedicated to acting in the public interest. Financial corruption is always news, as is nepotism, patronage appointments, logrolling, and "deals" in general. Decisions based, or thought to be based, on either self-interest or partisan concerns thus continue to be news whenever they occur, even though they long ago ceased to be novel events.

Politicians, politics, and democracy are also expected to be meritocratic; the regular activities of political machines are regularly exposed, and "machine" itself is a pejorative term. Although the news therefore regards civil-service officials more highly than "political appointees," the former are held to a very high standard of efficiency and performance; as a result, any deviant bureaucratic behavior becomes newsworthy. "Waste" is always an evil, whatever the amount; the mass of paperwork entailed by bureaucracy is a frequent story, and the additional paperwork generated by attempts to reduce the amount of paperwork is a humorous item, which has appeared in the news with regularity over the years. Officials, whether elected or appointed, are also expected to be spartan in their tastes; consequently, in 1977, Secretary of Health, Education, and Welfare Joseph Califano got into the news when he hired a chef for his official dining room. The story lasted longer than a concurrent report that he had hired a combination bodyguard-office manager, at almost four times the cook's salary.

The same high standards apply to citizens, however. Citizens should participate; and "grassroots activity" is one of the most complimentary terms in the vocabulary of the news, particularly when it takes place to foil politicians or bureaucrats, or to eliminate the need for government action. Ideally, citizens should help themselves without having to resort to government aid, and occasionally stories of such an occurrence suggest a revival of a past and now extinct tradition. As a result, the news seems to imply that the democratic ideal against which it measures reality is that of the rural town meeting—or rather, of a romanticized version of it. Citizen participation should also be as unselfish as that of politicians. Organized lobbying and the formation of pressure groups in behalf of citizens' self-interest is still reported in suspect tones, though not as suspect as when corporate lobbyists are covered.

The support for altruism correlates with an emphasis on what one might call the official norms of the American polity, which are derived largely from the Constitution. Consequently, the news endorses, or sets up as a standard, the formal norms of democracy and the formal structures of democratic institutions as established by the Founders. Concurrently, it treats as suspect the informal norms and structures that have developed in the polity to allocate power and resources; in effect, the news defends democratic theory against an almost inevitably inferior democratic practice.

In the process, the news keeps track of the violations of official norms, but it does so selectively. Over the years, the news has been perhaps most concerned with freedom of the press and related civil liberties; even recurring local violations, by school boards that censor library shelves, have often become national news. Violations of the civil liberties of radicals, of due process, habeas corpus, and other constitutional protections, particularly for criminals, are less newsworthy.

Another official norm to which the news pays frequent attention is racial integration. Activists who strive for the realization of democratic norms are often described in the news as extremists or militants, but the activists supporting racial integration were never so labeled, much to the dismay of southern television stations affiliated with the networks. Conversely, black-power activists were newsworthy in part because they rejected integration; they were almost uniformly labeled militants, with equally activist supporters of integration described as moderates.

Actually, the news tends to treat all formal governmental goal statements, and even campaign promises, as official values, and reports when these are violated. In particular, politicians who run campaigns emphasizing their honesty are closely watched, and the deviations from their own stated ideals by Eugene McCarthy, George McGovern, and Jimmy Carter consequently became headline news.

While—and perhaps because—the news consistently reports political and legal failures to achieve altruistic and official democracy, it concerns itself much less with the economic barriers that obstruct the realization of the ideal. Of course, the news is aware of candidates who are millionaires or who obtain substantial amounts of corporate or union campaign money, but it is less conscious of the relationship between poverty and powerlessness, or even of the difficulty that Americans of median income have in obtaining political access. That economic power affects the achievement of the democratic ideal continues to be viewed more as a campaign theme than as a fact of life, for in the altruistic and official democracy valued by the news, economics are—and should be—kept separate from politics.

The relative inattention to economic obstacles to democracy stems from the assumption that the polity and the economy are separate and independent of each other. Under ideal conditions, one is not supposed to affect or interfere with the other, although typically, government intervention in the economy is more newsworthy and serious than private industry's intervention in government. Accordingly, the news rarely notes the extent of public subsidy of private industry, and it continues to describe firms and institutions that are completely or partly subsidized by government funds as private—for example, Lockheed, many charitable organizations, and most privately run universities.

Responsible Capitalism

The underlying posture of the news toward the economy resembles that taken toward the polity: an optimistic faith that in the good society, businessmen and women will compete with each other in order to create increased prosperity for all, but that they will refrain from unreasonable profits and gross exploitation of workers or customers. Bigness is no more a virtue in business or union organization than in government, so that the small and family-owned firm is still sometimes presented as the ideal. While monopoly is clearly evil, there is little explicit or implicit criticism of the oligopolistic nature of much of today's economy. Unions and consumer organizations are accepted as countervailing pressures on business (although the former much less so than the latter), and strikes are frequently judged negatively, especially if they inconvenience "the public," contribute to inflation, or involve violence.

Economic growth is always a positive phenomenon, unless it brings about inflation or environmental pollution, leads to the dstruction of a historic landmark, or puts craftsmen or craftswomen out of work. In the past, when news anchors personally gave the stock market report, even the most detached ones looked cheerful when the market had had a good day, assuming this to be of universal benefit to the nation and the economy.

Like politicians, business officials are expected to be honest and efficient; but while corruption and bureaucratic misbehavior are as undesirable in business as in government, they are nevertheless tolerated to a somewhat greater extent in business. Actually, the news often fails to notice that corporations and other large private agencies are also bureaucracies given to red tape. Also, innovation and risk taking are seen as more desirable in business than in public agencies. Consequently, governmental demonstration projects must succeed the first time around, while the failure of business experiments is treated with greater tolerance, even if the public pays the bill in both instances.

Domestic news has by now acknowledged the necessity for the welfare state; even in the good society, the market cannot do everything. The term "welfare state" itself is reserved largely for foreign countries, however, and attitudes toward it are more clearly evident in foreign than in domestic stories. These tend to dwell more on its problems and failures than on its successes, most recently in Sweden, where the welfare state is particularly seen as a threat, from high tax rates and public control over investment, to the ability of the economy to provide sufficient incentives for economic growth. In America, the welfare state is expected to aid people who cannot participate in the market or who are hard-pressed; that government can provide useful services, or that it can sometimes do so more effectively than private enterprise, is not often acknowledged.

It is now accepted that the government must help the poor, but only the deserving poor, for "welfare cheaters" are a continuing menace and are more newsworthy than people—other than the very rich—who cheat on their taxes. Public welfare agencies are kept under closer scrutiny than others, so that, although the news reported on the "welfare mess" in the 1960s, it did not describe equivalent situations in other government agencies in the same way. There was, for example, no "defense mess," and what is "waste" in social programs is "cost overruns" in Pentagon programs.

American news is, of course, consistently critical of Communist and democratic-socialist economies. In fact, foreign news is more worried about the political and cultural shortcomings of socialism or communism. To be sure, both are suspect because public ownership and other socialist programs will do away with private property and impair productivity and growth; but descriptions of existing income distributions, in America and elsewhere, now regularly imply that economic inequality is undesirable, even if income redistribution is not the right solution. Still, the primary dangers of socialism are cultural homogeneity, the erosion of political liberties, and the burgeoning of bureaucracy.

Although domestic politicians who criticize governmental welfare measures as socialistic or communistic no longer get the attention they once did, domestic news also remains critical of American socialism. More correctly, the news ignores it, for socialist critiques of the American economy, as well as the activities of America's socialist parties and informal groups, are not newsworthy. The socialist factions in the protest movements of the 1960s and in the feminist and other movements of the 1970s have also been ignored.

Small-town Pastoralism

The rural and anti-industrial values that Thomas Jefferson is usually thought to have invented can also be found in the news, which favors small towns (agricultural or market) over other types of settlements. At one time, this preference was complemented by a celebration of the large city and of the vitality of its business and entertainment districts; but the end of this period can be dated almost exactly by *Life's* special issue on the cities, which appeared in December 1965.

Although the belief that cities should be fun places and that large, central business-district renewal projects should "revitalize" them still continues to be held, cities have been in the news almost entirely as problematic, with the major emphasis on racial conflict, crime, and fiscal insolvency. Suburbs are not often newsworthy, despite the fact that a near majority of Americans now live in them, and they, too, have generally received bad press. During the 1950s and 1960s, suburbs were viewed as breeding grounds of homogeneity, boredom, adultery, and other evils; since then, they have come into the news because they are suffering increasingly from "urban" problems, particularly crime, or because they keep out racial minorities and stand in the way of racial integration.

During the 1960s, new towns (like Columbia, Maryland) were welcomed precisely because they were expected to overcome the faults of both city and suburb, restoring the more intimate social relationships and sense of community ascribed to small towns; but that hope was lost when they also encountered fiscal problems and manifested racial conflict and other "urban" ills as well. As a result, the small town continues to reign supreme, not only in Charles Kuralt's classic CBS travelogue series, "On the Road" but also in television and magazine stories about "the good life" in America. Stories about city neighborhoods judge them by their ability to retain the cohesiveness, friendliness, and slow pace ascribed to small towns, and to the ethnic enclaves of the past.

Needless to say, the pastoral values underlying the news are romantic; they visualize rural and market towns as they were imagined to have existed in the past. Today's small towns are reported nostalgically; and their deaths, or their being swallowed up by the expanding suburbs, is a frequent and sentimental story. During the 1960s, the youthful exodus into the hinterlands of Vermont and California was first welcomed as a small-town revival. In recent years, the growth of small towns, especially in the South, has also been reported as a revival; but generally, economic growth is viewed as a danger to "community," even if it is valued in the abstract.

Small-town pastoralism is, at the same time, a specification of two more general values: the desirability both of nature and of smallness per se. The news dealt with the conflict between the preservation of nature and the activities of developers long before the environment and ecology became political issues; and more often than not, the news took at least an implicit stand against the developers. The postwar developers of suburbia were seen as despoiling the land in their rapacious search for profits; that they were concurrently providing houses for people was rarely noted.

The virtue of smallness comes through most clearly in stories that deal with the faults of bigness, for in the news, Big Government, Big Labor, and Big Business rarely have virtues. Bigness is feared, among other things, as impersonal and inhuman. In the news as well as in architecture, the ideal social organization should reflect a "human scale." The fear of bigness also reflects a fear of control, of privacy and individual freedom being ground under by organizations too large to notice, much less to value, the individual. As such, bigness is a major threat to individualism, an enduring value in the news, to be discussed below. Consequently, the news often contains stories about new technology that endangers the individual—notably the computer, which is viewed anthropomorphically, either as a robot that will deprive human beings of control over their own lives or as a machine endowed with human failings, which is therefore less of a threat. In any case, there is always room for a gleeful story about computers that break down. The news has, however, always paid attention to the dangers of new technology: when television sets were first mass-produced, they were viewed as dehumanizing because they robbed people of the art of conversation; related fears were expressed at the time of the institution of digit-dialing in telephones.

Conversely, the news celebrates old technology and mourns its passing, partly because it is tied to an era when life was thought to have been simpler, partly because it is viewed as being under more individual control. Sentimental features about the closing of a business based on craftsmanship and about the razing of architectural landmarks, including the industrial mills that were once hated symbols of an exploitative industrialism, are commonplace. Even more attention is paid to the berthing of an ocean liner or the elimination of an old railroad train; and the captain of an ocean liner is a far more admired figure than the pilot of a jumbo jet, even if both now use radar to steer their vehicles, and the vehicles themselves are both owned by large corporations.

Small-town pastoralism and old technology may in the end be surrogates for a more general value: an underlying respect for tradition of any kind, save perhaps discrimination against racial, sexual, and other minorities. Tradition is valued because it is known, predictable, and therefore orderly, and order is a major enduring news value. Novel phenomena are, despite their being the basic raw material of news, potential threats to order. Thus, California, which is, from the Eastern perspective of the news, still a new land, is viewed as the fountainhead of bizarre new ideas.

Individualism

One of the most important enduring news values is the preservation of the freedom of the individual against the encroachments of nation and society. The good society of the news is populated by individuals who participate in it, but on their own terms, acting in the public interest, but as they define it.

The ideal individual struggles successfully against adversity and overcomes more powerful forces. The news looks for people who act heroically during disasters, and it pays attention to people who conquer nature without hurting it: explorers, mountain climbers, astronauts, and scientists. "Self-made" men and women remain attractive, as do people who overcome poverty or bureaucracy. Still, the most pervasive way in which the news pays homage to the individual is by its focus on people rather than on groups.

Conversely, the news also continually deals with forces that may rob people of their initiative as individuals. The fear of new technology is, on one level, a fear of its ability to emasculate the individual; computers and data banks invade the privacy that enables people to act as individuals. Communism and socialism are viewed similarly, and capitalism is valued less for itself than for the freedom it offers to at least some individuals. During the 1950s, the suburbs were thought to induce conformity, which would stifle individuality; in recent years, various youth cultures and community developments in the Sunbelt have been criticized in the same fashion. The news values hard and task-oriented work, and is upset about the decline of the "work ethic."

Individualism is, in addition, a means of achieving cultural variety, and variety is in turn another weapon against the dangers both of bigness and conformity. The small town is the last hiding place of the stubborn eccentric, and ethnic enclaves consist of people who try to stave off complete Americanization. The news is fearful of mass society, although it neither uses that term nor worries that the masses will overwhelm high culture.

Moderatism

The idealization of the individual could result in praise for the rebel and the deviant, but this possibility is neutralized by an enduring value that discourages excess or extremism. Individualism that violates the law, the dominant mores, and enduring values is suspect; equally important, what is valued in individuals is discouraged in groups. Thus, groups that exhibit what is seen as extreme behavior are criticized in the news through pejorative adjectives or a satirical tone; in many spheres of human activity, polar opposites are questioned and moderate solutions are upheld.

For example, the news treats atheists as extremists and uses the same approach, if more gingerly, with religious fanatics. People who consume conspicuously are criticized, but so are people such as hippies, who turn their backs entirely on consumer goods. The news is scornful both of the overly academic scholar and the oversimplifying popularizer: it is kind neither to highbrows nor to lowbrows, to users of jargon or users of slang. College students who play when they should study receive disapproval, but so do "grinds." Lack of moderation is wrong, whether it involves excess or abstention.

The same value applies to politics. Political ideologists are suspect, but so are completely unprincipled politicians. The totally self-seeking are thought to be consumed by excessive ambition, but the complete do-gooders are not to be believed. Political candidates who talk only about issues may be described as dull; those who avoid issues entirely evoke doubts about their fitness for office. Poor speakers are thought to be unelectable, while demagogues are taken to be dangerous. Those who regularly follow party lines are viewed as hacks, and those who never do are called mavericks or loners—although these terms are pejorative only for the politically unsuccessful; the effective loner becomes a hero.

Insofar as the news has an ideology of its own, it is moderate. Since the ideology in the news is implicit, however, and not a deliberate or integrated doctrine, the political values may even be derivative, reflecting a belief in the virtue of moderation that extends across all human activities.

SOCIAL ORDER AND NATIONAL LEADERSHIP

If one looks at the actors and activities that have dominated the news over the years, it is possible to divide much of what appears on television and in the magazines, particularly as hard news, into two types of stories. One type can be called disorder news, which reports threats to various kinds of order, as well as measures taken to restore order. The second type deals with the routine activities of leading public officials: the day-to-day decisions, policy proposals, and recurring political arguments, as well as the periodic selection of new officials, both through election and appointment. These story types in turn suggest two additional values: the desirability of social order (but as will be seen, of a certain type) and the need for national leadership in maintaining that order.

Disorder and Order

Disorder stories fall into four major categories: natural, technological, social, and moral. Natural disorder news deals with natural disasters, such as floods and earthquakes, as well as industrial accidents that can be ascribed to natural forces, such as many but not all plane crashes or mine cave-ins. Technological disorder concerns accidents that cannot be ascribed to nature. Social disorder news deals with activities that disturb the public peace and may involve violence or the threat of violence against life or physical property; it also includes the deterioration of valued institutions, such as the nuclear two-parent family. Moral disorder news reports transgressions of laws and mores that do not necessarily endanger the social order.

These categories are not used by journalists, nor are they hard and fast. A major fire may first be reported as a natural or technological disaster, but if there is evidence of human failure or arson, it soon becomes a moral disorder story. Similarly, once social disorder ends, the news looks for the responsible parties and identifies agents of moral disorder. Conversely, when high officials are guilty of moral disorder, the news may raise the possibility of resulting social disorder. If people lose faith in their leaders, there is fear that the social fabric may unravel.

Social Disorder News

American news media have always emphasized stories of social disorder, both at home and abroad. Foreign news is limited to violent political disorder, but domestic news also keeps track of nonviolent and nonpolitical demonstrations. Conflict among public officials is reported so matter-of-factly that it is a routine activity story rather than disorder news; the conflict is expected; and because it involves officials rather than ordinary people, it is not treated as a threat to the public peace.

During the 1960s, domestic social disorder news was dominated by the ghetto disturbances and by antiwar marches, demonstrations, and "trashings." Marches and demonstrations are, from one point of view, protest activities, but the news almost always treated them as potential or actual dangers to the social order. In the beginning, the television cameras focused mainly on bearded and other unusual-looking participants who were, in those days, assumed to threaten the social order by their very appearance. Later, when demonstrations became a conventional strategy, they became particularly newsworthy when reporters noticed trouble.

At first, "trouble" was defined as stone throwing and other physical or verbal violence against the police, or fights between demonstrators and hecklers, often from the American Nazi party. Marches, especially those involving large numbers, were deemed potential threats to the social order because so many people were involved; consequently, trouble was almost inevitable, and if it did not take place, that fact was also newsworthy. "Violence," as well as trouble, was perceived as action against constituted legal authority; and until the 1968 Chicago Democratic Convention, police violence against the demonstrators was viewed as action taken to restore order and was rarely called violence. What the demonstrators described as police brutality was at best shown in passing on television, while day-to-day police brutality in the ghettos was not normally news, perhaps because it was routine.

The turning point in the treatment of antiwar demonstrators came in Chicago when the behavior of the police was reported almost universally as a "police riot." More important, perhaps, earlier in 1968, most national news media had been persuaded by the Tet offensive that the Vietnam War could or should not be continued. From then on, the news started to see the demonstrators more as protesters, and to pay closer attention to the middle-class, middle-aged, and conventionally dressed young marchers. Eventually, some demonstrations even began to be seen as responses to the moral disorder on the part of the president and his hawkish policy makers.

Disorder news could, of course, be analyzed as valuing disorder, and some critics of the news media have charged that overly liberal journalists have done so to justify the need for political change. Actually, however, domestic disorder stories are, except in unusual circumstances, as much concerned with the restoration of order by public officials as with the occurrence of disorder. For example, the Kerner Commission study of the network television coverage of the 1967 uprisings showed that only about 3 percent of the sequences were devoted to what it called riot actions, 2 percent more to injuries and deaths, and at least 34 percent to what I call order restoration.[2] Although the emphasis on order restoration could be explained by the inability of television to gain immediate camera access to the disorder, the newsmagazines were not hampered by such considerations. Even so, *Newsweek*'s ghetto-disturbance stories devoted four times as much text to police and army attempts to restore order as to descriptions of the disturbances.

After the disturbances had ended, the concern with order restoration continued, for television documentaries and special sections of the newsmagazines suggested, without condoning participants in the disturbances, that racial segregation and, to a lesser extent, economic inequality, had helped to bring them about, the implication being that government and economic reforms were necessary to prevent their recurrence. On both practical and moral grounds, the news argued for a more altruistic democracy and a more responsible capitalism. By the start of the 1970s, however, the fear of ghetto disorders had disappeared, and so had the pleas for reform, although they returned briefly after the looting that accompanied the 1977 power failure in New York City. This time, the looters were criticized more harshly than in the 1960s because they had taken advantage of the city's disability, were thought to be employed, and were taking luxury goods rather than necessities.

Another illustration of the value placed on order restoration can be found in the news about events that do not, on the surface, deal with disorder. A television report covering a demonstration outside the White House moments after Richard Nixon made his resignation speech emphasized that the demonstration was quiet and that there were no signs of incipient panic or violence. Likewise, in the hours after John Kennedy's assassination, network anchorpersons and reporters frequently pointed out that the country was not panicking. Later, I learned that they were, in fact, worried about possible panics and immediately looked for stories that would indicate that none were taking place. They also sought to allay panic by reporting that the transition of Lyndon Johnson to the presidency was taking place quickly and in an orderly fashion.[3] For the same reason, the anchorpersons also took pains to dispel a rumor that the Russians were about to take advantage of the president's death to launch a war.[4]

I do not mean to suggest, however, that the fears of a Russian move originated with the journalists; in describing Richard Nixon's inability to govern during his last days in the White House, Woodward and Bernstein suggest that then Secretary of State Henry Kissinger was considering "the possibility that some foreign power would do something foolish." Still, the fears expressed in the news underline the generic concern with order and suggest the extent to which order is thought to depend upon the president, which reflects, among other things, the value placed on his leadership.

Moral Disorder News

The moral disorder story is a hallowed tradition in modern American journalism, prototypically taking the form of exposés based on investigative reporting. Such exposés reveal instances of legal or moral transgression, particularly by public officials and other prestigious individuals who, by reason or virtue of their power and prestige, are not expected to misbehave.

The prime exposé of the 1970s was Watergate. Although defenders of the Nixon administration have accused the news media of exaggerating the transgressions involved in the events and of blowing up the story in order to drive a president disliked by many journalists out of office, the story was a prototypical exposé, which would have been dealt with in much the same manner had the scandals been committed by a more popular president. Later investigations of CIA and FBI scandals, which implicated Presidents Kennedy and Johnson, were carried out just as energetically. Some observers have also suggested that the news exaggerated Nixon's transgressions by combining individual and often unrelated activities into a single scandal; but exposés are, by their nature, structured to point the finger at a morally disorderly leader, and sometimes, investigative reporting efforts do not see the light of day until a villain is found. Traditionally, exposés have concentrated on politicians or other public officials resorting to nepotism, unethical campaign practices, bribery, and taking money out of the public till, although sometimes, exposés are more institutional, dealing with the failure of public agencies to serve their constituents or clients, or more frequently, with wasting the taxpayer's money.

Nevertheless, the vast majority of moral disorder stories do not involve investigative reporting; often they deal with routine phenomena, such as violent or nonviolent crime or political acts, which are treated as violations of altruistic democracy. Such common practices as logrolling, deals, patronage appointments, or the failure of election candidates to abide by campaign promises are reported in such a way as to indicate that these practices are immoral.

In most moral disorder stories, the values being violated are never made explicit, and that they are being violated is not discussed. Still, the participants in a moral disorder story know they are being identified as transgressors and react accordingly. After an election in New Jersey, supporters of the losing candidate, who was then on trial for bribery and had been accused of conducting a racist campaign, smashed television cameras and attacked reporters. The values in the news, against corruption and for racial integration, had led to campaign stories that the candidate and his supporters felt were responsible for his defeat.

News stories that are announced, or in Erving Goffman's terminology, "framed," as exposés make the search for moral disorder explicit, forcing those identified as transgressors into the difficult position of defending their practices, while at the same time reaffirming the moral values on which the exposé is based. Few people can do so without being defensive, particularly on television documentaries, which are television's primary genre for exposés. If the transgressors refuse to be interviewed, their refusal is also reported and becomes a virtual admission of guilt.

In such instances, the news media become guardians of a moral order; as a result, reporters are generally viewed as representatives of that order, even if they are not looking for moral disorder news. Consequently, when they, and especially television camera crews, arrive on a scene, people begin to perform not only physically for the camera but also morally, denying or eliminating behavior that could be judged as moral disorder. Beatings or tortures of prisoners did not take place in South Vietnam or the American South when cameras were present. Public and private agencies spruce up their physical environment when reporters are expected, just as the Chinese authorities temporarily "opened" their society when American television crews arrived to film life in China during and after President Nixon's visit. Berelson's classic study of the 1945 New York City newspaper strike showed that when the newspapers were not publishing, politicians sometimes ignored the honesty values that are defended in and guarded by the news media.[5]

The Nature of Order in the News

The frequent appearance of disorder stories suggests that order is an important value in the news, but order is a meaningless term unless one specifies what order and whose order is being valued. For one thing, there are different types of order; a society can have violence in the streets and a stable family life at home, or public peace and a high rate of family instability. Also, what order is will be judged differently by different people. To the affluent, the slums will appear orderly as long as there are no disturbances and crime does not spill over into wealthy districts; but for slum dwellers, order cannot exist until exploitation, as well as crime, is eliminated. For the parent generation, adolescent order exists when adolescents abide by parental rules; for the young people, order is also freedom of interference from adults.

WHAT ORDER IN THE NEWS?

The conception of order in the news varies with each type of disorder. In news about natural disasters, order is defined as the preservation of life and property; despite the concern for nature, flood stories do not often worry about how the flood may harm the river. Among technological disasters, plane crashes are usually more newsworthy than the winter breakdowns of tenement furnaces, even if they result in the same number of deaths. Yet, here as elsewhere, disorder news is affected by whose order is being upset.

Social disorder is generally defined as disorder in the public areas of the society. A protest march in which three people die would be headline national news, whereas a family murder that claimed three victims would be a local story. Disorders in affluent areas or elite institutions are more likely to be reported than their occurrence elsewhere. In the 1960s, the looting of a handful of stores on New York's Fifth Avenue received as much attention as a much larger looting spree taking place in a ghetto area that same day. Peaceful demonstrations on college campuses, especially elite ones, are usually more newsworthy than those in factories or prisons. But the major public area is the seat of government; thus, a trouble-free demonstration in front of a city hall or a police station is news, whereas that in front of a store is not.

Still, the most important criterion of worthiness is the target of the demonstration. Ultimately, social disorder is equated with political disorder; similarly, social order is viewed as the absence of violent or potentially violent threats to the authority of public officials, particularly the president. The antiwar demonstrations of the 1970s were covered as disorder stories because they were aimed at presidents, and campus protests against government war policies were more often reported than protests against college-administration policies. Likewise, the 1978 coal strike did not become a magazine cover story until it involved the president. Just as low-level public officials and corporate leaders get into the national news only when they quarrel with the president, the activities of ordinary people must also touch the Oval Office before they are newsworthy.

Even so, the conception of political order in the news transcends public officials and even the president. Now and then, such officials are themselves treated by the news as potential threats to order, either because they resort to "demagoguery," which may stir up the passions of their followers, or because they act in ways that may encourage ordinary people to question the legitimacy of authority, and subsequently to ignore the rules that underlie the political order. In the waning days of the Nixon administration, the news frequently expressed concern about the possibility and consequences of widespread cynicism toward and lack of trust for the presidency (rather than toward the incumbent president); and when Richard Nixon was reported to have underpaid his taxes, there were stories that speculated whether ordinary taxpayers would follow his example.

Beneath the concern for political order lies another, perhaps even deeper concern for social cohesion, which reflects fears that not only the official rules of the political order but also the informal rules of the social order are in danger of being disobeyed. This is apparent in the nonpolitical stories that either become or do not become news. Hippies and college dropouts of the 1960s were newsworthy in part because they rejected the so-called Protestant work ethic; even now, drug use by the young, and its consequences, is in the news more than alcohol use because it signifies a rejection of traditional methods of seeking oblivion or mind expansion. Indeed, the news evaluates the young almost entirely in terms of what adult rules they are in the process of rejecting, be they of dress, decorum, or sexual behavior. Rising divorce rates, falling rates of marriage and fertility, and increasing cohabitation without benefit of clergy, all of which suggests a rejection of the conventional rules of family life, are therefore more frequently in the news than family conflict (other than wife beating and child abuse). Whatever its effect on family life, conflict is not viewed as indicative of the decline of the family. The romanticization of the past as an era in which formal and informal rules *were* obeyed betrays the same fear of contemporary disintegration, and the frequent celebration of past ways in the news may reflect an implicit ideal for the future. As Eric Severaid put it during the live television coverage of the traditional royal pomp and circumstance of the marriage of Princess Anne of England in 1973: "A people needs the past to hold them together."

Moral disorder stories are, in the end, cued to much the same concern for social cohesion, particularly those stories that report violations of the mores rather than the laws. Such stories are based on the premise that the activities of public officials, public agencies, and corporations should derive from the same moral and ethical values that are supposed to apply to personal, familial, and friendship relations. Even if every political reporter knows that politicians cannot operate with the same ideal of honesty as friends, the failure of politicians to do so continues to be news. In fact, insofar as the news conceives of nation and society anthropomorphically, as having a will and as being held together by moral fibers, the social order persists because it is based on moral values, and the violation of these values is thus an invitation to political and social disintegration. In the last analysis, the values underlying social and moral disorder news are the same, although the two types of news differ in subject and object: social disorder news monitors the respect of citizens for authority, while moral disorder stories evaluate whether authority figures respect the rules of the citizenry.

WHOSE ORDER IN THE NEWS?

National news is ostensibly about and for the entire nation; therefore its values pertain to national order. Since one person's or group's order may be another's disorder, however, and since the news does not report equally about all parts of the nation or society, it cannot possibly value everyone's order. Thus, it is relevant to ask whose order is being valued.

Much of the answer has already been suggested. Most of the routine—

and thus, by presumption, orderly—activities that appear in the news are carried on by elected and appointed officials, whereas social and moral disorder news involves, by and large, ordinary people, many of them poor, black, and/or young. Moral disorder stories, however, also identify public officials who have violated the laws or the enduring values. In other words, the news supports those public officials who abide by the enduring values against misbehaving peers and deviant ordinary people.

In addition, the news upholds the legitimacy of holders of formal authority as long as they abide by the relevant enduring values, both in public and private realms. It also pays respect to the more prestigious professions, although its members must not only abide by the enduring values but must also carry out innovative activities. The news reports more about progress in physics than in plumbing, but it pays no more attention to the routine activities of physicists than of plumbers.

In social and economic class terms, then, the news especially values the order of the upper-class and upper middle-class sectors of society, though it may make fun of some of their very rich members. Although it does not often concern itself with either the social order or the values of the middle and working classes and the poor, it supports the classes when they respect the enduring values; but it can be critical of their popular culture, and among whites, their prejudice toward blacks.

The news also tends to value the social order of the middle-aged and old against the young. Most public officials, business leaders, and professionals do not act in newsworthy ways until they are in their fifties and sixties, so that the news cannot help but be dominated by this age group; even so, it is rarely reported that old leaders sometimes become senile in office. Similarly, the young are inevitably in the news because criminals or protesters are almost always youthful; even so, juvenile delinquency against adults is commonplace news, whereas adult delinquency against juveniles—other than child abuse—is much less so.

With some oversimplification, it would be fair to say that the news supports the social order of public, business and professional, upper middle-class, middle-aged, and white male sectors of society. Because the news emphasizes people over groups, it pays less attention to the institutionalized social order, except as reflected in its leaders; but obviously, the news is also generally supportive of governments and their agencies, private enterprise, the prestigious professions, and a variety of other national institutions, including the quality universities. But here, too, always with a proviso: obedience to the relevant enduring values. Equally obvious, however, is the fact that institutional obedience is monitored differentially, and the news is therefore much harsher on government than on the remaining sectors.

In short, when all other things are equal, the news pays most attention to and upholds the actions of elite individuals and elite institutions. It would be incorrect to say that the news is about elites per se or a single elite; rather, the news deals mostly with those who hold the power within various national or societal strata; with the most powerful officials in the most powerful agencies; with the coalition of upper-class and upper middle-class people that dominates the socioeconomic hierarchy; and with the late middle-aged cohort that has the most power among age groups.

Nevertheless, the news is not subservient to powerful individuals or groups, for it measures their behavior against a set of values that is assumed to transcend them. Moral disorder stories can bid the elites to relinquish, or at least hide, their moral deficiencies. To be sure, the values invoked in moral disorder stories are themselves often set by and shared by these elites. The president's policies are not often viewed from the perspectives of, or judged by, the values of low-income and moderate-income citizens; corporate officials are even less rarely judged by the values of employees or customers; or university presidents, by the values of students or campus janitors. Instead, the values in the news derive largely from reformers and reform movements, which are themselves elites. Still, the news is not simply a compliant supporter of elites or the Establishment or the ruling class; rather it views nation and society through its own set of values and with its own conception of the good social order.

Leadership

If the news values moral and social order, it also suggests how to maintain them, primarily through the availability of morally and otherwise competent leadership. The news focuses on leaders; and with some exceptions, public agencies and private organizations are represented by their leaders. In the past, magazine cover stories often reported national topics or issues in relation to an individual who played an instrumental or symbolic leadership role in them. When necessary, the news even helps to create leaders; in the 1960s, radical and black organizations functioning on the basis of participatory democracy sometimes complained that journalists would pick out one spokesperson on whom they would lavish most of their attention, thereby making a leader out of him or her.

Although several practical considerations encourage the news media to emphasize leaders, the news is also based on a theory of society that would argue, were it made explicit, that the social process, above all others, is shaped by leaders: by people who, either because of their political or managerial skills, or personal attributes that inspire others, move into positions of authority and make things happen.

Unlike sociology, which sees leadership as a role found in most groups and assumes that someone will inevitably take it, the news focuses instead on the personal qualities and psychological traits of the person taking it. Also, while sociology suggests that group members, in other than totalitarian situations, use formal and/or informal mechanisms for choosing leaders, thereafter influencing their actions, the news tends to treat group members as followers. Moreover, sociology proposes that institutions require and therefore generate leadership; the news, however, sees institutions as "blocks" to it. Whether sociologists or journalists are more correct is not at issue here, for both may be observing different aspects of the same phenomenon. Still, the news divides nation and society into leaders and followers, with leaders not only initiating but also being given credit for the activities of the followers. Washington stories routinely tell of the statements or actions of official leaders, while equally routinely ignoring the fact that these are often the work of subordinates. In fact, although the news objectively reports the orders that leaders give, it looks askance at the government bureaucrats who carry them out.

The foremost leader in America is the president, who is viewed as the ultimate protector of order. He is the final backstop for domestic tranquillity and the principal guardian of national security, his absence from the White House due to resignation or death evoking, as I indicated earlier, fears of an enemy attack or possible panic by a now leaderless populace. Through his own behavior and the concern he shows for the behavior of others, the president also becomes the nation's moral leader. He sets an example that might be followed by others: should he permit or condone corruption among his associates or appointees, he is suspected of moral disorder. Finally, he is the person who states and represents the national values, and he is the agent of the national will.

The news describes the president as the person who actually performs, or who is expected to perform, these functions. Stories that indicate that decisions are actually being made by others, sometimes even without the president's knowledge, are written to suggest that such delegation of power is a departure from the norm and a potential cause for alarm. When a president takes a vacation, the news questions his control over the government during his absence; a presidential illness is always a major story; and his death is the biggest story of all.

NOTES

1. Foreign news lends itself especially well to this analysis because of a special terminology that is rarely used in domestic news. Some foreign governments are

"juntas" or "regimes," but the news does not speak of the "Carter regime." Headlines and their television equivalents are also revealing, for when space is at a minimum, writers must often make value judgments as a kind of forced choice. Even so, the choice is not idiosyncratic. The People's Republic of China was often called Red China because three-letter words are prized by headline writers; however, no color was assigned to the Republic of China on Taiwan.

2. Twenty-three percent of the sequences depicted "control or containment"; 4 percent, arrests; and 7 percent, "conciliation." Simulmatics Corporation, "News Media Coverage of the 1967 Urban Riots," Final Report, mimeographed (New York: Simulmatics Corp., February 1, 1968), Table IV. The largest proportion of sequences was devoted to "Aftermath," defined as "scenes showing property damage, cleanup and normal activity," and thus a mixture of disorder and order-restoration news. Ibid., p. 18.

3. I gathered this information from ABC and NBC journalists while serving as an interviewer for a study of television's coverage of the assassination, directed by the late Louis Cowan and Paul Lazarsfeld.

4. A radio story I heard shortly after Gerald Ford's swearing-in noted that Richard Nixon's resignation was handed in at 11:35 A.M.; that Gerald Ford had not taken the oath of office until noon; and that technically speaking, therefore, the country was leaderless for twenty-five minutes. The reporter reassured his listeners, however, that if any foreign power had wanted to take advantage of a leaderless America to set off an international crisis, Mr. Ford would undoubtedly have taken the reins of office earlier so as to prevent it.

5. Bernard Berelson, "What 'Missing the Newspaper' Means," in *Communications Research, 1948–1949,* ed. Paul Lazarsfeld and Frank Stanton (New York: Harper & Brothers, 1949), 111–29.

· *Part Two* ·

URBAN POVERTY—THEORY AND POLICY

Part Two consists of four articles on poverty in America. The first is mainly theoretical; the others are more explicitly policy-oriented.

I begin with what is probably my most widely reprinted article. It is also among the very few I submitted to a "mainstream" sociological journal, since I was never comfortable writing in the research report format most academic journals require. One reason the *American Journal of Sociology* accepted my article was because the editor that year was a professional editor rather than an academic—the journal's short-lived experiment. A sequel to Chapter Four, which I wrote twenty years later, entitled "The Positive Functions of the Undeserving Poor," was rejected by the same journal, but quickly accepted by an academic journal not wedded to the research report.[1]

Like other articles I have written, "The Positive Functions of Poverty" started with a puzzle: why has poverty persisted so long even though almost everyone favors its abolition? The origin of that puzzle was the virtual end of the War on Poverty at the close of the 1960s, and the piece began with a hunch: poverty must have positive functions—useful effects for enough nonpoor people in the society—that enable it to persist. The rest was relatively easy: to make a list of these functions, the well-known economic (including Marxist) ones, as well as the lesser-known cultural, social, and political ones. The piece is largely an annotated list of these functions, although it ends on a political note. I argued that poverty will persist as long as it is functional, unless the poor obtain enough political power to alter their lowly position in the social hierarchy and, in the process, can eliminate or replace the functions they perform. The political ending fit the political climate of the 1960s, although I doubted that the poor would soon obtain the needed political power. (Readers who will look at the end of my 1994 sequel, published in *Politics and Society,* will see that it lacks a political ending, closing instead with predictions about the elimination, not of poverty, but of the poor.)

The article as well as its political ending also had another agenda: to show that Mertonian functionalism, which was at that time falling into disrepute because it was considered overly supportive of the status quo, could be adapted to more radical analyses and conclusions. Although my article occasioned some debate, including some partly justified critiques that I had mixed functions with causes, it did not radicalize or revive functionalism. Instead, many readers decided it was satire, which presumably meant they did not have to take it seriously. Nonetheless, it was written in dead earnest, as a completely straightforward analysis, even though the notion that pov-

---

1. It can also be found in my *War Against the Poor.* (New York: Basic Books, 1995.)

69

erty can be useful to many of the rest of us is morally absurd enough to lend itself to satire.

Chapter 5 is equally straightforward, and is one of many policy-oriented analyses of poverty that I wrote during the 1960s. This one began as invited testimony to one of many senatorial committees that investigated ghetto disorders during what was then called the "urban crisis." By today's standards, and even when I wrote the paper, I was wildly optimistic and overly hopeful, but after all I had a chance to influence the decisions a senatorial panel dominated by New Deal liberals would make about what really needed to be done to reduce poverty and segregation. Yet other parts of the article also predicted what would happen if nothing was done, and, sad to say, too many of my predictions have proved accurate.

Of course, the article left out political considerations, but an invited expert is not expected to discuss politics with a group of skilled politicians. Besides, there was then—as now—no way of coming up with an effective as well as politically and immediately feasible program, particularly of economic policies that would integrate poor blacks, or whites, into the mainstream economy.

I still believe that the programs that a small band of policy-oriented social scientists (of whom I was a part) advocated in the 1960s and in the years thereafter were justified. Experts and academics are able to advocate policies that appointed and elected officials cannot. Also, experts should say honestly what their expertise tells them about what must be done even if it is not politically feasible at the moment, future political feasibility being impossible to predict.

Still, neither we nor anyone else anticipated the backlash against what the War on Poverty did accomplish. Perhaps the backlash could have been avoided if that part of the economy most important in the lives of the white working class had not begun to decline in the late 1960s, even before the general economic turndown that the country experienced, beginning in the early 1970s. Hindsight suggests also that we were too naive about various aspects of the politics of social policy. Above all, we failed to combine our proposals for effective long-range programs with short-range ones, for politicians must have short-range policies for the next election.

Anticrime policy offers a good example. While it remains true that the root causes of street crime are lodged somewhere in poverty and inequality (even if we do not yet know exactly where) and must be eliminated with long-range antipoverty and economic reform policies, short-range programs to maximize the safety of the citizenry must be instituted simultaneously or earlier. Conservatives were able to understand the need for short-range programs, and thus not only filled the vacuum left by liberals with unnecessarily harsh and therefore often harmful measures, but could dismiss at the same time the validity of long-range programs—other than yet more incarceration and prison building. Ironically enough, the strongest defenders of long-range antipoverty programs as a weapon against street crime have been some big-city police chiefs, but even their appeals have not been heeded.

Chapter 6 is a policy article for the 1990s. The year after President Clinton won the 1992 election, it became apparent that he was planning to ignore the job-centered economic mandate that elected him, even though corporate downsizing was becoming worse. I wrote this article not only to suggest the need for political pressure to remind the president of what he had promised, but also to propose a lobby to serve the needs of the many workers, white-collar ones especially, who were not yet prepared to join unions. It was not an antiunion piece, although it was so interpreted in some union quarters. At this writing, the unemployment rate has been brought down significantly by the creation of many low-wage jobs, but I think the piece is still relevant. Consequently, I hope that the currently revitalizing union movement will not only be able to regain its lost membership, but will make unions more attractive to nonunion workers. Otherwise, I hope that someone else will invent employee organizations for them.

The article also had some unexpected action consequences, for it inspired a young activist lawyer, Sara Horowitz, to invent an organization called Working Today. It describes itself as "promoting the interests of America's independent workforce," among whom it includes freelancers, temps, part-time workers, and other contingent workers. Someday the organization may become big enough to pursue my original employee lobby idea.

The final article in this section is, like the first, an attempt to confront the reality of the end of the War on Poverty. This one is not a puzzle but the expression of a yearning. More concretely, it is an excerpt from a book entitled *More Equality,* that I published in 1973. My interest in equality goes back to my adolescence when I learned about the egalitarian kibbutz communities of Israel, but I began to write about American equality only during the late 1960s, including in such now-seemingly unlikely places as the Sunday Magazine of *The New York Times.*

The selection from that book, which appears here in Chapter 7, also reflects a related interest—utopian thought. It presents two scenarios, about the workings and consequences of economic equality and political equality in an obviously utopian society that has both.

My interest in utopian thinking was stimulated originally by some of the late nineteenth-century writers of novelistic utopias and the thinkers who influenced the invention of the kibbutz, as well as by David Riesman, who was then what would today be called a mentor of mine during my years at the University of Chicago. In this day and age, dystopias have unfortunately replaced utopias, but a revival of utopian thinking is highly desirable. This time, they must be designed for ordinary human beings rather than for the impossibly altruistic people who filled the utopian writings of the late nineteenth century.

Implementing utopia in actually existing societies is not a good idea, but what I think of as socially realistic utopian thought could be useful in inventing, developing, and discussing new policy ideas. Egalitarian utopias could shed new light on how to change today's dangerously inegalitarian America, as well as on turning inequality and the achievement of more equality into a viable political issue.

· 4 ·

The Positive Functions of Poverty

Over 20 years ago, Merton (1949, 71), analyzing the persistence of the urban political machine, wrote that because "we should ordinarily . . . expect persistent social patterns and social structures to perform positive functions which are at the time not adequately fulfilled by other existing patterns and structures . . . perhaps this publicly maligned organization is, under present conditions, satisfying basic latent functions." He pointed out how the machine provided central authority to get things done when a decentralized local government could not act, humanized the services of the impersonal bureaucracy for fearful citizens, offered concrete help (rather than law or justice) to the poor, and otherwise performed services needed or demanded by many people but considered unconventional or even illegal by formal public agencies.

This chapter is not concerned with the political machine, however, but with poverty, a social phenomenon that is as maligned as and far more persistent than the machine. Consequently, there may be some merit in applying functional analysis to poverty, to ask whether it too has positive functions that explain its persistence. Since functional analysis has itself taken on a maligned status among some American sociologists, a secondary purpose of this chapter is to ask whether it is still a useful approach.[1]

Functions

Merton (1949, 50) defined functions as "those observed consequences which make for the adaptation or adjustment of a given system; and dys-

This chapter was first published in *The American Journal of Sociology* 78, no. 2 (1972). Earlier versions of this paper were presented at a Vassar College conference on the War on Poverty in 1964, at the 7th World Congress of Sociology in 1971, and in *Social Policy* 2 (July–August 1971): 20–24. I am indebted to Peter Marris, Robert K. Merton, and S. M. Miller for helpful comments on earlier drafts of this paper.

functions, those observed consequences which lessen the adaptation or adjustment of the system." This definition does not specify the nature or scope of the system, but elsewhere in his classic paper "Manifest and Latent Functions," Merton indicated that social system was not a synonym for society, and that systems vary in size, requiring a functional analysis "to consider a *range* of units for which the item (or social phenomenon H.G.) has designated consequences: individuals in diverse statuses, subgroups, the larger social system and cultural systems" (1949, 51).

In discussing the functions of poverty, I shall identify functions for *groups* and *aggregates;* specifically, interest groups, socioeconomic classes, and other population aggregates, for example, those with shared values or similar statuses. This definitional approach is based on the assumption that almost every social system—and of course every society—is composed of groups or aggregates with different interests and values, so that, as Merton put it (1949, 51), "items may be functional for some individuals and subgroups and dysfunctional for others." Indeed, frequently one group's functions are another group's dysfunctions.[2] For example, the political machine analyzed by Merton was functional for the working class and business interests of the city but dysfunctional for many middle class and reform interests. Consequently, functions are defined as those observed consequences that are positive *as judged by the values of the group under analysis;* dysfunctions, as those which are negative by these values.[3] Because functions benefit the group in question and dysfunctions hurt it, I shall also describe functions and dysfunctions in the language of economic planning and systems analysis as benefits and costs.[4]

Identifying functions and dysfunctions for groups and aggregates rather than systems reduces the possibility that what is functional for one group in a multigroup system will be seen as being functional for the whole system, making it more difficult, for example, to suggest that a given phenomenon is functional for a corporation or political regime when it may in fact only be functional for their officers or leaders. Also, this approach precludes reaching a priori conclusions about two other important empirical questions raised by Merton (1949, 32–36), whether any phenomenon is ever functional or dysfunctional for an entire society, and, if functional, whether it is therefore indispensable to that society.

In a modern heterogeneous society, few phenomena are functional or dysfunctional for the society as a whole, and most result in benefits to some groups and costs to others. Given the level of differentiation in modern society, I am even skeptical whether one can empirically identify a social system called society. Society exists, of course, but it is closer to being a very large aggregate, and when sociologists talk about society as a system, they often really mean the nation, a system that, among other things, sets up boundaries and other distinguishing characteristics between societal aggregates.

I would also argue that no social phenomenon is indispensable: it may be too powerful or too highly valued to be eliminated, but in most instances, one can suggest what Merton calls "functional alternatives" or equivalents for a social phenomena, that is, other social patterns or policies that achieve the same functions but avoid the dysfunctions.

FUNCTIONS OF POVERTY

The conventional view of American poverty is so dedicated to identifying the dysfunctions of poverty, both for the poor and the nation, that at first glance it seems inconceivable to suggest that poverty could be functional for anyone. Of course, the slumlord and the loan shark are widely known to profit from the existence of poverty; but they are popularly viewed as evil men, and their activities are, at least in part, dysfunctional for the poor. However, what is less often recognized, at least in the conventional wisdom, is that poverty also makes possible the existence of expansion of "respectable" professions and occupations, for example, penology, criminology, social work, and public health. More recently, the poor have provided jobs for professional and paraprofessional "poverty warriors," as well as journalists and social scientists, this author included, who have supplied the information demanded when public curiosity about the poor developed in the 1960s.

Clearly, then, poverty and the poor may well serve a number of functions for many nonpoor groups in American society, and I shall describe 15 sets of such functions—economic, social, cultural, and political—that seem to me most significant.

Economic Functions

First, the existence of poverty makes sure that "dirty work" is done. Every economy has such work: physically dirty or dangerous, temporary, dead-end and underpaid, undignified, and menial jobs. These jobs can be filled by paying higher wages than for "clean" work, or by requiring people who have no other choice to do the dirty work and at low wages. In America, poverty functions to provide a low-wage labor pool that is willing—or, rather, unable to be unwilling—to perform dirty work at low cost. Indeed, this function is so important that in some Southern states, welfare

payments have been cut off during the summer months when the poor
are needed to work in the fields. Moreover, the late 1960s debate about
welfare—and about proposed substitutes such as the negative income tax
and the Family Assistance Plan—emphasized the impact of income grants
on work incentive, with opponents often arguing that such grants would
reduce the incentive of—actually, the pressure on—the poor to carry out
the needed dirty work if the wages therefore are no larger than the income
grant. Furthermore, many economic activities that involve dirty work depend heavily on the poor; restaurants, hospitals, parts of the garment industry, and industrial agriculture, among others, could not persist in their present form without their dependence on the substandard wages they pay to
their employees.

Second, the poor subsidize, directly and indirectly, many activities that
benefit the affluent.[5] For one thing, they have long supported both the
consumption and investment activities of the private economy by virtue of
the low wages they receive. This was openly recognized at the beginning
of the Industrial Revolution, when a French writer quoted by T. H. Marshall (n.d., 7) pointed out that "to assure and maintain the prosperities of
our industries, it is necessary that the workers should never acquire
wealth." Examples of this kind of subsidization abound even today; for example, domestics subsidize the upper middle and upper classes, making life
easier for their employers and freeing affluent women for a variety of professional, cultural, civic, or social activities. In addition, as Barry Schwartz
pointed out (personal communication), the low income of the poor enables
the rich to divert a higher proportion of their income to savings and investment, and thus to fuel economic growth. This, in turn, can produce higher
incomes for everybody, including the poor, although it does not necessarily
improve the position of the poor in the socioeconomic hierarchy, since the
benefits of economic growth are also distributed unequally.

At the same time, the poor subsidize the governmental economy. Because local property and sales taxes and the ungraduated income taxes levied by many states are regressive, the poor pay a higher percentage of their
income in taxes than the rest of the population, thus subsidizing the many
state and local governmental programs that serve more affluent taxpayers.[6]
In addition, the poor support medical innovation as patients in teaching
and research hospitals, and as guinea pigs in medical experiments, subsidizing the more affluent patients who alone can afford these innovations once
they are incorporated into medical practice.

Third, poverty creates jobs for a number of occupations and professions
that serve the poor, or shield the rest of the population from them. As already noted, penology would be miniscule without the poor, as would the

police, since the poor provide the majority of their "clients." Other activities that flourish because of the existence of poverty are the numbers game, the sale of heroin and cheap wines and liquors, pentecostal ministers, faith healers, prostitutes, pawn shops, and the peacetime army, which recruits its enlisted men mainly from among the poor.

Fourth, the poor buy goods that others do not want and thus prolong their economic usefulness, such as day-old bread, fruit and vegetables that would otherwise be thrown out, secondhand clothes, and deteriorating automobiles and buildings. They also provide incomes for doctors, lawyers, teachers, and others who are too old, poorly trained, or incompetent to attract more affluent clients.

Social and Cultural Functions

In addition, the poor perform a number of social and cultural functions:

Fifth, the poor can be identified and punished as alleged or real deviants in order to uphold the legitimacy of dominant norms (Macarov 1970, 31–33). The defenders of the desirability of hard work, thrift, honesty, and monogamy need people who can be accused of being lazy, spendthrift, dishonest, and promiscuous to justify these norms; and as Erikson (1964) and others following Durkheim have pointed out, the norms themselves are best legitimated by discovering violations.

Whether the poor actually violate these norms more than affluent people is still open to question. The working poor work harder and longer than high-status jobholders, and poor housewives must do more housework to keep their slum apartments clean than their middle-class peers in standard housing. The proportion of cheaters among welfare recipients is quite low and considerably lower than among income taxpayers.[7] Violent crime is higher among the poor, but the affluent commit a variety of white-collar crimes, and several studies of self-reported delinquency have concluded that middle-class youngsters are sometimes as delinquent as the poor. However, the poor are more likely to be caught when participating in deviant acts and, once caught, to be punished more often than middle-class transgressors. Moreover, they lack the political and cultural power to correct the stereotypes that affluent people hold of them, and thus continue to be thought of as lazy, spendthrift, etc., whatever the empirical evidence, by those who need living proof that deviance does not pay.[8] The actually or allegedly deviant poor have traditionally been described as undeserving and, in more recent terminology, culturally deprived or pathological.

Sixth, another group of poor, described as deserving because they are disabled or suffering from bad luck, provide the rest of the population with different emotional satisfactions; they evoke compassion, pity, and charity, thus allowing those who help them to feel that they are altruistic, moral, and practicing the Judeo-Christian ethic. The deserving poor also enable others to feel fortunate for being spared the deprivations that come with poverty.[9]

Seventh, as a converse of the fifth function described previously, the poor offer affluent people vicarious participation in the uninhibited sexual, alcoholic, and narcotic behavior in which many poor people are alleged to indulge, and which, being freed from the constraints of affluence and respectability, they are often thought to enjoy more than the middle classes. One of the popular beliefs about welfare recipients is that many are on a permanent sex-filled vacation. Although it may be true that the poor are more given to uninhibited behavior, studies by Rainwater (1970) and other observers of the lower class indicate that such behavior is as often motivated by despair as by lack of inhibition, and that it results less in pleasure than in a compulsive escape from grim reality. However, whether the poor actually have more sex and enjoy it more than affluent people is irrelevant; as long as the latter believe it to be so, they can share it vicariously and perhaps enviously when instances are reported in fictional, journalistic, or sociological and anthropological formats.

Eighth, poverty helps to guarantee the status of those who are not poor. In a stratified society, where social mobility is an especially important goal and class boundaries are fuzzy, people need to know quite urgently where they stand. As a result, the poor function as a reliable and relatively permanent measuring rod for status comparison, particularly for the working class, which must find and maintain status distinctions between itself and the poor, much as the aristocracy must find ways of distinguishing itself from the *nouveau riche.*

Ninth, the poor also assist in the upward mobility of the nonpoor, for, as Goode has pointed out (1967, 5), "the privileged . . . try systematically to prevent the talent of the less privileged from being recognized and developed." By being denied educational opportunities or being stereotyped as stupid or unteachable, the poor thus enable others to obtain the better jobs. Also, an unknown number of people have moved themselves or their children up in the socioeconomic hierarchy through the incomes earned from the provision of goods and services in the slums: by becoming policemen and teachers, owning "Mom and Pop" stores, or working in the various rackets that flourish in the slums.

In fact, members of almost every immigrant group have financed their upward mobility by providing retail goods and services, housing, entertainment, gambling, narcotics, etc., to later arrivals in America (or in the city), most recently to blacks, Mexicans, and Puerto Ricans. Other Americans, of both European and native origin, have financed their entry into the upper middle and upper classes by owning or managing the illegal institutions that serve the poor, as well as the legal but not respectable ones, such as slum housing.

Tenth, just as the poor contribute to the economic viability of a number of businesses and professions (see function 3 above), they also add to the social viability of noneconomic groups. For one thing, they help to keep the aristocracy busy, thus justifying its continued existence. "Society" uses the poor as clients of settlement houses and charity benefits; indeed, it must have the poor to practice its public-mindedness so as to demonstrate its superiority over the *nouveaux riches* who devote themselves to conspicuous consumption. The poor play a similar function for philanthropic enterprises at other levels of the socioeconomic hierarchy, including the mass of middle-class civic organizations and women's clubs engaged in volunteer work and fund-raising in almost every American community. Doing good among the poor has traditionally helped the church to find a method of expressing religious sentiments in action; in recent years, militant church activity among and for the poor has enabled the church to hold on to its more liberal and radical members who might otherwise have dropped out of organized religion altogether.

Eleventh, the poor perform several cultural functions. They have played an unsung role in the creation of "civilization," having supplied the construction labor for many of the monuments that are often identified as the noblest expressions and examples of civilization, for example, the Egyptian pyramids, Greek temples, and medieval churches.[10] Moreover, they have helped to create a goodly share of the surplus capital that funds the artists and intellectuals who make culture, and particularly "high" culture, possible in the first place.

Twelfth, the "low" culture created for or by the poor is often adopted by the more affluent. The rich collect artifacts from extinct folk cultures (although not only from poor ones), and almost all Americans listen to the jazz, blues, spirituals, and country music, which originated among the Southern poor—as well as rock, which was derived from similar sources. The protest of the poor sometimes becomes literature; in 1970, for example, poetry written by ghetto children became popular in sophisticated literary circles. The poor also serve as culture heroes and literary subjects, particularly, of course, for the Left, but the hobo, cowboy, hipster, and the mythical prostitute with a heart of gold have performed this function for a variety of groups.

Political Functions

Finally, the poor carry out a number of important political functions:

Thirteenth, the poor serve as symbolic constituencies and opponents for several political groups. For example, parts of the revolutionary Left could not exist without the poor, particularly now that the working class can no longer be perceived as the vanguard of the revolution. Conversely, conservative political groups need the "welfare chiselers" and others who "live off the taxpayer's hard-earned money" in order to justify their demands for reductions in welfare payments and tax relief. Moreover, the role of the poor in upholding dominant norms (see function 5 above) also has a significant political function. An economy based on the ideology of laissez-faire requires a deprived population that is allegedly unwilling to work; not only does the alleged moral inferiority of the poor reduce the moral pressure on the present political economy to eliminate poverty, but redistributive alternatives can be made to look quite unattractive if those who will benefit from them most can be described as lazy, spendthrift, dishonest, and promiscuous. Thus, conservatives and classical liberals would find it difficult to justify many of their political beliefs without the poor; but then so would modern liberals and socialists who seek to eliminate poverty.

Fourteenth, the poor, being powerless, can be made to absorb the economic and political costs of change and growth in American society. During the nineteenth century, they did the backbreaking work that built the cities; today, they are pushed out of their neighborhoods to make room for "progress." Urban renewal projects to hold middle-class taxpayers and stores in the city and expressways to enable suburbanites to commute downtown have typically been located in poor neighborhoods, since no other group will allow itself to be displaced. For much the same reason, urban universities, hospitals, and civic centers also expand into land occupied by the poor. The major costs of the industrialization of agriculture in America have been borne by the poor, who are pushed off the land without recompense, just as in earlier centuries in Europe, they bore the brunt of the transformation of agrarian societies into industrial ones. The poor have also paid a large share of the human cost of the growth of American power overseas, for they have provided many of the foot soldiers for Vietnam and other wars.

Fifteenth, the poor have played an important role in shaping the American political process; because they vote and participate less than other groups, the political system has often been free to ignore them. This has not only made American politics more centrist than would otherwise be the case, but it has also added to the stability of the political process. If the

15 percent of the population below the federal "poverty line" participated fully in the political process, they would almost certainly demand better jobs and higher incomes, which would require income redistribution and would thus generate further political conflict between the haves and the have-nots. Moreover, when the poor do participate, they often provide the Democrats with a captive constituency, for they can rarely support Republicans, lack parties of their own, and thus have no other place to go politically. This, in turn, has enabled the Democrats to count on the votes of the poor, allowing the party to be more responsive to voters who might otherwise switch to the Republicans—in recent years, for example, the white working class.

FUNCTIONAL ALTERNATIVES

I have described fifteen of the more important functions that the poor carry out in American society, enough to support the functionalist thesis that poverty survives in part because it is useful to a number of groups in society. This analysis is not intended to suggest that because it is functional, poverty *should* persist, or that it *must* persist. Whether it should persist is a normative question; whether it must, an analytic and empirical one, but the answer to both depends in part on whether the dysfunctions of poverty outweigh the functions. Obviously, poverty has many dysfunctions, mainly for the poor themselves but also for the more affluent. For example, their social order is upset by the pathology, crime, political protest, and disruption emanating from the poor, and the income of the affluent is affected by the taxes that must be levied to protect their social order. Whether the dysfunctions outweigh the functions is a question that clearly deserves study.

It is, however, possible to suggest alternatives for many of the functions of the poor. Thus, society's dirty work (function 1) could be done without poverty, some by automating it, the rest by paying the workers who do it decent wages, which would help considerably to cleanse that kind of work. Nor is it necessary for the poor to subsidize the activities they support through their low-wage jobs (function 2), for, like dirty work, many of these activities are essential enough to persist even if wages were raised. In both instances, however, costs would be driven up, resulting in higher prices to the customers and clients of dirty work and subsidized activity, with obvious dysfunctional consequences for more affluent people.

Alternative roles for the professionals who flourish because of the poor (function 3) are easy to suggest. Social workers could counsel the affluent, as most prefer to do anyway, and the police could devote themselves to traffic and organized crime. Fewer penologists would be employable, however, and pentecostal religion would probably not survive without the poor. Nor would parts of the second- and thirdhand market (function 4), although even affluent people sometimes buy used goods. Other roles would have to be found for badly trained or incompetent professionals now relegated to serving the poor, and someone else would have to pay their salaries.

Alternatives for the deviance-connected social functions (functions 5–7) can be found more easily and cheaply than for the economic functions. Other groups are already available to serve as deviants to uphold traditional morality, for example, entertainers, hippies—and adolescents in general. These same groups are also available as alleged or real orgiasts to provide vicarious participation in sexual fantasies. The blind and disabled function as objects of pity and charity, and the poor may therefore not even be needed for functions 5–7.

The status and mobility functions of the poor (functions 8 and 9) are far more difficult to substitute, however. In a hierarchical society, some people must be defined as inferior to everyone else with respect to a variety of attributes, and the poor perform this function more adequately than others. They could, however, perform it without being as poverty-stricken as they are, and one can conceive of a stratification system in which the people below the federal "poverty line" would receive 75% of the median income rather than 40% or less, as is now the case—even though they would still be last in the pecking order.[11] Needless to say, such a reduction of economic inequality would also require income redistribution. Given the opposition to income redistribution among more affluent people, however, it seems unlikely that the status functions of poverty can be replaced, and they—together with the economic functions of the poor, which are equally expensive to replace—may turn out to be the major obstacles to the elimination of poverty.

The role of the poor in the upward mobility of other groups could be maintained without their being so low in income. However, if their incomes were raised above subsistence levels, they would begin to generate capital so their own entrepreneurs could supply them with goods and services, thus competing with and perhaps rejecting "outside" suppliers. Indeed, this is already happening in a number of ghettoes, where blacks are replacing white storeowners.

Similarly, if the poor were more affluent, they would make less willing clients for upper- and middle-class philanthropic and religious groups (function 10), although as long as they are economically and otherwise unequal, this function need not disappear altogether. Moreover, some would still use the settlement houses and other philanthropic institutions to pursue individual upward mobility, as they do now.

The cultural functions (11 and 12) may not need to be replaced. In America, the labor unions have rarely allowed the poor to help build cultural monuments anyway, and there is sufficient surplus capital from other sources to subsidize the unprofitable components of high culture. Similarly, other deviant groups are available to innovate in popular culture and supply new culture heroes, for example, the hippies and members of other countercultures.

Some of the political functions of the poor would, however, be as difficult to replace as their economic and status functions. Although the poor could probably continue to serve as symbolic constituencies and opponents (function 13) if their incomes were raised while they remained unequal in other respects, increases in income are generally accompanied by increases in power as well. Consequently, once they were no longer so poor, people would be likely to resist paying the costs of growth and change (function 14); and it is difficult to find alternative groups who can be displaced for urban renewal and technological "progress." Of course, it is possible to design city-rebuilding and highway projects that properly reimburse the displaced people, but such projects would then become considerably more expensive, thus raising the price for those now benefiting from urban renewal and expressways. Alternatively, many might never be built, thus reducing the comfort and convenience of those beneficiaries. Similarly, if the poor were subjected to less economic pressure, they would probably be less willing to serve in the army, except at considerably higher pay, in which case war would become yet more costly and thus less popular politically. Alternatively, more servicemen would have to be recruited from the middle and upper classes, but in that case war would also become less popular.

The political stabilizing and "centering" role of the poor (function 15) probably cannot be substituted for at all, since no other group is willing to be disenfranchised or likely enough to remain apathetic so as to reduce the fragility of the political system. Moreover, if the poor were given higher incomes, they would probably become more active politically, thus adding their demands for more to those of other groups already putting pressure on the political allocators of resources. The poor might continue to remain loyal to the Democratic party, but like other moderate-income voters, they could also be attracted to the Republicans or to third parties. While improving the economic status of the presently poor would not necessarily drive the political system far to the left, it would enlarge the constituencies now demanding higher wages and more public funds. It is of course possible to add new powerless groups who do not vote or otherwise participate to the political mix and can thus serve as "ballast" in the polity, for example, by encouraging the import of new poor immigrants from Europe and elsewhere, except that the labor unions are probably strong enough to veto such a policy.

In sum, then, several of the most important functions of the poor cannot be replaced with alternatives, while some could be replaced, but almost always only at higher costs to other people, particularly more affluent ones. Consequently, *a functional analysis must conclude that poverty persists not only because it satisfies a number of functions but also because many of the functional alternatives to poverty would be quite dysfunctional for the more affluent members of society.*[12]

FUNCTIONAL ANALYSIS

I noted earlier that functional analysis had itself become a maligned phenomenon and that my secondary purpose was to demonstrate its continued usefulness. One reason for its presently low status is political; insofar as an analysis of functions, particularly latent functions, seems to justify what ought to be condemned, it appears to lend itself to the support of conservative ideological positions, although it can also have radical implications when it subverts the conventional wisdom. Still, as Merton has pointed out (1949, 43; 1961, 736–37), functional analysis per se is ideologically neutral, and "like other forms of sociological analysis, it can be infused with any of a wide range of sociological values" (1949, 40). This infusion depends, of course, on the purposes—and even the functions—of the functional analysis, for as Wirth (1936, xvii) suggested long ago, "every assertion of a 'fact' about the social world touches the interests of some individual or group," and even if functional analyses are conceived and conducted in a neutral manner, they are rarely interpreted in an ideological vacuum.

In one sense, my analysis is, however, neutral; if one makes no judgment as to whether poverty ought to be eliminated—and if one can subsequently avoid being accused of acquiescing in poverty—then the analysis suggests only that poverty exists because it is useful to many groups in society.[13] If one favors the elimination of poverty, however, then the analysis can have a variety of political implications, *depending in part on how completely it is carried out.*

If functional analysis only identifies the functions of social phenomena without mentioning their dysfunctions, then it may, intentionally or otherwise, agree with or support holders of conservative values. Thus, to say that the poor perform many functions for the rich might be interpreted or used to justify poverty, just as Davis and Moore's argument (1945) that social stratification is functional because it provides society with highly trained professionals could be taken to justify inequality.

Actually, the Davis and Moore analysis was conservative because it was incomplete; it did not identify the dysfunctions of inequality and failed to suggest functional alternatives, as Tumin (1953) and Schwartz (1955) have pointed out.[14] Once a functional analysis is made more complete by the addition of functional alternatives, however, it can take on a liberal and reform cast, because the alternatives often provide ameliorative policies that do not require any drastic change in the existing social order.

Even so, to make functional analysis complete requires yet another step, an examination of the functional alternatives themselves. My analysis suggests that the alternatives for poverty are themselves dysfunctional for the affluent population, and it ultimately comes to a conclusion that is not very different from that of radical sociologists. To wit: *that social phenomena that are functional for affluent groups and dysfunctional for poor ones persist; that when the elimination of such phenomena through functional alternatives generates dysfunctions for the affluent, they will continue to persist; and that phenomena like poverty can be eliminated only when they either become sufficiently dysfunctional for the affluent or when the poor can obtain enough power to change the system of social stratification.*[15]

NOTES

1. It also has the latent function, as S. M. Miller has suggested, of contributing to the long debate over the functional analysis of social stratification presented by Davis and Moore (1945).

2. Probably one of the few instances in which a phenomenon has the same function for two groups with different interests is when the survival of the system in which both participate is at stake. Thus, a wage increase can be functional for labor and dysfunctional for management (and consumers), but if the wage increase endangers the firm's survival, it is dysfunctional for labor as well. This assumes, however, that the firm's survival is valued by the workers, which may not always be the case, for example, when jobs are available elsewhere.

3. Merton (1949, 50) originally described functions and dysfunctions in terms of encouraging or hindering adaptation or adjustment to a system, although subsequently he has written that "dysfunction refers to the particular inadequacies of a particular part of the system for a designated requirement" (1961, 732). Since adaptation and adjustment to a system can have conservative ideological implications, Merton's later formulation and my own definitional approach make it easier to use functional analysis as an ideologically neutral or at least ideologically variable

method, insofar as the researcher can decide for himself whether he supports the values of the group under analysis.

4. It should be noted, however, that there are no absolute benefits and costs just as there are no absolute functions and dysfunctions; not only are one group's benefits often another group's costs, but every group defines benefits by its own manifest and latent values, and a social scientist or planner who has determined that certain phenomena provide beneficial consequences for a group may find that the group thinks otherwise. For example, during the 1960s, advocates of racial integration discovered that a significant portion of the black community no longer considered it a benefit but saw it rather as a policy to assimilate blacks into white society and to decimate the political power of the black community.

5. Of course, the poor do not actually subsidize the affluent. Rather, by being forced to work for low wages, they enable the affluent to use the money saved in this fashion for other purposes. The concept of subsidy used here thus assumes belief in a "just wage."

6. Pechman (1969) and Herriott and Miller (1971) found that the poor pay a higher proportion of their income in taxes than any other part of the population: 50 percent among people earning $2,000 or less according to the latter study.

7. Most official investigations of welfare cheating over the last quarter-century have concluded that less than 5 percent of recipients are on the rolls illegally, while it has been estimated that about a third of the population cheats in filing income tax returns.

8. Although this chapter deals with the functions of poverty for other groups, poverty has often been described as a motivating or character-building device for the poor themselves; and economic conservatives have argued that by generating the incentive to work, poverty encourages the poor to escape poverty. For an argument that work incentive is more enhanced by income than lack of it, see Gans (1971, 96).

9. One psychiatrist (Chernus 1967) has even proposed the fantastic hypothesis that the rich and the poor are engaged in a sadomasochistic relationship, the poor being supported financially by the rich so that they can gratify their sadistic needs.

10. Although this is not a contemporary function of poverty in America, it should be noted that today these monuments serve to attract and gratify American tourists.

11. In 1971, the median family income in the United States was about $10,000, and the federal poverty line for a family of four was set at just about $4,000. Of course, most of the poor were earning less than 40% of the median, and about a third of them, less than 20% of the median.

12. Or as Stein (1971, 171) put it: "If the non-poor make the rules . . . antipoverty efforts will only be made up to the point where the needs of the non-poor are satisfied, rather than the needs of the poor.

13. Of course, even in this case the analysis need not be purely neutral, but can be put to important policy uses, for example, by indicating more effectively than moral attacks on poverty the exact nature of the obstacles that must be overcome if poverty is to be eliminated. See also Merton (1961, 709–12).

14. Functional analysis can, of course, be conservative in value or have conservative implications for a number of other reasons, principally in its overt or covert comparison of the advantages of functions and disadvantages of dysfunctions, or in its attitudes toward the groups that are benefiting and paying the costs. Thus, a conservatively inclined policy researcher could conclude that the dysfunctions of poverty far outnumber the functions, but still decide that the needs of the poor are simply not as important or worthy as those of other groups, or of the country as a whole.

15. On the possibility of radical functional analysis, see Merton (1949, 40–43) and Gouldner (1970, 443). One difference between my analysis and the prevailing radical view is that most of the functions I have described are latent, whereas many radicals treat them as manifest: recognized and intended by an unjust economic system to oppress the poor. Practically speaking, however, this difference may be unimportant, for if unintended and unrecognized functions were recognized, many affluent people might then decide that they ought to be intended as well, so as to forestall a more expensive antipoverty effort that might be dysfunctional for the affluent.

REFERENCES

Chernus, J. "Cities: A Study in Sadomasochism." *Medical Opinion and Review* (May 1967): 104–9.

Davis, K., and W. E. Moore. "Some Principles of Stratification." *American Sociological Review* 10 (April 1945): 242–49.

Erikson, K. T. "Notes on the Sociology of Deviance." In *The Other Side,* edited by Howard S. Becker. New York: Free Press, 1964.

Gans, H. J. "Three Ways to Solve the Welfare Problem." *New York Times Magazine,* 7 March 1971, 26–27, 94–100.

Goode, W. J. "The Protection of the Inept." *American Sociological Review* 32 (February 1967): 5–19.

Gouldner, A. *The Coming Crisis of Western Sociology.* New York: Basic, 1970.

Herriot, A., and H. P. Miller. "Who Paid the Taxes in 1968." Paper prepared for the National Industrial Conference Board, 1971.

Macarov, D. *Incentives to Work.* San Francisco: Jossey-Bass, 1970.

Marshall, T. H. n.d. "Poverty and Inequality." Unpublished paper prepared for an American Academy of Arts and Sciences project on poverty and stratification.

Merton, R. K. "Manifest and Latent Functions." In *Social Theory and Social Structure.* Glencoe, Ill.: Free Press, 1949.

————. "Social Problems and Sociological Theory." In *Contemporary Social Problems,* edited by R. K. Merton and R. Nisbet. New York: Harcourt Brace, 1961.

Pechman, J. A. "The Rich, the Poor, and the Taxes They Pay." *Public Interest,* no. 17 (Fall 1969), 21–43.

Rainwater, L. *Behind Ghetto Walls.* Chicago: Aldine, 1970.

Schwartz, R. "Functional Alternatives to Inequality." *American Sociological Review* 20 (August 1955): 242–30.

Stein, B. *On Relief.* New York: Basic, 1971.

Tumin, M. B. "Some Principles of Stratification: A Critical Analysis." *American Sociological Review* 18 (August 1953): 387–93.

Wirth, L. "Preface." In *Ideology and Utopia,* by Karl Mannheim. New York: Harcourt Brace, 1936.

· 5 ·

THE FEDERAL ROLE IN SOLVING
AMERICA'S URBAN PROBLEMS

Cities today have many critical problems, but two are uppermost: poverty and segregation. My studies have convinced me that the urban crisis is that our cities are becoming the major place of residence for poor Americans, many of them nonwhite. I argue that this is *the* urban crisis partly because poverty amidst affluence, and segregation in a democracy, are social evils, but also because poverty and segregation cause, directly or indirectly, all the other problems of the city.

THE REAL CAUSES OF THE URBAN CRISIS

Poverty and segregation are the basic causes of slums, for when people cannot afford to pay for decent housing and are kept out of some areas by their color, they cannot help but live in overcrowded circumstances in the oldest and least desirable building of the city. And when men are unemployed or underemployed, whatever their race, they cannot play their proper familial roles, and this results in the broken families, illegitimacy, and welfare dependency currently found in both white and nonwhite poor families. Poverty and segregation breed despair and alienation, feelings of hopelessness that are soon translated into actions that then become social problems. Youngsters who see their elders without jobs or who discover that segregation means poor jobs even for the educated have little incentive to learn; they become school dropouts. Despair and hopelessness also express themselves in juvenile delinquency, sexual promiscuity, and crime, as well as in

---

This chapter is an abridged version of my testimony to the "Ribicoff Committee on the Crisis of the Cities," December 8, 1966. The full statement appears in *The Federal Role in Urban Affairs,* Hearings before the Subcommittee on Executive Reorganization, Committee on Government Operations, U.S. Senate, 89th Congress, Part 11, 2400–17. Washington: Government Printing Office, 1967.

pathological forms of escape—mental illness, alcoholism, and drug addiction—and the latter leads directly to yet more crime. Recently, despair has also produced rioting and looting, violence and property destruction.

These consequences of poverty and segregation are costly for the people who are driven to despairing behavior, for their fellow citizens, and for their communities. Poor people do not want to become school dropouts, unwed mothers, drug addicts, or rioters; they are literally forced into self-destructive and antisocial acts because, seeing no other choice, they grow desperate. These acts make for unsafe neighborhoods and streets, particularly in the slums, but also in more affluent neighborhoods. Our institutional ways of coping with desperate acts and desperate people—public welfare payments, police protection, prisons and rehabilitation centers, mental hospitals and addiction-treatment centers, among others—are expensive and must be funded from the public treasury, even though the poor people whom they "serve" pay little in taxes. An increase in the number of poor city dwellers thus means lower tax receipts and at the same time more costly municipal services. As a result, cities find themselves in financial straits.

Moreover, the spread of slums and of despairing acts by poor people encourages the suburban exodus of more affluent city dwellers, thus causing a further loss of tax revenue to the cities. The exodus also deprives central business districts of their most profitable customers, thus creating problems for downtown. And the more the cities become the home of the nonwhite poor, the less willing are the suburbs to cooperate in solving the problems of the metropolitan area. They become more resistant to racial integration, oppose metropolitan government and regional planning, and even refuse to participate in mass transit schemes for fear that they will bring in the urban poor. And this in turn accelerates the extent of suburbanization and the problems of physical and governmental sprawl.

In short, there are few urban problems that cannot somehow be traced to the twin evils of poverty and segregation. Moreover, these evils are not limited to the cities. The urban crisis is also a rural one, for many of the urban poor have come from rural areas to escape greater poverty and segregation there. The crisis is thus not urban, but national, both in origin and scope; it has little to do with the city and much more with social and economic inequalities in our society. Indeed, the crisis is, above all, economic, for many of the negative consequences of segregation are in reality the consequences of poverty. It is poverty, not race, that breaks up families, and it is poverty, not race, that creates the fears that drive more affluent whites to the suburbs. These fears are not of the Negro per se, but of the slum dweller, the poor Negro. It is a class fear more than a racial fear—the same class fear that led to discrimination against the Irish, Jews, Italians, and other European immigrants when they were poor.

That the fear is class-based is perhaps best illustrated by the fact that much of the opposition to present government efforts against poverty and segregation comes from people whom I would call the "not-so-affluent"—blue-collar and lower-level white-collar workers in the cities and suburbs who become anxious about the antipoverty program and the extension of equality to nonwhites and express it in counterdemonstrations, violence against civil-rights demonstrators, or backlash voting to force retrenchment in public efforts. If a person, whatever his color, is fearful that he many lose his job to the computer (or to a poorer person), or if he is anxious that the property value of his house (usually an old one) will go down as a result of Negro immigration or other urban change, he will inevitably feel threatened. This population, which is not half as affluent as we think, also suffers from social and economic inequality, and its protests are also part of the urban crisis. Its problems are less serious than those of the poor, but they are real, and the federal government must help to solve them, particularly if it is to provide political support for a federal program to stamp out poverty and segregation.

Urban poverty in turn is largely the result of unemployment and underemployment—of the lack of jobs and of being eligible only for insecure, underpaid, and dead-end jobs. Of course, some people are poor because they cannot work—for example, the aged and unmarried mothers; but the latter are in this condition mainly because when men are unreliable breadwinners, they have little incentive to marry, and women have equally little incentive to marry them or to stay married. Moreover, many unmarried mothers who raise their children on grants by Aid for Families of Dependent Children would much rather work if they could find jobs and if day-care facilities were available for their children.[1]

Some have argued that the real problems of the urban poor have nothing to do with unemployment; they are the result of slavery or cultural deprivation, which has created an apathetic population that is unwilling to work or is incapable of performing on the job. Admittedly, there are such cases, particularly among youngsters, but they are often the result, not of cultural inadequacy, but of two other factors. First, a youngster who has never worked before or has long ago given up the hope that anyone would give him a decent job is frightened, and the slightest sign of failure may cause him to lose hope and to drop out of the job just as he dropped out of school.

Second, and more important, the jobs in which poor youngsters fail most often turn out to be poorly paid or dead-end jobs that underemploy rather then employ them. In a society in which most people expect to have useful and dignified jobs, it should not be surprising that poor people would have similar expectations, and youngsters without family responsibilities may well be uninterested in a dead-end job. Although the social and emotional consequences of unemployment are now being recognized, little attention has so far been paid to the consequences of underemployment, even though these may be far worse. According to a finding from the H.A.R.Y.O.U. study, social pathology (delinquency, crime, illegitimacy, and homicide) in Central Harlem was related to and perhaps caused by poor jobs more than by unemployment, particularly since so many more people were holding poor jobs than were unemployed. As Kenneth Clark concluded: "Apparently the roots of social pathology in Central Harlem lie not primarily in unemployment [but] in the low status of the jobs held by the residents of the community."[2]

The fact that poor people can perform well in useful and dignified jobs is best illustrated by the experience of World War II, when defense plants hired the poor, the illiterate, the unemployed, and even the allegedly unemployable and put them to work without benefit of elaborate training, counseling, or educational schemes. Moreover, in doing so, the defense plants integrated poor people into the common war effort and thus made them part of American society in a way that we have not yet been able to—but must—duplicate today. Useful and dignified jobs are, after all, the way by which people judge whether or not they are wanted and needed by their society and by their family, and when they are faced with unemployment or underemployment, they realize quickly that they are being excluded from their society and thus turn to despair and desperate actions. *Ultimately, then, most of the problems of the poor can be traced to unemployment and underemployment, and these in turn are largely responsible for bringing about the crisis of the city.*

It should be stressed that most poor people live law-abiding and respectable lives without ever resorting to the desperate acts that become social problems for the city. Most keep their suffering to themselves, expressing it in the prevailing depression that students of slum life have observed or in emotional disturbances that cause pathology in the family, but are invisible outside the home. Moreover, it does not take many people to create a social problem. Only a small percentage of the poor are drug addicts, but they wreak great havoc on themselves and on those from whom they must steal to pay for their daily "fix"—and much of that theft is never reported to the police. Also, only a small proportion of slum dwellers is desperate enough to riot, although the rioters' actions are supported by a much larger number of people who share their feelings, but do not approve of their methods or are just not desperate or foolish enough to risk being arrested or shot at by the police.

THE GOALS OF A NATIONAL POLICY FOR THE CITIES

This analysis leads logically to the most important goal of future urban, or rather national, policy: *to make sure that the poor, the unemployed, and the underemployed obtain the incomes and jobs that will make them members of the affluent society and entitle them to the rights and privileges and the goods and services that affluent white Americans take for granted.* Once poor people, white and nonwhite, can obtain decent jobs and incomes, they can afford standard housing and will no longer be a captive market for slums and slumlords. Crime, delinquency, addiction, and violence will be reduced drastically; children will grow up in stable, two-parent families and will have the incentive to learn in school and to prepare themselves for a positive future. The cities will derive higher taxes from them; and the central business districts, more free-spending customers.

Moreover, once the majority of nonwhite people are on the way to affluence, they will no longer be so threatening to their white fellow citizens. When they do not need to resort to the desperate acts that stem from poverty, color will no longer be a symbol of poverty, the stereotype of the slum dweller will disappear, and so will many of the current objections to racial desegregation. Nonwhites will be able to move to the suburbs if they wish, and the opposition to a constructive city-suburb relationship will die down.

In effect, I suggest that if unemployment and other causes of poverty can be eliminated, segregation will eventually begin to disappear by itself. This does not mean giving up the struggle for integration, *but national strategy ought to emphasize the abolition of poverty in this generation, so that the children of today's Negro poor will be able to move into the mainstream of American society economically, socially, and politically. If these children can obtain decent jobs and incomes, so that being nonwhite is no longer viewed as equivalent to being lower class, much of the white support for segregation would begin to crumble. Once color is no longer an index of poverty and lower class status, it will cease to arouse white fears, so that open-housing laws can be enforced more easily and ultimately may even be unnecessary. Real integration could then be achieved, possibly even through voluntary means.*

The crucial question, then, is: How can this strategy be achieved?

Programs to End Poverty and Unemployment

Poverty is best eliminated by having more money, and for poor people who cannot work, income grants are the only solution. Old people can be helped by a significant increase in social-security payments and by equivalent grants for those not covered by social security. Other poor people who cannot work should also be supported by direct income grants, for these are not only a more effective way of reducing poverty than welfare or dependency payments but also less punitive and degrading, and they decrease the feeling of poor people that they are being officially labeled and stigmatized as poor and worthless.

Public welfare payments are based on the assumption that their recipients are unwilling to work and must therefore be "encouraged" by low payments to get off the rolls, by regulations that prescribe how the payments must be spent and how their recipients ought to live, and by investigators who invade their lives and their privacy to make sure the regulations are enforced. In a society where poverty is largely a result of job scarcity and racial discrimination, such treatment is unjustifiable. Dependency programs such as Aid to Families with Dependent Children are equally undesirable because they encourage families to separate in order to obtain payments. Since they are given to mothers rather than to families, they are particularly undesirable in the Negro community, for they maintain the superior economic and familial role of the mother and thus help to keep the Negro man in the inferior and marginal familial role he has occupied since slavery. A much better solution would be to provide job opportunities for the men and even for unmarried mothers who want to work. And all families would be aided significantly by a national program of family allowances, formulated so as to exclude all but the children of the rich. Family allowances, as Daniel P. Moynihan, Alvin Schorr, and others have pointed out, would help children, whether legitimate or illegitimate, and also provide needed aid to large families among the not-so-affluent who cannot afford to keep children in school or send them to college.

Unemployment compensation is superior to public welfare and A.F.D.C. because it goes to the man of the family, but it is presently too low, too short in duration, and it does not take cognizance of family size. Finally, the minimum wage, which is another form of income subsidy, is also too low, for the people who earn such a wage cannot possibly support a family, particularly in the cities, and those who receive it are in effect subsidizing the more affluent customers of the resulting goods or services. The minimum wage must either be raised or, in essential industries and public agencies that cannot operate at higher wage levels, be complemented by federal wage supplements that function like the recently approved rent supplements. Of course, new jobs will have to be found for those who are laid off when the minimum wage is raised.

Despite the need for family allowances and income grants for those who really cannot work, the most important program for abolishing poverty is eliminating unemployment and underemployment: for providing decent, useful, and well-paying jobs for all who want them. Job training, job counseling, better vocational education are all necessary, but they are all secondary; as I noted before, when useful jobs are available, people flock to them, and if the jobs pay well enough, they can find their way out of poverty with only little additional help.

JOB-TRAINING AND RETRAINING PROGRAMS

Where will more and better jobs come from, particularly in an automating society that no longer needs unskilled and even semiskilled workers in large numbers? One source is in the present shortage of skilled workers. Existing job-training and retraining programs should be expanded to give the unemployed and the underemployed a chance to fill these vacancies. This is no easy task, for job-training schemes work best on site, when the trainees have obtained the job. If they are only promised the hope of a job after they undergo training, they are likely to be less motivated, especially since they have often been disappointed by promises before. The job must be given before training begins, with some guarantee that the trainee will not be laid off for the slightest infraction of rules or malperformance. Some unemployed people need only to be taught new skills, but others have become so discouraged and cynical that they lack the faith in themselves and in their employers that is necessary to perform in and hold a job. Consequently, job-training programs must build in "tolerance," both for the youngster who is doubtful about himself and the job and for the employer who cannot, after all, afford to pay a poorly performing worker. Building in tolerance means, essentially, providing enough federal funds to help worker and employer in the early period when there are problems, giving both incentive and time to remain in the program. The opportunity to train for a guaranteed job should be given first to the presently unemployed, but it should be extended also to the underemployed who want better jobs, including people in the not-so-affluent category. Indeed, in the long run, all efforts should be made to eliminate jobs that provide only underemployment, using the blessings of automation to do away with as much of the dirty work of our society as possible.

EXPANSION OF NONPROFESSIONAL RANKS

Another, perhaps more important, source of employment is in newly created jobs of two types. One is "nonprofessional" jobs in what are often called the helping or caretaking services—in schools, hospitals, clinics, libraries, recreation centers, welfare and legal agencies, and the like—which would improve the quality of service by providing trained nonprofessionals to help understaffed, overworked professionals. For example, most hospitals are now run to reduce the workload on their harried staffs, rather than to extend maximum help to patients. Hospital staff should be enlarged so that more attention—which people need as much as they need surgery, medicine, or nursing—can be paid to patients. Hospital aides can help in this process, just as teaching aides can help teachers with large classes, paying more attention to slow learners.

Nonprofessionals are especially useful in agencies that provide services to poor people, for if the former are themselves poor people, they can understand, communicate with, and help clients more easily than professionals, who are almost always middle-class people. For example, a professional social worker wrote about the nonprofessional "indigenous home-makers" hired by New York's Mobilization for Youth.

> Indigenous people could teach professional staff a great deal if the latter were willing to learn. . . . They don't perceive people as problems. . . . I sometimes feel like an inhibiting influence when I go along to introduce a homemaker to a client. When I leave, they break out into their own language and vernacular. . . . Empathy rather than sympathy comes more naturally sometimes to the homemaker than the professional worker.[3]

Many communities, helped by federal grants, are now already hiring nonprofessionals for a variety of services. This program should be expanded greatly, for not only does it raise the quality of public services but it provides highly useful, dignified, and interesting jobs. If such jobs were combined with educational opportunities and scholarships, many high school dropouts may be encouraged to return to school and to prepare themselves for professional careers.

This expansion of nonprofessional job creation should take two forms. First, such jobs should not be limited to the antipoverty program, as is now largely the case, for the work to be done by trained professionals is needed in all public services, to raise the quality of such services for *all* Americans, rich and poor. Second, the federal government will have to find ways of persuading federal, state, and local agencies to improve their services with nonprofessional aid. This can best be done by developing new concepts of the good school, hospital, library, and the like, and by setting federal performance standards for these agencies that would require the use of non-professional workers. In addition, the federal government should provide grants to initiate the process of implementing these performance standards, enabling agencies to redesign their operations and to hire nonprofessionals.

Nonprofessional and other workers are also needed elsewhere. Daniel P. Moynihan has suggested that the United States Post Office restore the twice-a-day mail delivery and create fifty thousand new jobs in the process. Municipal agencies can use aides and researchers for a variety of duties; parks, playgrounds, and community centers could be maintained and serviced better if additional staff were available.

The second type of job to be created is for improving the public facilities in cities, suburbs, and elsewhere. All communities need more schools, hospitals, recreation centers, and parks, more highways and mass transit facilities, to name just a few. But perhaps the most important source of such jobs is in the area of housing and slum clearance and, more generally, in rebuilding our cities.

A JOB–CENTERED HOUSING AND URBAN–DEVELOPMENT PROGRAM

We have long believed that clearing slums and providing poor people with good housing and new community facilities alone would improve their living conditions and reduce their poverty. Our experience with urban renewal and public housing has shown, however, that these beliefs are without foundation and that a new housing policy is needed.

We need a national policy that begins with the assumption that *good housing does not cure poverty, but that curing poverty will enable people to afford good housing.* If poor people can obtain the incomes, jobs, and freedom of choice to allow them to afford decent homes in decent neighborhoods, slums and slum living will be eliminated almost automatically. This ought to be the main goal of national urban policy.

This goal can, however, be achieved in part through a housing and urban-development program, for building and rebuilding houses and community facilities is a labor-intensive activity and will create many jobs, particularly for unskilled and semiskilled people. Consequently, it is possible and desirable to kill two birds with one stone: to replace the slums with good housing and to create jobs in the process—jobs that will help people to move into such housing and into the affluent society.

Some of the new and rebuilt housing should be public housing, preferably on scattered sites, but as much as possible should be exactly the same government-supported "moderate"- and "middle"-income housing that is provided for other Americans, with poor people being enabled to live there through rent supplements. In other words, instead of putting poor people into special kinds of housing, the government should use most of its funds to construct more middle-income housing—and to encourage builders to construct it—and enable poor people to move into it as well through rent supplements to them or to builders.

This program calls for two concurrent schemes: to open the suburbs to some poor and nonwhite citizens and to rebuild the ghettos. Although some have argued that rebuilding the ghetto would perpetuate segregation and that future federally supported housing should be entirely integrated, others have argued that integration is unlikely to happen quickly, that it is principally of interest to middle-class nonwhites, and that if the majority of poor nonwhites is to be helped, the ghetto ought to be rebuilt for them and by them.

I believe that framing the issue in an either-or manner is dangerous and unnecessary; housing and integration are both important goals, and both must be pursued. Rebuilding the slums without integrating the suburbs is wrong, but integrating the suburbs without touching the ghetto means relegating many people to the slums for another generation, ignoring the desire of those who want to remain in familiar neighborhoods even if they are in the ghetto, and neglecting the needs of those who must have access to jobs in the inner city.

Integrating the suburbs is essential, particularly because industries and offices are moving out of the city at a rapid rate, and nonwhite people must have access to these jobs. But building integrated housing in the suburbs is difficult, for the opposition to "open housing" is intense and widespread and is not likely to decrease in the future. There are, however, ways of reducing this opposition. The federal government could make the stepped-up housing program attractive to the suburbs by paying for schools and other community facilities and by offering tax subsidies for municipal services so that suburbanites would receive some relief from rising property taxes. Conversely, the government could withhold school and other funds from the suburbs as long as they are segregated. Moreover, it could provide greater incentives to builders and thus obtain their political support for integrating the suburbs. If the plan to build new housing in the suburbs is massive enough, and builders and suburbs can be given incentives to erect integrated housing all over the metropolitan area, then no suburb can continue to attempt to remain racially "pure." Greater efforts to persuade private enterprise and the unions to integrate suburban job opportunities should also be made; and if all these efforts are coordinated, the badly needed federal open-housing requirement, whether by legislation or executive order, would be politically feasible much sooner.

Actually, the white fears over the consequences of suburban integration are highly exaggerated. Until many more suburban jobs for nonwhites are available, the nonwhite families who will be financially able and occupationally secure enough to move to predominantly white areas will be middle class and will be accepted more readily by whites of equal status. There is considerable evidence that housing integration is successful when whites and nonwhites are both middle class and the latter are in a minority.[4] Also, there is little likelihood that the nonwhite slum dwellers whom white suburbanites seem to fear will be able or willing to move to the suburbs in the near future in large numbers. Even if they could afford to do so, many would prefer to remain near inner-city jobs or in or near familiar neighborhoods. Indeed, a goodly number of such people have bought houses outside the ghetto, thus revitalizing older urban areas.

Even though all efforts must be made to hasten integration, probably the fastest and politically most feasible way of providing more employment and better housing to the urban poor is to rebuild the ghettos. This is the intent of the Model Cities program, of the Comsatlike Urban Development Corporation, which the president has been asked to establish, and of the Community Development Corporations proposed by Senator Robert F. Kennedy. All three are highly desirable programs. The Model Cities program is at present better in principle than in reality, for the funds now allocated and scheduled are too small to do any significant amount of rebuilding in any ghetto. Indeed, unless the funds are increased quickly, there is a danger that the Model Cities program will fall back on the routine of urban renewal and replace slums with housing for the more affluent, rather than for the poor. Since so little money is being provided to build or rehabilitate housing that poor people can afford, and since rent-supplement appropriations are also minuscule, the Model Cities program may falter, like urban renewal, because of the lack of relocation housing or because local agencies will be forced to rely on private enterprise to do the rebuilding, which means that, as in the case of urban renewal, the resulting housing will be out of the price range of poor people.

When President Johnson first proposed the Model Cities program, he insisted that it must "foster . . . widespread citizen participation—especially from the demonstration area—in planning and execution of the program" and offer maximum occasions for employing residents of the demonstration area in all phases of the program. The proposed Urban Development Corporation would provide the massive funds needed to provide inexpensive housing and ensure the creation of jobs in significant numbers.

Senator Kennedy's Community Development Corporation scheme is more emphatic on the use of housing programs as a source of jobs than even the Model Cities legislation and vests greater control of the rebuilding program with the residents of the slum areas than does the Urban Development Corporation. I am less sanguine than he, however, that "the great financial institutions" will invest their funds readily in Community Development Corporations, at least at the start, and I would question his suggestion that the Corporations "should need and receive no significantly greater subsidy than is ordinarily available to nonprofit housing corporations under present law." I would argue that these Corporations must be eligible for whatever federal subsidy is needed to make them successful, particularly if they are to be organized and managed by ghetto residents.

America's poor have been so often disappointed by government efforts to help them that they have become discouraged and even cynical and are reluctant to raise their hopes once more, for that is an emotionally risky step for people who have to live with constant disappointment. If funds are insufficient to get the Community Development Corporations off to a flying start and provide no clear evidence that they will improve the living conditions of a large number of people in a foreseeable future, few ghetto residents will have incentive to participate in or support the Corporations. Second, and equally important, the ghetto-rebuilding program has to be massive, whether done by Model Cities, the Urban Development Corporation, or the Community Development Corporations, so that enough jobs are created to make significant inroads on unemployment and underemployment—and so that the building trades unions can be motivated to integrate.

Moreover, building funds should be allocated so as to maximize the number of jobs, rather than to encourage the housing industry (and other industries interested in building housing) to develop new construction technologies that would lead to automated factories and a minimal number of new jobs. Modern methods of construction must be brought into the housing industry, of course, but if it is done in such a manner that the federal government only subsidizes the industry's automation, the job-creating efforts of the housing program will be minimal and the Urban Development Corporation will only be building better kinds of public housing to shelter the unemployed, leaving them as poor as before. This consequence must be avoided at all costs.

Rebuilding the houses and tenements of the ghetto is not enough; better neighborhoods and community conditions must also be created, and this process should be, as Senator Kennedy suggests, correlated with the rebuilding program. The usual physical facilities—schools, playgrounds, community centers, hospitals, and the like—that have often been scarce in the ghetto must be built, but, more important, they must be developed with programs, staffs, and client-involvement techniques so that they will address themselves to their areas' needs.

The most crucial such facility is probably the school. Shiny new buildings alone are insufficient; they must also be schools that will enable poor children to want to learn and to learn. This is no easy task, for since its inception more than a hundred years ago, the public school system has never learned how to teach poor children, mainly because it has not needed to do so. In the past, those who could not or would not learn what the schools taught dropped out quietly and went to work. Today, such children drop out less quietly, and they cannot find work. Consequently, the schools have to learn how to hold them, not only when they drop out physically, but long before, in the early elementary grades, when they begin to drop out in spirit. At present, many poor children, and not only in the ghetto, come to school knowing already from what they have seen in their neighborhoods that they are unlikely to be admitted to full membership in the affluent economy or the democratic society. As a result, they lack motivation to learn, and this motivation is reduced further by anachronistic, irrelevant, or dull curriculums and texts and by teachers who are either too poorly trained or too harried to understand them or to persuade them that they should learn.

The school's task will be much easier if employment programs are vast enough so that the next generation of children will realize they can obtain jobs—and membership in the affluent society—if they are willing to learn. As the Coleman report[5] pointed out, a Negro child's achievement is highly correlated with his feeling that he can control his own destiny, and that feeling—and the social and economic changes that are needed to create it—will motivate him more quickly and easily than the best curriculums and teachers. Even so, the schools must develop the teaching methods, the teachers, and, equally important, the school "climate" that will help children to learn. Such schools require smaller classes, better teachers, curriculums more relevant to the ideas and aspirations which the ghetto child brings to school, and more decentralized, less bureaucratized school systems which can permit experimentation and innovation, relate the school to the ghetto-rebuilding program, experiment with joint work–education programs, offer scholarships to adult dropouts who now want to go back to school, and even provide training for nonprofessionals working in the neighborhood agencies.

A quality education also means integrated education, for de facto segregated schools are as unequal as de jure segregated schools, and children who do not feel themselves to be equals cannot learn to become equals. In the ghetto, where school integration is impossible, more effective neighborhood participation in the school may give the children more feeling that they control their own destinies, but wherever possible schools and school-district boundaries must be located so that the student body will include children from outside the ghetto, particularly beyond the early elementary grades. In the long run, however, the federal government must help cities build educational parks—large campuses where children from many neighborhoods can go to school together and programs are designed for the particular needs and strengths of the park's service area. By centralizing facilities, it will be possible to decentralize services and programs, thus giving the students attending school in an educational park the quality education—special classes, teachers, and courses, for example—which cannot be offered in a set of individual schools, set far apart and isolated from one another.

Furthermore, all schools, inside the ghetto and out, must revamp their social studies programs to give students an opportunity to learn the problems as well as the ideals of American society. If children are to become intelligent adult citizens, white ones need to learn that the myths and stereotypes with which their elders reject the Negro poor are inaccurate, and Negro children need to learn that poverty and segregation are the result of more complex causes than a white conspiracy.

The rebuilt slum also needs nursery schools, day-care centers, and Head Start schools where working mothers and others can send their children to play and learn. It also needs better, cheaper, and more decentralized medical services: an expanded Medicaid program that covers all poor people, plus neighborhood clinics, group practice, and more hospitals. These should offer medical and psychiatric treatment under the same conditions as are (or ought to be) available to other Americans: no waiting lines, a stable and positive doctor-patient relationship, and the necessary specialists. Poverty and segregation have fostered a great deal of emotional disturbance and mental illness, and the services of psychotherapy, now barely available to middle-class people, must be extended to the poor. Neighborhood clinics must be established for this purpose, and less intensive counseling and helping can be provided by psychiatric aides, homemakers, and social workers able to practice their profession, rather than to act as budget investigators. The ghetto slum needs treatment centers for addicts most urgently, both to help the addicts, and if possible to cure them, and to protect ghetto residents from the problems they cause, although if proper help is provided the addicts, they will no longer need to steal or destroy property to pay for their drugs. Many of these facilities could be provided in one-stop neighborhood service centers, which should be constructed as part of the ghetto-rebuilding process and, wherever possible, staffed with trained nonprofessionals from the neighborhood.

Better shopping facilities are as important as new playgrounds, although, again, new buildings are less necessary than stores that serve their customers honestly and equitably and provide opportunities for ghetto residents to go into retail businesses. Moreover, the ghetto needs better police protection and sanitation, more extensive legal services, to be supplied through neighborhood law firms, and, as Watts has demonstrated, better mass transit facilities. Neighborhood municipal offices must be established to create better communication between city hall and the ghetto; and neighborhood planning offices, staffed in large part by residents to be trained in planning techniques, are essential if the ghetto is actually to rebuild itself. Such offices cannot, however, be mere branches of central agencies, for the ghetto must have power to implement its demands, and authority to develop plans for its future.

HELPING RURAL AREAS AND THE NOT–SO–AFFLUENT

Many of the urban poor escaped worse poverty in rural areas, and most left voluntarily, for the lure of the city's job opportunities is as strong for people in underdeveloped portions of America as for the people in the "developing" nations. Yet some want to stay in rural areas, and others would want to if they could earn a decent living. Consequently, rural programs are needed as part of the urban ones I have described, some to prevent involuntary city migration and help people stay on the land or in small towns.

Programs are also needed for people whom I called the not–so–affluent. Although they are not poor, they have difficulties in coping with the rising cost of living, with increased property taxes, disappearing jobs, and aging neighborhoods. They too cannot afford adequate medical and psychiatric service, and they worry about their children, for with factory jobs in increasingly short supply, these children must be educated for other kinds of work.

Needed Resources for Employment and Housing Programs

The economic, housing, and community programs I have suggested as necessary to help the cities are vast in scope and in the amount of effort, money, and innovation they require. It is easy to propose new programs but difficult to carry them out, particularly for four reasons: little is really known about the city and its problems; the technical personnel needed to develop and carry out most of the programs I have proposed are in short supply; the federal government is not organized to deal in a coordinated fashion with what is essentially a single set of interrelated problems; and it has never before been willing to appropriate the amount of money necessary to really solve these problems.

Although goodly sums have been spent for research in agriculture, defense, health, and other governmental activities, almost nothing has been done to study housing and community problems. Urban renewal has now been in existence for over fifteen years, but we still know little about its effects, its benefits, and its costs. We have not measured the consequences of slum clearance on the displaced; we have no idea how many middle-class people have actually been lured back to the city; and we do not even know how much downtown revitalization can be credited to urban-renewal activities. We debate the virtues of integration versus ghetto rebuilding, but we do not know how many ghetto residents want better housing while remaining in their present neighborhoods, how many want to live in urban areas beyond the ghetto, and how many want to move to the suburbs—or how many can afford any of these options. We know even fewer basic facts about the poor and the Negro populations: how many of them are permanently poor, and how many are just caught in a temporary squeeze. Nor do we know how much the exodus of white families to the suburbs is caused by racial change and racial fears, and how much by the desire to live in low-density new single-family houses that are normally available only in the suburbs. We do not know how many white families leave because of the quality of urban schools, or what kinds of schools would persuade them to stay. In short, we know equally little about the needs and wants of more affluent citizens.

Market researchers know pretty well who likes what kind of soap or aspirin, and the manufacturers of consumer products would not think of planning for their future production without such information; but government, federal, state, and local, knows almost nothing about the citizens for whom it plans and about needs that are much more important than soap or aspirin. And while there are ratings for every last television program, governments have no "ratings" for their "programs"; they must infer from election results how well these appeal to the "audience." We do not know how government programs really affect people at the grassroots level or whether they ever reach those grass roots. We build elaborate legislative and administrative safeguards into government programs against graft and corruption, but we rarely include research and evaluation techniques to make sure that these programs achieve the goals intended by legislation.

I am a researcher by profession and have a vested interest in more research. But I am not asking for more research per se or for more basic research, but for policy research, studies framed to answer the questions that must be answered to develop programs for the city and its peoples; and for program experimentation, for demonstrations and pilot projects to test many new program ideas.

A second need is for federally supported training activities to recruit and train the people needed to carry out programs. For example, rebuilding the ghetto slums requires not only masons and electricians but planners, manpower specialists, and job creators, doctors, nurses, psychiatrists, social workers, teachers, administrators, educational planners, municipal specialists, and many more. Both professionals (and nonprofessionals) must be trained to work for and with poor people rather than as experts who tell less-informed clients what to do.

A third need is to develop a federal administrative structure that can deal with the urban crisis in an integrated fashion. I am less concerned about internal contradictions within an agency—for example, that within the Housing and Home Finance Agency, the Federal Housing Administration was subsidizing the suburban exodus while the Urban Renewal Administration was trying to bring middle-class people back—than about the more general tendency of redefining social problems so that they fit the division of labor between the executive departments. This tendency may please the departments, but it often fails to solve the original problem and is particularly inappropriate for the urban condition. If the main problem is urban poverty, then it logically "belongs" to the Office of Economic Opportunity, but insofar as poverty is abolished by income grants, it also belongs to Health, Education, and Welfare, and insofar as it is eliminated by job creation and job training, it belongs as well to Labor, Commerce, and H.E.W. And if housing is to be a major source of jobs, then the problem belongs also to Housing and Urban Development, although the federal housing agency has traditionally been more concerned with producing housing than with creating jobs.

Obviously, the urban problem belongs to almost all agencies in the federal government, and because the parts of the problem are intricately interrelated, attempts have been made to coordinate the efforts of these agencies. Coordination has not been effective, however, because the problems of the city are so large, widespread, and diffuse and those charged with the task of coordinating are so powerless that individual agencies have done little more than pay lip service to coordination, and, like all agencies in and out of government, have spent most of their time and money pursuing their own favorite programs.

I have little faith in the coordination of existing agencies and would argue that because the urban problem is in reality a national problem it must be assigned to a separate governmental body which has the power to determine the needed programs, and the funds to create new ones where necessary, and can use relevant established federal agencies and their programs to help it. This governmental body could be a coordinating agency, provided it had the ability to establish needed new programs and to reformulate traditional programs of other federal agencies, but it must have the ability to shape the programs to the problem, rather than the other way around. Moreover, it must have more power than federal agencies do today to influence local activities; not to dictate to the states and the cities, but to set performance standards that would require them to concentrate on the problem if they are to receive funds, rather than, as now often happens, to divert federal funds to less important local concerns. Admittedly, such a governmental body would have tremendous power, but I can see no other solution if the urban-national problem is really to be solved. Moreover, if the job-creation and housing programs will involve private enterprise and the ghetto neighborhoods themselves, these will be able to provide a large measure of decentralization that reduces the power of the federal body.

The last but hardly the least need is for more federal funds. A variety of estimates suggest that it will take between $100 billion and $200 billion to eliminate poverty, but the federal government and the American people are still looking for magical ways of doing it cheaply. The unwillingness to spend what is needed results in large part from the fact that we have not spent very much in the past, and it is difficult to tear ourselves away from that comfortable tradition. For example, we have known for over a decade that huge sums are needed to replace the slums with good housing, but the federal government still spends less on housing than it takes in. William Wheaton wrote:

> The truth is that even in these days of reapportionment, the historic rural bias of our state legislatures and the Congress produces annual expenditures exceeding $5 billion each year for agricultural subsidies, largely directed to wealthy landowners, and literally nothing for housing and urban renewal. The President's budget message indicates that all programs of the Department of Housing and Urban Development *will show a net revenue to the federal government of approximately $100 million this year, as they have in almost every year for two decades.* In sum, nothing for housing and urban renewal, but billions for agriculture, highways and other less controversial objects. [Emphasis added.][6]

Admittedly, more money is spent for the poor than the funds allocated to O.E.O., but much of that money is used badly. The funds spent on public welfare do not reduce poverty; they only keep the poor in their present state. Millions are spent to prevent the import of heroin, but much less on the addicts. Every time a cache of heroin is confiscated, the price of the drug is driven up, and those who need it to exist must then drive up the crime rate, which then in turn requires the hiring of more policemen. It costs no more to create a job for a poor youngster than to put and keep him in jail, but we do too little of the former, and eventually we are often forced to do the latter.

Wiser spending, for programs that will reduce rather than maintain poverty, would help, but much more federal spending is essential. Private enterprise can help more with the antipoverty effort than it has so far, but moral appeals to business people cannot overcome the fact that the poor often are—or are thought to be—unprofitable or risky customers, even by government itself. After all, slumlords exist only because no one else has sought to house the poor and because respectable private firms can make money more easily by serving the affluent, particularly when government housing programs have been more inclined to subsidize building for the affluent than for the poor. Nor will appeals encourage private enterprise to create jobs, for we live in an era in which profit and productivity are most easily increased by replacing workers with machines.

I am not convinced, however, that poor people are really such unprofitable customers, except when they are treated as such and then revenge themselves by living up to expectations. Consequently, it should be possible to incorporate the poor people into the same production and consumption markets that serve other Americans, provided they have the jobs and incomes to participate in those markets.

The federal government's role ought to be to initiate and support this incorporation: to make the poor better customers and to make private enterprise better suppliers. Since private enterprise has usually been willing to engage in new ventures when financial incentives were available to reduce or eliminate the risks, the federal government ought to provide the funds needed to start private enterprise in the new ventures and continue to provide such funds until private enterprise can make a reasonable profit by its own efforts.

In addition to providing incentives, however, the federal government should also reduce the temptations that now encourage private enterprise to serve mainly the affluent. It can do so by re-evaluating all of its subsidization activities and by withdrawing its subsidies from those activities that can be carried on by private enterprise without federal help, particularly for products and services to the affluent, who need governmental subsidy less than the poor. Federal funds recouped in this fashion could then be diverted to solving the urban problem. But whatever the source of federal money, there is no other choice but for the federal government to fund and to set in motion the economic processes by which the poor and the cities must be helped. If the federal government will not do it, it will not be done.

The opponents of federal spending have argued vociferously that America cannot afford to eliminate poverty, that taxes must be spent on the war in Vietnam, or that they must be cut to retain private initiative; but they have been fighting all government programs that extend affluence to the less fortunate for generations. The money to mount an effective war on poverty and slums *is* available; A. Philip Randolph's *Freedom Budget*[7] demonstrated fully and impressively that these funds can come *just* from the increases in national production, what the Budget calls the "economic growth dividend," in the next ten years.

The real issue is not lack of money, but lack of political support to spend a share of American affluence to abolish poverty. All Americans support the War on Poverty in the abstract, but many are against specific programs as soon as these become effective or endanger existing privileges. Programs to help the poor are therefore controversial, and since the poor are a small and powerless portion of the national constituency and of most local constituencies as well, elected officials have little political incentive to propose or to support programs that are likely to generate opposition from larger and more powerful constituencies: the affluent and particularly the not-so-affluent.

How, then, can the massive expenditures needed to solve the urban crisis be justified, and how can the needed new legislation and programs be made politically feasible? One can argue that these programs are required on moral grounds, but the celebrated American generosity leans more toward charity than toward effective action and typically results in the minuscule federal programs now available; for example, for the War on Poverty or public housing. One can argue also that such programs are needed to save the cities, but the balance of power today lies with the suburbs, and with industry and offices streaming out of the city to join the suburbanites, they have less and less reason to feel that they need the city.

Ultimately, I suspect that an effective program must be justified on practical grounds: that the consequences of not mounting it will be far greater than the costs of doing something. If we as a society continue to promise equality to the poor, white and nonwhite, but continue to do little to bring it about, they are likely to give up the patience and self-discipline they have shown in the past. On the one hand, there may be more family breakups, crime, delinquency, and escape into alcohol, drugs, or mental illness; on the other hand, more group violence: more riots, more looting, and more destruction of property.

Coping with more pathology and violence will, of course, require large sums from the public treasury, even for stopgap measures like those we use today. But more important, the rise in pathology, violence, and public expenditures to control them will create a demand from other Americans for repressive action and for retrenchment in federal antipoverty and civil-rights programs. Whether we call it backlash or, with Louis Levine, "the opportunity for the fearful and hostile white to 'legitimately' reveal his bias,"[8] they will demand an end to federal efforts until Negroes stop engaging in desperate acts. But such demands can only generate more Negro hostility, and these will in turn produce yet more pathology and violence.

I believe that we are now at the beginning of such a process, and if it is permitted to continue, the country may be caught in a vicious circle that will spiral and escalate, until eventually America will be divided into a small but growing pathology-ridden and hostile "underclass" and a fearful and revenge-seeking majority, one predominantly Negro, the other mainly white. If this happens, American life may be marked by recurring riots, by full-fledged class warfare between the haves and the have-nots. Then the taste of affluence will be bitter, and the American way of life will not be worth living even for the rich.

NOTES

1. Helen I. Safa, *Profiles in Poverty* (Syracuse, N.Y.: Youth Development Center, 1966—mimeographed).

2. Harlem Youth Opportunities Unlimited, *Youth in the Ghetto* (New York: H.A.R.Y.O.U., 1964), 159. The correlation between social pathology and unemployment was only .07, but between pathology and unskilled workers, it was .64.

3. From an unpublished memorandum by Gertrude Goldberg, quoted in Frank Riessman, *The Revolution in Social Work: The New Nonprofessional* (New York: Mobilization for Youth, November 1963—mimeographed), 26, 35.

4. See, for example, Housing and Home Finance Agency, *Equal Opportunity in Housing* (Washington, D.C.: Government Printing Office, June 1964).

5. James S. Coleman, *et al., Equality of Educational Opportunity* (Washington, D.C.: Government Printing Office, 1966).

6. "Comments on the Demonstration Cities Program," *Journal of the American Institute of Planners,* XXXII (November 1966): 368.

7. *A 'Freedom Budget' for all Americans* (New York: A. Philip Randolph Institute, October 1966).

8. Louis Levine, *The Racial Crisis: Two Suggestions for a National Program* (New York: Center for Research and Education in American Liberties, Columbia University, 1966—mimeographed), 12.

· 6 ·

Time for an Employees' Lobby

B ill Clinton was elected president in large part because he proposed to
do something about the ever-declining number of full-time, decent
jobs—but since his election, he seems to have put aside this campaign
promise. He needs to be encouraged to remember it, and one way to encourage him is to establish a national lobby of employees.

Such an organization, which could also be called a jobs lobby, would
represent employed workers, whatever the shapes and colors of their col-
lars, as well as supervisory and managerial employees of all kinds. It would
speak for the jobless, as well, and for "contingent," "flexible," and other
involuntary part-time workers.

The principal purposes of the employees' lobby would be to pressure
governments and private enterprise to: (1) to develop short-term and long-
term policies to save jobs and create new ones, preferably civilian; (2) begin
considering long-term solutions for the continuing and seemingly permanent erosion of jobs; and (3) establish proper income support programs for
the underemployed and unemployed.

The employees' lobby should also place the jobs issue high on the public agenda, and educate the public both about the drastic changes our economy is facing and the need to address them politically. While many people
complain about what the disappearance of jobs has done to them and their
communities, amazingly little public discussion of *what to do about the problem* has appeared, in the news media, on the talk shows, among economists,
and above all in Congress and the White House. Admittedly, creating new
jobs may be the most difficult problem any political economy can face
today, but that does not justify virtually ignoring it. In fact, the widespread
opposition to NAFTA probably reflected in large part the Clinton administration's failure to address the jobs problem.

Perhaps the pervasive sidestepping of the issue, deliberate or otherwise,

This chapter was first published in *Social Policy* 24, no. 2 (1993): 35–38. © 1993 by Social
Policy Corporation, New York, N.Y. Reprinted with permission.

exists because the problem does not yet appear serious enough; after all, the *official* unemployment rate, which is too-seldom questioned, remains around 6.5 percent and implies that more than 90 percent of all those seeking work are employed. The *actual* rate, which includes the visibly discouraged jobless, estimates the invisibly discouraged who stopped looking for work long ago, and also counts the involuntary part-timers, is often thought to be about twice the official rate. (One early task of the employees' lobby will be to press for more accurate counting of the actually jobless, and monthly reporting of the number of the contingent and other underemployed workers.)

The jobs problem may also be ignored because there is still hope that prosperity *with* fuller employment is just around the corner. Many optimistic public officials and members of the business community seem to expect that with a variety of economic indicators rising again in 1994, the jobless rates will come down significantly. Even *if* these optimists are right, they must still consider the possibility that capitalism has "advanced" to the stage of jobless prosperity, which is good for corporate executives and stockholders but does nothing for unemployed, underemployed, or underpaid workers.

WHY ANOTHER LOBBY?

In a different world, the proper organization to deal with job erosion is not an employees' lobby but a workers' party. Because the United States has never had a significant workers' party, however, and because the long-established European ones are now losing steam, this does not seem to be a relevant solution. Nor are unions the answer, for their role and influence are still being reduced. Although they remain major lobbies for their workers, neither a single union or even a union of all unions seems likely to represent all employees in the United States today.

Would people join, support, or even lend their names to such a lobby? Predicting political participation is always a dangerous enterprise; most Americans do not participate in any political organization most of the time. Nonetheless, a sizable number of people, including those who want nothing to do with unions, might well support a lobby.

There are many people who at least have reason to support a lobby of employees. They include some of the people who have lost both their jobs and the likelihood they will ever find others, and the much larger number who lack full-time, secure, and decently paying jobs. The already unemployed have in the past often been too discouraged to be organizationally active, but perhaps the current emergence of self-support groups of the jobless suggests a change is in the offing.

Other possible supporters of an employees' lobby might include the relatives and friends of those who are unemployed or underemployed, as well as the many who are themselves threatened by future job loss. A 1993 study by the Families and Work Institute gave some sense of the scope of the problem: 42 percent of all workers in a national sample reportedly worked for companies undergoing temporary or permanent workforce reductions—nearly a majority of the employed labor force.

Finally, even the securely employed and the permanently tenured might back an employees' lobby, particularly if they realize that being well employed *now* no longer offers the security it once did. In addition, while they may not like lobbies *sui generis,* they may feel differently when they realize that their employers, whether in profit-making firms or nonprofit agencies, are generally members of *employers'* lobbies of one kind or another.

ACROSS CLASS AND IDEOLOGY

If a lobby is to obtain support from as many employees as possible, it must be a *multiclass* organization, appealing to workers ranging from the upper middle-class professional to the low-income domestic. It must also be *trans-ideological,* welcoming people of all political persuasions—and especially the apolitical. Any romantic hoping to transform the United States through a politically mobilized working class must go elsewhere.

How should such a lobby be structured? Should it have actual members or mostly nominal ones who are mainly available to be counted when numbers are needed? Should it be run by elected members or by professionals? Should it ally itself with one of the major parties or a third party; and how should it relate to labor unions and other groups with related interests? The right answer is the structure that is most successful at achieving the purposes of the lobby most quickly.

What would employees lobby *for?* Like other lobbies, an employees' lobby would have to offer policies. But while lobbies offer policies, they rarely invent new ones. Alternatives already are available to the last decade's policy of tax reduction for businesses and low interest rates that have obviously not been very successful. A detailed program would need to be worked out, but for starters I would point to five areas for development: (1) help for new business ventures, from public loans and loan guarantees to government-sponsored "industrial policies"; (2) public works (rebuilding bridges, developing modern databases, renewing urban schools, etc.); (3) work-time reduction and work sharing, giving current employees shorter work weeks, longer vacations, and earlier retirement, at the same time bringing more people into the workforce; (4) proper income support for the underemployed and unemployed, including welfare paid (as in Western Europe) at a supportive, not a punitive, rate; (5) democratizing the employer-employee relationship.

I am well aware that many of the policies in these five categories are currently considered not politically feasible. That's precisely why we need an employees' lobby: clearly, solutions are available and would become feasible if mainstream political support were mobilized for them.

An AARP for Employees?

In some respects, this is a strange time to propose a new citizen organization, for we live in an era of deep and pervasive skepticism about government, politics—and, in fact, anything beyond individual solutions to even the most public of problems. When combined with the economic and political difficulties of creating new jobs, it is risky to imagine finding a large enough group of Americans willing to begin to press for the search for new solutions.

Nonetheless, politics has always been unpredictable, and the only way to see if an employees' lobby would work is to try to start one. Who could have predicted that a national association of retired people, the AARP, would today be one of America's largest and most powerful lobbies?

What is needed first are starters. Perhaps there are enough blue-and white-collar unions and professional associations that are fed up with the lack of national inaction on jobs, or strong enough to concurrently reach out to nonunion and anti-union workers in a new way. In fact, some existing unions, especially those that know they are not likely to grow further as unions, might have the most immediate incentive to get an employees' lobby under way. Forward-looking union officials might also consider the possibility that a successful employees' lobby could generate new interest in unionization.

New ventures need more than just members; they also need funds. Eventually, the big consumer goods corporations might be desperate to support any venture that puts money into the pockets of the customers they need to buy their products, but that future is far off. Presumably, some unions might supply startup money, as might the usual funding sources for liberal causes—even if this must not end up as another exclusively liberal cause. And since many of the prospective members or supporters of an employees' lobby will be working, a small membership fee—like the $8 a year charged by the AARP—would not be unreasonable.

THE ECONOMIC FUTURE

Once upon a time, American economic growth could be relied on to produce new jobs almost automatically. In today's global economy, however, that automatic process seems to have disappeared. Consequently, Americans have to apply the lessons of democracy to take their economic future into their own hands, and make sure that government plays its role in supplying jobs, and incomes, for all.

There is, however, another scenario. Continuing to wait for the economy to supply jobs could someday bring about a society in which only a plurality of people still hold decent jobs, a large minority is underemployed, and another is unemployed. Such a society, which only promises more violent social strife and a deteriorating quality of life for everyone, must be avoided at all costs.

· 7 ·

SOME UTOPIAN SCENARIOS

Complete equality is a utopian idea, but utopian ideas are worth exploring to suggest future directions for existing society. This chapter presents two utopian scenarios, brief speculative sketches of hypothetical societies, both designed around a different kind of complete equality. The scenarios emphasize some of the consequences that would follow and the problems that would have to be solved under complete equality, because they are also intended to shed some light on the consequences and problems of policies for more equality.

Scenario is a popular term approximating what social scientists call models or simulations, and model building is common practice today in a number of social sciences. These models attempt to simulate existing societies, whereas utopian models must be speculative. Even though they should be grounded in current theoretical insights and empirical knowledge about the workings of existing societies, they have to depend heavily on thoughtful guessing about how institutions and people might behave under radically different circumstances, thus moving far beyond whatever is scientific in social science. Nevertheless, I think such "research" is useful for the social sciences because it requires the application of informed imagination to the study of society, which not only might encourage researchers to realize the relationist quality, to use Karl Mannheim's concept, of current social arrangements, but would also generate many new research questions about how existing society operates.

Properly speaking, utopian models should include three components: the *definition* of the egalitarian condition; the social, economic, and other *prerequisites* necessary to a society before such equality can exist; and the various *consequences* for other parts of the society that accompany the kind of equality under discussion. The scenarios I am presenting here do not measure up to this standard; they are exceedingly simple in conception and

---

This chapter is excerpted from Chapter 8 of *More Equality*. New York: Pantheon Books, 1973.

scope—preliminary illustrations of scenarios that ought to be constructed rather than finished products.

Finally, the scenarios are only partially utopian; in fact, they begin with the nonutopian premise that people in these hypothetical societies would pursue their self-interest as they do in existing ones. I set up this premise partly because I do not believe that utopias that assume a very different "human nature" are useful, and partly because one of my purposes in writing the scenarios was to discover the conflicts between complete equality and self-interest. The scenarios are only partially utopian in other ways as well, for I have tended to assume the presence of some exiting institutions, referring, for example, to corporations in an economically egalitarian society. This is in part intentional, for I assume that a large society will require corporations of some kind even if it is egalitarian, but this also reflects the primitive and incomplete design of my scenarios, for I have obviously not thought about what kind of economic organization is most congruent with equality.

The scenarios included here discuss only economic and political equality.

ECONOMIC EQUALITY

By economic equality, I mean here equality of income and wealth, leaving out equality of occupational status or equality in the workplace. For brevity's sake, I shall limit the scenario to one kind of income equality, in which everyone earns about the median income, thus leaving out such alternatives as the *kibbutz* in which economic equality is achieved by the communal provision of all goods and services and no one receives personal income, except for pocket money and vacation allowances; the socialist models involving public ownership of the economy; and the so-called Cuban model in which the state hopes to supply all basics such as bread and milk, shelter, medical services, and transportation for nothing, but continues wage and salary differentials.

There are even a number of median-income models, each with different social implications. One provides for wage and salary equality, which would probably make it difficult to recruit workers for onerous jobs and would require other rewards to demarcate status differences. Another, which I shall choose, maintains wage differentials, using the tax system to create equality. Even within this model, further distinctions must be made, based on the time period and the social unit for which equality is computed. Thus, incomes could be equalized every year, every *n*th year, or over a person's lifetime. In the latter case, people could draw most heavily on their lifetime income at the time they need it most, for example, while raising their families.

The social unit can be, among others, the household (assuming here it is equivalent to the nuclear family), or adult individuals (although one could also conceive of a model in which children obtained full income equality as well). Each of these would have different social consequences; with the household as the unit, present family arrangements would probably continue, at least if additional allowances were made for children, although children would be encouraged to set up new households more quickly, so that both the family of origin and that of procreation would be able to maximize their family income. If no extra money were allocated for children, fertility and family size might well decline, since some people would prefer to spend their limited income on other things; if allowances for children were included, some families might have more children than today, particularly since they would not be able to earn additional after-tax income through work or investment. However, if the allowances were set strictly in terms of the cost of raising children at different ages, so that they would not provide additional family income, fertility would not be affected. If individuals were the social unit, then people earning above the median might decide not to marry, though as long as two people could live more cheaply than one, the incentive not to marry would be slight. More important, people establish families mainly for noneconomic reasons, so that different egalitarian policies probably would have only a minor impact on family formation and size.

The economic-equality scenario developed here will assume the retention of wage differentials, with equality achieved annually or more often through the tax system, enabling all adult individuals to have equal incomes, with cost-level allowances for children determined both by their number and their age. Under such a scheme, women would obtain more equality than they have now, since after-tax family income would be the same whether they or their husbands worked, but they could also remain housewives, and family size would not ride on economic considerations.

Insofar as economic equality extended to wealth, families would no longer be able to pass their wealth on to the next generation and thus to perpetuate themselves as dynasties. In fact, unless some people had the power to send their children to the best schools, they could not pass on much of their own status, and if economic equality reduced incentives for education, as I suggest subsequently, then even less so. The extent to which the generational transmission of economic and social resources is important to family cohesion and structure is hard to estimate, but if it is important, parents would oppose any egalitarian scheme that prohibited it, and if it were instituted, some might not want to have children at all. If it is not important, then parents might take less interest in their children when they became adolescent, for if their children could not guarantee them immortality, they might have less need to shape their lives along parental lines. On the one hand, this might free adolescents from adult domination; on the other, it might increase the social distance between the two age groups once their lifestyles diverged. Younger children, however, would continue to be dependent on parents, and parents would thus have more incentive to shape them according to parental culture. In fact, they might exert more pressure on young children to be like themselves, knowing that they could not exert this pressure in adolescence. (This is the case among many working-class and poor families in our society, and it may be related to the fact that they have few resources to pass on to their children.)

Needless to say, an economically equal society would be very different in other respects from the present one, for poverty and great affluence—and all the pathology, problems, and conflict they generate—would be eliminated. If this scheme were implemented (as of this writing in 1972), a family of four would have an annual income between $15,000 and $20,000, plus its share of the redistributed wealth, and assuming no major change in price levels, everyone would be comfortably off if not affluent. But assuming also that the normal human desire for more income would continue, people would try to obtain further income in various ways. Suburban gardens would be planted with vegetables so as to allow expenditure of money income for other goods, people would exchange certain types of labor with each other, and barter of various kinds could be expected as well. People working in consumer-goods industries and stores would probably try to take home more of their employers' products than they do now, and firms that wanted to attract skilled workers when the supply was scarce would no doubt offer a variety of fringe benefits that added to real income, such as automobiles that could be used off the job and sales or other conferences at vacation resorts. Consequently, tax regulations would have to control such benefits so that they did not create excessive new inequalities. Individuals who could not restrain their need for more income might turn to bank robbery for this purpose, although their number would probably be small, for a society willing to establish economic equality would have various formal and informal ways of discouraging greed.

People would continue to work for noneconomic reasons alone—though surely not as hard—but since higher wages would bring them only more stratus and not more spending power, they would reject onerous jobs and flood the market for more desirable ones, thus forcing society to provide other incentives and sanctions to make sure the onerous work got done and supply-demand equilibrium was established for the more desirable jobs. Onerous jobs could be filled by reducing the number of work hours, but it is not clear whether corporations could be run by twenty-hour-a-week executives, or whether firms could operate with any degree of efficiency with employees working different numbers of hours. Moreover, the people with shorter work periods would have more time to grow vegetables or produce goods for barter. Symbolic rewards such as national honors might recruit some people for some jobs, but another solution would be to rotate desirable and undesirable jobs, as is done in the kibbutz. This is more difficult in a large society than in a community-sized one, and would reduce efficiency and productivity when well-trained people were lost by rotation. Of course, people could be allowed to work longer hours without additional recompense, and those who especially enjoyed their work might do so, but then they would shrink the supply of desirable jobs. Perhaps a better solution is the "industrial army" proposed by Edward Bellamy in his 1888 utopian novel, *Looking Backward,* in which every member of society was required to put in a period of years at the most onerous jobs before being free to look for work of his or her choice. Nevertheless, some necessary jobs might not be taken, and some people might have to be paid more to fill needed roles. If their number was small and they could not pass their higher incomes on to their children, such a deviation from complete equality would probably not be problematic, although if the deviants could also obtain more political power, the seeds of a new elite would have been sown.

With income equality, there would be little incentive to save and investment would have to become a public function, creating political problems to be discussed below. The market mechanism could probably determine investment for consumer goods and services, and costly personal services, such as medical care, could be provided publicly on the basis of need, but other public investment decisions are difficult to make on an egalitarian basis, since they often benefit some people more than others. For example, if income equality did away with private philanthropists who now subsidize expensive high culture and the government had to invest in the production of chamber music concerts, the few people attending such concerts would obtain high per capita benefits at the expense of the rest of the population. An egalitarian society might decide that such concerts would have to be abolished as one price of equality, and chamber music would be available only on records, or in private concerts given in people's living rooms.

If work ceases to be a source of higher income, educational motives will change. Some people will then decide to pursue the liberal arts education educators have always dreamed of, and those with shorter work weeks may go to school to keep busy, but many others will decide that education is unnecessary or unenjoyable, and a mechanism will have to be invented to make sure that the jobs requiring a great deal of prior education are filled. Most likely, the needed skills could be imparted through more on-the-job training, but the jobs that require intensive schooling could be filled only by paying people their full income for and while going to school. Society could, of course, provide everyone with a free college education, and even make it compulsory so as to postpone a rush on the labor market, but this would penalize students who did not want such an education and the teachers who would have to teach them; and if universities became, in effect, places that provided training for potential workers, they would be far more vocational than they are today.

Income equality would result in a radical change in the class structure, although wage differentials and the division of labor would maintain some kind of social differentiation and stratification. People holding the hardest-to-fill jobs would have the highest status, and if they were able to withhold their labor by striking, they would presumably have more political power than the rest of the population. Consequently, such a society would have to make sure that hard-to-fill jobs were kept at a minimum by job redefinition and work rationalization. Similarly, executives and others who have power over workers or whose decisions affect the economy and the society would still have more status, and would join the scarce workers at the top of the socioeconomic hierarchy, but their power to generate new inequality for themselves could be discouraged at least to some extent by job rotation, and by making them elected officials whose decisions were regulated by a constituency of workers and others. This would undoubtedly affect efficiency and productivity in some cases, but an egalitarian society would have to reconcile itself to such effects.

For the majority of people, status differences would no longer be determined by income or work, and new sources of differentiation would develop. For example, if people no longer clustered socially or residentially on the basis of income, they might do so by age, ethnic origin, religion, kind of education, and leisure interests. If reduction of work hours became the major incentive to fill needed jobs, the people working the fewest hours would not only have the most status but would be sure to congregate socially and residentially, since a lifestyle based on a twenty-hour work week would be quite different from one based on a work week of thirty to thirty-five hours, and people with a lot of free time would associate with each other to develop common ways of spending that free time. The ways in which people chose their neighbors and communities would thus change drastically.

Moreover, with income equality, money would be too scarce to justify the building of large houses as indicators of status; except for the few who wanted to spend extra amounts of money or their own labor for distinctive housing, most people would live in much more uniform dwellings than now. In fact, housing would be designed more to fit age and family-size needs, since people could save money by buying less housing space when they were single or old, which would in turn encourage further current trends of residential clustering by position in the life cycle.

If community and housing choices were no longer made on the basis of present class and status considerations, many people would become more mobile. A Boston Brahmin might stay in his hometown because, even with a lower income, he would still derive some status from his historical family background and his connections, but more people than ever would head for warmer and pleasanter climates, particularly to regions where they could live with lower heating bills and grow more of their own food. In fact, family farming might undergo a small renaissance.

With income differences eliminated by taxation, politics would cease to be a conflict between the haves and the have nots, although traditional political differences—for example, between producers and consumers, landlords and tenants, or urban and rural residents—would persist. New ones would develop as well; for example, if people congregated in terms of interests, communities of sports enthusiasts would fight with communities of hobbyists over public investments for their respective leisure pursuits, and within the former, golfers would fight with hikers about whether open space should be devoted to golf courses or wilderness areas. People who worked full-time would ask government to prevent those with more spare time from earning extra income by producing goods for barter, or to grant them public benefits that would add an equivalent amount to their own incomes. And since full-time workers would constitute a political majority, they would have the power to achieve their demands, at least if democracy means majority rule. People who are politically powerful by virtue of high positions in the economy would also attempt to get extra benefits, although if their numbers were small and if politicians did not depend on them or their companies for campaign funds, their political power would be much less than it is today. But perhaps the major political struggles would be over public investment, with all groups trying to pressure government for decisions that would mean extra benefits for them, and here too, their numerical power as well as their organizational skill would determine to what extent public decisions were deflected from egalitarian principles.

In order to maintain economic equality, the best solution for government would be to transfer as many of its regulatory powers to bureaucracies that did not need to respond to the electorate, but this would make the society less democratic and the bureaucracies too powerful. Indeed, unless all citizens accepted the desirability of economic equality, a conflict might soon arise between egalitarian and democratic principles. But even if this did not happen, government itself would have to proliferate, since it would be saddled with the responsibility of keeping the economy egalitarian. Although such proliferation is less dangerous than today's opponents of equality suggest, and, if government is democratic, less dangerous than the proliferation of corporations large enough to free themselves from control by customers, investors, or political regulators, it does put more power into the hands of a monopolistic institution, and monopoly power is dangerous for equality whether in private or in public hands.

It is possible, of course, to argue that the benefits of economic equality, particularly for the population that now earns less than the median, outweigh any of these costs, but such costs are inevitable, and who is to bear them is itself a major political issue. Once-poor people might well favor a government that obtained a median income for them, even if government officials lived better than they, but people who had to give up some income would not share their opinion, and intellectuals would suffer if government were powerful enough to restrict criticism and civil liberties. Whether it is possible to create political and bureaucratic mechanisms that would enable government to protect equality without accruing unequal powers and privileges is perhaps one of the most important unanswered questions in designing an economically egalitarian scenario.

POLITICAL EQUALITY

A politically egalitarian scenario is much harder to describe than an economically egalitarian one, for power is less easily divided than money, and any large society with a division of labor requires some delegation of authority, which can result in inequality. In fact, complete political equality probably requires the breakup of the nation-state, for if people were to have equal amounts of power in determining their fate, they would have to live in small communities with direct democracy, or at least a low degree of representative democracy. Moreover, such communities would have to be fairly homogeneous in population, for direct democracy can work only when it is grounded on a considerable degree of consensus, and with heterogeneity, majorities could create inequality for minorities. Smallness and homogeneity go together, for only a small community can develop the cohesion that will motivate people to give up benefits for the sake of others, for example, to allow children to train themselves for jobs not needed by the community, which with respect to artists and scientists has been a problem even in the relatively homogeneous kibbutz. Such communities would either have to be so poor that the mere struggle for survival made the community's well-being every person's self-interest, or so affluent that no one had scarce resources or skills the control of which could become a source of extra power.

In addition, politically egalitarian communities would need to be economically self-sufficient, for they cannot long maintain political equality if they become involved in relationships with other communities, unless these are also egalitarian. For example, if a community had to earn part of its living by trading with other communities, then those people and firms carrying out the trade would obtain a degree of economic power that would soon translate itself into political power, although this might be ameliorated if the economic enterprises of the community were publicly owned. Consequently, complete political equality would probably be best achieved by farming communities that could feed themselves, but the attainment of such equality would mean a lower standard of living for everyone—provided, of course, that the individual communities would refrain from making war on each other to enrich themselves.

Whether or not people would partake of the opportunity for political equality in small communities is another question. The kibbutz experience suggests that people would participate in issues critical to the survival of the community and issues in which they were personally interested, leaving the rest of the decision making to elected representatives or to self-selected individuals who enjoy politics. Given the smallness of the community, access to and control over such representatives would be easy, so that they would always have a good sense of what their constituents wanted or would accept and would not be likely to disobey the general will when it manifested itself.

In a large, heterogeneous nation-state, complete political equality is probably unattainable, but scenarios for maximizing it can be suggested. For this purpose, it is useful to distinguish between equality of participation, equality of access to political representatives, and equality of control over them. Equality of participation begins with the right of one person to have one vote and to have the opportunity to vote more often than at biennial and quadriennial elections. Voting could be equalized simply by creating election districts of roughly equal size, instituting proportional representation, and funding election campaigns with federal monies. However, voting is only one kind of participation, and not a very effective one at that, for it is available only infrequently and gives voters little choice except between rival candidates.

The most effective form of participation is the exertion of political pressure, but this is difficult to equalize. It might be possible to equalize the *ability* to exert pressure, which would probably require economic and educational equality for all citizens, as well as methods of encouraging and giving added weight to pressure from unorganized citizens and of discouraging and discounting that of organized groups. Even if this were feasible, the *willingness* to exert pressure would also have to be equalized, and this is far more difficult, for it is a function of individual and group needs. People who wanted something from government or were dissatisfied with its performance would be willing to engage in pressure activities, thus gaining a political advantage over people who wanted nothing or were satisfied. Consequently, a politically egalitarian society would probably have to minimize the opportunity for pressure politics, emphasizing instead elections and other forms of feedback in which everyone not only could but had to participate.

Involuntary participation could be created by frequent elections and referenda. Modern communications technology even makes it possible to design a feedback system by which people voice their opinions once a month or even once a week, either by telephone or by a device attached to the television set. This, of course, assumes that everyone has access to a telephone or television set and is available to "cast" an opinion at the required time. An alternative approach is to establish a national opinion poll that interviews a sample of citizens frequently and regularly to get their reactions to current issues and upcoming decisions, with the sample large enough to narrow the amount of error and make sure that the entire opinion spectrum is adequately represented for statistical and political purposes.

Whatever the scheme, public opinion would thus supply more feedback to government, provided that government was required to take it into account. Even so, a number of problems would have to be dealt with. First and most important, insofar as a vote or opinion is affected by the nature of the ballot or the poller's questions, the people who made up the ballot or the questions would have the power to shape the feedback. The power of the news media would also be enhanced, for most people get from them the information on which to base their vote or opinion. However, unless the right to frame voting alternatives and poll questions was itself democratically determined, and news about all alternatives was widely disseminated, a feedback scheme would not provide greater political equality, and could easily become a mockery of the democratic process, as it often has been in dictatorships that conduct carefully supervised elections and referenda. Second, a feedback scheme can only work if everyone is required to vote, for if voting or participating in a poll is voluntary, people may not express themselves on issues that do not interest them, and a minority of the population or an interest group mounting a campaign to arouse its constituents can thus swing the "election." Third, any feedback results that are evaluated by majority rule will mean less equality for the "losers." In a society where government plays a minor role, this is not very important, but in an egalitarian society, government plays a major role and many phases of social life will automatically be politicized, so that devices for guaranteeing the representation and rights of numerical minorities must be provided.

If government decisions were required to follow the results of these feedback schemes, people would have not only more equality of participation but also more equality of access. Still, such access would be indirect, and if political pressure was to be discouraged, direct access would have to be also. Assuming for the moment that ways could be found to allow direct access without its leading to unequal pressure politics, such access could be equalized only to a limited extent. In a large society, it is obviously impossible to give every citizen equal access to his or her political representative, for no representative will have time to see everybody. Access could be equalized by reducing the size of political units, for example, if congressional districts were reduced to one-fifth or one-tenth of their present size; but this would require a much larger Congress, thus reducing even further the already small amount of power of an individual representative. Moreover, giving every citizen equal access to a representative might not properly equalize access, for an individual citizen would then have more access than one who represented others, for example, an organizational leader or a company president. Insofar as such people are themselves properly elected representatives of other citizens, they deserve more access than the individual who speaks only for himself or herself.

Equal access does not guarantee equal control, however, for even if everyone could make contact with his or her representative, that representative could not grant all wishes equally without bankrupting the public treasury or acceding to contradictory demands. In a large, heterogeneous society, a political representative must therefore be free to decide whose demands will be granted, thus automatically reducing the equality of those whose demands are rejected. Some correction of this result is possible by making sure that at least all major interest groups obtain access and control, so as to correct the present situation in which affluent and organized interest groups can "buy" a congressman or senator but less affluent and less organized interest groups cannot. Under completely egalitarian conditions, all interest groups should have their own representative, which would also require an enlargement of Congress. A yet more difficult problem stems from the fact that every person "belongs" to a number of interest groups because of the multiplicity of roles that exists in modern society, and a completely egalitarian polity requires a political system where all such roles have access and control, so that an individual would be represented as a worker, parent, church member, hobbyist, and so on. In theory, it might be possible to design a political system with several legislatures, each concerned with a specific role, but ultimately, a central legislature and executive would have to establish priorities among roles and make final decisions.

Another approach to equalizing control is to reduce the differences between the citizen and the politician, and one way of doing this is by lot, or by random selection of politicians from among the citizenry. If all citizens are equally capable of exercising their democratic rights, then presumably they are also equally capable of representing other citizens and could therefore be assigned to political office from the population by random selection. Thus citizens would be put directly in control, although, in a heterogeneous society, the political results would not be much different from electing professional politicians, since the randomly chosen citizens would have to act much the same way, given the heterogeneity of their constituencies. If anything, they might be less effective at dealing with their role or their constituents until they had learned the ropes. Nonprofessional politicians now are elected to office in small towns and suburbs and, though politician enough to stand for election, are amateurs at the start, but ultimately their behavior is much the same as that of professionals.

As for the consequences of political equality, an egalitarian polity would find it more difficult to make decisions, for once more people obtained political access and control, more alternatives and interests have to be considered—and placated—and often politicians would find it impossible to make decisions, or would make them only by setting their constituencies against each other so as to give themselves more freedom to maneuver. In fact, an egalitarian polity can probably work only if society is more homogeneous than it is today, and if fewer conflicts and contradictions have to be dealt with in reaching decisions. Consequently, political equality would have to be preceded by economic equality, thus eliminating one major source of heterogeneity and contradiction. Conversely, political equality would itself encourage more economic equality, insofar as poorer citizens would be able to put pressure on government for income and other forms of redistribution, and the affluent would have lost much of the political power that now enables them to prevent economic equality.

The nature and extent of political participation would depend on whether the polity had to require involuntary participation and discourage pressure in order to remain egalitarian. If the freedom to exert pressure could be preserved, individuals and groups with demands or dissatisfactions would obviously participate more than the rest of the population, as in existing societies. If participation had to be limited to involuntary feedback, people with intensely felt demands and dissatisfactions would be restricted to private grumbling, although it is hard to imagine that such grumbling would not become a form of feedback if it was widespread.

Insofar as involuntary participation provided everyone the feeling of having a voice in the governance of society, trust in government should be higher than in existing societies, at least among people whose opinions coincided with government decisions. If popular feedback was combined with majority rule, however, the people whose opinions frequently place them in the minority might quickly lose faith in the democratic character of the feedback machinery, and in the responsiveness of government as well. Public trust would therefore depend to a considerable extent on the ability of government to take minority opinions into account and to reconcile conflicting demands. In fact, the people whose opinions were powerless and whose demands were unsatisfied might come to believe that political equality, which did not benefit them, was a sham, and they might become even more distrustful of government than in existing and unequal societies. Moreover, because society would be completely politicized and almost every matter would wind up before the politicians, everyday life would become more disputatious—and newspapers and television news programs longer. If trust in government's ability to deal with conflicting political demands evaporated, the society might well become highly polarized, and in a crisis, a demagogue who promised simple solutions to complex questions might obtain considerable support, at least for a while. Whereas an egalitarian polity could realize the fondest expectations of democratic theory, it would also raise popular expectations for governmental performance, and when high expectations could not be met, such a polity might be quite fragile.

Finally, the recruitment of politicians would probably change; as more people became part of the political process, they would support politicians more like themselves, and the demographic makeup of Congress would be more similar to that of the total population than at present. Politicians would have to be more astute—and perhaps more manipulative—in order to cope with the greater amount of feedback and access, and they would not have time to be technical experts on any of the issues with which they have to deal. Consequently, politicians would have to rely more on assistants who were technical experts; but expertise would be highly politicized, and much more knowledge would be needed about the effects of various decisions for specific goals and values so that the technical experts could give the right kind of political advice to the politicians for whom they worked.

Realistic Scenarios

Although the preceding scenarios have been unabashedly utopian, it is also possible to develop more realistic egalitarian scenarios, which work out the prerequisites and consequences of varying degrees of more equality, and ultimately, such scenarios will be more useful for egalitarian policy than utopian ones. Still, they are also harder to write, for to be useful they will have to determine the impact of a specific egalitarian proposal on existing society at a given point in time. Such specificity is premature, although if and when the political climate encourages egalitarian ideas, realistic scenarios ought to be formulated to help the policy makers who must write the legislation and administrative guidelines for more equality.

ETHNICITY, ETHNIC GROUPS, AND IMMIGRATION

Part Three's last essay makes the point that many of today's researchers of ethnicity and immigration begin their research careers by studying their own ethnic or racial group—and I was no different from anyone else. In my case, the story (told in the autobiographical Appendix A) begins with adolescent struggles over my Jewish identity, which then turned into potential research projects when I was in high school. Subsequently, during my course work at the University of Chicago, I discovered the "Chicago School's" pioneering sociological research on ethnic acculturation and assimilation. I developed an interest in these two ethnic processes and originally wanted to write my master's thesis on how the Yiddish theater dealt with them in the plays it presented during regular visits to Chicago.

That project foundered, among other reasons, because the usually impoverished Yiddish theater lacked spare scripts that it could loan to a graduate student—the photocopier having not yet been invented. Some years later, I interviewed a number of English-speaking Jewish comedians instead, including Mickey Katz (whose reputation has undergone a recent revival), about whom I published an article in 1953. However, my first ethnic research project—my second ethnographic study—was on the Jews of Park Forest, Illinois—a new community that later became famous as the place where William H. Whyte, Jr., discovered the "Organization Man."

I had gone to Park Forest originally in 1949 to do fieldwork (my first study) for a master's thesis on political participation. However, while living there—or rather "renting" a corner of the living room of an equally impecunious fellow graduate student—I became curious about how the new town's Jews had found each other, come together, and literally organized themselves. I also watched how they were affected by and dealt with living in a non-Jewish community, a big change at least for those who had grown up in predominantly Jewish Chicago neighborhoods.

My research was, I learned later, the first study of suburban Jewish living in America, and in 1951, a young social scientist turned magazine editor named Nathan Glazer, whom I had originally met when he was working with David Riesman on *The Lonely Crowd,* invited me to write an article about it for *Commentary,* then a liberal Jewish magazine. It was my first publication, and appears here as the first part of Chapter Eight. Starting my writing career by appearing in *Commentary* was a stroke of good luck, for Glazer's rewriting and editing helped me begin to write more clearly, although I have still not fully mastered that skill today.

I went back to Park Forest in 1956 to see what had happened to Park Forest's Jewish community, and that story appears here as the second part of Chapter Eight. (In 1957, when I went to Levittown, New Jersey, I once more watched a Jewish community in formation, and that study is reported in Chapter 4 of *The Levittowners*.)

One aspect of Jewish acculturation, which I began to think about in Park Forest, I called "symbolic Judaism," and I wrote about it in another article I contributed to *Commentary* in 1955. Like many of every researcher's early ideas, that one was also stored in the back of my head, and twenty years later, in 1979, it blossomed into the more general notion of "symbolic ethnicity," the transformation of ethnic heritages into a variety of ethnic symbols and consumer products, which is presented in Chapter Nine. In 1996 I published a postmortem to the original piece that also responds to some of the critiques of symbolic ethnicity; it appears here as an epilogue to Chapter Nine.

I have continued to write about the acculturation of European immigrants, but the first (Asian-American) students from the so-called post-1965 immigration whose ethnographic dissertations I sponsored at Columbia University evoked my curiosity about America's latest newcomers. However, the article reprinted as Chapter Ten was generated mainly by the arrival of economic "downsizing," and my fear that many of the already Americanized children of the poorer new immigrants would reject the low pay and other forms of exploitation to which the immigrants themselves had, like earlier newcomers to the United States, had to resign themselves. Instead, I thought many would wind up on the jobless lines.

Like much social science research, this article turned out to be time-bound, for at this writing, lack of jobs is a lesser problem than lack of adequately paying jobs. Still, if the children of the newcomers refuse such jobs as demeaning for the Americans they perceive themselves to be, they will suffer from somewhat the same kind of second generation decline I discussed in this essay.

Although the acculturation of the new immigrants struck me as not taking a drastically different path from that of the Europeans who began to come here in the 1870s, many of the young sociologists from among the new immigration disagreed sharply. They have been arguing that the findings of the Chicago sociologists and their intellectual descendants were no longer applicable, if they had ever been so, and that the descendants of the new immigrants would remain more loyal to their old country culture and social institutions than the children of the European immigrants.

I think the young researchers are wrong, believing as I do that the power of the American Dream and its promise of upward mobility, the cultural, sexual, and other freedoms available in America, and the persuasiveness of American popular culture would be as attractive to the children of the new immigrants, if not the immigrants themselves, as they had been to previous sets of newcomers and their children. Who is right will not be known until enough of the immigrants' children have become adults and parents sometime in the twenty-first century, but the issue is the subject of my final chapter in Part Three.

In that chapter, I also return to an old intellectual love from graduate school days, the Mannheimian sociology of knowledge, applying it to look at whether the origins and values of the new researchers could have produced what I consider to be their misperception about the end of acculturation. The article is one of my most recent, and I hope that it stimulates empirical research into how the researchers' origins and values, in immigration research as in other fields, affect their—or rather our—findings and conclusions.

· 8 ·

THE BIRTH AND GROWTH OF A SUBURBAN JEWISH COMMUNITY

In November 1949, the author of this article completed a study of the Jews of Park Forest, Illinois. The study had one especially intriguing aspect under its very eyes—in the midst of answering questionnaires, as it were—Park Forest's Jews gave birth to a young, awkward, but unmistakable Jewish community. It was an entirely natural birth, and the witnessing of it was an illuminating introduction to some of the whys and wherefores of Jewish life and of present-day Judaism in America.

Obviously Park Forest is not Flatbush or Scarsdale or Detroit—so undoubtedly there are limitations in what it has to teach us. On the other hand, when we think of the present composition of American Jewry—which is by and large second generation, mostly business and professional in occupation, and overwhelmingly middle class—perhaps Park Forest is not so atypical after all. What we can see happening there may be chiefly different from what is occurring in other locales only in being more visible and accessible to the student. Park Forest may thus turn out to be a by-no-means unrepresentative Jewish neighborhood in today's rapidly changing American scene. Here, in any case, is what happened, and how.

I

Park Forest is a garden-apartment housing project located thirty miles south of Chicago. The project, privately developed, was started in 1947, when

---

This chapter is a combination of two articles from *Commentary*; the first entitled "Park Forest: Birth of a Jewish Community," which appeared in April 1951; the second here renumbered as Part II with the original title, in February 1957. Reprinted with permission. A more formal research report on this study appears as "The Origin and Growth of a Jewish Community in the Suburbs," in *The Jews,* edited by M. Sklare, 205–48. Glencoe, Ill.: The Free Press, 1958.

the Chicago housing shortage was at its height. The first tenants moved in on August 30, 1948, and for two years they continued to come in as new sections of the village were completed. By November 1949, there were 2,000 families—nearly 8,000 people—renting garden apartments at $75 to $100 per month. One hundred and forty-one of these families were Jewish. Of these, about thirty had not been in the village long enough to have relations with the other Jewish families; another fifteen were "mixed marriages," with both husband and wife having rejected any identification as Jews; and the remainder, approximately one hundred families (including a few mixed marriages), 5 percent of the project, formed a fledgling "Jewish community."

In Park Forest the accent is on youth: the project naturally attracted the people most sorely pressed for housing: veterans with children. The men average thirty to thirty-five years of age, the women somewhat less (anyone over forty is generally considered old). Most of the men are at the beginning of their careers, in professional, sales, administrative, and other business fields. (Only four of the men interviewed owned their own businesses.) Although not long removed from the GI Bill of Rights, they were in 1949 already earning from $4,000 to $10,000 a year—most of them perhaps around $5,000. Few of the men, and few of the wives even, are without some college experience, and educationally, the Jews as a whole stand even higher than the rest of the Park Forest community. Ninety percent of the Jewish men interviewed have college training, 60 percent hold degrees, and no less than 36 percent have graduate degrees.

The Jews of Park Forest dress as do the other Park Foresters, enjoy similar leisure-time activities, read the same newspapers, look at the same movies, hear the same radio programs—in short, they participate with other Park Foresters in American middle-class culture. They observe few traditional Jewish religious practices; the village's isolation from synagogues and kosher food shops has probably discouraged observant Jews from becoming tenants, and brought problems to those few who did.

Not only do Park Forest Jews live like other Park Foresters, they live with them. Whereas most American cities have "neighborhoods" dominated by one ethnic group or another—in atmosphere and institutions, if not in numbers—this is not true of Park Forest. Most Park Foresters live in what are called "courts"—*culs de sac* surrounded in circular fashion by twenty to forty two-story garden apartments. Each "apartment" is actually a house, built together with five or seven others into a single unit. Privacy is at a minimum, and each court is almost an independent social unit. Many of the Park Foresters find all their friends in their own court—but this is not the case with the Jews. The Jewish families are scattered all over the village, and only rarely are two Jewish families to be found in adjacent apartments. Yet in just one year, a Jewish community consisting of informal groups of friends, a B'nai B'rith lodge, a National Council of Jewish Women chapter, a Sunday school, and even a Board of Jewish Education had emerged.

How did this happen?

Finding Jewish Neighbors

From the very beginning it seemed to be important to Jewish Park Foresters to "recognize" whether or not any of their neighbors were Jewish. And the widespread labeling, in America and Europe, of certain Mediterranean-Armenoid facial features as "Jewish," plus the monopolization of certain surnames by Jews, has resulted in a stereotypical formula of recognition, used by Jews and non-Jews, which is accurate more often than not.

One early resident related: "I saw Mrs. F. in the court a couple of times. . . . I thought she looked Jewish. With me, there's no mistaking it. Then someone told me her name, and I went up to talk to her. Finally we talked about something Jewish, and that was it."

"Jewish mannerisms" were also used to establish, or at least guess at, the other person's Jewishness. "The woman across the street, her actions were typical New York, so we recognized them as Jewish immediately." People very skillfully explored each other through conversations, attempting to discover whether the other person was Jewish or not, and offering clues to their own Jewishness. "She's been told I'm Jewish, and I know she's Jewish, we haven't discussed it, but she uses Jewish expressions she wouldn't use in front of other people." Others turned the conversation to favorite foods: "It was a slow process, we told them what kind of food we like, corned beef, lox. . . ." Sometimes there are no symbols or formulas that can be applied, and people find out by accident: "I asked before Passover if they wanted macaroons, and we found out."

Many Jewish Park Foresters had known each other previously, had mutual friends or acquaintances elsewhere, or bore introductions from mutual friends to "go look up so-and-so when you get to Park Forest." The people with such previous contacts, however loose these may have been, quickly established friendships and often became "charter members" of social circles that then attracted strangers. In this respect, the Jews differ sharply from other Park Foresters, most of whom knew no one and had no "introduction" to anyone when they arrived in the village. (Even in cities as large as New York and Chicago, a surprisingly large number of Jews know or know of each other, because there are relatively few groups that they join, few temples that they can belong to, and few neighborhoods in which they choose to live.)

Barely had this informal network of friendships and acquaintances sprung up from the first Jews moving into Park Forest (it did not, of course, preclude friendships with non-Jewish neighbors—though these, as we shall see later, were rather different in quality from the friendships with Jews), when two formal Jewish organizations were set up—a chapter of the B'nai B'rith and a chapter of the National Council of Jewish Women. Both enrolled only about forty members—those who, for various motives and reasons, were "organization-minded," and those, especially women, who had no Jewish neighbors and wanted to meet Jews from other parts of the village.

Both almost immediately found a purpose: "doing something" about the Jewish children of the growing Park Forest community. And through them steps were soon taken to establish the single most important Jewish institution in Park Forest: the Sunday school.

By June 1949, less than a year after the first residents moved in, the chapters of the B'nai B'rith and National Council of Jewish Women were already fairly well established. Eighty-six Jewish families were now living in the rapidly growing project. Passover had come and gone; the handful of Jewish people who observed it in the traditional way had banded together to order *matzos* and all the trimmings from Chicago. The men who had organized the B'nai B'rith lodge and now formed its ruling clique had begun to talk of a congregation. Some of them were "Jewish professionals," men who make their careers within the American Jewish community; others were men who had been active in big-city Jewish affairs and whose social life had been oriented around a congregation and its activities. But it was generally agreed that Park Forest's prime problem was a Sunday school for the forty-odd eligible children then in the village, and for the others who were to come.

Organizing a Sunday School

The B'nai B'rith leadership met one evening and sketched out the organization of a Sunday school as part of a congregation—Reform or Conservative, it was not yet clear—to be established in the village. At a meeting with a delegation of women from the Council, however, the latter refused to help organize a congregation, insisting that what Park Forest needed was a Sunday school now, and a congregation later, perhaps. One man said of the women: "They don't care for Jewish values, but they recognize that they are Jewish and they need a Sunday school because the kids ask for it.

. . . They want a non-sectarian school." The women, on the other hand, accused the men of trying to take over the community for their own political ambitions, of wanting a "Jewish Community Incorporated."

Eventually a steering committee of four men and four women was formed to proceed with the organization of a Sunday school. While the administrative organization and the budget were being prepared, largely by the men, the school's curriculum was left to a young Chicago rabbi who had become interested in Park Forest. Quite unexpectedly to some, he supported the women in their rejection of a congregation, and formulated instead a Sunday school that would involve the parents in their children's Jewish education: "As we train the children," he told the parents, "you will have to train yourselves. . . . You'll have to move toward a community center and a synagogue eventually." The parents' major contribution would be to prevent such inconsistencies as would be apt to arise from not practicing at home the content of the Sunday school curriculum.

At a meeting of parents, there was a sharp reaction to the rabbi's plans. A large number of those present objected to the curriculum proposed; they wanted a "secular" Sunday school, one that would teach the child *about* Jewish traditions, but which would not put pressure on the parents to *observe* these traditions in the home. For the reasons that they did not want a congregation, they did not want a school that would involve them either. The committee resigned, and a new committee was formed.

But exactly what type of "Jewish content" should be brought into the school, and how? The new committee did not have sufficient Jewish background to set up any kind of Jewish curriculum, secular or otherwise, and called for aid from a Jewish professional family that lived in Park Forest, the husband a group worker, and his wife a trained Sunday school principal. The group worker was finally successful in devising a formula that reconciled the two sides, and the basis of the reconciliation is revealing:

> The children will not be taught that parents have to light candles; the children will be informed of the background of candles. . . . We're teaching the child not that he must do these things, we just teach him the customs. . . . Why, we even teach them the customs of the Negro Jews . . . and that the customs have been observed for many years, and are being modified.

A Community for Adults or Children?

In "Yankee City's" Jewish community[1] the conflict over the synagogue was between generations, the foreign-born and the first-generation

American. In Park Forest, where almost everyone is native-born, the conflict over the Sunday school was of a different nature: it was between those who wanted what may be called an *adult-oriented* community and those who wanted a *child-oriented* one.

The adult-oriented community is the traditional (but not necessarily Orthodox) one whose activities are focused around its congregation of adults, and in which the role of the children is to become Jewish adults and assume an adult role. The men who wanted a congregation, with its Sunday school, were thinking of such an adult Jewish community, training its children for eventual membership in the organized Jewish group. In a child-oriented community, the community's energy is focused almost exclusively around the children, around their problems and needs as Jewish children—but, of course, as the adults see these needs. Thus, the women wanted a school for the children and, as became clear, not one that would involve the adults in Jewish community life.

The focus of Park Forest's problem—and conflicts—lies in the family. The Sunday school, much as other Jewish institutions, is recognizably an ethnic rather than a religious institution—more correctly, an American reaction to an ethnic situation—which transmits ethnic behavior and identity; the Jewish home, however, is run by American middle-class behavior patterns. The women feared that the contradictions between the traditional Jewish home, whose features are now incorporated in the Sunday school curriculum, and the American home, which embodies their primary present-day values, would lead to family tensions. So, although they wanted their children to learn about traditional Jewish life, they did not want it brought home.

The situation in Park Forest, then, is that many parents reject involvement in the cultural-religious aspects of the Jewish tradition for themselves as adults, while they demand that their children involve themselves to the extent of learning about this tradition, without, however, getting so involved as to wish to practice it. The fruit of this might well be a Judaism that ends rather than begins with Bar Mitzvah.

THE GOALS OF SUNDAY SCHOOL

Why, however, did the parents want the children to go to Sunday school at all?

First, and quite important, was the fact that the children, in contrast to the parents of Park Forest, having found their friends within the court without concern for ethnic origin, would see their non-Jewish friends leave for school on Sunday mornings. As one mother explained: "Our kids want to get dressed up and go to church too. The Sunday school [the Jewish one] will give them something to do." A few children were actually sent to the Protestant Sunday school a couple of times, but the overwhelming majority of the parents found this intolerable, so the pressure from the children was translated into parental demand for a Jewish Sunday school.

Second, and this is perhaps the more important reason, the parents wanted to send their children to Sunday school because they wanted to make them aware of their ethnic identity, to acquaint them with Jewishness through Jewish history and customs. (Quite frequently, this explanation was complemented by the qualification, ". . . so that later he can choose what he wants to be." The notion that the Jewish child would have a choice between being Jewish or not Jewish, a decision he would make in adolescence or early adulthood, was voiced even by parents who admitted their own continuing confusion as to how to act, and as to the identity they had and wanted to have.)

But why become aware of ethnic identity and of "Jewish customs"? Because parents want their Jewish identity explained to their children, often as a *defense* against hardships they might run into because they are Jews. Representative of this rather widespread sentiment was the comment:

> A Jewish child, he's something different, he's never one of the boys in a Gentile group, even if he's the best guy, he's one of the outsiders, the first to get abused, and if he doesn't know why, it's going to be a shock. It's part of his training, the Sunday school, he needs it.

A number of parents of six- and seven-year-olds were particularly clear in their hopeful expectation that Sunday school would supply the children with answers about their identity. It seems to be at that age that questions first develop in the children's play groups as to what they are, in terms of religion or nationality. Sometimes the children are stimulated by a remark made in school or kindergarten, sometimes by something overheard in parents' conversation. One child may thus discover that he is Protestant, and that there are also Catholics and Jews. He brings this information to the group, which then tries to apply these newly discovered categories to its members. Soon the children come home and ask their parents what they are, and are they Jewish, and perhaps even "Papa, why do I have to be Jewish?" Here the Sunday school is asked to come to the rescue. One father reported of his son now in Sunday school: "He can probably tell me more than I can tell him."

CELEBRATING JEWISH HOLIDAYS

It is not only the Sunday school that is child-oriented. The entire community shows itself child-oriented: during the first fourteen months of existence, the largest part of its organized adult activities was for the children. B'nai B'rith nearly collapsed because its leadership was drawn off into the task of establishing the Sunday school; and after the school had been set up, the lodge immediately went to work on a Chanukah party, which it hoped to make an annual event. Even among those who wished to found a congregation, a goodly portion explained they wanted it exclusively for the sake of the children: "I don't believe in praying . . . in God . . . I want it for my son and daughter. I want them to know what it's like. I have had the background . . . I remember I enjoyed it at the time."

The Jewish holidays have become perhaps the chief mechanism of teaching and reinforcing Jewish identity. All the "happy" holidays— Pesach, Purim, Sukkoth, and Chanukah, especially the last—are emphasized and made into children's festivals. At Chanukah time 1948, when the Park Forest Jewish community consisted of less than twenty families, the problem of Chanukah versus Christmas first presented itself to Jewish parents. A year later, the problem loomed so large in everyone's mind that people discussed it wherever they gathered. The women's Council devoted its November meeting to "Techniques of Chanukah Celebration," that is, techniques of competing with Christmas.

By late November, the non-Jewish friends of the Jewish children are eagerly awaiting Christmas and Santa Claus. Naturally, the Jewish children are inclined to join in these expectations, and ask their parents for Christmas trees. In 1948 and 1949, the parents acted quickly. One mother explained: "The F.'s had a big menorah in their window, that was very fine, maybe I'll do the same next year. . . . I could put my little menorah up there, I could wire it, is that O.K., we could have different color lights—no that's too much like Christmas." Another parent said: "My child wanted a Christmas tree and we talked her out of it. . . . I make a fuss about Chanukah to combat Christmas, I build up Chanukah and she appreciates it just as much."

Other parents told how they decorated the menorah, and even the entire house, and used electric candles instead of wax ones. They tried hard to emphasize and advertise Chanukah to the child, and at the same time to exclude the Christmas tree and its related symbols from his environment. Parents were very bitter about the Jewish families who displayed Christmas trees. "In our house we do certain things, and in other Jewish houses they don't, and the children ask questions. . . . It's very confusing."

In the process of making a children's holiday in December (or sometimes in November) just as good as the Christian one, the parents' adult participation in the holiday is forgotten, and Chanukah, more than any other holiday, becomes completely child-oriented. In this, ironically, the fate of Chanukah closely resembles that of the American Christmas, which has tended to be transformed from a solemn religious festival to a day of delights for children.

Meanwhile, the adults were not nearly so lavish in providing for their own needs as Jews.

Park Forest has a number of families, either Reform or mildly Conservative, whose social life before moving to Park Forest took place largely in or near the congregation of their choice. Some of these people did not hesitate long before joining a wealthy congregation in Chicago Heights—especially those whose own income and social position were more or less equal to that of the Heights community. In addition there are a number of families, probably less than ten, who have maintained enough of the traditional system of religious attitudes and ritual practices to be called Orthodox or Conservative. They favor the establishment of a congregation, preferably Orthodox or Conservative, in the village.

But for the remainder, the large majority of the Jews, religious institutions and practices play no role. Of forty-odd families interviewed, more than half reported that they observed no customs or holidays, and had not attended synagogues or temples "for years." Ten reported attending High Holiday services only; seven attended on High Holidays, some other holidays, and a few Friday evenings during the year.

For the majority of Park Foresters, the problems of traditional observance (such as the kosher home) or of attending religious services simply do not exist. They spend Friday nights as others do in Park Forest, entertaining, or going out occasionally when Saturday is not a workday for the man of the house, or staying at home if it is. Saturdays are reserved for work around the house, shopping, visiting, and taking care of the little things suburbanites have no time for during the week.

There are, however, two religious patterns that are still being observed, not universally but by many. First, as has been indicated, there are those holidays and traditions that concern the children. Second are those aspects of death and birth that relate the Jew to his parents. Several of the men remarked matter-of-factly that they were not interested in religious observances, but added just as matter-of-factly, "except of course *Yortzeit*" (anniversary of the death of a parent). Another said: "The only thing we did—at my son's birth we had a rabbi at the circumcision, mostly for my wife's parents, they would have felt bad." (Circumcision is probably all but universal. As for Bar Mitzvah, [at the time of this writing in 1950] as yet there are almost no children as old as thirteen.)

Some people celebrate the Jewish holidays by spending them with parents or in-laws, not as religious holidays but as family get-togethers. One woman explained, jokingly: "I believe Rosh Hashanah should be two days, Passover too, for practical purposes. One day we go to his family, the other to mine."

There have been some attempts to establish the beginnings of a religious institutional system in Park Forest. In January 1949, when the Jewish population did not exceed twenty-five families, the group already had a rabbi-substitute, a gregarious "Jewish professional" who roamed through the Jewish community and from his Conservative background ministered to occasional religious needs. "Someone needed Hebrew writing on a tombstone, they were told to call me, someone else wanted *Yizkor* [prayer for the dead] or *Yortzeit* services, they called me."

Before Rosh Hashanah 1949, two men, one an early comer, the other just arrived, tried independently to set up a *minyan* (minimal group of ten) for the High Holidays. Since communication between Jewish tenants in the older courts and the newer ones had not yet been established, these men never knew of each other's attempts. Both were unsuccessful. Various groups have talked sporadically about setting up a regular congregation.[2] Most interesting in this demand for a congregation is the reason given by many supporters: "They'll have more respect for us, to show that we have arrived, that we're not merely a bunch of individuals."

The "they" referred, of course, to the non-Jewish neighbors. This congregation movement was thus born not entirely of religious impulse, but of one that attempted to demonstrate the solidarity and respectability of the Jewish community to the rest of Park Forest. Significantly enough, the area of Park Forest in which this congregation movement sprang up was populated by a large number of small-towners and Southerners who, from the first, indicated that they did not think favorably of Jews.

Uninterested as Park Foresters may be in "the Jewish heritage," they are nevertheless very much Jews. Clearly and unmistakably, that is, they remain both matter-of-factly and by conscious design, members of identifiably Jewish groups. This Jewish group may be another Jewish couple with whom they spend much of their time; it may be a regular and more or less stable group that gathers, in full or in part, almost every weekend and on special occasions. These groups make up the informal Jewish community, the "spontaneous" community that did not require professionals and organizers to be created.

For the most part, this informal community exists at night. In the daytime, when only housewives and the children inhabit Park Forest, the Jewish housewife participates in the general court social life. She interrupts her household duties to chat with a neighbor, while "visiting" over a morning cup of coffee or while watching the children in the afternoon. In most cases, there is no distinction here between the Jewish and the non-Jewish housewife; they belong together to the bridge and sewing clubs that have been established in many courts. There are a few courts in which religious or ethnic cliques of women have formed, and where "visiting" is restricted to such groups. In most courts, however, there are few ethnic distinctions in daytime social life. This applies even more to the men when they participate with other men in court life on weekends (and occasional evenings) through athletic teams and poker clubs. As one of the women observed: "The boys are real friendly. I imagine they don't think about it [ethnic distinctions], but the women have different feelings. Women have little to do; they talk about it in the afternoons."

At night, however, in the social relations among "couples," the Jewish husband and wife turn to other Jews for friendship and recreational partnership. As one person summarized it: "My real close friends, my after-dark friends, are mostly Jewish; my daytime friends are Gentile." Of thirty Jewish residents who listed the names of Park Foresters they see regularly, ten named only Jews; ten named mostly Jews, and one or two non-Jews; ten named a majority of non-Jews or only non-Jews. And many of the people who named both Jews and non-Jews pointed out, like the person quoted above, that their most intimate friends were Jewish.

THE IN-GROUPS AND THE OUT-GROUPS

There are, of course, all types of friendship circles in this informal Jewish community. One of the largest groups is made up predominantly of older, well-to-do Park Foresters, many of them previously active in big-city Jewish congregations and groups. Most of these men are employed by business or industry, or in the nonacademic professions (medicine, dentistry, law, engineering). A second group consists largely of young academic intellectuals (research scientists, teachers, writers) and their wives. A third is made up of people who have only recently emerged from lower middle-class Jewish neighborhoods, and are just exploring, with occasional distaste, the life of the middle- or upper middle-class American Jew. And there are many others.

It is easy to explain the tendency to find friends in one's own group, even when this takes one from one's own front door, as it does in Park

Forest. As the Park Foresters say, "It's easier being with Jews"—it is psychologically more accommodating, and there is less strain in achieving an informal, relaxed relationship with other Jews: "You can give vent to your feelings. If you talk to a Christian and say you don't believe in this, you are doing it as a Jew; with Jewish friends you can tell them point blank what you feel."

The in-group attitude, and the anti-out-group feeling that often goes with it, are expressed most frequently at the informal parties and gatherings where the intimate atmosphere and the absence of non-Jews create a suitable environment. Often these feelings are verbalized through the Jewish joke—which generally expresses aspects of the Jew's attitude toward himself, his group, and the out-group—or through remarks about the *goyim* [non-Jews]. At parties that are predominantly Jewish, it is of course necessary to find out if everyone is Jewish before such attitudes can become overt.

One man, who had been converted to Judaism in his twenties, when he was married to a Jewish girl, became disturbed, at an informal party, over a discussion of how to inculcate Judaism into the children, "and keep them away from the *goyim*," and felt it time to announce that he had been until a number of years ago a member of a Christian denomination. The declaration broke up the party, and upset many people. After that he felt: "From now on, they'll be on their guard with me, they've lost their liberty of expression, they don't express themselves without restriction now. At a party, if anybody says something, everybody looks to see if I've been offended and people are taken into a corner and told about me." This man has adopted the Jewish religion, is bringing up his children as Jews, and has been more active than the average person in Jewish community life. Yet he is no longer a member of the Jewish in-group, although he remains a member both of the Jewish community and his smaller Jewish group. In his presence, the group sheds the informality and intimacy of the in-group, and is "on guard."

There are many Jewish Park Foresters who reject these in-group attitudes as "chauvinistic," and when asked about their friends, are quick to reply that they do not distinguish between Jews and non-Jews in choosing friends. Yet as one said: "The funny thing is, most of our friends are Jewish even though we say we don't care." And to quote another: "I think we should try to have friends that aren't Jewish. I don't like the fact that all my friends are Jewish."

But these Jewish Park Foresters, too, feel that they differ from the majority of the non-Jewish Park Foresters—and not only because their friends are Jews. The focus of these feelings of difference was summarized by one person:

> I have a friend who is not Jewish who told me how fortunate I was in being born Jewish. Otherwise I might be one of the sixteen to eighteen out of twenty Gentiles without a social conscience and liberal tendencies; he is cruel and apathetic. . . . Being Jewish, most of the Jews, nine out of ten, are sympathetic with other problems, they sympathize, have more culture and a better education; strictly from the social and cultural stand-point a man is lucky to be born a Jew.

These feelings have a basis in Park Forest reality. The Jews are distinguished by a feeling of "social consciousness," by concern over political and social problems, by a tendency toward a humanistic agnosticism, and by an interest in more "highbrow" leisure activities: foreign films, classical music, the fine arts, and in general the liberal intellectual-aesthetic leisure culture of America, and perhaps the Western world. There seem to be proportionately more Jews than non-Jews in Park Forest who participate in this culture. Jews who seek other people with whom they can share these attitudes and interests tend to find other Jews. This culture—which includes an important proportion of Park Forest's Jews—itself is largely devoid of Jewish content, and the Jews who come together in it would seem to do so not primarily because they are Jews but because they share a culture. When Jewish problems are discussed by these people (and they are discussed), they are seen from a generalized worldview, rather than from an in-group perspective.

Just as Jews form a large proportion of those interested in "culture," they form a large proportion of those interested in the self-government of Park Forest, and in other local activities. Although in November 1949 the Jews made up only 9 percent of Park Forest's population, eleven of thirty-seven candidates in the first two village elections were Jewish. All but one member of the first Board of Education, and half of the original six-man Board of Trustees that runs the village, are Jewish. The community newspaper was started by a group of women many of whom were Jewish; the American Veterans Committee and the local affiliate of the Democratic party were organized with the help of a number of Jewish men.

Non-Jewish Park Forest

If for a moment we take a broader view and consider non-Jewish Park Forest, we discover that the Jewish community is only one of three quite similarly organized ethnic-religious groups. Both the large Catholic group (close to 25 percent of the village population is Catholic) and the smaller Lutheran one also consist of a religious body, men's and women's social organizations, and a more or less extensive informal community. The two Christian groups, unlike the Jewish one, are organized primarily for adult activities, but also emphasize the Sunday school. Both communities developed much more quickly than the Jewish one—largely because there was much less internal disagreement as to what to do and how to proceed—and both were in 1949 already engaged in building programs. The Catholic and Lutheran groups are primarily religious bodies (although they are in part ethnic groups), and have fewer members who reject the group culture. Those who do reject it can quite easily "resign" and become part of the large amorphous body of Americans not strongly identified by religious or ethnic group, something that is much more difficult for the Jew.

In its first year, the Jewish community was very sensitive to the problem of anti-Semitism. Just as every newly arrived tenant would try to recognize other Jews, he would also try to discover the attitudes of non-Jewish neighbors toward Jews. This led quickly to the sprouting of a grapevine that transmitted actual cases, suspicions, and imagined occurrences of anti-Semitism throughout the Jewish community, and sometimes dominated conversation among Jews. A number of people complained strongly that there was a great deal too much talk about anti-Semitism.

Actually, there has probably been very little anti-Semitism in Park Forest. In the interviewing, which covered thirty-five of the fifty-five courts occupied by November 1949, only seven people from seven different courts mentioned incidents they considered to be anti-Semitic. For the most part, these were cases of exclusion, Jewish women (and sometimes children) being left out of some formal and informal activities of the Christian members of the court. There are a number of courts where Jewish and non-Jewish women have split off into separate cliques. It would perhaps be surprising to expect these rather traditional forms of segregation to be absent, especially since Park Forest harbors so many people from different parts of the country, including small-town people from regions generally not friendly to Jews. And one must always ask how much this segregation results from the tendency, described above, of Jews to seek each other out as friends. And it seems certainly true that if anti-Semitism played any role in the formation of the community, it was the fear and expectation of anti-Semitism rather than actual experience of anti-Semitism in Park Forest, on the part of either children or parents.

On the other hand, there are many "liberals" in Park Forest, so that friendly and unquestioned social mixing of Jews and non-Jews is perhaps more common here than elsewhere. This spirit is perhaps typified by an incident that occurred early in the life of the village. A door-to-door salesman asked a non-Jewish resident to point out the Jews in the court because he did not want to sell to Jews. The next day the company was requested not to send any more salesmen to the village.

The Child-Oriented Community

Park Forest is a new and growing community; it has changed since this study was made, and will continue to change in the future as its present tenants are replaced by others or decide to stay and settle down. Nevertheless, the Jewish community has already become oriented around a number of elements that are not likely to change.

Whereas their parents were not only socially "clannish" but culturally different from their non-Jewish neighbors, the adult Jews of Park Forest are "clannish" but culturally not very different. (Or, rather, their cultural distinctiveness, when it exists, is not along Jewish lines.) Their adjustment to American society and their present status can be described as one of cultural assimilation and continued social distinctiveness. Thus, the Jews of Park Forest remain an ethnic group, albeit different from the parental one.

It is this feeling of Jewish togetherness, to sum up, which provides the impetus for a child-oriented community—for the parents' insistence on a Sunday school, their transformation and use of the Chanukah holiday, and the unending attempt to indoctrinate the child with a sense of Jewishness.

It is noteworthy that whereas in most cultures the transmission of the group's *esprit de corps* is carried out unconsciously through the children's imitation of, and partial participation in, adult activities, in Park Forest this transmission has become conscious, has become indoctrination—without the parents accepting for themselves the things they are passing on. This no doubt affects the very process of transmission, the thing transmitted, as well as the way the child receives it. Nevertheless, the transmission does take place. Child orientation is the mechanism that would seem to guarantee the existence of the ethnic group for another generation, even when the adult carriers of the group's culture are ambivalent about it, or have rejected it. So long as Judaism is the curriculum for teaching and transmitting Jewishness, the traditional behavior patterns will be studied, discussed, and taught. However, the high cultural assimilation of the group makes improbable the incorporation of traditional Jewish elements into the rules of daily life.

A major force in the development of the Park Forest Jewish community has been the "Jewish professional," who so far has been the spearhead, "the catalytic agent," as one called himself, in the process of community formation. It was Jewish professionals who helped bring the Jews together, ministered to their early religious needs, started the men's social organization, tried to organize a congregation, helped in forming the Sunday school, resolved the crisis that resulted, and have since supervised Jewish education in the village.

The Jewish professional is a new man on the Jewish scene. He is not a rabbi, but a leader of adults, a youth worker, a teacher, a fund-raiser, a social worker, a contact man, a community relations director, etc. The Jewish professional may not have special training in how to start a Jewish community, but he is expert at being Jewish, something other Park Forest Jews are not. Sometimes this expert Jewishness is a part of his background, and his reason for becoming a professional; sometimes it is the result of a desire to work in the Jewish community, among Jews rather than non-Jews. Sometimes the expert's Jewishness may be only a career, and the professional's activities in these organizations are for him a means of advancing in his career. Whatever his motives, however, the Jewish professional, rather than the rabbi, would seem to have taken over the initiatory role and the largest part of the work of creating the formal Jewish community. In the informal community, his influence is much smaller.

A final factor for an understanding of the Park Forest Jewish community is the sexual division of social labor that takes place within it. The Jewish informal community is based on the Jewish woman. It is she who generally inaugurates and stimulates acquaintances and friendships, who founds the social circles and sets their pattern and content. She has in addition the opportunity of establishing all-female groups, which reinforce the groups of couples. Most of the men seem to lay less emphasis on ethnic association, and although there are some all-Jewish male groups, male activities are more likely to take place in groups that more or less ignore ethnic distinctions. Perhaps that is why the B'nai B'rith lodge has been less successful than the women's group in uniting its membership into an active and developing organization. The larger concern of the women with Jewish education, and their more intense interest in the Sunday school, obviously arise from the fact that the women generally have the major role in bringing up the child. In general, the women live a greater part of their life within the Jewish group; and are more concerned with it and about it than the men. In Park Forest, and presumably in communities like it, they seem to be the most influential element in determining the nature of "Jewish" activities. At a somewhat later stage, these activities may be handed over to the men.

As to how representative the events and processes that took place in this one Jewish community are, the writer would not be able to hazard a guess, and certainly his study, of a single community and not comparative, would throw little light on this question. But his impression is that it is very unlikely that they are unique to Park Forest. Perhaps in other American Jewish communities, these developments are masked by the fact that the group is not so distinctively limited to young married couples with one or two children as it is in Park Forest. In all of them, however, it would seem reasonable to suppose that developments such as have been described must play an increasingly important role in the future Jewish community life in America. Certainly, it would not be claiming too much to suggest that the Park Forest Jewish community offers much illustrative and prophetic material as to the next major stage in the process of Jewish adjustments to American society: the stage in which it is the relations between the second and third generations, both American-born, not the relations between a foreign-born first and a native-born second generation, that are the crucial ones.

II
Progress of a Suburban Jewish Community

By May 1955, when I returned to Park Forest for a short visit, the town had become famous as a prototype of postwar suburbanization and as a model for builders of new towns elsewhere. Park Forest now had 24,000 residents, about half of whom owned their homes. There were five shopping centers, with close to one hundred stores and two professional buildings, five elementary schools, and six churches. Six more congregations were planning to build churches of their own.

The Jewish community had likewise grown. It now comprised between six to seven hundred families and, along with a congregation employing a full-time rabbi, it had two Sunday schools and three new women's groups: the Temple Sisterhood, a B'nai B'rith Auxiliary, and a Hadassah group. The Temple building had just been dedicated, and all the evidence suggested that it was now the Jewish community's central institution. I was curious to find out why Park Forest's Jews had changed their minds about a congregation, and, even more important, why they had turned—apparently—from a child- into an adult-oriented Jewish community within the five years since I had last visited them. I also wanted to see what their development into a seemingly representative suburban Jewish community revealed about the postwar growth of Jewish communities generally, and to what extent this growth bore out the claims of a recent revival of Jewish institutional and community life in this country.

In the course of my visit in 1955, I spoke with a dozen of the Jewish community's leaders and analyzed Temple membership records; subsequently, I obtained more information by correspondence and other means. I must, however, emphasize that, unlike my 1951 report, this present one is not based on a formal sociological study (although two important community leaders representing rival points of view, having seen it in an early draft, do consider the article to be an objective picture of the community as it was in 1955).

Although by 1950 the Park Forest builders had put up and rented all the apartments in their development—and from then on built only one-family homes, which they sold—the influx of Jewish residents continued in roughly the same proportion as before, maintaining the Jewish representation in Park Forest at just below 10 percent of the total. Community leaders, talking to me in 1955, felt that there was little difference between the older and the newer residents. The newcomers included proportionately fewer Ph.D.'s, but more M.D.'s, dentists, and businessmen. (A sizable proportion of the stores and professional offices in Park Forest's shopping centers were owned or managed by Jews.) It was guessed that the newer residents had slightly higher earnings than the 1949 group, whose median family income was about $6400.[3] The newer residents were also said to be predominantly second-generation Jews whose parents had come from Eastern Europe; in fact, some people thought that these newcomers knew more Yiddish than the earlier settlers did. On the whole, then, Park Forest Jewry could still be described as a community of young middle- and upper middle-class professionals, businessmen, and better paid white-collar workers, with children mostly of preschool or elementary school age.

The Park Forest Congregation

In 1949 two separate attempts at organizing local High Holiday services had failed; in 1950 renewed attempts to hold such services proved more successful. Shortly thereafter, the group of men that had tried to set up a congregation in 1949 founded the Reform Temple Beth Sholom. Late in 1951 enough families had joined the Temple to permit it to engage a full-time rabbi. Soon a building committee was organized and the first fund-raising letters were sent out. Support was slow in coming, but finally in 1954 a $70,000 temple was built with the help of a large mortgage and sizable contributions from the officers of American Community Builders (the developers) and their contractors, as well as smaller ones from about 20 percent of the Jewish residents of Park Forest.

In 1955, the paid-up membership of the Temple's congregation numbered 240 families, which constituted about 35 to 40 percent of the total Jewish community. The Temple's religious orientation could best be described as "East European Reform," for it combined Reform permissiveness about religious practices in the home with a quasi-Conservative array of ceremonials, Hebrew reading, and responsive singing at services. The nature of this synthesis was typified by the Temple kitchen, which was not kept kosher but did not serve pork. The rabbi described the services and their ritualistic emphasis as a "warm, liberal kind of Reform," which he thought would prove agreeable to both people used to Reform and those used to Conservative practices. The rabbi's background reflected that of his congregants; reared in a traditional East European milieu, he had been trained in an Orthodox seminary but had later changed over to Reform.

In 1955, Friday night services generally attracted from fifty to seventy-five people. There was a core of forty (more or less) regular worshippers—about 3 percent of the adult community—the rest being observers of *yahrzeit*, new members, and visitors. Bar Mitzvahs would bring enough people from Chicago to double or triple attendance, and High Holiday services attracted six hundred worshippers—about half the adult Jewish community.

The Temple's religious and cultural functions ran second to its social ones. Soon after its founding, a Sisterhood had been organized that by 1955 had enrolled about half the adult Jewish women in the congregation. Of these, a hundred—15 percent—were described as "active" by the president of the group. The Sisterhood's main ostensible function was fund-raising, for which purpose it sponsored luncheons, dinners, dances, bazaars, and other affairs. These were well attended. It was reported, for example, that in 1955 Purim services had attracted fewer than fifty worshippers, but that a Purim dance the same evening was attended by three hundred and fifty people. Other social functions were equally popular, and the high point of the annual fund-raising campaign was a bazaar to which the many businessmen and merchandisers in Park Forest's Jewish community contributed goods that were sold at bargain prices for the Temple's benefit. People critical of this "social emphasis" pointed out that the social hall in the basement claimed more space in the Temple than anything else.

In order to attract as many residents as possible, the Temple had set membership fees below what was needed to meet expenditures; this brought recurrent financial problems. Because of these, and because the organizers of the Sisterhood programs came from the highest income strata of the Jewish community, the price of active participation in the social activities revolving around the Temple was rather high. One of the Sisterhood leaders estimated that faithful attendance at the various affairs had cost her family about $600 in the past year, in addition to the hundred-dollar Temple membership fee. She explained: "Many of the gals in the $6000–$7000 income bracket can't afford to join us. They join the Temple and the Sisterhood but they explain they don't have time to participate, or give some reason like that. Most of the gals have accepted the fact that they can't afford it; only a few get obnoxious about it. But to those who can afford it, we don't have to sell the Sisterhood. I myself have played this game for years, and since my husband works in the community, we have to do it for professional reasons anyway."

Hence the social climate of the Temple and its Sisterhood was definitely upper middle class. For some of the active members, it served, perhaps, as preparation for the country-club style of life they would enter when they moved—as many would eventually—to a higher-income suburban community.

The Sisterhood was not only the upper middle-class Jewish women's club, but its members were the most active in helping the rabbi and keeping the routine work of the Temple going. Nonetheless, the lay leadership of the Temple was still male, and was composed for the most part of executives in Chicago commerce and industry, businessmen, lawyers, and doctors. As officers and board members of the Temple (and, in several cases, husbands of Sisterhood leaders), their share of the contributions to defray the operating costs and sustain the building program was the largest. The Temple was said to be "run," however, by the small group that had founded it, which included some "Jewish professionals" employed in the Chicago offices of national Jewish organizations. This group was supported by the president of American Community Builders, who holds a high position in the American (and world) Jewish community. A man vitally interested in the local Jewish community, he had donated a great deal of money to the Temple and was said to wield considerable influence in its affairs.

A Temple Affiliated Sunday School

While the Temple provided religious services and a modest lecture program, the Jewish education of the children remained in the hands of the community Sunday school, which had no organizational ties with the Temple. This school, which I described in Part I, had been under the direction of the Park Forest Board of Jewish Education since 1949. By 1954 to 1955, its enrollment had increased from an original thirty-five to a total of 385 students, who made up an estimated 85 to 90 percent of the eligible Jewish children in the village. Classes still met in the public schools on Sundays, and smaller groups of children attended weekday Hebrew classes. The school considered itself a community institution, without denominational affiliation. Its faculty prided itself on teaching the children something about the diversity of Jewish worship, believing that its function was to provide information about all Jewish denominations to students who might one day decide to choose other than Reform. At the same time, the school encouraged its pupils to attend the Temple. The latter's rabbi was a member of the faculty, preparing the older children for Bar Mitzvah. The teaching staff in general considered intellectual training and achievement a major objective; community leaders spoke highly of the school's curriculum and standards of instruction.

This emphasis on denominational diversity and intellectual standards was not coincidental, for it represented to a considerable extent the objectives of the two groups actively supporting the school. The first such group was made up primarily of academic or publicly employed professionals as scientists, research workers, teachers, and public administrators. These people belonged, or were on their way to belonging, to the upper middle class, but moved in a different social world from that of the Temple leaders, by whom they were characterized as "intellectuals"; they, in turn, described the Temple leaders as "businessmen and country-clubbers." Neither characterization was quite accurate, but it sufficed. The academic professionals—as we shall call them—were not much interested in religious or other involvement for themselves, but wanted their children to have good Jewish educations and were strongly in favor of the school's emphasis on intellectual achievement. The second, smaller group supporting the Sunday school was composed of people from more traditional backgrounds whose sympathies lay with Conservative rather than Reform practice. Many of these were lower middle-class, white-collar workers, and among them were to be found those Jews of Park Forest who retained patterns of immigrant culture to the greatest extent. The school's denominational neutrality, as well as its serious interest in Judaic traditions, is what gained it their support.

In 1949, even before the Temple was established, its founders fought for a Sunday school affiliated with it. After the Temple had been organized, they tried repeatedly to arrange for an affiliated school, but not until 1954 did the lay board of the Temple yield. Shortly thereafter the present rabbi was hired, partly because of his extensive training as a religious educator, on the understanding that he would set up a congregational school. After a few unsuccessful attempts to attach the community Sunday school to itself, the Temple announced the formation of a school of its own in March 1955, with classes to begin in September. When I returned to Park Forest in May

1955, the Jewish community, facing the prospect of two Sunday schools, was once again split into opposing camps.

The main argument, in public, involved the relations of the two schools to the Temple. The leaders of the new Sunday school objected to the community school's denominational neutrality, arguing that it was teaching the children *about* Judaism rather than emphasizing its practice. The rabbi illustrated the difference this way: "The community school teaches that Jews light candles on Friday night, and that the children *can* do this, but don't have to. Our curriculum will be more emphatic—we say you *ought* to do it."

To this argument, the community school retorted that, having only a single synagogue, the community needed a school that taught something about the views of all the Jewish denominations. A pamphlet issued during the controversy said:

> It [the school] emphasizes those elements of Judaism which are basically acceptable to all elements of Jewry. Differences of practice which exist are taught in a democratic climate encouraging acceptance of the diversity of opinion . . . a child who shares the experience with his parents in a Temple and further enriches himself in an independent school will have deeper insight than can be obtained from . . . a single viewpoint.

Underlying these public differences was the question that had been debated in 1949: Should the school teach children in a way that would encourage and press the parents to take part in community religious life, or should it teach them in a way that would leave parents uninvolved if they so chose? This question was basic to the larger problem of adult- versus child-orientation.

Children in Adult Roles

Although the community school staff was of two minds on the question, their school permitted the parents of its students to eschew all Jewish religious or cultural involvement. As one of the school's lay leaders pointed out:

> Its purpose is education, and the parents are not involved unless they want to be. Religion for the parents is not necessarily the main end of life; we want a school for our children.

The Temple, intended by its founders to be adult-oriented, explicitly sought the participation of parents in its new school and in the Temple. The rabbi explained:

> My primary interest is in the adults, and I am opposed to a child-centered
> Judaism. However, here the people seem to be mainly interested in the
> education of the children. . . . We hope, though, the children will bring
> the parents . . . perhaps they will return the parents to Jewish life.

However, the rabbi did not expect that this would happen. Indeed, he felt that the indifference of Park Forest parents to Judaic practice was such as to require the Temple to take a more active role in training their children for religious participation—and that he himself had to assume the role of a surrogate father. He explained:

> I want to make a personal contact with the children, otherwise I only get
> the volitional ones, and that's not many. . . . I want to be able to identify
> with the children. . . . I want them to accept the synagogue in their lives
> and come to services.

Nor did the Temple seek to draw in children only in order to teach them; it also wanted—and needed—to have them take the place of their nonobservant parents at Saturday services. The rabbi pointed out: "The school's program will be a worship curriculum. The children will have to come and help prepare services. . . . The Saturday morning services will be a part of their education."

This curriculum, in addition to its educational function, would provide a larger number of worshippers for the Temple. More important, by giving children the role, if not the status, of adults at the Saturday services, the Temple could maintain itself as an adult-oriented institution.

What had happened between 1949 and 1955 was therefore not a turnabout from child orientation to adult orientation. Rather, both the community school and the Temple, with its own new school, had resigned themselves to the essential unwillingness of adults to participate in formal Jewish religious and cultural activities. The Temple was able to operate as if it were an adult-oriented institution, while adjusting at the same time to the reality of the child-oriented community, by giving the children a quasi-adult role. Facing a choice between adhering to its traditional position or surrendering this for the assurance of community support—and survival—the Temple had chosen the latter.

Were the later Jewish arrivals in Park Forest—who presumably represented a majority of the Temple members—really as child-oriented as the settlers of 1948–49, or was the Temple responding only to the demands of the earlier group? This could not be determined in a brief study. However, one of the newcomers, a leader in the Sisterhood, said: "People here don't need to join the congregation . . . until their children are old enough to join the Sunday school and if there were no children, there would be no Temple or Jewish organizations."

Another leader said that though people without school-age children were asked to join the congregation, they were not expected to do so. This observation was borne out by a study of the congregational membership. Of one hundred and eight member families known to have children, 85 percent had at least one child of Sunday school age. This does not itself prove that the presence of eligible children was responsible for Temple membership, but data for a group of fifty new and old residents who recently bought homes in Park Forest tend to bear this hypothesis out. Thirteen of the twenty-six families with school-age children—50 percent—had joined the Temple, but of the seventeen families without eligible children, only three—18 percent—had joined.[4] These data, taken together with the community's indifference to religious activities, except on the High Holidays, suggest that most Park Forest Jewish parents could still be described as child-oriented.

It will take some time to discover whether the children are going to accept the quasi-adult functions planned for them in the Temple. If they do, the synagogue will be able to continue as a religious institution without reliance on the parents. If they do not, or if the children try to get their parents to attend synagogue regularly along with them, the parents may in the end be forced to choose between a child-oriented and an adult-oriented Jewish community more squarely than they have until now.

The controversy over the two schools was brief and ended shortly before spring registration. While child versus adult orientation was an underlying factor in the public debates, parents probably made their choice on the basis of more tangible considerations. For one thing, the Temple school offered free tuition to the children of members, which made a financial difference to families with two or more children. Then there was the fact that the congregation played a symbolic role as a community focus for the Jewish people. The Temple building, where classes would be held, also gave parents an opportunity to point out to their children that "they had a church now, too, just like their non-Jewish friends." On top of all this, the rabbi loomed as a welcome figure of authority to parents who wanted their children to be taught to feel Jewish, but could not or would not do the teaching themselves. The rabbi's authority—and his visibility as a Jewish symbol—was probably more convincing to parents than the community school staff's professed aim of exposing students to "a broad cross-section of Jewish thought"—especially to parents less concerned to have their children achieve an intellectual grasp of Judaism than to immerse them in a Jewish atmosphere and surround them with Jewish symbols.

One might say, then, that as the parents saw it, the community school emphasized Judaism as such, while the Temple school stressed identification with the Jewish community and its symbols—that is, with "Jewishness." This difference probably influenced the parents' choice, and their preference for the Temple school and "Jewishness" seems to be in accord with overall trends in the American Jewish community.[5]

The difference in prestige between the two schools was undoubtedly an additional factor in the parents' choice. The congregation's social program clearly stamped it as being upper middle class, whereas the community school sponsored no social activities to speak of. After its connection with the Temple was severed, the community school began to negotiate with a lower middle-class Orthodox synagogue in a nearby community for a place in which to hold Bar Mitzvah services for its thirteen-year-olds.

At the beginning of the 1955–56 academic year, it looked as though the Temple school had proven to be more attractive than the community school to the majority of Park Forest Jews. It counted a student body of over five hundred, while the community school had only about 125 students from eighty families closely identified with its cultural objectives. (If we knew exactly why so many Jewish parents chose the Temple school over the older community school, we should possess an important clue to their attitude toward Jewish education and to what Jewish life meant for them.) At the end of the academic year, I heard later, the future of the community school was for a time in doubt, and it was able to survive thanks only to donations from loyal supporters and voluntary salary cuts on the part of the staff. The school was now in the position of many another intellectually oriented group in America: it had enough members to justify its existence and propagate its point of view, but the small scale of its operations burdened it with chronic financial problems that constantly threatened its survival—despite the loyalty of its supporters.

From the Informal to the Formal Jewish Community

In 1955, then, Park Forest provided an example of the rapid growth of a postwar suburban Jewish community. Whether it is a representative example, only time and further study can tell, although reports from other communities suggest many similarities with Park Forest.

The rise of these suburban Jewish communities, with their greater organizing energy and higher participation rates as compared with urban communities, has been explained as the symptom of a "Jewish revival"—

that is, as a reversal of the trends toward ever greater cultural assimilation observable in the Jewish communities of the cities. To determine whether this explanation is correct for Park Forest would require a thoroughgoing study of the factors that have made its Jewish community what it is today. At this point it is possible only to speculate.

The major factors that "explain" Park Forest's Jewish community in 1955 seem to me to be five: the suburban environment; the social activity patterns that go with upper middle-class aspirations; the pressure on Jewish residents for participation; the flexibility of the Temple in serving their new requirements; and above all, the common desire to provide children with a Jewish environment.

The young Jews who moved to Park Forest were probably neither more nor less identified with and concerned about Judaism and Jewishness than their friends who remained in Chicago. But in Park Forest they found they could no longer live as before. In the city they had lived so much *with* Jews that there was little need to worry about living *as* Jews. But in Park Forest their neighbors were as likely as not to be not Jewish, and the latter's proximity made them conscious of the difference, all the more so as they felt that these neighbors saw and treated them *as* Jews.

One response to the new suburban circumstances was to transfer some of the social relations they had maintained informally with other Jews in the city into the more formal context of organized groups and Temple activities; the latter also became an avenue for meeting and associating with fellow Jews with whom they might otherwise have had no relations.

The Jews who most conspicuously made this shift to formal or organizational social life tended to belong to the higher income classes. They were responding not only to life among non-Jews, but to a new way of life that was associated with their rise into the professional and managerial upper-middle classes. Studies have shown time and again that participation in the activities of voluntary organizations increases as one goes up the socioeconomic ladder: community service has long been an integral part of the upper middle-class way of life in America. It is true that Jews in this country maintained a multitude of ethnic and religious organizations long before they aspired to upper middle-class ways. But as they have moved up the socioeconomic ladder, their organizations and the pattern of activities connected with them have gradually been altered to conform to the general American pattern for their new social position. Thus in Park Forest, where much of the activity of the voluntary organizations was in the hands of the women, it was patterned to a considerable extent on the secular upper middle-class clubs—and, in its social side, on the extracurricular life of the higher-status college campus. In many ways, the relation of the Sisterhood to the Temple resembled that of a sorority to its college community.

Many Jewish residents were not always as ready to contribute funds to the building up of the Jewish community, affix their signatures to membership cards, and in general work as volunteers, as they were to attend parties and dances. Often, people took part only after community leaders had exerted considerable pressure upon them. To organize this captive audience—as Nathan Glazer aptly calls it—required constant appeals to the self-interest of the individual Jew as well as to his "community spirit." Even so, interest in the community tended to remain sluggish. Only a handful of people organized the Temple; fund-raising for its building was planned by a professional public relations counsel, and involved dinners, the sending of letters, and considerable personal coaxing. It is said that the contributions of no more than fifty people really built the Temple.

Much of this pressure came from the "Jewish professionals" in the community. Their persistence, and the support given them by the Jewish officers of American Community Builders, undoubtedly hastened the growth of the Jewish organizations. Perhaps without them the Temple would not have been started, so great was the indifference—it is said—of Park Forest's Jewish community at large. It may be that the presence and effect of the leadership provided by the "Jewish professionals" distinguishes Park Forest somewhat from other Jewish suburban communities. However, the pressure for participation is a familiar phenomenon in other communities, and the resistance to it in these is just as ambiguous as it seems to be in Park Forest.

Living among non-Jews as they do, suburban Jews can't and won't surrender completely the allegiance, no matter how tenuous, they retain to the formal Jewish community. Despite complaints, even from some leaders, that the community was overorganized and that there was too much fund-raising, the mood of the Park Forest Jewish group was such that its members continued to be amenable to community pressure, though sometimes only grudgingly. It might be said that while the community's interest in the institutions developed by its leaders was weak enough to require the application of pressure, its cohesion as a Jewish group was sufficiently strong to tolerate this pressure.

It remains nonetheless true that the basic, underlying impulse for the establishment of a formal Jewish community in Park Forest was the desire of parents who felt themselves to be Jews to have their children grow up feeling Jewish too. Because parents could not or would not provide a Jewish atmosphere and cultural environment at home, they supported the community's organizations, schools, and Temple—and endured the community's pressures. While some kind of Jewish community would probably have been set up in Park Forest even without this motive, such a community, lacking this concern about the children, would have had fewer organizations, a much smaller scale of participation, no synagogue building or permanent rabbi, and perhaps no congregation.[7]

Finally, the community has taken its present form largely because of the capacity of the Temple to respond to the demands of its members and adapt itself to the new Jewish situation in the suburbs. Thus the Temple was able to overcome the loss of its original function as an adult house of worship and study by requiring that the children make up a large part of its congregation at services. At the same time, it has been able to retain adult support by ceasing to insist upon the attendance of adults and resting content with their presence in large numbers only on the High Holidays. On the other hand, the Temple attracts adults by offering itself as a center of voluntary social activities. In doing so, it also acknowledges the major role women now play in the formal Jewish community, and provides them with an opportunity to participate in what was previously a male organization. The men still make the major decisions regarding the operation of the Temple, but have otherwise retreated into the background. The gap left by their withdrawal from religious affairs, and by the women's lack of familiarity with such affairs, has been filled in large part by an increase in the functions and authority of the rabbi.

But the Temple could not have sustained its present level of operations and retained the community support it needed if it had not eventually set up a school—which remains the primary institution for the Jewish residents of Park Forest. The Temple's need to compete with the community Sunday school can thus be understood as a matter of institutional survival, although its rapid triumph in that competition can only be explained by its capacity to satisfy the present desires of the Jewish residents of Park Forest.

The Suburbanization of Jewish Life

It seems clear that what has happened in the Park Forest Jewish community over the past six years is not a "revival" of Jewish-centered life, but rather the adaptation of Jewish life to the suburban environment. Jewish life has become more visible because it has been taken out of the rather isolated urban Jewish neighborhood, because its participants have attained a social and economic level where organized communal activity is more highly prized, and because parents require institutions and visible symbols with which to maintain and reinforce the Jewish identification of their children.

In the course of this transformation of their lives as Jews, the Jews of

Park Forest have probably not become more religious or more interested in Judaic culture. They may have become a more cohesive community, but the cohesion rests primarily on the parents' desire to confirm the Jewish identity of their children, and it may fall off when this is assured. Moreover, it must be remembered that this report has been focused on the 40 percent of the Jews of Park Forest who belong to the Temple, the 10 percent who support the Board of Jewish Education, the 15 percent active in the Sisterhood, and the 3 percent who attend services regularly. These, though probably larger than the equivalent minorities in the city, are still minorities as regards the total Jewish community. The majority of Park Forest's Jews have not been considered in this study: they are Jews whose chief connection with the formal Jewish community (which may well be only a temporary one) consists in sending their children to its Sunday school.

The community revolves around its Sunday school students, and changes in the community may be expected when enough of these students reach the age of Bar Mitzvah. Unless they continue their Jewish education, or unless they are replaced by a new crop of youngsters, the Temple may have to seek new functions or else lose much of its support. According to the evidence provided by older communities, one such new function could be to provide a social center for those teenagers who want it and whose parents do not want to expose them to the possibility of intermarriage.

Whether the Temple would succeed in holding the Jewish teenagers in this way depends to some extent on the latter's relations with their non-Jewish contemporaries. But in the long run, holding on to today's children—and, indirectly, to their parents—hinges to a considerable extent on the way in which the Temple, the Sunday schools, and the parents themselves—as well as the secular institutions of the community—influence the youngsters' feeling of Jewishness over the nest few years.

NOTES

1. W. Lloyd Warner and Leo Srole, *The Social Systems of American Ethnic Groups* (New Haven, Conn.: Yale University Press, 1945).

2. In November 1950, after the completion of this study, a congregation was finally organized.

3. This was partially supported by the report that in 1954, when the developers opened a subdivision of more expensive ($19,000) homes, there was such a rush of Jewish newcomers, as well as of other Jews who had been living in rented apartments in Park Forest, that part of the section became (or seemed about to become) a densely settled Jewish neighborhood, and was banteringly described as "little Jerusalem" by Jews themselves.

4. The remaining seven families were "mixed marriages." Mixed-marriage families made up 14 percent of this sample, the same proportion as was found in the 100-family sample studied in 1949. As in 1949, however, there were probably still other mixed-marriage families in Park Forest that had renounced all Jewish identification.

5. For a sociological definition of latter-day Judaism and "Jewishness," and a discussion of these overall trends, see "American Jewry, Present and Future," by the same author, in *Commentary* (May 1956).

6. The present rabbi had directed a campus Hillel foundation before coming to Park Forest, and while this was not a factor in his selection, it may have been one in his ability to gain the community's support as rapidly as he did.

7. It is interesting to note that the two largest Christian congregations in the village, the Catholics and the United Protestants, began their building program with schools and have not yet constructed church buildings. (To some extent, this is probably a matter of economic allocation, for school buildings can be used for services whereas churches cannot easily be used for teaching.) Whether or not this is a reflection of Catholic and Protestant child orientation, I do not know.

· 9 ·

SYMBOLIC ETHNICITY

The Future of Ethnic Groups and Cultures in America

One of the more notable recent changes in America has been the re-newed interest in ethnicity, which some observers of the American scene have described as an ethnic revival. This chapter argues that there has been no revival, and that acculturation and assimilation continue to take place. Among third- and fourth-generation "ethnics" (the grandchildren and great-grandchildren of Europeans who came to American during the "new immigration"), a new kind of ethnic involvement may be occurring, which emphasizes concern with identity, with the feeling of being Jewish or Italian, etc. Since ethnic identity needs are neither intense nor frequent in this generation, however, ethnics do not need either ethnic cultures or organizations: instead, they resort to the use of ethnic symbols. As a result, ethnicity may be turning into symbolic ethnicity, an ethnicity of last resort, which could, nevertheless, persist for generations.

Identity cannot exist apart from a group, and symbols are themselves a part of culture, but ethnic identity and symbolic ethnicity require very different ethnic organizations and cultures than existed among earlier generations. Moreover, the symbols third-generation ethnics use to express their identity are more visible than the ethnic cultures and organizations of the first- and second-generation ethnics. What appears to be an ethnic revival may therefore be only a more visible form of long-standing phenomena, or of a new stage of acculturation and assimilation. Symbolic ethnicity may also have wider ramifications, however, for David Riesman has suggested that "being American has some of the same episodic qualities as being eth-

This chapter first appeared in H. Gans, N. Glazer, J. Gusfield, and C. Jencks, eds. *On the Making of America: Essays in Honor of David Riesman*. (Philadelphia: University of Pennsylvania Press, 1979); and the epilogue in Werner Sollors, ed., *Theories of Ethnicity: A Classical Reader*. (London: Macmillan Press Ltd., 1996). Reprinted with permission.

nic."[1] In effect, both kinds of being are also new ways of striving for individualism.

ACCULTURATION AND ASSIMILATION[2]

The dominant sociological approach to ethnicity has long taken the form of what Neil Sandberg aptly called "straight-line theory," in which acculturation and assimilation are viewed as secular trends that culminate in the eventual absorption of the ethnic group into the larger culture and general population.[3] Straight-line theory in turn is based on melting pot theory, which implies the disappearance of the ethnic groups into a single host society. Even so, it does not accept the values of the melting pot theorists, since its conceptualizers could have used terms like cultural and social liberation from immigrant ways of life, but did not.

In recent years, straight-line theory has been questioned on many grounds. For one thing, many observers have properly noted that even if America might have been a melting pot early in the twentieth century, the massive immigration from Europe and elsewhere has since then influenced the dominant groups, summarily labeled "WASP," and has also decimated their cultural, if not their political and financial, power, so that today America is a mosaic, as Andrew Greeley has put it, of subgroups and subcultures.[4] Still, this criticism does not necessarily deny the validity of straight-line theory, since ethnics can also be absorbed into a pluralistic set of subcultures and subgroups, differentiated by age, income, education, occupation, religion, region, and the like.

A second criticism of straight-line theory has centered on its treatment of all ethnic groups as essentially similar, and its failure, specifically, to distinguish between religious groups, like the Jews, and nationality groups, like the Italians, Poles, etc. Jews, for example, are a "peoplehood" with a religious and cultural tradition of thousands of years, but without an "old country" to which they owe allegiance or nostalgia, while Italians, Poles, and other participants in the "new immigration" came from parts of Europe that in some cases did not even become nations until after the immigrants had arrived in America.

That there are differences between the Jews and the other "new" immigrants cannot be questioned, but at the same time, the empirical evidence also suggests that acculturation and assimilation affected them quite similarly. (Indeed, one major difference may have been that Jews were already urbanized and thus entered the American social structure at a somewhat higher level than the other new immigrants, who were mostly landless laborers and poor peasants.) Nonetheless, straight-line theory can be faulted for virtually ignoring the fact that immigrants arrived here with two kinds of ethnic cultures, sacred and secular; that they were Jews from Eastern—and Western—Europe, and Catholics from Italy, Poland, and elsewhere. (Sacred cultures are, however, themselves affected by national and regional considerations; for example, Italian Catholicism differed in some respects from German or Polish, as did Eastern European Judaism from Western.)

While acculturation and assimilation have affected both sacred and secular cultures, they have affected the latter more than the former, for acculturation has particularly eroded the secular cultures that Jews and Catholics brought from Europe. Their religions have also changed in America, and religious observance has decreased, more so among Jews than among Catholics, although Catholic observance has begun to fall off greatly in recent years. Consequently, the similar American experience of Catholic and Jewish ethnics suggests that the comparative analysis of straight-line theory is justified, as long as the analysis compares both sacred and secular cultures.

Two further critiques virtually reject straight-line theory altogether. In an insightful paper, William Yancey and his colleagues argued that contemporary ethnicity bears little relation to the ancestral European heritage, but exists because it is functional for meeting present "exigencies of survival," particularly for working-class Americans.[5] Their argument does not invalidate straight-line theory but corrects it by suggesting that acculturation and assimilation, current ethnic organizations and cultures, as well as new forms of ethnicity, must be understood as responses to current needs rather than departures from past traditions.

The other critique takes the opposite position; it points to the persistence of the European heritage, argues that the extent of acculturation and assimilation have been overestimated, and questions the rapid decline and eventual extinction of ethnicity posited by some straight-line theorists. These critics call attention to studies indicating that ethnic cultures and organizations are still functioning, that exogamous marriage remains a practice of numerical minorities, that ethnic differences in various behavior patterns and attitudes can be identified, that ethnic groups continue to act as political interest groups, and that ethnic pride remains strong.[6]

The social phenomena that these defenders of ethnicity identify exist; the only question is how they are to be interpreted. Straight-line theory postulates a process, and cross-sectional studies do not pre-empt the possibility of a continuing trend. Also, like Yancey and his co-authors, some of the critics are looking primarily at poorer ethnics, who have been less touched by acculturation and assimilation than middle-class ethnics, and who have in some cases used ethnicity and ethnic organization as a psychological and political defense against the injustices that they suffer in an unequal society.[7] In fact, much of the contemporary behavior described as "ethnic" strikes me as working-class behavior, which differs only slightly among various ethnic groups, and then largely because of variations in the structure of opportunities open to people in America, and in the peasant traditions their ancestors brought over from the old country, which were themselves responses to European opportunity structures. In other words, ethnicity is largely a working-class style.[8]

Much the same observation applies to ethnic political activity. Urban political life, particularly among working-class people, has always been structured by and through ethnicity, and while ethnic political activity may have increased in the last decade, it has taken place around working-class issues rather than ethnic ones. During the 1960s, urban working-class Catholic ethnics began to politicize themselves in response to black militancy, the expansion of black ghettoes, and government integration policies that they perceived as publicly legitimated black invasions of ethnic neighborhoods, but which threatened them as working-class homeowners who could not afford to move to the suburbs. Similarly, working- and lower-middle-class Catholic ethnics banded together in the suburbs to fight against higher public school taxes, since they could not afford to pay them while they also had to pay for parochial schools. Even so, these political activities have been *pan-ethnic,* rather than ethnic, since they often involved coalitions of ethnic groups that once considered each other enemies but were now united by common economic and other interests. The extent to which these pan-ethnic coalitions reflect class rather than ethnic interests is illustrated by the 1968 election campaign of New York City's Mario Proccaccino against John Lindsay. Although an Italian, he ran as a "candidate of the little people" against what he called the "limousine liberals."

The fact that pan-ethnic coalitions have developed most readily in conflicts over racial issues also suggests that in politics, ethnicity can sometimes serve as a convenient mask for antiblack endeavors, or for political activities that have negative consequences for blacks. While attitude polls indicate that ethnics are often more tolerant racially than other Americans, working-class urban ethnics are also more likely to be threatened, as homeowners and jobholders, by black demands, and may favor specific antiblack policies, not because they are "racists," but because their own class interests force them to oppose black demands.

In addition, part of what appears as an increase in ethnic political activity is actually an increase in the visibility of ethnic politics. When the pan-ethnic coalitions began to copy the political methods of the civil rights and antiwar movements, their protests became newsworthy and were disseminated all over the country by the mass media. At about the same time, the economic and geographic mobility of Catholic ethnic groups enabled non-Irish Catholic politicians to win important state and national electoral posts for the first time, and their victories were defined as ethnic triumphs, even though they did not rely on ethnic constituents alone and were not elected on the basis of ethnic issues.

The final, equally direct, criticism of straight-line theory has questioned the continued relevance of the theory, either because of the phenomenon of third-generation return, or because of the emergence of ethnic revivals. Thus, Marcus Hansen argued that acculturation and assimilation were temporary processes, because the third generation could afford to remember an ancestral culture that the traumatic Americanization process forced the immigrant and second generations to forget.[9] Hansen's hypothesis can be questioned on several grounds, however. His data, the founding of Swedish and other historical associations in the Midwest, provided slender evidence of a widespread third-generation return, particularly among nonacademic ethnics; in addition, his theory was static, for Hansen never indicated what would happen in the fourth generation, or what processes were involved in the return that would enable it to survive into the future.[10]

The notion of an ethnic revival has so far been propounded mostly by journalists and essayists, who have supplied impressionistic accounts or case studies of the emergence of new ethnic organizations and the revitalization of old ones.[11] Since the third and fourth generation ethnics who are presumably participating in this revival are scattered all over suburbia, there has so far been little systematic research among this population, so that the validity of the revival notion has not yet been properly tested.

The evidence I have seen does not convince me that a revival is taking place. Instead, recent changes can be explained in two ways, neither of which conflicts with straight-line theory: (1) today's ethnics have become more visible as a result of upward mobility; and (2) they are adopting the new form of ethnic behavior and affiliation I call "symbolic ethnicity."

THE VISIBILITY OF ETHNICITY

The recent upward social, and centrifugal geographic, mobility of ethnics, particularly Catholics, has finally enabled them to enter the middle and upper-middle classes, where they have been noticed by the national mass media, which monitor primarily these strata. In the process they have also become more noticeable to other Americans. The newly visible may not participate more in ethnic groups and cultures than before, but their new visibility makes it appear as if ethnicity had been revived.

I noted earlier the arrival of non-Irish Catholic politicians on the national scene. An equally visible phenomenon has been the entry of Catholic ethnic intellectuals into the academy and its flourishing print culture. To be sure, the scholars are publishing more energetically than their predecessors, who had to rely on small and poverty-stricken ethnic publishing houses, but they are essentially doing what ethnic scholars have always done, only more visibly. Perhaps their energy has also been spurred in part by the need, as academics, to publish so that they do not perish, as well as by their desire to counteract the anti-ethnic prejudices and the entrenched vestiges of the melting pot ideal that still prevail in the more prestigious universities. In some cases, they are also fighting a political battle, because their writings often defend conservative political positions against what they perceive—I think wrongly—as the powerful liberal or radical academic majority. Paradoxically, a good deal of their writing has been nostalgic, celebrating the immigrant culture and its Gemeinschaft at the same time that young Catholic ethnics are going to college partly in order to escape the restrictive pressures of that Gemeinschaft. (Incidentally, an interesting study could be made of the extent to which writers from different ethnic groups, of both fiction and nonfiction, are pursuing nostalgic, contemporary, or future-oriented approaches to ethnicity, comparing different ethnic groups, by time of arrival and position in the society today, on this basis.)

What has happened in the academy has also happened in literature and show business. For example, although popular comedy has long been a predominantly Eastern European Jewish occupation, the first generations of Jewish comic stars had to suppress their ethnicity and even had to change their names, much as did the first generation of academic stars in the prestigious universities. Unlike Jack Benny, Eddie Cantor, George Burns, George Jessel, and others, the comics of today do not need to hide their origins, and beginning perhaps with Lenny Bruce and Sam Levinson, comics like Buddy Hackett, Robert Klein, Don Rickles, and Joan Rivers have used explicitly Jewish material in entertaining the predominantly non-Jewish mass media audience.[12]

Undoubtedly, some of these academics, writers, and entertainers have undergone a kind of third-generation return in this process. Some have reembraced their ethnicity solely to spur their careers, but others have experienced a personal conversion. Even so, an empirical study would probably show that in most cases their ethnic attitudes have not changed; either they have acted more publicly and thus visibly than they did in the past, or in responding to a hospitable cultural climate, they have openly followed ethnic impulses that they had previously suppressed.

A similar analysis may explain the resurgence of traditionalism among some Jews and Protestants. In both instances largely middle-class young people are perceived as having become newly orthodox (or fundamentalist), and in some cases this is undoubtedly true. Religious conversions may have increased in the last decade, partly because of the ideological and other turbulence of the 1960s, but also because the postwar affluence spawned a cohort of parents who were so upwardly mobile that they were too busy to pay attention to their children. These children developed a strong need for substitute parental guidance, which later manifested itself by their joining the theocratic Gemeinschafts that can be found among virtually all of the recent neotraditional movements. Converts are, however, also the most visible, since they tend to be leaders and are thus most often monitored by the mass media. At the same time, they have been joined by less visible young people who were already orthodox, but perhaps quiescently so, either because orthodoxy was in disrepute among their peers while they were growing up, or because they were uncomfortable in orthodox groups dominated by old people.[13] Only empirical research can indicate the proportions of third-generation returnees and already orthodox people in these groups, but in any case, it seems wrong on the part of enthusiastic observers of a religious revival to group the neotraditionalists with earlier traditional groups, such as the Chassidim, the non-Chassidic Orthodox Jews living in such enclaves as New York City's Boro Park, and rural groups like the Amish.[14] These groups have survived by insulating themselves from the larger society, rarely take in converts, and thus have also insulated themselves from the neotraditionalists.

ETHNICITY IN THE
THIRD GENERATION

The second explanation for the changes that have been taking place among third-generation ethnics will take up most of the rest of this chapter; it deals with what is happening among the less visible population, the large mass of predominantly middle-class third- and fourth-generation ethnics, who have not been studied enough either by journalists or by social scientists.[15]

In the absence of systematic research, it is difficult even to discern what has actually been happening, but several observers have described the same ethnic behavior in different words. Michael Novak has coined the phrase "voluntary ethnicity"; Samuel Eisenstadt has talked about "Jewish diversity"; Allan Silver about "individualism as a valid mode of Jewishness"; and Geoffrey Bock about "public Jewishness."[16] What these observers agree on is that today's young ethnics are finding new ways of being ethnics, which I shall later label "symbolic ethnicity."

I start my analysis with the assumption, taken from straight-line theory, that acculturation and assimilation are continuing among the third and fourth generations.[17] If these concepts were quantified, one might find that upwardly mobile working-class groups are moving out of ethnic cultures and groups faster than other ethnics as they try to enter the middle class, whereas those already in the middle class are now acculturating and assimilating at a slower rate, partly because they have already moved out of ethnic cultures and groups to a considerable extent, but also because they are finding that middle-class life is sufficiently pluralistic and their ethnicity sufficiently cost-free that they do not have to give it up deliberately.

In any case, for the third generation, the secular ethnic cultures that the immigrants brought with them are now only an ancestral memory, or an exotic tradition to be savored once in a while in a museum or at an ethnic festival. The same is true of the "Americanization cultures," the immigrant experience and adjustment in America, which William Kornblum suggested may have been more important in the lives of the first two generations than the ethnic cultures themselves. The old ethnic cultures serve no useful function for third-generation ethnics who lack direct and indirect ties to the old country, and neither need nor have much knowledge about it. Similarly, the Americanization cultures have little meaning for people who grew up without the familial conflict over European and American ways that beset their fathers and mothers: the second generation that fought with and was often ashamed of immigrant parents.

Assimilation is still continuing, for it has always progressed more slowly than acculturation. If one distinguishes between primary and secondary assimilation, that is, movement out of ethnic primary and secondary groups, the third generation is now beginning to move into nonethnic primary groups.[18] Although researchers are still debating just how much intermarriage is taking place, it is rising in the third generation for both Catholic ethnic groups and Jews, and friendship choices appear to follow the same pattern.[19]

The departure out of secondary groups has already proceeded much further. Most third-generation ethnics have little reason, or occasion, to depend on, or even interact with, other ethnics in important secondary-group activities. Ethnic occupational specialization, segregation, and self-segregation are fast disappearing, with some notable exceptions in the large cities. Since the third generation probably works, like other Americans, largely for corporate employers, past occupational ties between ethnics are no longer relevant. Insofar as they live largely in the suburbs, third-generation ethnics get together with their fellow homeowners for political and civic activities, and are not likely to encounter ethnic political organizations, balanced tickets, or even politicians who pursue ethnic constituencies.

Except in suburbs where old discrimination and segregation patterns still survive, social life takes place without ethnic clustering, and Catholics are not likely to find ethnic subgroups in the Church. Third-generation Jews, on the other hand, particularly those who live in older upper middle-class suburbs where segregation continues, if politely, probably still continue to restrict much of their social life to other Jews, although they have long ago forgotten the secular divisions between German (and other Western) and Eastern European Jews, and among the latter, between "Litwaks" and "Galizianer." The religious distinction between German Reform Judaism and Eastern European Conservatism has also virtually disappeared, for the second generation that moved to the suburbs after World War II already chose its denomination on the basis of status rather than national origin.[20] In fact, the Kennedy-Herberg prediction that eventually American religious life would take the form of a triple melting pot has not come to pass, if only because people, especially in the suburbs, use denominations within the major religions for status differentiation.

Nevertheless, while ethnic ties continue to wane for the third generation, people of this generation continue to perceive themselves as ethnics, whether they define ethnicity in sacred or secular terms. Jews continue to remain Jews because the sacred and secular elements of their culture are strongly intertwined, but the Catholic ethnics also retain their secular or national identity, even though it is separate from their religion.

My hypothesis is that in this generation, people are less and less interested in their ethnic cultures and organizations—both sacred and secular—and are instead more concerned with maintaining their ethnic identity, with the feeling of being Jewish or Italian or Polish, and with finding ways of feeling and expressing that identity in suitable ways. By identity, I mean here simply the sociopsychological elements that accompany role behavior, and the ethnic role is today less of an ascriptive than a voluntary role that people assume alongside other roles. To be sure, ethnics are still identified as such by others, particularly on the basis of name, but the behavioral expectations that once went with identification by others have declined sharply, so that ethnics have some choice about when and how to play ethnic roles. Moreover, as ethnic cultures and organizations decline further, fewer ethnic roles are prescribed, thus increasing the degree to which people have freedom of role definition.

Ethnic identity can be expressed in either action or feeling, or combinations of these, and the kinds of situations in which it is expressed are nearly limitless. Third-generation ethnics can join an ethnic organization or take part in formal or informal organizations composed largely of fellow ethnics, but they can also find their identity by "affiliating" with an abstract collectivity that does not exist as an interacting group. That collectivity, moreover, can be mythic or real, contemporary or historical. On the one hand, Jews can express their identity as synagogue members, or as participants in a consciousness-raising group consisting mostly of Jewish women. On the other hand, they can also identify with the Jewish people as a long-suffering collectivity that has been credited with inventing monotheism. If they are not religious, they can identify with Jewish liberal or socialist political cultures, or with a population that has produced many prominent intellectuals and artists in the last hundred years. Similar choices are open to Catholic ethnics. In the third generation, Italians can identify through membership in Italian groups, or by strong feelings for various themes in Italian or Neapolitan or Sicilian culture, and much the same possibilities exist for Catholics whose ancestors came over from other countries.

Needless to say, ethnic identity is not a new or a third-generation phenomenon, for ethnics have always had an ethnic identity, but in the past it was largely taken for granted, since it was anchored to groups and roles, and was rarely a matter of choice. When people lived in an ethnic neighborhood, worked with fellow ethnics, and voted for ethnic politicians, there was little need to be concerned with identity except during conflict with other ethnic groups. Furthermore, the everyday roles people played were often defined for them by others as ethnic. Being a dry-goods merchant was often a Jewish role; restaurant owners were assumed to be Greek, and bartenders, Irish.

The third generation has grown up without assigned roles or groups that anchor ethnicity, so that identity can no longer be taken for granted. People can, of course, give up their identity, but if they continue to feel it, they must make it more explicit than it was in the past, and must even look for ways of expressing it. This has two important consequences for ethnic behavior. First, given the degree to which the third generation has acculturated and assimilated, most people look for easy and intermittent ways of expressing their identity, for ways that do not conflict with other ways of life. As a result, they refrain from ethnic behavior that requires an arduous or time-consuming commitment, either to a culture that must be practiced constantly, or to organizations that demand active membership. Second, because people's concern is with identity, rather than with cultural practices or group relationships, they are free to look for ways of expressing that identity which suits them best, thus opening up the possibility of voluntary, diverse, or individualistic ethnicity. Any mode of expressing ethnic identity is valid as long as it enhances the feeling of being ethnic, and any cultural pattern or organization that nourishes that feeling is therefore relevant, providing only that enough people make the same choices when identity expression is a group enterprise.

In other words, as the functions of ethnic cultures and groups diminish and identity becomes the primary way of being ethnic, ethnicity takes on an expressive rather than instrumental function in people's lives, becoming more of a leisure-time activity and losing its relevance, say, to earning a living or regulating family life. Expressive behavior can take many forms, but it often involves the use of symbols—and symbols as signs rather than as myths.[21] Ethnic symbols are frequently individual cultural practices that are taken from the older ethnic culture; they are "abstracted" from that culture and pulled out of its original moorings, so to speak, to become stand-ins for it. And if a label is useful to describe the third generation's pursuit of identity, I propose the term "symbolic ethnicity."

SYMBOLIC ETHNICITY

Symbolic ethnicity can be expressed in a myriad of ways, but above all, I suspect, it is characterized by a nostalgic allegiance to the culture of the immigrant generation, or that of the old country: a love for and a pride in a tradition that can be felt without having to be incorporated into everyday behavior. The feelings can be directed at a generalized tradition, or at specific ones: a desire for the cohesive extended immigrant family, or the obedience of children to parental authority, or the unambiguous orthodoxy of immigrant religion, or the old-fashioned despotic benevolence of the machine politician. People may even sincerely desire to "return" to these imagined pasts, which are conveniently cleansed of the complexities that accompanied them in the real past, but while they may soon realize that they cannot go back, they may not surrender the wish. Or else they displace that wish on churches, schools, and the mass media, asking them to recreate a tradition, or rather, to create a symbolic tradition, even while their familial, occupational, religious, and political lives are pragmatic responses to the imperatives of their roles and positions in local and national hierarchical social structures.

All of the cultural patterns that are transformed into symbols are themselves guided by a common pragmatic imperative: they must be visible and clear in meaning to large numbers of third-generation ethnics, and they must be easily expressed and felt, without requiring undue interference in other aspects of life. For example, Jews have abstracted *rites de passage* and individual holidays out of the traditional religion and given them greater importance, such as the *Bar Mitzvah* and *Bas Mitzvah* (the parallel ceremony for thirteen-year-old girls that was actually invented in America). Similarly, Chanukah, a minor holiday in the religious calendar, has become a major one in popular practice, partly since it lends itself to impressing Jewish identity on the children. *Rites de passage* and holidays are ceremonial, and thus symbolic to begin with; equally importantly, they do not take much time, do not upset the everyday routine, and also become an occasion for reassembling on a regular basis family members who are rarely seen. Catholic ethnics pay special attention to the feast days of saints affiliated with their ethnic group, or attend ethnic festivals that take place in the area of first settlement or in ethnic churches.

Consumer goods, notably foods, are another ready source for ethnic symbols, and in the last decades the food industry has developed a large variety of easily cooked ethnic foods, as well as other edibles that need no cooking—for example, chocolate matzohs that are sold as gifts at Passover. The response to symbolic ethnicity may even be spreading into the mass media, for films and television programs with ethnic characters are on the increase. The characters are not very ethnic in their behavior, and may only have ethnic names—for example, Lieutenant Colombo, Fonzi, or Rhoda Goldstein—but in that respect that are not very different from the ethnic audiences who watch them.

Symbolic ethnicity also takes political forms, through identification or involvement with national politicians and international issues that are sufficiently remote to become symbols. As politicians from non-Irish ethnic backgrounds achieve high national or state office, they become identity symbols for members of their group, supplying feelings of pride over their success. For example, Michael Dukakis, ex-governor of Massachusetts, and John Brademas, congressman from Indiana, may currently serve this function for Greeks, being the first members of the ethnic group to be elected to high office—other than Spiro Agnew, who, however, changed both his name and his religion before entering politics. That such politicians do not represent ethnic constituencies, and thus do not become involved in ethnic political disputes, only enhances their symbolic function, unlike local ethnic politicians, who are still elected for instrumental bread-and-butter reasons and thus become embroiled in conflicts that detract from their being symbols of ethnic pride. Thus, there was little pride in New York's Jewish community when Abe Beame was elected the first Jewish mayor of the city in 1973; in fact, some New York Jews opposed his election on the ground that any new difficulties facing the city during his administration would be blamed on the Jews. As it happened, the city's financial crisis turned disastrous while Beame was in office, and although he was widely criticized for his role in it, he was not attacked as a Jew, and was in fact succeeded by another Jewish mayor, Ed Koch.

Symbolic ethnicity can be practiced as well through politically and geographically even more distant phenomena, such as nationalist movements in the old country. Jews are not interested in their old countries, except to struggle against the maltreatment of Jews in Eastern Europe, but they have sent large amounts of money to Israel, and political pressure to Washington, since the establishment of the state. While their major concern has undoubtedly been to stave off Israel's destruction, they might also have felt that their own identity would be affected by such a disaster. Even if the survival of Israel is guaranteed in the future, however, it is possible that as allegiances toward organized local Jewish communities in America weaken, Israel becomes a substitute community to satisfy identity needs. Similar mechanisms may be at work among other ethnic groups who have recently taken an interest in their ancestral countries—for example, the Welsh and the Armenians—and among those groups whose old countries are involved in internal conflict—for example, the Irish, and Greeks and Turks since the Cyprus war of 1973.

Old countries are particularly useful as identity symbols because they are far away and cannot make arduous demands on American ethnics; even sending large amounts of money is ultimately an easy way to help, unless the donors are making major economic sacrifices. Moreover, American ethnics can identify with their perception of the old country or homeland, transforming it into a symbol, which leaves out those domestic or foreign problems that could become sources of conflict for Americans. For example, most American Jews who support Israel pay little attention to its purely domestic policies; they are concerned with its preservation as a state and a Jewish homeland, and see the country mainly as a Zionist symbol.

The symbolic functions of old countries are facilitated further when interest in them is historical, when ethnics develop an interest in their old countries as they were during or before the time of the ancestral departure. Marcus Hansen's notion of third-generation return was actually based on the emergence of interest in Swedish history, which suggests that the third-generation return may itself be only another variety of symbolic ethnicity. The third generation can obviously attend to the past with less emotional risk than first- and second-generation people, who are still trying to escape it, but even so, an interest in ethnic history is a return only chronologically.

Conversely, a new symbol may be appearing among Jews: the Holocaust, which has become a historic example of ethnic-group destruction that can now serve as a warning sign for possible future threats. The interest of American Jews in the Holocaust has increased considerably since the end of World War II; when I studied the Jews of Park Forest in 1949–1950, it was almost never mentioned, and its memory played no part whatsoever in the creation of a Jewish community there. The lack of attention to the Holocaust at that time may, as Nathan Glazer suggested, reflect the fact that American Jews were busy with creating new Jewish communities in the suburbs.[22] It is also possible that people ignored the Holocaust then because the literature detailing its horrors had not yet been written, although since many second-generation American Jews had relatives who died in the Nazi camps, it seems more likely that people repressed thinking about it until it had become a more historical, and therefore a less immediately traumatic, event. As a result, the Holocaust may now be serving as a new symbol for the threat of group destruction, a symbol required, on the one hand, by the fact that rising intermarriage rates and the continued decline of interest and participation in Jewish religion are producing real fears about the disappearance of American Jewry altogether; and on the other hand, by the concurrent fact that American anti-Semitism is no longer the serious threat to group survival that it was for first- and second-generation Jews.

Somewhat the same process appears to be taking place among some young Armenians who are now reviving the history of the Turkish massacre of Armenians some sixty years later, at a time when acculturation and assimilation are beginning to make inroads into the Armenian community in America. Still, good empirical data about the extent of the concern both with the Holocaust and the Turkish massacre are lacking, and neither may be as widespread among third-generation Jews and Armenians as among their professional and voluntary organizational leaders. Conversely, the 1978 NBC miniseries "The Holocaust" may be both an effect of rising interest in the tragedy and a cause of further interest, eve if NBC commissioned the series in the hope of duplicating the earlier success of "Roots."

Most of the symbols used by third-generation ethnics are, however, more prosaic. Jews who take vacations in Israel and Catholic ethnics who go back to their ancestral countries may make these visits in part to satisfy identity needs. Some agnostic Jewish college students appear to have transformed Yom Kippur into a symbol of their Jewishness and stay away from classes even though they do not go to synagogue. It is even possible that the recent public emergence of Polish and other ethnic jokes serves some symbolic functions. Sandberg found that his Polish respondents were not particularly upset by Polish jokes, and perhaps third-generation Poles tell them to each other as negative symbols, which indicate to them what Polishness is not, and concurrently enable them to express their distaste for the butts of these jokes: Poles of an earlier generation or lower socioeconomic status.[23]

I suggested previously that ethnicity per se had become more visible, but many of the symbols used by the third generation are also visible to the rest of America, not only because the middle-class people who use them are more visible than their poorer ancestors; but because the national media are more adept at communicating symbols than the ethnic cultures and organizations of earlier generations. The visibility of symbolic ethnicity provides further support for the existence of an ethnic revival, but what appears to be a revival is probably the emergence of a new form of acculturation and assimilation that is taking place under the gaze of the rest of society.

Incidentally, even though the mass media play a major role in enhancing the visibility of ethnicity and communicating ethnic symbols, they do not play this role because they are themselves ethnic institutions. True, the mass media, like other entertainment industries, continue to be dominated by Jews (although less so than in the past), but for reasons connected with anti-Semitism, or the fear of it, they have generally leaned over backward to keep Jewish characters and Jewish fare out of their offerings, at least until recently. Even now, a quantitative analysis of major ethnic characters in comedy, drama, and other entertainment genres would surely show that Catholic ethnics outnumber Jewish ones. Perhaps the Jews who write or produce so much of the media fare are especially sensitive to ethnic themes and symbols; my own hypothesis, however, is that they are, in this case as in others, simply responding to new cultural tendencies, if only because they must continually innovate. In fact, the arrival of ethnic characters followed the emergence and heightened visibility of ethnic politics in the late 1960s, and the men and women who write the entertainment fare probably took inspiration from news stories they saw on television or read in the papers.

I have suggested that symbolic ethnicity must be relatively effortless, but while this is probably true for the majority of third-generation ethnics, it is possible that more intense identity needs may produce a more intense form of symbolic ethnicity. Thus, Paul Ritterband has suggested that some aspects of the contemporary neotraditional movement among Jews may be in part symbolic, in that the movement is more concerned with strengthening feelings of Jewish identity and a sense of historic continuity than with perpetuating an Orthodox culture. Drawing on the distinction between *Halachah* (law) and *Aggadah* (myth), he suggests that such leading figures of the movement as Martin Buber and Abraham Heschel developed what he calls a new mythic culture, which manifests little relationship with an allegiance to the existing law-centered Orthodox Judaism. Consequently, it would be useful to study the members of this movement to discover to what extent they are pursuing new ways of being good Jews, and to what extent they want to perpetuate the laws and other dictates of Orthodoxy.

I noted earlier that identity cannot exist apart from a group and that symbols are themselves part of a culture, and in that sense, symbolic ethnicity can be viewed as an indicator of the persistence of ethnic groups and cultures. Symbolic ethnicity, however, does not require functioning groups or networks; feelings of identity can be developed by allegiances to symbolic groups that never meet, or to collectivities that meet only occasionally and exist as groups only for the handful of officers that keep them going. By the same token, symbolic ethnicity does not need a practiced culture, even if the symbols are borrowed from it. To be sure, symbolic culture is as much culture as practiced culture, but the latter persists only to supply symbols to the former. Indeed, practiced culture may need to persist, for some, because people do not borrow their symbols from extinct cultures that survive only in museums. And insofar as the borrowed materials come from the practiced culture of the immigrant generation, they make it appear as if an ethnic revival were taking place.

Then, too, it should be noted that even symbolic ethnicity may be relevant for only some of the descendants of the immigrants. As intermarriage continues, the number of people with parents from the same secular ethnic group will continue to decline, and by the time the fourth generation of the old immigration reaches adulthood, such people may be a minority. Most Catholic ethnics will be hybrid, and will have difficulty developing an ethnic identity. For example, how would the son of an Italian mother and Irish father who has married a woman of Polish-German ancestry determine his ethnicity, and what would he and his wife tell their children? Even if they were willing, would they be able to decide on their, and their children's, ethnicity; and in that case, how would they rank or synthesize their diverse backgrounds? These questions are empirical, and urgently need to be studied, but I would suggest that there are only three possibilities. Either the parents choose the single ethnic identity they find most satisfying, or they encourage the children to become what I earlier called panethnics, or they cope with diversity by ignoring it, and raise their children as nonethnics.

The Emergence of Symbolic Ethnicity

The preceding observations have suggested that symbolic ethnicity is a new phenomenon that comes into being in the third generation, but it is probably of earlier vintage and may have already begun to emerge among the immigrants themselves. After all, many of the participants in the new immigration were oppressed economically, politically, and culturally in their old countries, and could not have had much affection even for the villages and regions they were leaving. Consequently, it is entirely possible that they began to jettison the old culture and to stay away from ethnic organizations other than churches and unions the moment they came to America, saving only their primary groups, their ties to relatives still left in Europe, and their identity. In small-town America, where immigrants were a numerically unimportant minority, the pressure for immediate acculturation and assimilation was much greater than in the cities, but even in the latter, the seeds for symbolic ethnicity may have been sown earlier than previously thought.

Conversely, despite all the pressures toward Americanization and the prejudice and discrimination experienced by the immigrants, they were never faced with conditions that required or encouraged them to give up their ethnicity entirely. Of course, some of the earliest Jewish arrivals to America had become Quakers and Episcopalians before the end of the nineteenth century, but the economic conditions that persuaded the Jamaican Chinese in Kingston to become Creole, and the social isolation that forced Italians in Sydney, Australia, to abolish the traditional familial male-female role segregation shortly after arriving, have never been part of the American experience.[24]

Some conditions for the emergence of symbolic ethnicity were present from the beginning, for American ethnics have always been characterized by freedom of ethnic expression, which stimulated both the ethnic diversity and the right to find one's own way of being ethnic that are crucial to symbolic ethnicity. Although sacred and secular ethnic organizations that insisted that only one mode of being ethnic was legitimate have always existed in America, they have not been able to enforce their norms, in part because they have always had to compete with other ethnic organizations. Even in ethnic neighborhoods where conformity was expected and social control was pervasive, people had some freedom of choice about ethnic cultural practices. For example, the second-generation Boston Italians I studied had to conform to many family and peer-group norms, but they were free to ignore ethnic secondary groups, and to drop or alter Italian cultural practices according to their own preference.

Ethnic diversity within the group was probably encouraged by the absence of a state religion and national and local heads of ethnic communities. For example, American Jewry never had a chief rabbi, or even chief Orthodox, Conservative, and Reform rabbis, and the European practice of local Jewish communities electing or appointing local laymen as presidents was not carried across the ocean.[25] Catholic ethnics had to obey the cardinal or bishop heading their diocese, of course, but in those communities where the diocese insisted on an Irish church, the other ethnic groups, notably the Italians, kept their distance from the church, and only in the parochial schools was there any attempt to root out secular ethnic patterns. The absence of strong unifying institutions thus created the opportunity for diversity and freedom from the beginning, and undoubtedly facilitated the departure from ethnic cultures and organizations.

Among the Jews, symbolic ethnicity may have been fostered early by self-selection among Jewish emigrants. As Liebman pointed out, the massive Eastern European immigration to America did not include the rabbis and scholars who practiced what he called an elite religion in the old countries; as a result, the immigrants established what he called a folk religion in America instead, with indigenous rabbis who were elected or appointed by individual congregations and were more permissive in allowing, or too weak to prevent, deviations from religious orthodoxy, even of the milder folk variety.[26] Indeed, the development of a folk religion may have encouraged religious and secular diversity among Jews from the very beginning.

Still, perhaps the most important factor in the development of symbolic ethnicity was probably the awareness, which I think many second-generation people had already reached, that neither the practice of ethnic culture nor participation in ethnic organizations was essential to being and feeling ethnic. For Jews, living in a Jewish neighborhood or working with Jews every day was enough to maintain Jewish identity. When younger second-generation Jews moved to suburbia in large numbers after World War II, many wound up in communities in which they were a small numerical minority, but they quickly established an informal Jewish community of neighborly relations, and then built synagogues and community centers to formalize and supplement the informal community. At the time, many observers interpreted the feverish building as a religious revival, but for most Jews the synagogue was a symbol that could serve as a means of expressing identity without requiring more than occasional participation in its activities.[27] Thus, my observations among the second-generation Jews of Park Forest and other suburbs led me to think, as far back as the mid-1950s, that among Jews, at least, the shift to symbolic ethnicity was already under way.[28]

Suburban Jews also built synagogues and centers to help them implant a Jewish identity among their children, and to hold back primary assimilation, particularly intermarriage. Jewish parents sent their teenagers into Jewish organizations so that they would date other Jews, and then to colleges where they would be most likely to find Jewish spouses. Rising intermarriage rates suggest, however, that their efforts were not always success-ful, but also that their fears of the consequences of intermarriage were exaggerated. By now, many Jewish parents realize that intermarriage need not inevitably lead to surrender of Jewish identity. Non-Jewish spouses of third-generation Jews sometimes convert to Judaism, more frequently adopt some trappings of Jewish culture and pay homage to Jewish symbols, and even raise their children as Jews, thus suggesting that even with third-generation intermarriage, the next generation will still consider itself to be Jewish.[29]

Actually, if being Jewish need only mean feeling Jewish and attending to Jewish symbols, the transmission of Jewish identity to the next genera-tion is fairly easily achieved, even by non-Jewish parents. Although little is known about socialization for Jewish identity, it may require only a mini-mum of parental action, no cultural or organizational affiliation, and per-haps not even a Jewish education for the children. Some evidence suggests that at about age five, children begin to ask themselves, their peers, and their parents what they are, and being told that they are Jewish may be sufficient to plant the seeds of Jewish identity.[30]

Needless to say, a person's ethnic identity is not firmly established at five and can weaken or disappear in later years. Even when this does not happen, adolescents and adults often develop doubts about their ethnic identity, and particularly about their ability to pass it on to their children.[31] I have the impression that ambivalence about one's identity is weaker among third-generation Jews than it was among their parents, if only be-cause ethnic identity is now not burdensome or beset with major social and economic costs. Still, unless strong incentives or pressures develop to encourage Jews to give up their identity, it seems likely that they will retain it in the fourth generation, especially since the demands of symbolic ethnic-ity are light enough not to cause conflict with other, more highly valued, identities and activities.

Some of these observations apply equally well to third-generation Catholic ethnics, especially those who live in the suburbs. They still attend church more frequently than Jews attend synagogue, generally marry Cath-olics, and are unlikely to give up their Catholic identity. They do not, how-ever, feel a strong need to perpetuate their secular ethnicity, so that, for example, Italian parents do not press their adolescent children to date other Italians. Even so, it is possible that identity may also be transmitted to chil-dren by others besides parents, for example, grandparents and peers. In any case, Sandberg has shown that fourth-generation Poles still retain their Pol-ish identity, and Crispino has found the same among Italians.[32]

As intermarriage increases, however, it will be important to discover which ethnic identity, if any, is transmitted to children by intermarried Catholic ethnics; whether mothers and fathers play different roles in identity transmission; and how grandparents and close friends act in this connection. Similar questions could be asked of hybrid ethnics, although it seems unlikely that they could even decide which of their many ancestries they should pass on to their children.

THE FUTURE OF ETHNICITY

The emergence of symbolic ethnicity naturally raises the question of its persistence into the fifth and sixth generations. Although the Catholic and Jewish religions are certain to endure, it appears that as religion becomes less important to people, they, too, will be eroded by acculturation and assimilation. Even now synagogues see most of their worshippers no more than once or twice a year, and presumably the same trend will appear, perhaps more slowly, among Catholics and Protestants as well.

Whether the secular forms of ethnicity can survive beyond the fourth generation is somewhat less certain. One possibility is that symbolic ethnicity will itself decline as acculturation and assimilation continue, and then disappear as erstwhile ethnics forget their secular ethnic identity to blend into one or another subcultural melting pot. The other possibility is that symbolic ethnicity is a steady-state phenomenon that can persist into the fifth and sixth generations.

Obviously this question can only be guessed at, but my hypothesis is that symbolic ethnicity may persist. The continued existence of Germans, Scandinavians, and Irish after five or more generations in America suggests that in the large cities and suburbs, at least, they have remained ethnic because they have long practiced symbolic ethnicity.[33] Consequently, there is good reason to believe that the same process will also take place among ethnics of the new immigration.

Ethnic behavior, attitudes, and even identity are, however, determined not only by what goes on among the ethnics, but also by developments in the larger society, and especially by how that society will treat ethnics in the future: what costs it will levy and what benefits it will award to them as ethnics. At present, the costs of being and feeling ethnic are slight. The changes that the immigrants and their descendants wrought in America now make it unnecessary for ethnics to surrender their ethnicity to gain upward mobility, and today ethnics are admitted virtually everywhere, provided they meet economic and status requirements, except at the very highest levels of the economic, political, and cultural hierarchies. Moreover, since World War II, the ethnics have been able to shoulder blacks and other racial minorities with the deviant and scapegoat functions they performed in an earlier America, so that ethnic prejudice and "institutional ethnism" are no longer significant, except, again, at the very top of the societal hierarchies.

To be sure, some ethnic scapegoating persists at other levels of these hierarchies; American Catholics are still blamed for the policies of the Vatican, Italo-Americans are criticized for the Mafia, and urban ethnics generally have been portrayed as racists by a sometime coalition of white and black Protestant, Jewish, and other upper middle-class cosmopolitans. But none of these phenomena, however repugnant, strike me as serious enough to persuade anyone to hide his or her ethnicity. White working-class men, and perhaps others, still use ethnic stereotypes to trade insults, but this practice serves functions other than the maintenance of prejudice or inequality.

At the same time, the larger society also seems to offer some benefits for being ethnic. Americans increasingly perceive themselves as undergoing cultural homogenization, and whether or not this perception is justified, they are constantly looking for new ways to establish their differences from each other. Meanwhile, the social, cultural, and political turbulence of the last decade and the concurrent delegitimation of many American institutions have also cast doubt on some of the other ways by which people identify themselves and differentiate themselves from each other. Ethnicity, now that it is respectable and no longer a major cause of conflict, seems therefore to be ideally suited to serve as a distinguishing characteristic. Moreover, in a mobile society, people who often find themselves living in communities of strangers tend to look for commonalities that make strangers into neighbors, and shared ethnicity may provide mobile people with at least an initial excuse to get together. Finally, as long as the European immigration into America continues, people will still be perceived, classified, and ranked at least in part by ethnic origin. Consequently, external forces exist to complement internal identity needs, and unless there is a drastic change in the allocation of costs and benefits with respect to ethnicity, it seems likely that the larger society will also encourage the persistence of symbolic ethnicity.

Needless to say, it is always possible that future economic and political conditions in American society will create a demand for new scapegoats, and if ethnics are forced into this role, so that ethnicity once more levies costs, present tendencies will be interrupted. Under such conditions, some ethnics will try to assimilate faster and pass out of all ethnic roles, while others will revitalize the ethnic group socially and culturally, if only for self-protection. Still, the chance that Catholic ethnics will be scapegoated more than today seems very slight. A serious economic crisis could, however, result in a resurgence of anti-Semitism, in part because of the affluence of many American Jews, and in part because of their visibly influential role in some occupations, notably mass communications.

If present societal trends continue, however, symbolic ethnicity should become the dominant way of being ethnic by the time the fourth generation of the new immigration matures into adulthood, and this in turn will have consequences for the structure of American ethnic groups. For one thing, as secondary and primary assimilation continue, and ethnic networks weaken and unravel, it may be more accurate to speak of ethnic aggregates rather than groups. More importantly, since symbolic ethnicity does not depend on ethnic cultures and organizations, their future decline and disappearance must be expected, particularly those cultural patterns that interfere with other aspects of life and those organizations that require active membership.

Few such patterns and organizations are left in any case, and leaders of the remaining organizations have long been complaining bitterly over what they perceive as the cultural and organizational apathy of ethnics. They also criticize the resort to symbolic ethnicity, identifying it as an effortless way of being ethnic that further threatens their own persistence. Even so, attacking people as apathetic or lazy and calling on them to revive the practices and loyalties of the past have never been effective for engendering support, and reflect instead the desperation of organizations that cannot offer new incentives that would enable them to recruit members.

Some cultural patterns and organizations will survive. Patterns that lend themselves to transformation into symbols and easy practice, such as annual holidays, should persist. So will organizations that create and distribute symbols, or "ethnic goods," such as foodstuffs or written materials, but need few or no members and can function with small staffs and low overhead. In all likelihood, most ethnic organizations will eventually realize that in order to survive, they must deal mainly in symbols, using them to generate enough support to fund other activities as well.

Symbols do not arise in a vacuum, however, but are grounded in larger cultures. Moreover, insofar as ethnicity involves the notion of a heritage and an actual or imagined gloried past, contemporary symbols depend on older cultures. What kinds of symbols future generations of ethnics will want can hardly be predicted now, but undoubtedly some will want nostalgia, while others will use ethnicity as a substitute or indicator for other goals or purposes. Even now, ethnicity has served as an intentional or unintentional cover for racism, conservative political and economic ideologies, and the defense of familial and local structures and values against national forces and tendencies that drive American society further from *Gemeinschaft* and closer to a nationally homogeneous *Gesellschaft*.[34]

The demand for current ethnic symbols may require the maintenance of at least some old cultural practices, possibly as hobbies, and through the work of ethnic scholars who keep old practices alive by studying them. It is even possible that the organizations that attempt to maintain the old cultures will support themselves in part by supplying ethnic nostalgia, and some ethnics may aid such organizations if only to assuage their guilt at having given up ancestral practices.

Still, the history of religion and nationalism, as well as events of recent years, should remind us that the social process sometimes moves in dialectical ways, and that acculturative and assimilative actions by a majority occasionally generate revivalistic reactions by a minority. As a result, even ethnic aggregates in which the vast majority maintains its identity in symbolic ways will probably always bring forth small pockets of neotraditionalism—of rebel converts to sacred and secular ways of the past. They may not influence the behavior of the majority, but they are almost always highly visible, and will thus continue to play a role in the ethnicity of the future.

SYMBOLIC ETHNICITY AND STRAIGHT-LINE THEORY

The third and fourth generations' concern with ethnic identity and its expression through symbols seems to me to fit straight-line theory, for symbolic ethnicity cannot be considered as evidence either of a third-generation return or of a revival. Instead, it constitutes only another point in the secular trend that is drawn, implicitly, in straight-line theory, although it could also be a point at which the declining secular trend begins to level off and perhaps to straighten out.

In reality, of course, the straight line has never been quite straight, for even if it accurately graphs the dominant ethnic experience, it ignores the ethnic groups who still continue to make small bumps and waves in the line. Among these are various urban and rural ethnic enclaves, notably among the poor; the new European immigrants who help to keep these enclaves from disappearing; the groups that successfully segregate themselves from the rest of American society in deliberately enclosed enclaves; and the rebel converts to sacred and secular ways of the past who will presumably continue to appear.

Finally, even if I am right to predict that symbolic ethnicity can persist into the fifth and sixth generations, I would be foolish to suggest that it is a permanent phenomenon. Although all Americans, save the Indians, came here as immigrants and are thus in one sense ethnics, people who arrived in the seventeenth and eighteenth centuries, and before the mid-nineteenth-century old immigration, are, except in some rural enclaves, no longer ethnics even if they know where their emigrant ancestors came from. Admittedly, in recent years some upper-class WASPs have begun to consider themselves to be ethnics, but they have done so as a reaction to their loss of cultural power, and the feeling of being a minority that has accompanied this loss, and they have not identified themselves by their European origins.

The history of groups whose ancestors arrived here seven or more generations ago suggests that, eventually, the ethnics of the new immigration will be like them; they may retain American forms of the religions that their ancestors brought to America, but their secular cultures will be only a dim memory, and their identity will bear only the minutest trace, if that, of their national origins. Ultimately, then, the secular trend of straight-line theory will hit very close to zero, and the basic postulates of the theory will turn out to have been accurate—unless, of course, by then America, and the ways it makes Americans, have altered drastically in some now unpredictable manner.

NOTES

This paper was stimulated by S. H. Eisenstadt's talk at Columbia University in November 1975 on "Unity and Diversity in Contemporary Jewish Society." I am grateful to many people for helpful comments on an earlier draft of the paper, notably Harold Abramson, Richard Alba, James Crispino, Nathan Glazer, Milton Gordon, Andrew Greeley, William Kornblum, Peter Marris, Michael Novak, David Riesman, Paul Ritterband, Allan Silver, and John Slawson.

1. Personal communication. Incidentally, David Riesman is now credited with having invented the term "ethnicity" as it is currently used. (Hereafter, I shall omit personal communication notes, but most of the individuals mentioned in the text supplied ideas or data through personal communication.)

2. For the sake of brevity, I employ these terms rather than Gordon's more detailed concepts. Milton Gordon, *Assimilation in American Life* (New York: Oxford University Press, 1964), chap. 3.

3. Neil C. Sandberg, *Ethnic Identity and Assimilation: The Polish-American Community* (New York: Praeger, 1974). The primary empirical application of straight-line theory is probably still W. Lloyd Warner and Leo Srole, *The Social Systems of American Ethnic Groups* (New Haven, Conn.: Yale University Press, 1945).

4. See, for example, Andrew Greeley, *Ethnicity in the United States* (New York: Wiley, 1974), chap. 1.

5. W. Yancey, E. Ericksen, and R. Juliani, "Emergent Ethnicity: A Review and

Reformulation," *American Sociological Review* 41 (1976): 391–403; words quoted on p. 400.

6. The major works include Greeley, *Ethnicity in the United States*; Harold J. Abramson, *Ethnic Diversity in Catholic America* (New York: Wiley, 1973); and Nathan Glazer and Daniel P. Moynihan, *Beyond the Melting Pot,* 2nd ed. (Cambridge: MIT Press, 1970).

7. Class differences in the degree of acculturation and assimilation were first noted by Warner and Srole, *Social Systems*; for some recent data among Poles, see Sandberg, *Ethnic Identity.*

8. Herbert J. Gans, *The Urban Villagers* (New York: Free Press, 1962), chap. 11. See also Dennis Wrong, "How Important is Social Class," in *The World of the Blue Collar Worker,* ed. Irving Howe (New York: Quadrangle, 1972), 297–309; William Kornblum, *Blue Collar Community* (Chicago: University of Chicago Press, 1974); and Stephen Steinberg, *The Academic Melting Pot* (New Brunswick, N.J.: Transaction Books, 1977).

9. Marcus L. Hansen, *The Problem of the Third Generation Immigrant* (Rock Island, Ill.: Augustana Historical Society, 1938); and "The Third Generation in America," *Commentary* 14 (1952): 492–500.

10. See also Harold J. Abramson, "The Religioethnic Factor and American Experience: Another Look at the Three-Generations Hypothesis," *Ethnicity* 2 (1975): 163–77.

11. One of the most influential works has been Michael Novak, *The Rise of the Unmeltable Ethnics* (New York: Macmillan, 1971).

12. See Phil Berger, *The Last Laugh* (New York: Morrow, 1975).

13. Similarly, studies of the radical movements of the 1960s have shown that they included many people who themselves grew up in radical families.

14. See, for example, Egon Mayer, "Modern Jewish Orthodoxy in Post Modern America: A Case Study of the Jewish Community in Boro Park" (Ph.D. diss., Rutgers University, 1974).

15. Perhaps the first, and now not sufficiently remembered, study of third-generation Jews was Judith Kramer and Seymour Leventman, *The Children of the Gilded Ghetto* (New Haven, Conn.: Yale University Press, 1961).

16. Geoffrey Bock, "The Jewish Schooling of American Jews" (Ph.D. diss., Harvard University, 1976).

17. I also make the assumption that generation is an important determinant of ethnic behavior, but I am aware that it is less important than I sometimes imply; that there are large differences in the experience of a generation within and between ethnic groups; and that the immigrants' age of arrival in the United States affected both their acculturation and that of their descendants.

18. The notion of primary assimilation extends Gordon's concept of marital assimilation to include movement out of the extended family, friendship circles, and other peer groups. In describing marital assimilation, Gordon did, however, mention the primary group as well. Gordon, *Assimilation in American Life,* p. 80.

19. The major debate at present is between Abramson and Alba, the former

viewing the amount of intermarriage among Catholic ethnics as low; and the latter, as high. See Abramson, *Ethnic Diversity in Catholic America*: and Richard Alba, "Social Assimilation of American Catholic National-Origin Groups." *American Sociological Review* 41 (1976): 1030–46.

20. See, for example, Marshall Sklare and Joseph Greenblum, *Jewish Identity on the Suburban Frontier* (New York: Basic Books, 1967); Herbert J. Gans, "The Origin and Growth of a Jewish Community in the Suburbs: A Study of the Jews of Park Forest," in *The Jews: Social Pattern of an American Group* ed. Marshall Sklare (New York: Free Press, 1958), 205–48; and Herbert J. Gans, *The Levittowners* (New York: Pantheon, 1967), 73–80. These findings may not apply to communities with significant numbers of German Jews with Reform leanings. There are few Orthodox Jews in the suburbs, except in those surrounding New York City.

21. My use of the word "symbol" here follows Lloyd Warner's concept of symbolic behavior. See W. Lloyd Warner, *American Life: Dream and Reality* (Chicago: University of Chicago Press, 1953), chap. 1.

22. See Nathan Glazer, *American Judaism,* 2d. ed. (Chicago: University of Chicago Press, 1972), 114–15.

23. Sandberg, *Ethnic Identity,* Table 5-20. Understandably enough, working-class Poles felt more offended by these jokes. Table 5-19.

24. On the Jamaica Chinese, see Orlando Patterson, *Ethnic Chauvinism* (New York: Stein and Day, 1977), chap 5; on the Sydney Italians, see Rina Huber, *From Pasta to Pavlova* (St. Lucia: University of Queensland Press, 1977), part 3.

25. For a study of one unsuccessful attempt to establish a community presidency, see Arthur A. Goren, *New York Jews and the Quest for Community* (New York: Columbia University Press, 1970).

26. Charles S. Liebman, *The Ambivalent American Jew* (Philadelphia: Jewish Publication Society of America, 1973), chap. 3. Liebman noted that the few elite rabbis who did come to America quickly sensed they were in alien territory and returned to Eastern Europe. The survivors of the Holocaust who came to America after World War II were too few and too late to do more than influence the remaining Jewish Orthodox organizations.

27. Gans, "The Origin of a Jewish Community in the Suburbs."

28. See Herbert J. Gans, "American Jewry: Present and Future," *Commentary* 21 (1956): 422–30, which includes a discussion of "symbolic Judaism."

29. Fred S. Sherrow, "Patterns of Religious Intermarriage among American College Graduates" (Ph.D. diss., Columbia University, 1971).

30. See, for example, Mary E. Goodman. *Race Awareness in Young Children* (Cambridge: Addison-Wesley, 1952).

31. Sklare and Greenblum, *Jewish Identity on the Suburban Frontier,* p. 331.

32. Sandberg, *Ethnic Identity*; and James Crispino, *The Assimilation of Ethnic Groups: The Italian Case* (New York: Center for Migration Studies, 1979).

33. Unfortunately, too little attention has been devoted by sociologists to ethnicity among descendants of the old immigration.

34. The Ethnic Millions Political Action Committee (EMPAC), founded by Mi-

chael Novak, described itself as a "national civil rights committee, dedicated to a politics of family and neighborhood, to equality and fairness, to a new America." Conversely, Patterson sees ethnicity as a major obstacle to the achievement of a universalist, and socialist, humanism. Patterson, *Ethnic Chauvinism*.

Nearly two decades have gone by since I first published this paper, and many new, then unpredictable, phenomena have taken place, including the growth of the global economy and its weakening of the American economy, the extent of the post-1965 immigration and its illegal portion, as well as the just beginning negative reaction of economically squeezed and culturally threatened native-born Americans to it. Some of the trends discussed in the original chapter have persisted or have increased, for example the Jewish reactions, symbolic and otherwise, to the Holocaust. Other trends, important in 1979, like the so-called ethnic revival among European ethnics, have been forgotten. Although I do not lack for temptation to update everything I wrote then, I do lack space, and I will limit myself to seven issues from the original paper that I feel are of importance in 1995. Many of these concern ethnic and straight-line theory more than the concept of symbolic ethnicity.

First, symbolic ethnicity seems to have become a useful concept. While I have not tracked its use, over the years a number of scholars have verified its existence empirically.[1] To be sure, the concept has been repeatedly criticized as representing an inauthentic, trivial, or shallow kind of ethnicity, and authors have criticized me as well for appearing to advocate that kind of ethnicity.[2] Nonetheless, when I wrote this paper, I intended the term to be purely descriptive and analytic, making no value judgment about its desirability. This intention continues.

Indeed, I was surprised how often I was misread, even by social scientists, for while I can understand an advocate of ethnic organizations disapproving the concept, I was a bit nonplussed by authors writing in this vein as social scientists. However, ethnic research has never been noted for its interest in empirical objectivity, and too many ethnic researchers write as defenders of ethnic groups and traditions they are studying, without indicating, or perhaps even being aware, that they are taking a stand.[3]

In addition, I was misunderstood, but that is a normal experience in an author's life. Some of the misunderstandings might have been avoided if the original article had emphasized the symbolic element as merely a *necessary* factor in symbolic ethnicity, symbols being ever present in all forms of ethnicity. However, the lack of involvement in organized ethnic groups or cultures is the *sufficient* factor without which symbolic ethnicity as I conceive it is impossible.

Second, my formulation of symbolic ethnicity was also a statement about 'straight-line theory.' Originally, I viewed symbolic ethnicity as a stage in that theory, and ended the paper by raising the possibility that the

195

secular trend of straight-line theory would end with the final disappearance of the ethnic groups I was discussing, that is, the white Europeans. Although I was not alone, I failed to realize that other groups might have had different experiences because while they also had distinctive ethnic cultures and organizations, they were also racial groups.[4]

In the late 1970s, straight-line theory was still the reigning paradigm in ethnic studies, though its hegemony was clearly declining.[5] Today, straight-line theory is not only no longer dominant, but it is thought to be empirically invalid as well as being normatively undesirable. Instead, the reigning paradigm argues that, ethnicity being a constructed notion, people are able to construct, reconstruct, or invent a variety of ethnicities that can follow any 'line,' or none at all.[6]

I have never been persuaded by this total rejection of straight-line theory. While people *can* construct or invent their own ethnicity, the materials which they use in doing so have to come from what they know about their own or another ethnicity. Moreover, since acculturation and assimilation continue to take place, what they know differs from what their parents or other ancestors knew. It is therefore unlikely, if not impossible, for them to reconstruct even pale imitations of the ethnic groups or cultures of their immigrant ancestors, except perhaps as museum exhibits, or as events at an ethnic festival.

Likewise, no one can invent an ethnic group or culture that is not their own. The many intermarried ethnics now to be found in America can borrow from the ethnicity of their spouses and in-laws, but such borrowings are apt to be meager, since exogamous spouses are usually marginal to their own ethnic origins.[7]

Third, despite the decline of straight-line theory in social science thought, the theory seems to be applicable to the post-1965 immigrants for, with some exceptions, the children of the new immigrants are acculturating in much the same way as did the Europeans decades earlier.[8] Concurrently, these children are also constructing and inventing ethnic patterns that fit their perception of the economy and society they live in, and are inventing ethnic identities that earlier immigrants may not have needed. If current conditions continue, the spread and intensity of 'identity politics' may increase for some, particularly the immigrants who must deal concurrently with their ethnicity and their racial origins, and with the reactions of white nonimmigrant America to them. However, it may still be possible that the old patterns of straight-line theory, as well as the symbolic ethnicity I saw among the European third generation, will occur among the third generation of the new immigrants.

Indeed, it is even possible that by the time the third generation becomes adult, the bipolar redefinition of race into black and nonblack that is now beginning in those parts of the country that have been the main hosts for immigrants will have become fully established, and that what are now perceived as racial differences between, for example, Asian-Americans and Caucasian-Americans will no longer be noted, at least when class differences are minimal.[9]

Still, the notion that ethnicity would someday end in a totally melted American pot is not considered possible by anyone in the last decade of the twentieth century, although half a century from now straight-line theory may be once again on top of the heap. But we know now, more than we did 50 years ago, how much the requirements of national economies, polities and ideologies influence the struggles between theories, including empirically grounded ones. And no one can predict what disasters or persecutions, or the now unpredictable arrivals of new and distinctive immigrants will do to ethnicity and theories about it.

Fourth, the current—and long overdue—study of the economic roles of immigrants and ethnic groups raises new issues about the future of straight-line theory. For example, Alejandro Portes and Nin Zhou's notion of segmented assimilation not only calls attention to the variety of scenarios, particularly economic ones, currently experienced by different immigrant groups, but it also raises questions for the future.[10]

One question concerns the fate of ethnic economic enclaves, niches and the ethnic markets created by immigrant languages and immigrant food habits, as well as the likelihood of persistence over several generations. Although some ethnic economic niches that began early in the twentieth century have survived nearly 100 years later, no one can predict what the new global economy will do to them, and to new ones. For example, the children of some poorer immigrants, especially dark-skinned ones may not even have work, joining poor native-born blacks and Hispanics in unemployment.[11]

Most likely, economic segmentation in production will coexist with acculturation and the beginning of social assimilation in consumption. Thus, many members of the second generation may still work with fellow ethnics but their lifestyles will be predominantly American, and many nonblack and nonpoor children of immigrants may join mainstream suburban American society.[12]

Fifth, with the new and desirable emphasis on agency and choice in ethnicity and thus on the construction of ethnicity, it is possible that my speculations in the original article about the resort to symbolic ethnicity before the third generation may be supported by new historical research. Even immigrants who do not like their fellow immigrants, or who resign from the power struggles and other conflicts that beset ethnic organizations, or want nothing to do with the religious institutions which control ethnic culture among some immigrant groups, could develop the distanced ethnicity possible via symbolic ethnicity, and that can come at any time.[13] Here, too, however, race cannot be ignored, for as long as whites perceive immigrants or their children as nonwhite, the latter will be forced to maintain some contact with their fellows, if only for reasons of security.

Sixth, I wish I could add more here about the development of symbolic ethnicity and especially its persistence, but it is too early to answer such questions, since adult fourth-generation European ethnics do not yet show up in studies. Moreover, the research among fifth, sixth, seventh and later generations, for example, of Germans and Scandinavians that I had advocated in the original article still remains to be undertaken. Pockets of German and Scandinavian communities continue to exist in various parts of the country, however, and obviously they must act or feel ethnically in some respect to be visible to the rest of the population. Conversely, the rising intermarriage rates in all third generations, their meager connections to any single ethnicity, and the increasing scarcity of "pure" ethnics reported by Alba and others also means that pockets of the other European immigrant populations, especially those not supplemented by newcomers after 1965, will be shrinking continually.[14]

Bakalian reminded us, however, that symbolic ethnicity can persist independently of any immediate demand for symbolic products. She observed that ethnic groups now preserve some of their cultural heritage through what she called "knowledge banks," such as university chairs in ethnic studies, ethnic museums, or wings at larger museums, although such banks are apt to preserve ethnic high and elite national culture rather than popular, everyday or even peasant culture.[15] Nonetheless, her observation suggests that symbolic ethnicity does not require a living ethnic group or culture, and can be pursued through ethnic "museum culture" whether it flourishes in museums, research monographs or CD-ROMS, data banks, and their yet unknown technological descendants.

Perhaps the most interesting innovation in symbolic ethnicity since I first wrote in 1979 stems from the widespread marketing of ethnic products and even ideas all over America. As a result, Americans can now indulge in being or feeling ethnic in many ethnic groups, and can change from one ethnic group to another when they so choose. Whether they opt to eat in Ethiopian restaurants or buy Peruvian crafts in import stores, and then shift to Vietnamese restaurants and Indian crafts the next time, even the descendants of immigrants who arrived on the Mayflower can enjoy ethnic symbols. To be sure, this phenomenon is "symbolic multiethnicity" and probably differs from the more typical symbolic ethnicity discussed in the original article.[16]

Seventh, I hope, naturally, that future ethnic researchers will undertake more systematic studies of symbolic ethnicity.[17] Such studies should move beyond verifying the existence, and persistence of symbolic ethnicity, and determine how it operates, sociologically, intellectually, and emotionally, with an eye also to understanding its functions and dysfunctions, i.e., consequences for different people and strata, and its prerequisites, e.g., what kind of ethnic group or culture it requires to sustain it, if any. Later in the twenty-first century, similar studies can be conducted among the descendants of the various post-1965 immigrants. Perhaps some researchers can also use these and other data to identify new bumps in straight-line theory, or new lines that are no longer even straight, and speculate about the likelihood of an ending of ethnicity, if there should be one, as predicted by classical straight-line theory.

Such an ending could probably not occur in the twenty-first century, even if no further immigration took place. But if it did occur, the outcome might even resemble the "new American," albeit one more heterogeneous in class and race, and less godlike in morality than the new American about whom Crevecoeur and Zangwill wrote so long ago.[18]

NOTES

1. Those who found it useful include James Crispino, *The Assimilation of Ethnic Groups: The Italian Case* (Staten Island, N.Y.: Center for Migration Studies, 1980); Richard Alba, *Ethnic Identity: The Transformation of White America* (New Haven, Conn.: Yale University Press, 1990); Mary C. Waters, *Ethnic Options* (Berkeley: University of California Press, 1990); and Anny Bakalian, *Armenian-Americans: From Being to Feeling Armenian* (New Brunswick, N.J.: Transaction Publishers, 1993).

The only study I know of that did not find the concept relevant was Peter Kivisto and Ben Nefzger. "Symbolic Ethnicity and American Jews: The Relationship of Ethnic Identity to Behavior and Group Affiliation," *Social Science Journal* 30 (1993): 1–12. However, the two researchers studied a well-organized Jewish community in a small town, where for social control reasons alone, I would imagine practicing symbolic ethnicity to be impossible.

2. I have not kept track of such critics either. Conversely, Jenna Joselit wrote of my parallel notion of "symbolic Judaism" in an almost celebratory tone, describing this form of Judaism as "an inchoate and at times ineptly rendered but consistently heartfelt and deeply intended emotional and cultural sensibility." Jenna W. Joselit, *The Wonders of America: Reinventing Jewish Culture 1880–1950* (New York: Hill & Wang, 1994), 133.

3. Most of the time, I suspect they assume the desirability of the ethnic group or culture *a priori,* ignoring that other value judgments are possible. After all, why would they study their own ethnic group if not to help ensure its survival and persistence.

4. I failed to do so in 1979, but now, ethnic researchers must follow the lead of Ruben Rambaut and Mary Waters, among others, and pay special attention to the many nonwhite immigrants who must also deal with racism as they maintain, or give up, their ethnic cultures.

I did at least note that some white ethnics also had distinctive religions, but even today, some ethnic researchers still conflate such groups, for example, Jews and various Eastern Orthodox groups, with mainstream Protestant or Catholic ethnic groups. The more recent arrival or visibility of Buddhists, Hindus, Moslems, and others may finally end this conflation, and perhaps someone will even study ethnics who are also atheists. On some similarities between ethnic and religious acculturation, see my "Symbolic Ethnicity and Symbolic Religiosity: Toward a Comparison of Ethnic and Religious Acculturation," *Ethnic and Racial Studies* 17 (1994): 577–92.

5. Actually, the interest I expressed in straight-line theory in the original paper also reflected the fact that in the mid-1950s, I had already written about "symbolic Judaism," an earlier version of symbolic ethnicity, and at that time, straight-line theory had no real competition in the academy. The earlier articles appeared in *Commentary*; for citations, see note 20 of the original paper.

6. See e.g. Werner Sollors, ed., *The Invention of Ethnicity* (New York: Oxford University Press, 1989); and Kathleen N. Conzen, *et al., "*The Invention of Ethnicity: A Perspective from the US" *Journal of American Ethnic History* 12 (1992): 3–41. I defended what I now called "bumpy-line theory" in an invited comment: "Comment: Ethnic Invention and Acculturation: A Bumpy-Line Approach," pp. 43–52.

7. Today, Americans can also choose their own religions, save those not accepting converts, and in each case the converts have to learn as much of the secular ethnic cultures that are practiced by these religions so as to prevent being socially isolated. Still, new Moslems do not have to, and cannot become Arab-Americans. However, it is surely no coincidence that ethnic groups lack institutions to encourage and manage conversions.

8. Unfortunately, there is so far mainly anecdotal data, much of which is personal observations of researchers among their students. For early evidence of acculturation among the children of the first (pre-1965) Cuban immigrants, see Eleanor Rogg, *The Assimilation of Cuban Exiles: The Role of Community and Class* (New York: Abingdon, 1974).

9. This would not be entirely novel, since native-born WASPs originally opposed the poor Jews, Catholics and others who came to America from Eastern and Southern Europe after the Civil War as different, i.e., "swarthy," races. They stopped doing so, however, once the newcomers spoke English and earned sufficient incomes from respectable jobs. In the process, old differences in hair color, head shapes or other physical details originally defined as racial were no longer visi-

ble, and now the descendants of these newcomers are "white ethnics" who feel entitled to oppose those of different "race." Actually, the swarthy immigrants were anti-black even before native-born whites began to treat them as whites.

10. Alejandro Portes and Min Zhou, "The New Second Generation: Segmented Assimilation and its Variants," *Annals of the American Academy of Political and Social Science* 530 (1993): 74–96.

11. Herbert J. Gans, "Second-Generation Decline: Scenarios for the Economic and Ethic Futures of the post-1965 American Immigrants," *Ethnic and Racial Studies* 15 (1992): 173–92.

12. In this connection, Mary Waters rightly wonders whether middle-class West Indian immigrants who now use Caribbean cultures and dialects to prevent their being confused with African-Americans will be able to pass this pattern on to the second generation, since this requires the latter's being willing, and more important, able, to maintain the immigrant dialects. Mary C. Waters, "Ethnic and Racial Identities of Second Generation Black Immigrants in New York City," *International Migration Review* (Special issue: "The New Second Generation" ed. by Alejandro Portes) 23 (1994): 795–820. Of course, second-generation West Indians may invent new ways of distinguishing themselves from African Americans, if they choose to do so.

13. Joselit's *The Wonders of America* is full of examples of the early construction of Jewish symbols and the invention of symbolic products. However, these appear to be Americanized European-Jewish practices and products, or Jewish version of American ones, but they were intended for use in Jewish groups, and thus fail to meet the sufficient factor in my definition of symbolic ethnicity.

14. Alba, *Ethnic Identity.*

15. Bakalian, *Armenian-Americans,* 439–40.

16. I say probably because too little is still known about the subjective aspects of symbolic ethnicity. In any case, symbolic multiethnicity is a worthy research topic of its own. Nor should it be forgotten that all the symbols involved create jobs for someone, either in the old country or an immigrant in the United States, in the latter case supporting some kind of ethnic economic niche.

17. Actually, it is the fourth generation of the later European immigration, since the descendants of the Europeans who came around the middle of the nineteenth century, and even of the first of the Eastern and Southern Europeans who arrived in 1870 and 1880 must now be of a later generation. However, they do not seem to be visible, and thus difficult for researchers to study.

18. On these two writers, see Werner Sollors, *Beyond Ethnicity: Consent and Descent in American Culture* (New York: Oxford University Press, 1986), especially pp. 61–81. Both writers were indulging in nationalist teleology reflecting both the chauvinism and idealism of American exceptionalism. When I raise the possibility of the end of ethnicity, I see it as one of several alternative cultural–structural extrapolations, modeled on that done by demographic forecasters but based on the data on acculturation and assimilation that social scientists have accumulated during this century.

· 10 ·

SECOND-GENERATION DECLINE

Scenarios for the Economic and Ethnic Futures
of Post-1965 American Immigrants

The children of the latest "new immigration" that began after 1965 are now in school, some are already in the labor force, and by the mid-1990s their numbers will begin to increase rapidly.[1] Their entry into that force raises a host of significant questions about their economic future, questions that are relevant both to public policy and ethnic theory.

Specifically, this chapter is impelled by the fear of "second-generation decline," that is, if the American economy is not growing, some members of the second generation, especially those whose parents did not themselves escape poverty, could in adulthood finish in persistent poverty because they will either not be asked, or will be reluctant, to work at immigrant wages and hours as their parents did but will lack the job opportunities, skills, and connections to do better.

Thus, they—including the Vietnamese and other Asian-Americans, Salvadorans and other Central and Latin Americans, as well as Haitians and others from the Caribbean, Africa and elsewhere—may join blacks, and the Puerto Rican, Mexican, and other "Hispanics", who came to the cities at an earlier time, as well as "Anglos" (in some places) as excluded from, or marginal to, the economy. Indeed, even much of the joblessness, pathology, and crime of today's urban poor is associated with second-generation decline on the part of young blacks and Hispanics whose parents came to the cities a generation or longer ago and who are unable or unwilling to work in "immigrant" jobs but are excluded, for skill or other reasons, from better jobs.[2]

This chapter was first published in *Ethnic and Racial Studies* 15, no. 2 (1992): 173–92. © 1992 by Routledge. Reprinted with permission.

Moreover, when the next spurt of economic growth rolls around, the second generation of the current immigration, as well as poor blacks and Hispanics, may be further marginalized by a new wave of immigrants ready to work in "un-American" conditions. Bringing new workers ready to work at low wages and for long hours into urban areas from peasant areas overseas—as in the past from rural America—is an old American technique for renewing economic growth quickly and cheaply.

The theoretical concerns of this chapter are not limited to second-generation decline but extend also to the relations between ethnicity and economy. Specifically, I am interested in the theories of acculturation and assimilation that were first developed in connection with the southern and eastern European immigration of about 1880 to 1925. These theories were formulated during a time in which the American economy was growing more or less continuously, especially with the employment of immigrant physical labor.[3] Today, however, that economy has changed and the need for large amounts of physical labor has ended. This raises the questions of whether and how immigrant acculturation and assimilation will be affected by the change in the economy, if at all, particularly among the non-Caucasian immigrant population.

For example, the "straight-line" assimilation theory associated with Warner and Srole (1945), in which each native-born generation acculturates further and raises its status *vis-à-vis* the previous one is an almost entirely sociocultural theory that pays little attention to the economy in which the immigrants and their descendants work. Looking back now on the classic research conducted in Yankee City, this emphasis seems strange, because the empirical work for the study took place between 1930 and 1935, in Newburyport, Massachusetts, never an affluent city at best. None the less, Warner and Srole said little about whether and how the economy and economic problems affected ethnic upward mobility and the Great Depression is not even an item in the book's index. In fact, Warner and Srole (1945, 2) seem to assume that the state of the economy is not relevant, for they introduce the book as telling "part of the magnificent history of the adjustment of ethnic groups to American life," and go on to predict that "oncoming generations of new ethnics will . . . climb to the same heights that generations of earlier groups have achieved."

It is most likely that the book, which began as Srole's doctoral dissertation, reflects not the Depression era but the upward mobility of the second generation of the affluent 1920s, as well as the personal optimism of its authors and their colleagues. However, straight-line theory is still being applied, and its subsequent users, this author included, never built economic factors into it. Even so, it has remained valid for most immigrant populations so far (Alba 1990; Waters 1990).

To be sure, the line of the theory has not always been straight—bumpy-line theory might be a more apt term. Moreover, the line will not necessarily "decline" into final and complete assimilation and acculturation, and it is possible, perhaps even likely, that ethnic groups reach plateaux after several generations in which they still name themselves as members of an ethnic group but indulge mainly in a familial and leisure-time ethnicity that I have called symbolic (Gans 1979). Finally, changing economic and political conditions can produce generational "returns," or at least interruptions in acculturation and assimilation processes, although the history of the descendants of the 1880–1925 immigrants suggests that straight- or bumpy-line theory operates quite independently of the economy, with assimilation and acculturation continuing even during economic downturns.

Straight-line theory has been under considerable attack in recent decades, not for ignoring the economy or even for distorting what has actually happened over the generations, but because it has conjured up too many impersonal and permanent forces or "structures," not left enough room for human choice or "agency," and, perhaps most important, for ignoring the possibility of ethnic identity without much ethnic behavior or group participation. The new theorists are correct in pointing out that people construct their own ethnicity (e.g., Yancey, Ericksen, and Juliani 1976) or invent it (Sollors 1989), but these theorists have not paid enough attention to the fact that people also construct their own acculturation and assimilation. Thus, whatever the faults of straight-line theory, including its lack of interest in identity, the outcome predicted by it—rapid cultural Americanization and slower familial and social assimilation—is still taking place and may be occurring also among the new post-1965 immigrants.

So far the evidence for what is happening to the second generation is mostly anecdotal, and besides, that generation is still mainly composed of children and adolescents. It is, however, maturing into adulthood at a time when the lower or "secondary" sectors of the national economy, and especially the urban economies in which immigrant parents are working, are no longer growing as they were during the last European immigration. Moreover, many of the immigrants are dark-skinned and non-Caucasian and suffer from various kinds of ethnic and racial discrimination, which now seem more permanent than those suffered by the white southern and eastern Europeans when they were characterized as races.[4] While dark-skinned immigrants from overseas cultures will also acculturate, racial discrimination will not encourage their assimilation, at least not into white society. As a result, a number of questions can be raised about acculturation and assimilation, identity construction, and other processes of ethnic adaptation among the second generation.[5]

Since this chapter is largely about the unknown future, it is organized in terms of "scenarios" for the economic future of the second generation, three positive for that generation and three negative, followed by a discussion of the primary policy and theoretical questions that they raise. The three positive scenarios focus around the role of education, ethnic succession, and niche improvement, respectively; the three negative ones deal with their opposites: educational failure, the stalling of the ethnic succession, and niche shrinkage.[6]

THE POSITIVE SCENARIOS

Education-Driven Upward Mobility

The extent to which education is a significant mechanism for upward mobility is difficult to ascertain. At the turn of the century, when less than 5 percent of all Americans—and even fewer members of the second-generation ethnics—graduated from high school, even a high school diploma must have made a big difference, especially for people who had no other resources for finding jobs and had no niches into which to enter. Today, high-school diplomas are virtually taken for granted, and the college degree is quickly becoming a prerequisite for stable white-collar employment. Only a limited number of postgraduate professional and technical specialties are so short of workers that a degree in them can still guarantee upward movement via education alone.

Popular conceptions of the acculturation process have often ignored this reality, and instead assumed that the children of the European immigrants used education to move out of immigrant poverty. In fact, however, education was a major factor for the upward mobility of only a minority of the second generation, including some but by no means all of the Jews (Steinberg, 1989, ch. 3). For most other descendants of European immigrants, education probably did not make a major difference until the third and fourth generation (Greeley 1974, 72).

This scenario may be repeated once more. Today's Asian-American second generation is currently being slotted into the role of the European Jews in the contemporary version of the ethnic-success myth, although (as among the Jews) only a minority of the Asian-Americans can live up to the myth. In today's economy, as in past eras, it is the children of middle-class immigrants, Asian-American and other, who are most likely to be able to use education in upward mobility.

This time, the scenario may also apply to especially talented young people from non–middle-class homes, who will do so well in high school that they will be able to go to better-quality colleges, on scholarship or otherwise, and then on to professional or graduate school.[7] Institutions of higher education, public or private, are now so concerned with student-body diversity, not to mention affirmative action, that they are opening their doors even to children of the immigrant poor.

A related but numerically more important version of this scenario can be constructed for the many immigrant children who will use high school graduation, technical training and perhaps some years of college to help them find, or qualify them for, jobs better than those now being held by their parents, including stable and well-paid blue- and white-collar jobs in the mainstream economy. If the economy is healthy, they will probably constitute at least the plurality of the second generation.

In the longer run, education may become a more important means for upward mobility than it is today for, as firms become larger, the global economy more competitive, and the division of labour more specialized, the most up-to-date technical or professional education will become an ever-greater job prerequisite, while parental social status may become less important.[8] For example, banks will be able to survive only with the most talented executives, and past requirements like an Ivy League background will pale into insignificance.

Succession-Driven Upward Mobility

During the European immigration, a typical second-generation scenario was the move into the relatively secure but low-status blue- and white-collar jobs that WASPs and the descendants of earlier immigrations would no longer accept because they could find better-paying and more pleasant work.[9] For that generation and its children, this kind of ethnic succession never ended, so that by the 1980s, white ethnics who were still in blue-collar and non professional white-collar occupations probably held the best jobs in these strata.

Many of the kinds of jobs the second generations took over, first in the 1920s and then massively in the 1940s, have been disappearing in the last two decades, either moving out of the United States into lower-wage countries, or eliminated altogether by the computer. Thus, the ethnic-succession scenario may be coming to an end in the manufacturing sector, although it will continue in two other sectors. One is the service sector, where immigrants, or the children of immigrants, are eligible as soon as they speak English and can live up to the status-based work and behavioral codes in service firms.[10]

A second sector that may open up to the children of the new immigration consists of the small manufacturing and service firms that have sprung up to fill gaps created by the departure of large ones overseas. So far, many of these firms seem able to survive only as long as they can hire immigrants at low wages and with inferior working conditions. These include the sweatshops that have replaced the old "garment district" firms of New York and other American cities. In other industries they may be illegal firms, or legal firms staffed with illegal immigrants. Whether such firms can find sufficiently stable roles in their industries to hire second-generation people at higher wages remains to be seen.

Niche Improvement

The final scenario for second-generation upward mobility is to remain in and improve the economic niches that their parents occupied when they came to America (Waldinger 1986). Many children of European immigrants took this route, staying in parental retail stores, taverns, contracting businesses and the like, both in their own ethnic neighborhoods, black ghettos and elsewhere. Their 'choice' (and it would be interesting to discover whether they chose or had to stay in ethnic niches) became part of the American ethnic-success myth when the family food store became a regional supermarket chain; the small-town dry-goods store, a big-city department store; and the local contractor, a national development and construction company.

In most instances, the immigrant establishments grew more modestly, with the second generation perhaps taking over as owners but letting others, often from a later wave of the European immigration as well as blacks, Hispanics and others, do the work that required long hours and physical labor.

A parallel working-class version of this scenario, closer to niche retention than improvement, had immigrants in good industrial and municipal jobs pass these onto their children. Sometimes the jobs were virtually heritable via parental seniority or union rules, and sometimes there were informal arrangements in which managements seeking long-term stability encouraged their best workers to bring other family members into the firm (Newman 1988, 182). Similar arrangements were found in some public agencies, notably police and fire departments.

The retail scenario is likely to be played out again among the children of immigrant store-owners, although this time round, petty retailing may be a less successful niche, in part because of the continually growing role of national chains. However, since the large retail chains tend to locate in the suburbs and some shun the cities altogether, they have left an urban retail vacuum that is in part being filled by immigrants, and which the immigrants can at least try to hand down to their children. The expansion of the black ghettos has not only enabled a few black businesses to establish themselves, but it has also opened up new business opportunities for Korean, Indian, Yemenite, and other immigrant storekeepers, and presumably at least some of them will pass their stores on to their descendants.

New retail niches were also created in the 1980s as a result of the decision of young professionals to remain urban. For example, since many of these professionals as well as others in New York City's upper middle class, adopted "health diets," Korean immigrants were able to develop urban fruit and vegetable retailing into a flourishing business.[11] This may have been an unusual instance of being in a profitable place at the right time, however. Moreover, the Korean storekeepers, many of whom had themselves obtained college and professional degrees in Korea, are sending their children to college here and may not even want the next generation to take over the store. Similar preferences can be found among other immigrant groups; Soviet Jews are an example (Gold 1989, 429).

In addition, the long hours required by storekeeping may discourage members of the second generation from continuing with the family stores, if they have any choices. This depends, however, on alternative opportunities, such as white-collar and technical jobs in manufacturing and service firms, or positions in public bureaucracies. Perhaps some second-generation people will find or develop opportunities in wholesale or chain retailing or more prestigious forms of petty retailing, so that the children of these immigrants will move out of corner grocery shops and news dealerships into appliance or clothing stores.

The old working-class scenario is probably nearly irrelevant now, since civil service, affirmative action, the declining power of unions, and other factors have reduced the heritability of all jobs considerably, including the ethnic niches established by the European immigrants in factories and public agencies.

THE NEGATIVE SCENARIOS

Educational Failure

Most European immigrants who were not from urban or middle-class backgrounds put little emphasis on their children's education. Just the reverse: children were expected to leave school as quickly as legally and otherwise possible so that they could contribute to the family income. This pattern began to change in the 1960s, when future-oriented working-class parents first began to realize that their children would need to go to college if they wanted to get better jobs. Lack of money, opportunity, and cultural factors seem to have held back many of the young people, however, for the ethnic working class had not yet caught up with the middle class in college entry and completion, except perhaps at community and four-year city colleges.

Meanwhile, educational success and the correct educational credentials become more important in the job market, but it is already evident that for some of the children of the new immigrants, school success and even a high school diploma are not in the offing. Studies of school performance are only just beginning and many of the data are in the form of grades rather than measurements of actual performance but they suggest that, as before, the children of urban and even nonurban middle-class parents perform the best, with the children of poor peasants and others from preindustrial cultures—as well as those from families disrupted by the Vietnam war—having the hardest time (Rumbaut and Ima 1988; Rambaut 1990). Thus, the Asian-American success myth notwithstanding, Asian-American children from poor and poorly educated homes do not always obtain good grades, although they do far better than the children of Latin and Central American immigrants.

The Stalling of Ethnic Succession

When access to better jobs is difficult or when jobs are scarce, ethnic succession slows down. People hold on to their jobs as best they can, and the groups next in line in the queue have to wait. This pattern is most graphically illustrated by the length of time Italian-Americans have held on to both low- and high-level jobs in organized crime. Being unable or unwilling to find alternate careers, they have let blacks and Hispanics, as well as newer immigrants, replace them mainly in the lower level and more dangerous jobs in organized crime, notably drug selling.

I have seen no studies of the extent to which succession has ended in the legal economy, but the journalistic and impressionistic evidence suggests that the progress of the urban queue has slowed, except when firms use retirement, union busting, and other devices to force higher-paid workers out in favor of lower-paid ones. As long as jobs remain scarce, this pattern will also affect, and shrink, the fortunes of the second generation.

Niche Shrinkage

When jobs become scarce and the queue stops moving up, immigrant niches are also affected. They may not improve so as to provide job opportunities at decent wages, and they may even shrink, for a variety of reasons. Even in the best of times, ethnic retailing shrinks because of the loss of its most loyal customers, its own immigrants. Those of the second generation generally speak English and are thus not limited to the ethnic enclave; nor will they be as loyal to ethnic institutions or goods. They will not often read ethnic newspapers and will shop at the supermarket rather than at the ethnic corner shop. If the original supply of immigrants is not replenished by newcomers, retail and service activities will decline considerably, unless they can, like today's Asian-American restaurants, attract nonethnic customers.

The other reason for niche shrinkage is competition; not only can employers look for new immigrants who will work at immigrant wages, but new immigrants can themselves become employers, at least in industries that require little skill and low initial capital. Thus, they can compete with existing firms. For example, just about every post-1965 immigrant group in New York City has gone into construction, and not only within its own ethnic enclaves. As a result, it seems unlikely that any single immigrant group can achieve the kind of success needed to improve the niche significantly, and provide enough good jobs for the second generation, and perhaps in industries other than construction.

SECOND-GENERATION DECLINE

Business cycles go up and down, but the long-term periods of economic growth, the first that began after the Civil War and the second that started after World War II, are not likely to return soon. The first helped to spur the arrival of the new European immigrants and enabled them to find more or less steady jobs so that many of them or their children could escape poverty by the end of the 1920s. The second enabled the descendants of that immigration to move at least into the upper working and lower middle classes, and in many cases, firmly into the middle classes.

Even if periods of long-term economic growth return, they will probably not be equally labor-intensive. No one expects a revival in physical labor, and even many low-level service jobs may be computerized, sent abroad, or left undone. Such trends have special meaning for the new immigration and its second generation since, among other things, they could lead to what I have earlier called second-generation decline. This could happen if the children of the immigrants, having shed the immigrant parental work norms, do not find the income, job security and working conditions they expect but are not asked to take, or they turn down, jobs involving minimal security, low wages, long hours, and unpleasant working conditions, because they have become sufficiently Americanized in their work and status expectations to reject immigrant jobs.

This fate is most likely to affect the children of illegal and undocumented immigrants. Although anyone born in the United States of America is automatically an American citizen, the children of illegal newcomers are apt to come from poor homes, because their parents' origins and legal status gave them access mainly to low-wage work.

Two separate processes are involved in second-generation decline. Either the second generation can be offered immigrant jobs and can accept them or turn them down, or the children of the immigrants can be denied the opportunity to make this choice. Who will have which of these choices and who then makes what choice remains to be seen, although such studies could be done now among the children of black migrants and of pre-1965 immigrants from Mexico or Puerto Rico.

If the young people are offered immigrant jobs, there are some good reasons why they might turn them down. They come to the world of work with American standards, and may not even be familiar with the old-country conditions (or those in the Deep South) by which immigrants and southern migrants judged the urban job market. Nor do they have the long-range goals that persuaded their parents to work long hours at low wages; they know they cannot be deported and are here to stay in America, and most likely they are not obliged to send money to relatives left in the old country. From their perspective, immigrant jobs are demeaning; moreover, illegal jobs and scams may pay more and look better socially—especially when peer pressure is also present.

Whatever the processes that might then be at work, however, the first to experience second-generation decline would be poor young men with dark skin, if only because, all other things being equal, they seem to be the first to be extruded from the labor market when there are more workers than jobs (Wilson 1987, p. 43).[12] Labor markets change, however, and they could also begin to extrude poor young Asians and whites of the second generation.

As long as they are young and single, and either do not have or can avoid family obligations, these young men could choose instead to hustle or work in the underworld economy, accepting steady immigrant and immigrant-like jobs only if and when they marry and have children to support. They can also remain unmarried and live off various women, or combine this with occasional jobs and hustles. Of course, they can also enter the drug trade, whether or not they also hold other jobs on the side.

In effect, some of the immigrants' children might react in the same way as poor young urban whites, blacks, and Hispanics who have not been offered or have turned down jobs of the kind that their immigrant or migrant parents took readily when they first arrived in American cities (Sullivan 1989). One likely result of second-generation decline is higher unemployment among that generation; another is the possibility of more crime, alcoholism, drug use, as well as increases in the other pathologies that go with poverty—and with the frustration of rising expectation.[13]

Indeed, second-generation decline is likely to produce an early convergence between the present American poor and some second-generation poor, for if immigrant parents are unable or unwilling to enforce strict school—and homework—discipline, if language problems cannot be overcome, or if the youngsters, especially those who have difficulty in school early on, see that their occupational futures are not promising, they may begin to get low grades, reject schooling, and eventually drop out or get themselves pushed out of the school system.[14] Should they join the poor black, Hispanic, and other youngsters in standing jobless on street corners, they will quickly be reclassified from being the children of praiseworthy immigrants to being undeserving members of the so-called underclass.

SOME POLICY AND THEORY QUESTIONS

Since most immigrants' children are now in school and not yet in the labor force, it is essential that the school careers and the future job possibilities of these children be understood as comprehensively as possible. The most urgent priority is to study—and then find help for—the children who are not likely to find a decent job either in an ethnic niche or in the mainstream economy. I am probably being over optimistic, but since there is still some interest in helping the immigrants, and since poor ones have not yet been dismissed by assignment to the underclass, perhaps some way can be discovered to divert those who are heading toward unemployment and/or the underworld before they leave school. The most important aspect of that diversion has to be a jobs policy: to discover what kinds of jobs these young people will take, and then to create them if they are not already available. If the diversion is successful, perhaps something can also be learned to help the black, Hispanic, and Anglo youngsters who are now heading for school and economic failure in large numbers.

Many other questions, of both policy and theoretical relevance, need to be asked about the new immigrants and their children, but in what follows I will limit myself almost entirely to the poor among them. *First,* has selective migration been operating in the post-1965 immigration, and if so, is the poverty-stricken second generation apt to be less energetic and ambitious in adulthood than its parents? Or have immigrants been successful mainly because they came when jobs were available, while the second generation is less so because opportunities are scarcer? Is ambition spurred less when there is less to be ambitious about?

One of the differences between the last European immigration and the post-1965 one is that it is easier for many of the immigrants or their children to go back to the old country. Travel time is less now, even if travel costs may not be, especially for the poor. Whether any members of the second generation are able or willing to go back to the old country if there is no economic future here remains to be seen. Perhaps sojourning, a temporary stay in the United States of America, and the back-and-forth migrations of Puerto Ricans will become more widespread among other ethnic groups.[15]

What about the differences between immigrants who came for political reasons and those who came for economic ones? Assuming that the former would go home if they could, would their children look at the old country through similar eyes? Do poor political refugees who have any chance of going home try to insulate their children from American culture and to maintain old-country work habits and standards? Or will poor political refugees, or their children, find economic reasons to stay here anyway?

In all these cases, what immigrants want is not necessarily what their children do; thus, it is also necessary to ask who is, and who is not, able to keep their children from becoming Americanized, including also attitudes about work and income expectations. This is probably affected, too, by the peer groups that the young people encounter, and the economic future they see for themselves. One study of poor Haitian immigrants, who are identified with a country that seems to mean little to their children, has suggested that the children are moving into the American black community, although the study did not report whether this had economic causes (Woldemikael 1989). Now, Waters (1991) has found the same pattern among other poor black West Indians. Conversely, the New York Chassidic community has insulated itself from America more successfully than perhaps even the Amish, but because their insulation also means that they will not work for non-Chassidim, they do not have enough jobs for all who need work, and many are on welfare.[16]

The post-1965 immigration also differs in class and race from the

1880–1925 one. This time, the proportion of immigrants of middle-class origin is higher, and this should affect the economic expectations—and perhaps success—of their children. Whether they will also be subject to second-generation decline, or whether this danger is limited to the children of the poor will have to be looked at—especially if and when the American economy is weak.

Today's immigrants are also far more diverse racially and ethnically. Many of the European immigrants of the 1880–1925 period looked "swarthy" to the WASPs and the earlier northern European immigrants, but their skin color seemed to lighten as they moved up in the economy. How today's second generation will be defined, and will define itself, is still unpredictable; even the variables that will influence definition and self-definition are not yet known. Once upon a time, Asian-Americans constituted a "yellow horde" in the eyes of whites; today their skin color seems to be irrelevant, at least as long as they are middle class.[17]

Indeed, as long as class remains crucial to economic success, it may also shape who is defined and self-defined as a desirable or undesirable race and ethnic group. However, white definitional patterns also depend in part on the white ability to distinguish the middle class from the poor. As far as self-definition is concerned, Waters (1991) has found that middle-class West Indian young people tend to remain West Indian, at least in identity and social ties, both to retain their status and to discourage whites from treating them as American (read poor) blacks. Presumably the West Indian accent also helps. Conversely, "Anglos" have a much harder time telling Asian-Americans apart, as they do Central and Latin American as well as Caribbean "Hispanics." However, in judging Hispanics, skin color may be more significant than class.

What role, if any, does gender play? The European immigrants were thought to be patriarchally organized, and since many of the women did not work outside the home, and poor immigrant women appear to have an easier time in getting jobs than do men; it is they who work in the sweatshops and as domestics. What tolerance the second generation has for such jobs remains to be seen. Women who do not want to hold "immigrant jobs" may not end up on a street corner or in the drug industry, but what will they do? Whether they can avoid the single-parent family status found among poor American women may depend on how well women are sheltered by their ethnic culture, including even its patriarchal dominance patterns, nominal or real, if such persist into the second generation.

What roles do various aspects of ethnicity play? Does the cohesion of an ethnic enclave, or the attractiveness of the ethnic culture, help poor children hold on to old work habits, or slow down their Americanization when that is occupationally useful? Will kin reciprocity patterns, mutual benefit associations and other ethnic sources of capital, as well as the availability of low-cost familiar labor, disappear by the second generation? Or can that generation obtain bank loans to go into business?

Among the poorer members of the second generation, will ethnic support systems or other features of ethnicity exist to help them through the crises of poverty, and will they therefore have an easier time than appears to be the case among blacks and Hispanics, skin color being held equal? The experiences of poor immigrants in the nineteenth century as well as today would indicate a negative answer, since the destructiveness of poverty seems to overcome the strength of ethnicity, even if poor ethnics suffered less than poor blacks because of lesser racial discrimination.

Finally, what can be learned about acculturation: the effects of America, both formal Americanization, for example, through schooling, and the informal kind, through peers, the media, and the many other cultural influences that will impinge on the second generation? Here, the validity of straight-line theory is at issue, for this theory would argue that acculturation begins the moment immigrants arrive in America and accelerates in the second generation, albeit inside ethnic families and networks.

Those who emphasize that ethnicity is a matter of self-selection or invention might disagree, but in the end only empirical research can tell. On the one hand, ethnic diversity is of a higher national value these days than it was during the 1880–1925 immigration, when the pressures toward Americanization were strong, and not only if upward mobility was to be achieved.

However, in those days the cultural differences between the immigrants and the native born were more sharply defined. Since the end of World War II, and to some extent before, American popular culture and the consumer goods of the American Dream have been diffused internationally. Robert Waldinger suggested that because many of today's immigrants—especially those coming from Latin and Central America—are already familiar with much of American culture, the amount and stress of cultural change may be reduced.

Conversely, given the value now placed on ethnic diversity, and the possibility that upward mobility is no longer automatically available to the Americanized ethnic, perhaps some immigrants may try to persuade their children—or the children may persuade themselves—to hold on deliberately to all or some of the ethnic culture, language included, although today it is also possible to be mainly American in culture but to be so in Spanish.[19]

In effect, immigrants or their children may resort to "delayed acculturation," as an insulation from American work and consumption expectations so that they will not reject immigrant economic niches (Gold 1989, 421–2), or in the case of the West Indians studied by Waters, to prevent identification with a racial group of lower status. Part of the new immigrant success myth is that Asian-American parents make their children study harder than is required by American school standards, and while some do it to ensure their children's upward mobility, others may be trying to delay their acculturation as well (Rumbaut 1990, 23).

These patterns are not new.[20] Poor black and Hispanic parents have insulated their children so that they devote themselves to school rather than to the adolescent street culture of the ghetto or barrio, and at the turn of the century, some eastern European Jews and other immigrants delayed their children's acculturation in the same way with the same purpose, although we do not know how many tried and succeeded and how many failed.

Findings about this practice were not incorporated in straight-line theory, but, probably because of its macrosociological bias, this theory has never concerned itself enough with the microsociology of how the immigrants and their children actually acculturated.[21]

Whether delayed acculturation works on any but a small scale or with a very insulated population in unlikely, and success probably depends on at least four factors. First, parents have to be able to offer some reasonable assurance of future occupational and other payoff; second, the young people have to appreciate the parental effort and have enough reasons—or lack of choice—to obey,[22] third, they must be able and willing to cope with countervailing pressure from peers, and, fourth, they have to resist the sheer attractiveness of American culture, especially for young people.

Ethnic researchers nostalgic for old-country cultures have often underestimated that attractiveness. It exists in part because American culture is in many ways a youth culture, and such a culture is still lacking in most of the countries from which the immigrants came.[23] America also holds out freedoms to young people unavailable in the old country; among others, the ability to choose one's own friends, including dates sans chaperons and even sexual partners; the right of young people to develop their own interests, cultural and occupational; and the freedom of young women from the dictates of either a patriarchal or matriarchal family.[24] In fact, the perceived attractiveness of American culture substitutes in part for the dim economic future that faces some poor young immigrants, and thus may help to generate second-generation decline.

The attractions of America become even stronger if the immigrants do not plan to go back to the old country. In that case, the country and the immigrant culture quickly become irrelevant for the second generation— and the more so if the immigrants were exploited there and have little positive to pass on about it to their children, other than their family structure and norms.

This is why acculturation seem to have proceeded quickly in the past, and why I would be inclined to think that it will do so again in the future, more or less as predicted by straight-line theory. However, today's second generation is growing up in a different economy and a different culture, and perhaps this time, the acculturation will be more partial or segmental, or what Rumbaut has called bicultural.

In fact, people do not acculturate into an entire culture, which only exists in textbooks. This is especially true in America, which is too diverse to be a single culture even for textbook purposes. Perhaps researchers who study today's second generation will be able to break the host country down into the institutional and cultural sectors that are most relevant to the lives of that generation, and the processes that will shape their relationships in and to these sectors.

In any case, the term acculturation is probably too narrow, for ultimately it describes a process that combines adaptation with learning. As such, it is no different from the "urbanization" of a rural migrant, or from the learning of newly minted American PhDs when they start teaching or working in a corporation. Straight-line theory's teleological programme hid the similarities between acculturation and other kinds of forced and voluntary learning.

CONCLUSION

Both the Warner–Srole straight-line theory and the more recent construction-of-ethnicity theories appeared during a period of affluence and economic optimism, encouraging ethnics, on the one hand, to acculturate and assimilate into the affluent melting pot, and, on the other, to construct their ethnicity and their identity largely by non–economic criteria. However, many of the post-1965 immigrants are coming into a different economy, in which selective migration may count for nothing after the first generation, and traditional opportunities for the upward mobility of later generations could be absent for some or many. Indeed, straight-line theory could be turned on its head, with the people who have secured an economically viable ethnic or other niche acculturating less than did the European second and third generations.

Conversely, those without such a niche or other opportunities, who acculturate out of their parent's immigrant jobs and end up experiencing the poverty and joblessness of second-generation decline might become more American faster than other second-generation ethnics, but they would be turning straight-line theory on its head in another direction, of downward mobility. If I am right, then past and present ethnic theorizing would need to be reevaluated, and the interrelationships between ethnicity and economy would have to be given more emphasis than they have been in the theorizing of the last half century.

In any case, the popular optimism about new immigrant economic successes ought to be replaced by reliable information about which members of which groups actually succeed and why—and what can be done for the rest. The cities cannot stand a cohort of immigrants' children who will join very poor blacks, Hispanics, and Anglos on the corner or in the lines of the welfare agencies.

ACKNOWLEDGMENTS

I am grateful to Rubén Rumbaut, Roger Waldinger, and Mary Waters for helpful comments on an earlier version of this article.

NOTES

1. Traditionally, new immigration has referred to the Europeans who came from about 1880 to 1925 but they stopped being new with the arrival of the Nazi refugees in the 1930s and the Displaced Persons who came after World War II. The terms *new* and *old* have long ago lost meaning, and I will be discussing the second generation of the post-1965 immigration.

2. On the comparison of migrant blacks and their "native-born" children, see Lieberson (1980) and the research summarized in Wilson (1987, 177–8).

3. Perhaps it would be more correct to say that these theories, which were initiated by the Chicago School of Sociology, paid particular attention to upward mobility, and therefore did not notice the downward phases of the business cycle during this period.

4. The relative success of the Chinese, Japanese, and Koreans, who are non-Caucasian but also light-skinned, may thus not be accidental.

5. In an era in which downward mobility is being experienced by virtually all classes (Newman 1988), the connection between ethnicity and downward mobility can no longer be ignored.

6. My analysis focuses on the scenarios, but the various members of a second-generation group can follow different scenarios.

7. Many will probably go to work in the more practical, less prestigious professions, in which skill is not affected significantly by language ability or parental social status, such as engineering, accounting, dentistry, computer science, and a variety

of public service professions. All but the first also attracted the first college-attending generations of the Europe immigration able to obtain a professional or technical degree. Then as now, the law, the academy, and often also medicine operate with an informal prerequisite that students should have college-educated parents of upper middle-class status.

8. Parental social status may still influence the quality of preprofessional school-ing, however, and as a result, occupational and parental status may remain corre-lated.

9. This succession scenario sometimes already began with the immigrants themselves, who could compete for the dirtiest jobs in mining, the steel industry, etc., while the women worked in textile mills, food processing, and other lowest-level "pink collar" work. (Howe 1977). Ironically, these jobs were at times taken from blacks, who then got them back when the ethnic-succession process reached them once more during and after World War II, only to lose them again after 1965, either to deindustrialization or to the new immigrants who could be paid less.

10. In this case, they may once again be taking jobs away from blacks and His-panics who, as Bourgois (1991) explained in a powerful but yet unpublished paper, are sometimes unable or unwilling to follow these works, and especially deference, codes.

11. Their ascent was also aided by the fact that the children of Italian and Jewish fruit and vegetable retailers did not move into the parental businesses, presumably because of long hours, low profits, and poor working conditions. The same fate may overtake today's Korean immigrant storekeepers.

12. For some early data that second-generation Filipinos, Mexicans, and other Hispanics do more poorly in the second generation than other immigrants, see Gil-bertson and Waldinger (1993). However, their data showed that judging by per-capita income, intergenerational decline is taking place in the third generation, in this case among Mexican-Americans (*ibid,* Tables 5 and 6).

13. Another possible effect is disillusionment with the United States, which might be expressed not in the desire to leave but a romantic or nostalgic view of the old country they have never known, or the politicized, almost nationalistic, ethnicity, rarely found among the descendants of the European immigrants, but vis-ible among Mexican Americans, Puerto Ricans, and others. The Chicano and Lat-ino movements, for example, attract mainly the middle-class second and third gen-eration, but much of their anger expresses the poverty and deprivation among their fellow ethnics. These movements are, needless to say, very different from the politi-cal parties that Asian, African, and other immigrants bring with them, and that are concerned with changing governments and economics in the countries of origin.

14. Rumbaut (1991) referred to studies that have found that Mexican-born im-migrants do better in school and are less likely to drop out than American-born students of Mexican origin.

15. Roger Waldinger argued (in personal communication) that the ending of the last European immigration in 1925 helped the second generation because of the lack of competition from newcomers. The continuation of the present immigra-

tion, illegal and legal, may alter the situation for today's second generation—and, of course for poor blacks and Hispanics.

16. This raises the question of what the Chassidim will do if there are further welfare cutbacks, or when they have to register for workfare jobs.

17. But what if Japan were to become an economic enemy of the United States in the future; would the Japanese then turn into an economic yellow horde in white eyes?

18. There are scattered data to suggest that women held more power in the immigrant family than they or their husbands will admit publicly. Moreover, among the later generations, women do more of the "kin work," thus doing more also to help maintain the ethnic group (di Leonardo, 1984).

19. Rumbaut has suggested (personal communication) that among the California youngsters he is studying, acculturation may be bicultural as well as bilingual, replacing the straight-line theory pattern he calls "subjective Americanization."

20. Gibson (1989) has described this practice as accommodation without assimilation, but it seems to be similar to the acculturation without (social) assimilation that took place among the 1880–1925 immigration and has long been reported by writers following straight-line theory.

21. Needless to say, the new immigrations provide a rare opportunity for microsociological ethnographic and interview studies among the immigrants and their children about all aspects of adapting to America, including the amount and degree of acculturation in the first and second generation. None of these could be conducted during the 1880–1925 immigration itself, and few were conducted afterward because of the macrosociological emphases of the early ethnic studies.

22. This is, of course, directly contradicted by the ability of the Chassidic community to insulate its young people even without a promising economic future, but the Chassidim are a fundamentalist religious group and only secondarily an ethnic group.

23. This raises an interesting question about the extent of cross-cultural differences in national pressures and incentives for acculturation, and not only between the United States and Europe.

24. Rogg (1974) reported that familial tensions between Cuban adults and teenagers about chaperons on dates developed shortly after they arrived. Evidently it did not take the young women, themselves immigrants, long to accept the desirability of romantic activities without chaperons.

REFERENCES

Alba, Richard D. *Ethnic Identity: The Transformation of White America.* New Haven, Conn.: Yale University Press, 1990.

Bourgois, Philippe. "In Search of Respect: The New Service Economy and the Crack Alternative in Spanish Harlem," Working paper no. 21. New York: Russell Sage Foundation, May 1991.

Di Leonardo, Micaela. *The Varieties of Italian Ethnic Experience; Kinship, Class and Gender among Italian Americans.* Ithaca, N.Y.: Cornell University Press, 1984.

Gans, Herbert J. "Symbolic ethnicity: the future of ethnic groups and cultures in America." *Ethnic and Racial Studies* 2, no. 1 (1979): 1–20.

Gibson, M. A. *Accommodation Without Assimilation: Sikh Immigrants in an American High School.* Ithaca, N.Y.: Cornell University Press, 1989.

Gilbertson, Greta, and Roger Waldinger. "Ethnic Differences in the United States." Unpublished paper, April 1991.

Gold, Steven J. "Differential Adjustment among New Immigrant Family Members." *Journal of Contemporary Ethnography* 17, no. 4 (1989): 406–34.

Greeley, Andrew M. *Ethnicity in the United States: A Preliminary Reconnaissance.* New York: Wiley Interscience, 1974.

Howe, Louisa K. *Pink Collar Workers: Inside the World of Women's Work.* New York: Putnam 1977.

Lieberson, Stanley. *A Piece of the Pie: Black and White Immigrants since 1880.* Berkeley: University of California Press, 1980.

Newman, Katherine S. *Falling from Grace: The Experience of Downward Mobility in the American Middle Class.* New York: Free Press, 1988.

Rogg, Eleanor M. *The Assimilation of Cuban Exiles: The Role of Community and Class.* New York: Abingdon, 1974.

Rumbaut, Rubén G. "Immigrant Students in California Public Schools: A Summary of Current Knowledge." Baltimore, Md.: Johns Hopkins University Center for Research on Effective Schooling for Disadvantaged Students, Report no. 11, August 1990.

―――. "Passages to America: Perspectives on the New Immigration." In *America at Century's End,* edited by Alan Wolfe, Berkeley: University of California Press, 1991.

Rumbaut, Rubén and Kenji Ima. "The Adaptation of Southeast Asian Refugee Youth: A Comparative Study." Washington, D.C.: U.S. Office of Refugee Settlement, 1988.

Sollors, Werner, (ed.) *The Invention of Ethnicity.* New York: Oxford, 1989.

Steinberg, Stephen. *The Ethnic Myth: Race, Ethnicity and Class in America,* 2d ed. Boston: Beacon Press, 1989.

Sullivan, Mercer L. *"Getting Paid": Youth Crime and Work in the Inner City.* Ithaca, N.Y.: Cornell University Press, 1989.

Waldinger, Roger. *Through the Eye of the Needle: Immigrants and Enterprise in*

New York's Garment District. New York: New York University Press, 1986.

Warner, W. Lloyd, and Leo Srole. *The Social Systems of American Ethnic Groups.* New Haven, Conn.: Yale University Press, 1945.

Waters, Mary C. *Ethnic Options: Choosing Identities in America.* Berkeley: University of California Press, 1990.

———. "The Intersection between Race and Ethnicity: Generational Changes among Caribbean Immigrants to the United States." Unpublished paper delivered at the meeting of the American Sociologial Association, Cincinnati, Ohio, 23 August 1991.

Wilson, William J. *The Truly Disadvantaged: The Inner City, the Underclass, and Public Policy.* Chicago, Ill.: University of Chicago Press, 1987.

Woldemikael, Tekle M. *Becoming Black American: Haitians and American Institutions in Evanston, Illinois.* New York: AMS Press, 1989.

Yancey, William, Eugene Ericksen, and Richard Juliani. "Emergent Ethnicity: A Review and Reformulation." *American Sociological Review* 41, no. 3 (1976): 391–403.

· 11 ·

TOWARD A RECONCILIATION OF "ASSIMILATION" AND "PLURALISM"

The Interplay of Acculturation and Ethnic Retention

For much of the last half of the twentieth century, sociologists of ethnicity have been classified into two positions that are usually described as assimilationist or pluralist.[1] The positions have long been widely used, but even so they suffer from at least three conceptual and other shortcomings.

First, the empirical researchers placed in one or the other position are frequently conflated with the normative thinkers so that the former are then wrongly characterized as favoring the normative position. Sometimes empirical researchers are even being accused of hiding their norms behind empirical language. A possible solution, for which it is probably too late, would be to use different concepts for empirical and normative purposes. In any case, my purpose in writing this chapter is strictly empirical.

Second, even among empirical researchers, the discussion about whether the descendants of the now "old" European immigration and the mainly non-European members of today's "new" immigration are assimilating socially, economically, and culturally or whether they are retaining significant ties to their ethnic heritage has become polar. As a result, what is in reality a range of adaptations is sometimes turned into a dichotomy—and a moral one—with the alleged assimilationists, and particularly "straight-line theorists," becoming the villains in a social scientific morality play.

Third, the labels attached to each position are adding to the polarization, for they are misleading. The so-called assimilationists have actually been emphasizing acculturation (becoming American culturally but not necessarily socially), while pluralism has taken on such a multiplicity of

From C. Hirschman, J. DeWind, and P. Kasinitz, ed. *Becoming American.* (Working Title) New York: Russell Sage Foundation, 1999. Reprinted with permission.

meanings that it is no longer useful as an empirical concept. Consequently, I will call the latter—i.e., those who seek to avoid acculturation and to retain their ethnic ties—*ethnic retentionists,* and shall hereafter write about acculturationists and retentionists.

When positions are polarized and start hardening into theoretical ones inured to further data, empirical research—and straight thinking with it—suffer.[2] Before the study of the new immigration is distorted in this fashion, the either-or polarization should be put to rest as soon as possible.

Fortunately, the polarization is almost entirely unnecessary, and this essay suggests a reconciliation between the two positions.[3] It does so by using two arguments. One argument is that, if acculturation is distinguished from assimilation, it is clear that acculturation begins in the immigrant generation, although researchers may qualify it as "partial" or "additive" (Gibson 1988). It is not accompanied by assimilation, however. Even the third generation, which may have become almost entirely acculturated, still retains a significant number of ethnic social ties, particularly familial ones, and has not assimilated. However, this is not at odds with ethnic retention theory, for most of its advocates are concerned mainly with the retention of ethnic social ties, and place less emphasis on cultural retention.

The other argument suggests that whatever empirical differences remain between the two empirical positions may be a result of differences both in the research and in the researchers, particularly those collecting their own survey, interview, or ethnographic data. The original students of the European immigration who developed the acculturationist position probably obtained much of their data from second-generation adults, while the data about the new immigration is coming mainly from first-generation adults. Although studies of the second generation are becoming increasingly popular already, these have been conducted so far mainly among schoolchildren and teenagers who still live with their parents and are under more retentionist pressures from their parents than they will experience later.

Furthermore, the major researchers and theorists of the European immigration were, as Merton (1973) put it, outsiders, who were neither members of, nor had any great personal interest in, the groups they studied. Many of their contemporary successors are, however, insiders, who often come from the ethnic groups they are studying and are often personally concerned with the survival of these groups. Thus, as a result of who was studied and of the perspectives of the two cohorts of researchers has come an overly acculturationist theory of the old immigration and an overly retentionist theory of the new immigration.

Like Merton, I use insiders and outsiders as empirical concepts, and the observations made here and later in this chapter are not intended as criticism of either. The research of both is needed for the full understanding of any set of immigrants or other group.[4]

ACCULTURATION AND ASSIMILATION

My distinction between acculturation and assimilation is hardly original, for it was conventional usage at the University of Chicago in the late 1940s. I use it here because I consider it more helpful to understanding immigrants and their descendants than the single concept used by Alba and Nee (1997) or the overly detailed seven-item concept proposed by Gordon (1964). The Chicago distinction, of which both Gordon and Alba and Nee are aware, is based on the difference between culture and society, and accordingly, acculturation refers mainly to the newcomers' adoption of the culture, i.e., behavior patterns or practices, values, rules, and symbols of the host society (or rather an overly homogenized and reified conception of it). Assimilation, on the other hand, refers to the newcomers' move out of formal and informal ethnic associations and other social institutions into the host society's nonethnic ones.[5]

The major virtue of the original Chicago distinction is to underline the generations of empirical research demonstrating that acculturation and assimilation operate at different speeds (Rosenthal 1960). By the third generation, the descendants of the newcomers are culturally almost entirely American, and often lack interest in or even knowledge of their ancestors' origins. Still, the opportunity for any but the most formal or superficial assimilation into American primary and secondary groups may not even become available until the third generation.

There are at least two reasons why acculturation is always a faster process than assimilation. That ever-changing mix of old WASP and modern immigrant features that we call American culture is an immensely powerful attractive force for immigrants—and was already powerful even when the mass media came in the form of silent movies.[6] Therefore, it easily entices the children of most immigrants, particularly those coming from societies that lack their own commercial popular cultures and that force these children to behave like little adults. Indeed, historically few ethnic cultures have been able to compete with American popular culture, and even religious groups that keep their young people separate from it, like the Amish and Chassidim, must provide some form of substitute. This could change, at least for today's immigrants who come from countries with their own commercial popular cultures, although for the moment, most of the world's popular cultures are still young enough to be influenced by, or to be imitations of, American popular culture.[7]

Second, ethnics can acculturate on their own, but they cannot assimilate unless they are given permission to enter the "American" group or institution.[8] Since discrimination and other reasons often lead to the denial of that permission to the immigrant and even the second generation, assimilation will always be slower than acculturation.[9]

When the assimilation-acculturation distinction is used in research, researchers will immediately notice the virtually inevitable lag of assimilation behind acculturation. If researchers' personal values do not influence data collection, and all other things are equal, empirically inclined retentionists should come up with virtually the same results as their acculturationist peers: that little assimilation is taking place even as the old country culture erodes. In that case, however, the empirical differences between the acculturationists and retentionists begin to shrink, at least if conceptual differences do not get into the way. Moreover, even the normative dispute should decline, at least among retentionists who place great value on the survival of the ethnic community but are less concerned with the preservation of the immigrant culture.

To be sure, the distinction between the cultural and social I have drawn here cannot always be applied empirically, for the retention of the ethnic community also involves the retention of some ethnic cultural practices, particularly those that are intrinsic to ethnic institutions, such as the family and other primary groups, and therefore cannot be ended without virtually destroying these groups. For example, if members of the second generation remain loyal to the immigrant family and honor the obligations it demands, these members must also retain some cultural practices they might otherwise shed. Thus, members of the second generation may retain the ethnic language because this is how they communicate with the parent generation.[10]

If ethnic researchers did not rely so often on overly simple survey research, however, and if the bilingual second generation were asked such questions as whether it retained its bilingualism voluntarily or involuntarily, the researchers might discover that language retention is not necessarily a rejection of acculturation but a prerequisite for maintaining familial relations. If researchers were to ask second-generation ethnics what they would do if they had a choice, many might indicate that they would give up the ethnic language, along with "meaningless" and "boring" family practices that were brought over from the old country.

In other words, involuntary retention of the ethnic language is an indicator of ethnic retention only if interviewees indicate they would also retain the language voluntarily; otherwise, involuntary retention should be coded as an indicator and correlate of family obligations.[11] Likewise, young second-generation women who honor the parental taboo against outmarriage have to forgo some acculturation involuntarily, such as American dating practices that they might choose if they were free to do so.

One reason students of ethnicity may not have been concerned with the voluntary-involuntary distinction in the retention of culture and ethnic attachments may lie in the failure of existing theories to encourage such a distinction. The theorizing of the acculturationists has not made much room for motive or intent of any kind, mainly because the Chicago school from which they are descended has thought in terms of impersonal processes rather than of human agents and choices. In addition, the early researchers, to be discussed further below, who were consciously or unconsciously in favor of "Americanization" (which sometimes included both acculturation and assimilation) probably assumed that immigrants and their descendants wanted to become Americans as quickly and completely as possible, an assumption that may have been justified among many of the immigrants to whom researchers from this school had access, particularly those who were refugees from political oppression or economic hopelessness. No one now knows whom they could not study, however, but presumably many of those uninterested in Americanization were not available for study because they did not speak English or went back to the old country.

Conversely, the retentionists, past and present, have had no interest in whether cultural retention is voluntary or not, because their assumption, and their normative predisposition, is that retention continues to exist. Thus, they would not be inclined to ask how many second-generation youngsters endured immigrant cultural practices mainly so as not to annoy parents or dishonor grandparents.

Similar questions can be raised about the school performance studies that now still dominate the study of the second generation. Some of these studies indicate that youngsters who are integrated into the ethnic community, or continue to speak the immigrant language, often do better in American schools than their less integrated or less bilingual peers (Portes and Schauffler 1994; Rumbaut 1994, 1995; Shou and Bankston 1994). Still, no one can yet tell whether their bilingualism is voluntary, although they may be too young to have a choice between voluntary and involuntary bilingualism especially in immigrant groups that harbor hopes of returning to the old country.

Moreover, since much of the evidence of school performance comes from a mixture of school grade reports and survey data using single indicators, it is too early to determine conclusively that bilingualism, other kinds of cultural retention, or community integration are significant causes of better school performance. Other correlated variables may be at play, and besides, studies of second-generation youngsters can never fully determine how much their performance is a result of parental pressure to achieve family upward mobility that the immigrants themselves could not achieve. The fact that school performance declines with the third generation among some immigrant groups that have already been here for several generations (e.g., Rumbaut 1990) suggests once more that immigrants may be different from their American descendants.

Be that as it may, however, the ethnic retention of the first generation can be reconciled with whatever acculturation takes place among its members at the same time. In fact, the two processes can probably be shown to take place concurrently—if researchers ask questions about both.[12] Even in the second generation, when acculturation usually increases, ethnic retention will still exist, some of it voluntary and probably more of it involuntary. The two processes can still coexist in the third generation, for even if its members should repeat the experience of the European immigrants and begin to assimilate, they will retain a number of ethnic relationships and some associated ethnic practices. Furthermore, since so many members of the new immigration are nonwhite, the grandchildren, particularly of black immigrants, will likely still suffer from racial discrimination, and are thus sure to retain yet other ethnic relationships and practices, even if not always voluntarily. The extent to which this will happen depends on the state of future American race relations (Gans 1999).

ETHNIC RECONSTRUCTION AND INVENTION

The reconciliation of acculturationists and retentionists can also be extended to what might be called the post-acculturationist school of ethnic reconstructers and inventors. That school, as typified by Yancey, Ericksen, and Juliani (1976), Sollors (1989), Conzen et al. (1992), and their colleagues participated in a debate over the later generations of the old immigration before the new immigration became visible to researchers and so far has not yet extended its empirical work to the new one. Nonetheless, the same debate may someday be revived among the descendants of the new immigrants to argue that ethnic culture does not become a victim of acculturation, but is reconstructed or invented anew all the time.[13]

The extension of my reconciliation would begin by questioning the assumption of the original ethnic researchers that immigrants come to the

United States with an old country culture, which is so homogenous and holistic that it could be codified in a textbook. In reality, however, there is no textbook or even an oral version thereof, for every immigrant family comes with its own ethnic practices, which are most likely a mix of handed-down memories of family, community, and regional practices.[14] These the family then adapts to America, negotiating with advocates of traditionalism and change in the family and in the (American) community. Indeed, holding the loyalty of the young in the second generation—and even more so in later ones—is apt to require not just negotiation but the very reconstruction and invention that Yancey, Conzen, Sollors, and their colleagues proposed.

Even so, what families and other groups carrying out ethnic practices reconstruct and invest begins with what the older people know and ends with what the younger ones objecting to the old country practices are willing to accept, especially with the younger usually being more American, modern, or prestigious.

As a result, what looks like reconstruction or invention to one school of researchers, including reconstruction for the sake of ethnic retention, may not always be very different from what looks like acculturation to the acculturationists. This applies particularly to those researchers whose preference for macrosociological analysis blinds them to the microsocial bits and pieces that actually go into macrosociological processes. For example, "Bas Mitzvah," the Jewish initiation rite for 13-year-old girls, was invented in the United States to legitimate the role of women in the Jewish community, but it was also an instance of acculturation that reduced the traditional patriarchal inequality of European Jewish religious practices.[15] My favorite secular example is from the second-generation Italian Americans I studied in Boston (Gans 1962) who invented their own Italian Thanksgiving dinner by serving turkey with their favorite holiday pasta dishes, combining a very American food, and holiday, with their list of old country dishes and celebrations.

IDENTITY AS ACCULTURATION OR RETENTION

One of the current buzzwords in immigration and ethnic research (and politics) is *identity,* which is often assumed to be an automatic instance of retention. Systematic research into identity, ethnic and racial, among members of the new immigration is just beginning, and operational and other definitions of the term remain scarce.[16] I would prefer to limit identity to strongly held feelings and associated actions concerning some aspect of ethnicity, but most studies so far have looked at identity as less intense feelings or practices, such as self-naming (Alba 1990, see also Waters 1990) or self-identification (e.g., Rumbaut 1994).[17] Consequently, no one yet knows whether personal or group identity is associated with either retention or acculturation, not to mention assimilation.

The development of identity feelings and actions that began in the 1980s among the new immigrants has been most visible in some cities and university campuses. Indeed, it could be an aftermath of student versions of the African-American Black Power movement of the 1960s, or perhaps also of an emerging identity movement among American intellectuals, artists, and academics from European ethnic groups that same decade, which was properly but incorrectly interpreted as a larger ethnic revival among "white ethnics" (Gans 1979). However, what might today be called identity has long expressed itself on a small scale on factory floors and other work places where minor conflicts of various kinds have often been displaced on ethnic joking (Halle 1984, 181). Overt ethnic conflicts, including violent ones, in which ethnic identity also plays a role, have been part of American history for a long time.

It is too early to tell what forms today's major expressions of identity—personal, group or both—will take among the new immigrants and the second generation because most members of the latter are still too young for college or the workplace. In addition, identities may change in the passage from adolescence to adulthood. Perhaps some of these expressions will be associated with cultural retention and an effort to resist the temptations of assimilation that are sometimes available to nonwhite second-generation college students heading for predominantly white campuses. Moreover, identities can also be reactions to events in the larger society, so that, for example, the resurgence of ethnic identity feelings among California Mexicans could be a response to that state's anti-immigrant politics (Rumbaut 1997).

Alba (1990) and Waters (1990) had already indicated that ethnic self-naming or self-identification is usually accompanied by continued acculturation and assimilation, including intermarriage. However, even the more intense search for personal identity, either at the level of feelings or action, can be an accompaniment to acculturation and even assimilation, with identity becoming an actual or symbolic substitute for ethnic cultural practices and affiliations. In fact, developing an identity or getting involved in identity groups can sometimes be easier, especially for the second generation, than trying to fight the temptations of acculturation or retaining "boring" ethnic practices. In any case, there need be no inherent contradiction between identity and acculturation, and the two processes can operate independently.

Moreover, the history of the European immigrants suggests that identity is more apt to develop among ethnics living amidst nonethnics, as on college campuses, in multiethnic neighborhoods or in ethnic areas fighting external threats such as the arrival of low-status newcomers. Conversely, people who are embedded in homogeneous ethnic neighborhoods or organizations and have little to do with nonethnics do not even need to be aware of their identity. A good example is New York City's socialist movement, which was so heavily Jewish that immigrants and second-generation Jews in the movement had no reason to pay attention to their ethnic identity.[18]

Ethnic identity is even compatible with assimilation. For example, ethnic group leaders may lead public lives in the ethnic community while devoting part of their private life to assimilatory activities, including those leading to their upward mobility. Furthermore, since part of their ethnic leadership requires them to associate with leaders from the dominant groups in society, they may even be participating in some on-the-job assimilation, voluntary and involuntary, if only in order to be able to work with leaders of dominant groups (e.g., Kasinitz 1992).

Racial minorities diverge in these respects from ethnic groups, because racial identity, or at least racial pride, is almost always required to fuel the struggles against the white majority. Immigrants who are also members of racial minorities may be shedding their old country culture, but whatever their ethnic identity, the racial identity they have had to develop in the United States may have unexpected implications for their ethnic identity (e.g., Rumbaut 1997).

Since immigrants and the next generation are apt to be involved in future conflicts over multiculturalism, culture wars, and identity politics, researchers will have many opportunities to chart the connections between these activities, acculturation and ethnic retention. They can also observe whether and how seemingly dissimilar reactions can occur concurrently.

IMMIGRATION AND ETHNIC RESEARCHERS

A final way of approaching the reconciliation of the acculturationists and retentionists involves the researchers themselves. We, the people who are doing the actual research, too often leave ourselves out of the analysis because the field still retains remnants of the asocial positivism, once dominant in the social sciences, which ignored the social beings who were doing the research. The moment the researchers understand that they are an intrinsic part of their own research, however, and those concerned with the European immigration and today's newcomers are compared, two differences that can affect their findings, and thus also their respective positions, become apparent.[19]

First, the two sets of researchers have studied immigrants at different times; and second, they are themselves different in origin and values. With some exceptions, the researchers who studied the European immigrants did not really begin their empirical research until the 1920s, at least forty years after the first eastern and southern Europeans arrived in large numbers. The major empirical study of the Chicago school, Louis Wirth's *The Ghetto,* was published in 1928; and the major ethnic volume of the 1930s Yankee City studies of W. Lloyd Warner and his associates, by Warner and Srole, appeared in 1945. The first major sociological study of Italians in America was by Ware (1935); the second, by Child, appeared in 1943.[20]

Moreover, only a few of the sociologists of the time came from eastern or southern European backgrounds and thus did not speak, or were encouraged to learn, the immigrant languages. As a result, the researchers probably got most of their data from the second generation, including much of what they learned about the immigrants. Consequently, the picture of a homogeneous and holistic immigrant culture was most likely affected by nostalgic recall.

More important, what was most visible to the researchers among the second generation was its public acculturation rather than its more private ethnic retention. In addition, as I pointed out earlier, the researchers could not have met many of the most determined retentionists, since these would have returned to the old country before World War I. However, they also saw no social assimilation, either because it did not exist sufficiently often, or because they failed to notice it, or both.[21]

It is no wonder then, that the early researchers supported the assimilationist theory Robert Park had first developed in the 1910s, although that Park, if not his actual students, influenced the next generation of ethnic researchers was surely relevant as well.

Furthermore, the European immigrants came to America at a time of rapid and almost continuous economic growth. While some worked in ethnic enclaves and never had to learn English, many were employed in the larger American economy. Economic growth encouraged departure from the ethnic enclave, however, and that in turn encouraged acculturation. To be sure, the business cycle did not abate when the immigrants came, but no social scientists were around to study how the immigrants fared during the terrible depression of the 1890s, or even during the one that followed just after World War I. Admittedly, the Yankee City studies took place during the Great Depression, and no one has yet figured out how and why the ethnics of Newburyport, Massachusetts, hardly an affluent city even in better times, continued to acculturate, and to provide one of the models for straight-line theory.

The researchers who are now studying the new immigration report on a very different set of newcomers. For one thing, they began their research much more quickly than the earlier researchers, and have obtained their data directly from the first generation. Moreover, that first generation is very different from the one written about by the researchers of the old European immigration. Among other things, many are also middle class and highly educated, especially among the Southeast Asian, South Asian, Middle Eastern, and Caribbean immigrations, and thus very different from the almost entirely poor and often illiterate immigrants that came from Europe a century or more ago.

Since today's researchers are studying the immigrants, they naturally see more retention than acculturation (Alba and Nee 1997, 850). Because so many are nonwhite, they will experience even less social assimilation; and because the parts of the economy in which many of today's immigrants work are growing less slowly or more irregularly than those of a century ago, they will experience less economic assimilation too.[22] In addition, the researchers are obtaining more accurate pictures of the old country cultures (few as preindustrial as those left behind by the old European immigrants) than the museum-like versions the first ethnic researchers learned from the second generation they studied.

But because today's researchers are seeing first-generation life up close, they also see its dynamic qualities, the immigrants' need or temptation to change practices and associates in unpredictable ways to respond to the opportunities or exigencies of the moment, and to retreat to the bosom of the ethnic or racial group when dominant group politics turns against them or other disasters strike. Last but not least, as I suggested previously, the second generation they now see still lives largely at home, and must obey ethnic and other parental dictates.

No wonder, then, that theories of assimilation make little sense to many of today's researchers, and that some feel the need to express their doubts about such theories. They see little or no acculturation among the first generation, and even less assimilation. In the second generation, they are gathering evidence of ethnic retention, especially among middle-class youngsters (e.g., Rumbaut 1995), even as they report the acculturation and attempted assimilation of lower-class adolescents, for example, West Indians and Vietnamese, who reject their old country origin to join (or try to join) native-born neighborhood gangs (Woldemikael 1989; Zhou and Bankston 1994).

All this differs sharply from most of the findings reported about the earlier immigrants—and the assimilation or straight-line theory applied to them. While the rejection of straight-line theory by today's researchers is understandable, it may also be somewhat premature, and may yet be contradicted when today's second generation reaches the same life-cycle position as the second generation studied by the researchers of the old immigration.

The Researchers, Old and New

There is, however, yet another set of reasons why today's ethnic researchers see so much ethnic retention where their predecessors saw acculturation. The first ethnic researchers were largely *outsiders vis à vis* the people they studied; today's are more often *insiders,* and that difference further helps to explain their divergent findings.[23]

The distinction between insiders and outsiders is not as hard and fast as, and also more complex than, the two terms make it appear; accordingly, the terms are also not easily defined. For my purposes here, insiders and outsiders can be defined—overly simply to be sure—either by their ancestry or their values, or by both criteria.[24] If the definition emphasizes ancestry, the issue is whether or not the researchers share the ethnic, racial, or other origins of the people they study. When the researchers cannot be asked directly, last names sometimes offer a clue to ancestry.

If the values criterion is applied, the issue is whether the researchers favor ethnic retention, cultural and/or social, or whether, whatever their values as outsiders, they are neutral toward and unconcerned with the groups' ethnic futures. This criterion is fairly easy to apply in empirical research if and when researchers build their values explicitly into their research questions or state them openly. The task becomes more complicated when values must be inferred from the theoretical and empirical questions researchers ask or the concepts and frames they use.[25]

The studies of researchers remain to be done, and what follows here is a set of hypotheses about the insider-outsider status of the two eras of immigrant researchers, with an emphasis on the sociologists among them who conducted empirical studies.

Most of the researchers who first studied the European immigration were outsiders—and for two good reasons. *First,* American empirical sociology did not exist when the European immigration began in the 1870s. Indeed, much of the Chicago School immigration research took place in and after the 1920s, when Congress ended the European immigration. *Sec-*

ond, the European immigrant groups were too poor to have their own social science researchers.[26] In fact, it took most of two or three generations—
and the help of the "G.I. Bill" after World War II—to choose social science
research careers.

As a result, the pioneer immigrant researchers, for example, Robert
Park, Ernest Burgess, W. I. Thomas, Caroline Ware, and Lloyd Warner,
were mostly WASPs, although hardly in the upper class. Almost all were
also assimilationists, but not necessarily deliberate ones. If they favored the
Americanization of the immigrants, they unthinkingly reflected both the
conventional wisdom and values of their era and their class, particularly in
the decades when a kind of retentionist alternative was mainly to be found
in anthropology.

Rather, they were researchers who considered themselves value-neu-
tral even if they were not. Too many sometimes used the racist vocabulary
then still applied to immigrants and their descendants, and most ignored
the nonwhite immigrants who also came to America during the European
immigration (DeWind and Kasinitz 1997, 1104).[27]

A few of the first empirical researchers were insiders by background,
for example, Louis Wirth and Leo Srole who were Jewish, but virtually
all were outsiders in terms of their values.[28] After World War II, however,
sociologists from a variety of ethnic backgrounds and predominantly from
the second generation, undertook empirical research. A large number applied outsider values, including those who wrote only about their own
group, as well as those who moved into comparative ethnic research, for
example, Milton Gordon and Tamotsu Shibutani; and in the next cohort,
Steven Steinberg and Mary Waters, among others.[29]

Concurrently, however, other sociologists of ethnic origin from the
same post-World War II cohorts have written as apparent or actual retentionists. Although they may report evidence of acculturation, they emphasize exceptions or accompany their findings with warnings that the ethnic
community—or in the case of Jews, the religious one—must act to stop
these trends. In the Jewish community, they have sometimes been described as survivalists, and include Stephen Cohen, Nathan Glazer, and
Marshall Sklare. Like-minded researchers from other ethnic groups are, for
example, Richard Gambino, Andrew Greeley, and Peter Kivisto.[30]

The students of the new immigration seem to be following a speeded-
up version of the pattern that developed among their European predecessors. The first researchers were once more outsiders, among them Edna
Bonacich, Ivan Light, Philip Kasinitz, and Roger Waldinger. However, the
newcomers of middle-class origin often included some social science researchers or sent their young people, a few from the 1.5 generation, into

graduate sociology programs. Many have come from Southeast Asian families, among them Won Moo Hurh, Illsoo Kim, Pyong Gap Min, and Min Zhou, although South Asian, Middle Eastern, African, Latino, and Caribbean researchers have also entered the field.

The immigrant, 1.5, or second-generation newcomers are insiders by ancestry, and many study, or begin their careers by studying, their own groups. As early as 1984, 86 percent of the references in a "Selected Bibliography on Korean-Americans" bore Korean or other Southeast Asian names (Hurh and Kim, 1984, 259–71).[31] My impression, which still requires empirical testing, is that many often follow insider values as well.

This pattern is continuing among new cohorts of young researchers in the 1990s. Thus, a study of 138 researchers applying for grants (most for dissertations) to the Social Science Research Council's Migration Division in 1997 showed that 53 percent were studying their own groups; 18 percent were looking at groups other than their own, and 29 percent were writing on general or comparative topics.[32] However, among the 65 applicants whose racial or ethnic background suggested that they or their parents were newcomers, 80 percent were studying their own group, and 20 percent were writing on general topics.[33] No one was studying groups other than their own.

There are two exceptions to the insider pattern described here. One is disciplinary, for only a fifth of all political scientists applying to SSRC but 70 percent of the sociologists were studying their own group.[34] While it is possible that disciplinary career pressures account for this difference, a more likely explanation is self-recruitment. Sociology has always attracted significant numbers of immigrants or their descendants, at least in the twentieth century.[35]

The other exception to the insider pattern described here is associated particularly with poor or non-English speaking immigrant groups that have not yet produced social science researchers. Thus, the earliest student of such poor Southeast Asian groups as the Hmong, the Laotians, and the Cambodians, has been the Cuban immigrant Rubén Rumbaut, although his comparative study was initially planned to include a sample of Cuban immigrants as well.[36] The first writings about the Russian newcomers have come from native-born American researchers such as Rita Simon, Nancy Foner, and Steven Gold. Some groups have been studied by both insiders and outsiders, for example, Mexicans, Puerto Ricans, West Indians, and South Asians.

Since most of the newcomer studies are about the immigrants, research about them will necessarily yield a predominance of retentionist findings, since few newcomers, at least among the adults, will have had time for much acculturation—or for attaining a position allowing them to assimilate into American groups. That so many of the researchers are insiders only reinforces this pattern, especially if and when the insiders also adhere to retentionist values. Still, even outsiders who study the first generation are likely to find more retention than acculturation, not to mention assimilation.

Various other characteristics of the new immigration research can be explained by the fact that the subjects of study are immigrants. One is the emphasis on so-called entrepreneurial activities, since immigrants with any kind of capital have traditionally turned to storekeeping or petty manufacturing, using their profits to educate their children for higher-status jobs. Most likely, they are also more often retentionists than people who go to seek their fortune in the larger economy—if only for the instrumental reason that their incomes often depend on their fellow immigrants.[37]

The second generation, once grown into adulthood, will, however, have some choice between various kinds of retention and acculturation. Those who intermarry, particularly with whites, can even achieve assimilationist goals, thus overturning the old finding derived from the European immigration that intermarriage and other kind of social assimilation are only available to later generations.

Unless political or economic conditions bring about a sudden halt to further immigration, many of today's immigrant groups are going to be replenished by further sets of newcomers just as the second generation of the post-1965 arrivals begin to enter adulthood. Nonetheless, their degree of choice about retention and acculturation should not be affected by the concurrent replenishment process.[38] As a result, whether the researchers who study this second generation are outsiders or insiders, in background and/or values, will begin to matter, for the researchers could use their values, theories, and concepts to produce findings that diverge, at least to some extent, from the behavior and values of the people they study.[39] Still, what they could do in theory is no guide to what they do in practice. After all, it is also possible that the second generation of researchers who will begin to appear in visible numbers some time early in the 21st century will not consist of the same kinds of insiders and outsiders as today's researchers.

CONCLUSION

The study of the new immigration is only just beginning, and as already indicated, most of the ideas about the second generation so far have been based on data about schoolchildren. "So far" is an important qualifier, however, and as immigration research expands, and the second and then the third generation grow to adulthood, studies of the new immigration are apt to come up with other findings than today's. Although we now know how much assimilation depends on economic and political processes that either make immigrants and their descendants attractive or threatening to other Americans, the findings about acculturation may in the longer run not be very different from those accumulated about the European immigration.

They cannot be the same findings because America and the world have changed drastically since the Europeans came to America. In addition, while the Europeans were also viewed as darker races when they arrived, they were able to become white more easily than many of today's "nonwhite" immigrants.

My personal hunch is that, in the long run, students of the new immigration will report many of the past findings of rapid acculturation and slower assimilation. However, as long as researchers are divided into insiders and outsiders, a modified version of the present division between acculturationists, value-neutrals, and retentionists will also continue.

Whatever the disadvantages of that tripartite division and the disagreements it generates, there are also advantages. Despite the wish of some sociologists for less "fragmentation" and for the restoration of a "core," such a core is also apt to be dominated by one paradigm or "school," with a decline of vitality as one result.

The reappearance of a "core" in immigration research seems unlikely, however, and the present diversity of researchers and frames may even increase. The members of this diverse field should therefore know—or learn—how to understand their differences, and understand also how much they themselves contribute to divergent findings and theories.

Consequently, they must transcend the largely dismal record of self-awareness and self-examination encouraged by positivism and scientism, and begin instead to study their own research—and themselves—as a regular part of their research. If socially structured, such reflexivity will help make sure that differences of findings or perspectives do not turn into polarization and transform disagreeing researchers into enemies or villains.

In the long run, the danger of polarization should decline as the proportion of insider and outsider researchers is more balanced, and the special contributions each can make are realized. In addition, the continuing diversity of the American population, enhanced no doubt by future sets of newcomers, will not be kind to theoretical and other intellectual polarizations among the researchers.

NOTES

My thanks to Richard Alba, Margaret Chin, Stephen Cornell, Jennifer Lee, Roger Waldinger, and an anonymous reviewer for helpful comments on earlier versions of this paper.

1. The same division has existed among sociologists studying religions associated with ethnic groups, such as Judaism.

2. I should note that such theoretical polarization is more likely if it accords with or accompanies political-ideological polarization, for example, about issues that divide the Left and Right, or those involving race, nationalism, and other subjects being debated or fought over in the larger society.

3. This paper was partly inspired by the comprehensive analytic defense of assimilation by Alba and Nee (1997) and its earlier version (Alba and Nee 1995). The inspiration stems from Alba and Nee's choice of a single concept, assimilation, to cover all the various cultural, social, and other processes that it entails. It set me off on an intellectual path that led to some related and many unrelated ideas, but did much to stimulate the observations and hypotheses of this paper.

4. In the long run, more balance between insider and outsider research is desirable. At present such balance is impossible, either because not enough outsiders or insiders are studying particular groups, for example, or because no insider researchers yet exist. Moreover, in some cases, outsider research cannot even be undertaken, because some immigrant groups do not make themselves accessible to interviewing and other face-to-face research by outsiders.

5. Although I was a graduate student at the University in the late 1940s, I did not know the origin of the distinction, and some additional research for this paper has not reduced my ignorance. Robert Park had already distinguished between the two terms 25 years earlier, but saw both as referring to culture, pointing out that "ethnologists" used acculturation for "primitive societies" while sociologists, who studied "historical peoples," used the term assimilation (Park and Burgess 1921, 771). They even indicated briefly that "social structure changes more slowly than material culture," but illustrated their thesis with examples from preindustrial societies (op. cit., 745–50).

Perhaps the coteaching by the University's sociologists and cultural anthropologists that began in the mid 1940s, as well as the increasingly visible acculturation of the descendants of the European immigrants as well as the continued social discrimination against them produced the distinction that I was taught. However, the earliest publication using it that I could find was Erich Rosenthal (1960), a teacher of mine in the 1940s.

6. In fact, the first movie theaters, actually only storefronts, were set up in early twentieth-century immigrant neighborhoods like New York City's Lower East Side.

7. As a result, some researchers of the new immigration suggest that the newcomers are already somewhat familiar with American culture before they come. This raises the fascinating question of what, and how much, the American culture

transmitted over the mass media, which is mostly entertainment, teaches prospective newcomers about the United States and how to live in it. It also supplies a new site and population to study the old question of what effects the mass media have on people's behavior and values. My thinking about these matters has been helped by personal communication with Robert Smith and Roger Waldinger.

8. For an earlier, somewhat similar, analysis that distinguishes between the acceptance of newcomers depending on whether they are superordinate or subordinate to the indigenous population, see Lieberson 1961.

9. When newcomers are denied assimilation for a long time, ethnic and racial minorities often set up parallel institutions that are similar to those that have rejected them, for example, country clubs, debutante balls, and other organizations and activities that help to demarcate high status. Researchers will have to find out whether this pattern will be repeated among the newcomers—and what variations will occur among the many Asian-Americans who are marrying native-born whites.

10. Likewise, Steinberg (1989) has shown that sometimes the third generation remains loyal to some family practices only until the grandparents die.

11. Hurh and Kim (1967, 27) call attention to other involuntary factors, such as ethnic segregation and economic and ecological conditions in the host society.

12. Here is a good example of where polarization can hurt research, since generally each "side" is likely to ask only questions that reflect its own hypotheses.

13. Strictly speaking, the advocates of reconstruction and invention were at odds with what Alba and Nee (1997) call canonical assimilation theory.

14. The immigrants may share similar national, or homeland, loyalties, but only if and when they come from functioning nations, or feel allegiance to a common homeland. Many of the newcomers arrive, just as did many of the European immigrants, with hatred of a nation-state that oppressed or exploited them, or from countries in which identification with the nation-state was limited to urban residents or members of the dominant "tribes."

15. See Joselit (1994) for a veritable catalog of Jewish-American ethnic inventions that Americanize and acculturate Jewish religious and secular practices brought over from Europe, as well as other inventions that "Judaize" American practices that had found favor with the immigrants and their children as they moved up the American class structure.

16. For useful discussions of the problems of defining and of researching identity, see e.g., Alba and Nee (1995, 93) and Yinger (1994, 156–57).

17. I would also want to distinguish what people name themselves for outside consumption, e.g., if asked while performing a variety of roles in the larger society, and for inside consumption, how they would describe or name their in-group identity.

18. Admittedly, socialist ideology did not encourage interest in ethnicity and ethnic identity, despite the later amalgamation of socialist and nationalist goals, e.g., in Zionism. Also, actual socialist organizations, particularly outside New York City, divided themselves along ethnic group lines.

19. My argument here is based on a sociology of knowledge approach based on

the work of Karl Mannheim (1936), which emphasizes that research theories and findings reflect the researchers' "perspectives," which in turn result in part from where they stand *vis à vis* the people studied—and I would add the methods and concepts used to study them.

20. A third, Whyte's classic *Street Corner Society* appeared the same year, but while the fieldwork was done among Boston's North End immigrant and second-generation Italians and the book is still widely read half a century later, it is not normally read as an ethnic study.

21. They could, of course, have noticed it among the descendants of the earlier European immigration, from Ireland and Northern Europe, but the Chicago School was so concerned with studying the new immigrants that, for example, Park and Burgess (1921) never mentioned the earlier arrivals at all in their various lengthy discussions of assimilation and Americanization.

22. Some of the retention among Southeast Asians, South Asians, and Caribbeans is deliberate, established to maintain their economic position and social status in an America in which nonwhites are often almost automatically assigned to the working or lower classes (e.g., Gibson 1988; Waters 1996).

23. I am indebted to Merton's classic essay (1973), even though I use somewhat different conceptions of insiders and outsiders.

24. Needless to say, a full definition would require yet other criteria, as well as the generational, class, and other factors that qualify their ancestry and impinge on their values.

25. Other conceptions and definitions of the two types of researchers deal with the quality and kinds of insights, theories, and findings each is best able to develop. Merton raised these issues in his 1973 article, but they are beyond the scope of this analysis.

26. For this reason alone, it would be interesting to study the novelists, journalists, and other writers who undertook quasi-sociological research among their own peoples.

27. Some were opposed to immigration and the European immigrants and believed in the genetic inferiority of the European immigrants and blacks. The immigration researchers were probably less guilty of what we now call racism than some of their fellow social scientists, but retrospectively, it is difficult to establish who simply repeated the conventional wisdom of the WASP intellectual and professional strata of the day and who was guilty of more personal and more extreme racism. It is, however, possible to identify the researchers who were politically active to restrict immigration or discriminate against blacks.

28. This is particularly true of Wirth, whose 1928 book about Chicago's West Side Jewish ghetto was often openly critical of many of the Eastern European Jews he studied. Actually, as a middle-class German Jew, Wirth was an outsider by origin as well, since at that time, the class, religious, and ethnic differences, not to mention antagonisms, between Jews from eastern and western Europe were considerable. Perhaps he is best classified as a hostile insider.

29. Some began by studying their own group and then moved on to others or to more comparative research, among them Richard Alba and this author.

30. Many little-known ethnic researchers write in retentionist tones about their own ethnic groups, but their works are often published by ethnic presses that generally do not reach the national research community.

31. Most of the remaining 14 percent of the citations were American or other "Anglo" names.

32. This pattern is only somewhat stronger among the applicants for dissertation grants, presumably the youngest. Of the 88 whose topics I could classify, 58 percent were studying their own groups and 18 percent other groups, with the remaining 24 percent researching general/comparative topics.

The data on which this analysis is based come from the proposal titles and subtitles, as well as the ethnic/racial self-identifications, of the year's 150 grant applicants, minus the 18 in which I was unable to determine whether they were studying individual groups or not. I am grateful to Josh DeWind, who directs the SSRC Migration Division, who proposed analyzing the SSRC applicants, provided a first rough count, and then made the data available for my analysis.

33. I selected this group from applicants who identified themselves as Latino, Asian (including South Asian), Caribbean, and African.

34. The remaining 81 percent of the 16 political scientists were studying general topics. (Even so, three of the eight political scientists whom I identified as newcomers were studying their own groups.)

Conversely, among the 37 sociologists (who are the subjects of this part of the paper), 19 percent were looking at groups other than their own and 11 percent were researching general topics. Among sociologists I classified as newcomers, who constituted 24 of the 37, all but one were studying their own group.

35. The children of some recent immigrants, e.g., Koreans and Vietnamese, interested in American history might have problems finding enough study topics in the short history of their groups in America. In any case, this kind of analysis must be undertaken for all the social science disciplines.

36. None of the SSRC applicants indicated they were studying Hmong, Cambodians, Vietnamese, and Laotians, but not all the applicants specified in their subtitles which Asians or Asian-Americans they were studying. Even so, judging by last names at least, Korean researchers were the largest number of Asian researchers, although not all indicated they were studying Korean populations.

37. Entrepreneurs are also easier to study, being fewer in number, more visible, and more concentrated than immigrants who have gone to work in the larger economy.

38. Here I disagree with some researchers, including Alba and Nee (1997, 843) who believe that the constant replenishment by new immigrants will slow down acculturation. The new immigrants will surely replenish immigrant institutions deserted by earlier arrivals, and, if poor, they could hamper the assimilation of the upwardly mobile children of today's newcomers. Still, the social rejection and economic exploitation of the latest fellow immigrants seems to continue with every generation of every new immigration.

39. By then, disciplinary differences among researchers may also have to be con-

sidered, at least if anthropologists studying the United States maintain their current preoccupations with and sympathies for preindustrial or exotic culture, and are thus more likely to be retentionist than the sociologists.

REFERENCES

Alba, Richard D. *Ethnic Identity: The Transformation of White America.* New Haven, Conn.: Yale University Press, 1990.

Alba, Richard D., and Victor Nee. "The Assimilation of Immigrant Groups: Concept, Theory and Evidence." Paper presented to the Social Science Research Council Conference, "Becoming American/ America Becoming," (December) 1995.

———. "Rethinking Assimilation Theory for a New Era of Immigration, 1997.

———. *"International Migration Review* 31, no. 4 (1997): 826–74.

Child, Irvin L. *Italian or American?* New Haven, Conn.: Yale University Press, 1943.

Conzen, Kathleen N. *et. al.* "The Invention of Ethnicity: A Perspective from the U.S.A." *Journal of American Ethnic History* 12, no. 1 (1992): 3–41.

DeWind, Josh, and Philip Kasinitz. "Everything Old is New Again." *International Migration Review* 31, no. 4 (1997): 1096–111.

Gans, Herbert J. *The Urban Villagers.* New York: Free Press, 1962.

———. "Symbolic Ethnicity." *Ethnic and Racial Studies* 2, no. 1 (1979): 1–20.

———. "Second-Generation Decline: Scenarios for the Economic and Ethnic Futures of the Post-1965 American Immigrants." *Ethnic and Racial Studies* 15, no. 2 (1992): 173–92.

———. "The Possibility of a New Racial Hierarchy in the 21st Century United States." In *Cultural Territories of Race,* edited by Michelle Lamont. Chicago: University of Chicago Press and New York: Russell Sage Foundation, 1999.

Gibson, Margaret A. *Accommodation with Assimilation: Sikh Immigrants in an American High School.* Ithaca, N.Y.: Cornell University Press, 1988.

Gordon, Milton M. *Assimilaiton in American Life: The Role of Race, Religion and National Origins.* New York: Oxford University Press, 1964.

Halle, David. *America's Working Man.* Chicago: University of Chicago Press, 1984.

Hurh, Won Moo, and Kwang Chung Kim. *Korean Immigrants in America.* Rutherford N.J.: Fairleigh Dickinson University Press, 1984.

Joselit, Jenna W. *The Wonders of America: Reinventing Jewish Culture, 1880–1950.* New York: Hill & Wang, 1994.

Kasinitz, Phillip. *Caribbean New York: Black Immigrants and the Politics of Race.* Ithaca, N.Y.: Cornell University Press, 1992.

Lieberson, Stanley. "A Societal Theory of Race and Ethnic Relations." *American Sociological Review* 21 (1961): 902–10.

Mannheim, Karl. *Ideology and Utopia.* New York: Harcourt Brace, 1936.

Merton, Robert K. "The Perspectives of 'Insiders' and 'Outsiders'." In *The Sociology of Science: Theoretical and Empirical Investigations,* 99–136, edited by Norman W. Storer. Chicago: University of Chicago Press, 1973.

Park, Robert E., and Ernest W. Burgess. *Introduction to the Science of Sociology.* Chicago: University of Chicago Press, 1921.

Portes, Alejandro, and Richard Schauffler. "Language and the Second Generation." *International Migration Review* 28, no. 4 (1994): 640–61.

Rosenthal, Erich. "Acculturation without Assimilation? The Jewish Community in Chicago." *American Journal of Sociology* 66 (1960): 275–88.

Rumbaut, Rubén G. "Immigrant Students in California Public Schools: A Summary of Current Knowledge." Baltimore, Md.: Johns Hopkins University Center for Research on Effective Schooling for Disadvantaged Students, Report No. 11, 1990.

———. "The Crucible Within: Ethnic Identity, Self-esteem and Segmented Assimilation among Children of Immigrants." *International Migration Review* 28, no. 1 (1994): 748–94.

———. "The New Californians: Comparative Research Findings on the Educational Progress of Immigrant Children." In *California's Immigrant Children: Theory, Research and Implications for Educational Policy,* edited by Rubén G. Rumbaut and Wayne A. Cornelius, chapter 2. San Diego: Center for U.S.-Mexican Studies, University of California, 1995.

———. "Paradoxes (and Orthodoxies) of Assimilation." *Sociological Perspectives* 40, no. 3 (1997): 483–551.

Sollors, Werner, ed. *The Invention of Ethnicity.* New York: Oxford University Press, 1989.

Steinberg, Stephen. *The Ethnic Myth.* Boston: Beacon Press, 1989.

Ware, Caroline. *Greenwich Village, 1920–1930.* Boston: Houghton Mifflin, 1935.

Warner, W. Lloyd, and Leo Srole. *The Social Systems of American Ethnic Groups.* New Haven, Conn.: Yale University Press, 1945.

Waters, Mary. *Ethnic Options: Choosing Identities in America.* Berkeley: University of California Press, 1990.

———. "Ethnic and Racial Identities of Second-Generation Black Immigrants in New York City." In *The Second Generation,* edited by Alejandro Portes, Chapter 8. New York: Russell Sage Foundation 1996.

Whyte, William F., Jr. *Street Corner Society.* Chicago: University of Chicago Press, 1943.

Wirth, Louis. *The Ghetto.* Chicago: University of Chicago Press, 1928.

Woldemikael, Tekle M. *Becoming Black American: Haitians and American Institutions in Evanston, Illinois.* New York: AMS Press, 1989.

Yancey, William, Eugene Ericksen, and Richard Juliani. "Emergent Ethnicity: A Review and Reformulation." *American Sociological Review* 41, no. 3 (1976): 391–403.

Yinger, Milton J. *Ethnicity: Source of Strength? Source of Conflict?* Albany, N.Y.: SUNY Press, 1994.

Zhou, Min, and Carl L. Bankston. "Social Capital and the Adaptation of the Second Generation: The Case of Vietnamese Youth." *International Migration Review* 28, no. 4 (1994): 821–45.

· *Part Four* ·

SOCIOLOGY IN AMERICA

I received my Ph.D. in the late 1950s, shortly after the post-World War II period of affluence arrived in the social sciences. As a result, jobs and research opportunities were plentiful, and I was able to work as a researcher on my projects, with lots of time to write, for the next 14 years. Unlike today's sociologists, many of whom start teaching right after they obtain their doctorates, I did not take a full-time teaching position until 1971. However, I was always teaching on the side while earning my living as a researcher—and a prolific young writer who research organizations hired in part because my writings provided them with useful publicity.

The sudden affluence in the social sciences also had desirable cultural and political consequences, for as it turned out, sociology was the social science of choice among many of the liveliest young students, activists, and researchers of the 1950s and 1960s. During the 1960s especially, the younger and politically involved sociologists (including this author) were full of hope about the present relevance and future vitality of their discipline. Much of the nonempirical writing about sociology dealt with competing ways of understanding society, and these ways frequently involved or included debates between the advocates and critics of the New Left and their sociological peers and equivalents. (If it had not been so out-of-date, I would have included my own 1965–66 debate with Tom Hayden, Staughton Lynd, and James Weinstein in *Studies on the Left*.)

By the mid 1970s, the enthusiasm for and enrollments in sociology were on the decline, although it was not until the early 1980s that occasional articles about what was sometimes described as sociology's "doldrums" began to appear. I did some informal speech making on this topic myself, and one of my favorite points, then as now, was that in order for sociology to flourish, it must prove useful and helpful for understanding America not only to the students that come to our classes—and to the parents that often pay for them—but also to the public that pays indirectly for our research and writing. (At present, enrollments in sociology have risen again, in some places to record heights, but as I suggested in the Preface, sociology's rationale is still questioned. Its reputation is still poor, especially among journalists and other nonacademics, even though we are regularly consulted and asked for quotes by many journalists.)

For reasons having nothing to do with any of the above, in 1986 I was elected the president of the American Sociological Association, and my first and most important duty was to plan the president's portion of the association's 1988 annual meeting. Feeling that I should select a theme of interest for the meeting of appeal to everyone rather than just to colleagues in one of my own specialties, I chose "Sociology in America"; my own agenda however, was to consider in what ways sociology was and was not being useful to the country.

Presidential meeting themes are usually presented most fully by the presidents themselves in their presidential addresses. Mine discussed what I thought was good and bad about sociology, and proposed ways in which the discipline could be more useful to the general public, as well as the country.

American academic meetings are so organized that presidents only make their presidential addresses a few days before their terms end, and, intentionally or otherwise, are thus unable to do anything about what they propose in these addresses. In addition, they cannot, at least in sociology, try to continue what they start by influencing the choice of their successors. Their presidential addresses turn into the lead articles of the next volume of the official flagship journal, *The American Sociological Review,* but whether these influence the future of their discipline has not yet been studied. In any case, my lead article is reprinted here as Chapter Twelve.

My presidency, however, led to my continuing interest in the future of the discipline, leading to a number of short articles in the association's newsletter and the other two pieces included here. The first of these stems directly from my concern about sociology's usefulness to the general public, and more specifically, from discussions over the years with students and others about which books by sociologists are read by that public.

Consequently, I tried to find out! While—as newspaper and magazine publishers discovered long ago—it is virtually impossible to find out what people actually read, I could find out what books written by sociologists have sold the most copies. Even that was immensely difficult, and the numbers themselves are sufficiently ambiguous that I published only a rank order of the nearly 60 such books (not counting texts) that have sold 40,000 copies or more since the end of World War II. I had always known that Riesman, Glazer, and Denney's *The Lonely Crowd* was the top best-seller, and that Liebow's *Tally's Corner* was next, but many other books have sold very well, as readers can discover from the table included in Chapter Thirteen.

The last chapter stemmed more indirectly from my concern about sociology's usefulness, and began with another hunch. This time the hunch was a doubt; namely, that sociologists were failing to develop a cumulatively growing research and theoretical literature that was constantly increasing the total amount of sociological knowledge. Instead, they were regularly rediscovering old findings, and as I argue in Chapter Fourteen, the rediscovery starts anew every twenty years—that being the age, roughly speaking, of the oldest books and articles that prominent researchers, in the fields I know best, cite or refer to in the bibliographies of their books. (One of the researchers whose bibliographies I analyzed was my own, and I found myself as guilty of the same practice as everyone else.)

My bibliographic measure is an imperfect test of my hunch, and part of the reason for the two-decade span is that theories, concepts, and sometimes almost entire vocabularies change. Another reason is social change, but even so, much of the social world we study changes slowly, and it is surely not totally renewed every twenty years. If sociologists had any incentive to be more efficient, and if academic disciplines did not reward researchers merely for coining new words for old phenomena, the same number of researchers could produce more in the way of useful new findings, empirical and theoretical. Incidentally, I suspect equivalent inefficiencies can be found in other disciplines, though no one outside sociology has so far replicated my study.

Admittedly, efficiency is not an unalloyed benefit, but if the prophets of declining resources are correct, and disciplines and researchers must compete more energetically for fewer research funds in the future, social science research may have to become more efficient just to ensure its continued existence.

· 12 ·

SOCIOLOGY IN AMERICA

The Discipline and the Public

When I first began to think about the presidential address, I planned to choose one of the research areas in which I've worked all of my professional life. I considered a paper on Sociology and the City, urban sociology currently being in an exciting intellectual transition, and also one on Poverty and Inequality, a topic about which sociologists have far more to contribute than they now do. I would also have liked to discuss Sociology and the Mass Media, an ever more significant field, which still has not received the attention and respect from the discipline that it deserves.

Instead of writing a paper that might have been relevant to only some colleagues, however, I chose a topic in which all of us are or should be interested—the discipline.[1] More particularly, I want to discuss our relations with America's nonsociologists, the *lay public:* both the very large general public and the smaller well-educated one, which does much of the country's professional-level analytic and creative work. Since the lay public includes the country's entire population, less the approximately 20,000 sociologists, my topic is also an intrinsic part of Sociology in America.

Although I shall concentrate on what we still need to do to serve the lay public and the institutions in which it is involved, in many respects we are doing better than we have in the past. Sociology has established a presence in many kinds of policy analysis and is moving into large numbers of other so-called practice areas, even if our ideas continue to be largely absent from the country's political thinking. As best I can tell from energetic but unsystematic observation, the news media pay more attention to us than before, and some journalists now want sociological angles on feature stories they are covering. Slowly but surely they are also becoming interested in

This chapter was first published as "The American Sociological Association 1988 Presidential Address." *The American Sociological Review* 54, no. 1 (1989): 1–16.

sociological research. We even show up as sympathetic characters in occasional popular novels and films, although we continue to play villains and fools in high culture. I have the impression that the majority of the literary community still believes that only it can analyze society.

When one talks with publishers of general, nonacademic books as well as with editors and writers for so-called serious magazines and with foundation heads, the picture also remains discouraging. Too many people still dislike sociology or, worse still, are not interested in it. To be sure, often they react to caricatures of sociology, but the very fact that they are not motivated to go beyond caricatures is itself depressing. In effect, we play a smaller part in the country's intellectual life than we should.

Many sociologists find nothing wrong with this state of affairs. For them, sociology is a social science with emphasis on the science, and reaching out to, or obtaining the attention of, the lay public is irrelevant. Others hold a stronger version of this point of view; being in touch with the laity, except when necessary for earning a living, impedes the progress of scientific research. Colleagues who feel most strongly speak of vulgarizing sociology or pandering to the uninformed.

I believe that these feelings are mistaken. Maintaining some relationship with the American public is part of our responsibility as members of society and as recipients of its funds, public or private, whether as tuition payments, salaries, grants, or contacts. Moreover, when members of the lay public feel that our work is useful or enlightening or both, they have an incentive to give us their cultural and political support if we need it—when issues like student interest in sociology, the allocation of research funds, and freedom of research are at stake. The rest of the essay will show that paying more attention to lay America can be done without pandering.

This essay has three major parts. The first describes some of the research needed to analyze sociology's roles in America, for without it we cannot fully understand how we can best reach out to the lay public. The second part discusses some ways in which we can now improve our relations with the public. The last part concerns sociology itself, offering some ideas on what we can do better for ourselves even as we do better by the public.[2]

Before I start I must define the term "we." I use it broadly, referring to "we the discipline" and "we the collectivity," knowing all the while that the discipline is highly diverse while the collectivity is far from a functioning sociopolitical entity. "We" is therefore mainly a shorthand about how numbers of us act or how we should all act, but I must apologize to sociology's practitioners that my "we" is mostly the academic discipline and collectivity, they being what I know best.

STUDYING SOCIOLOGY IN AMERICA

My initial topic is researching Sociology in America. At one level, I see the topic as a set of studies in the sociology of knowledge that tries to understand where we are coming from and going and how we are tied to the main structures and hierarchies of American society. In the process, we should identify our employers, sponsors, funders, supporters, and allies, as well as our clients or constituents—and our possible victims. In short, we must understand whose sides we have been on, purposely or accidentally (Becker 1967).

At another level, Sociology in America is evaluative, the application of our analytic tools and our values to understand and assess what we are doing for and to the country, as well as to all the sectors on which we might impinge, from underdogs to top dogs, for instance. We need to know whom we help and whom we injure and damage, intentionally and unintentionally, so that we can figure out what we should be doing and not doing in behalf of a better society, however "better" may be defined.

"Sociology in America" is a good title for an ASA annual meeting theme, but the topic could also be called sociology and society, in part to emphasize that it must be cross-national and cross-cultural as well (Kohn 1987). A first priority is conceptualizing the basic subject, and many alternatives are possible. One can begin by looking for and at sociology's *contributions,* identifying activities and institutions in which sociologists have participated directly or in which their work has been used indirectly. A major problem with looking at contributions is that we tend to forget the negative ones and the ones we fail to make, but this problem can be corrected.

A slightly different approach would be to ask what *roles* sociology has played and is playing, adding the evaluative element by also asking how well these roles were played, and which should be played in the future. Some roles are self-evident, but the concept allows us to wonder whether, for example, we somehow also represent particular interest groups, or falling, not to mention rising, classes. Or are we mainly one of a set of academics whose role it is to add a touch of cultural polish and a smidgen of social conscience to the socialization of young Americans able and willing to go to college? Yet how do we fit into the scheme of things when we play what I think of as the Martian role, distancing ourselves and going to Erving Goffman's backstage—or back of it—to report on how society or some of its constituent parts operate.

My own thinking takes me in the direction of *effects* concepts, because what matters most is not what we have done but how our work has affected others. Somewhat the same outcome as a study of effects can be achieved by the use of functional analysis, for functions are operationalized as consequences—as long as we always inquire into functions and dysfunctions of what for whom, and assume the possibility that some of our activities are functional mainly for ourselves. Alternatively, one can look at sociology's benefits and costs—if these are not treated solely as quantitative concepts. We must also remember that researchers will not always agree on what is beneficial and costly, and that the determination of benefits and costs must reflect the views of all those who actually win and lose. Moreover, we must never exclude the possibility that our work has neither significant benefits nor costs—nor major independent effects. We are, after all, only 20,000 in a country of 230 million.

I am aware of all the methodological difficulties of studying effects, functions, and benefits and costs, but we *must* discover what impact we have had. Furthermore, any properly sociological effects study has to examine the agents and processes that have shaped sociology to achieve whatever impacts it is having. Thus, a study of sociology's impact on America must be preceded by research on America's impacts on sociology (Gouldner 1970; Vidich and Lyman 1985). However, if we analyze the roles we have played, we must likewise ask who helped us play these roles and how we were invited or shoehorned into them.

Needless to say, there are other conceptual schemes for looking at sociology in America, but whatever the schemes, the questions I have raised also have to be answered historically. In fact, it may be strategic to begin with historical analyses because the historical view can give us a better fix on the primary theoretical and empirical issues on which we must concentrate in order to understand the present.

Although the teaching of sociology has still not obtained enough respect from the discipline, the fact remains that virtually all academic sociologists, including those at the most elite research universities, earn their living by teaching. Consequently, one of the first and most important questions to be researched concerns the effects, and thus also the effectiveness, of our teaching.

ASA estimates that 75 percent of America's sociologists—or 15,000—are still academics. If each teaches four courses a year, and many unfortunately teach many more, that comes to 60,000 courses a year, and of these the most frequently taught continue to be introductory, marriage and the family, and social problems. Although studies have been made of the major texts used in these courses, we ought to start finding out what is actually being *taught* in them: not only what kinds of sociology, but what descriptions of and prescriptions for American society. For example, a multicampus sample of marriage and the family courses could be analyzed to identify what models of marriage and the family sociologists teach, and what postures they encourage students to take toward them, explicitly or implicitly. To what extent do we teach conformity to the culturally dominant models, and if we suggest the desirability of sociopolitical change, what new or old models do we have in mind?

After that, we ought to begin on the more urgent but also more complex task of looking at what students *learn* from these basic courses, for their own lives and their citizen roles, to see if we can establish findings about the effects of their exposure to sociology. Since sociology has begun to drift down to the high schools, similar research can be done there. Schools not being the only teaching institutions in America, however, someone should also take a look to see whether sociology has yet had any visible impact on the country's news and entertainment media.

Parallel kinds of research can be undertaken among sociological practitioners. Indeed, now is an ideal time to begin, for before-and-after studies should immediately be conducted at some of the many public agencies and private companies that are first hiring sociologists, so that we can learn what early effects they are having. Now that sociologists are being employed in market research, for example, it would be useful to look at a sample of firms to discover what, if anything, the sociologists do differently—and with what effects—from the previous market researchers who have generally been MBA's and psychologists. Do sociological market researchers have more empathy for the subjects of market research than had their predecessors, and what effects does this have on their work, the resulting firm policies, and the profits? Or are sociologists in big organizations more likely to practice what their organizations prescribe rather than what their discipline has trained them to practice? Incidentally, an interesting study of *academic* practitioners, the increasing number of sociologists who become deans and provosts of their universities, could be done to see what, if anything, they do differently because they are sociologists.

The effects studies of the greatest urgency are those with potential public policy significance. I will limit myself to two examples. One is the roles and functions sociology has played in past culture-of-poverty research and is now playing in the study of what is currently called the underclass. We could begin, for example, with the effects the most widely read new sociological book of the last two years, William J. Wilson's *The Truly Disadvantaged* (1987), has had for the public understanding of the underclass, and for the policies needed to bring it into the country's mainstream. As sociological underclass research proliferates, however, we must also look at what we may be doing against the people now assigned to that class.

The term *underclass* was first used in recent times by Gunnar Myrdal

(1963) as an economic concept for describing a set of people being driven to the edges or out of the economy. While most current underclass research seems to be in the hands of economists, they have generally adopted a different definition, perhaps of journalistic origin, in which the members of that class are also associated with a variety of criminal, pathological, or stigmatized activities and are generally black or Hispanic.

No laws prevent us from studying the impact of economists along side of, or in comparison to, our own, and many questions deserve answering. Do studies using the underclass concept call attention to people who need economic and other kinds of aid? Or are researchers primarily giving scientific legitimization to the latest buzzword for the undeserving poor and concurrently helping to disseminate a new code word for the covert expression of racial hostility? More generally, what role do researchers play in the emergence of a new public stereotype, and how can they prevent a social science generalization or an ideal type from being interpreted as a stereotype?

To the extent that underclass studies are seen and used by social workers and other street-level bureaucrats as well as policy makers, we have to ask whether these studies mainly help the people assigned to the underclass or help government to control them? Once again, what sides are we on, intentionally and unintentionally, as we study this newest "hot" topic? Perhaps the biggest problem stems from unintentional "put-downs" of poor people, because of either lack of researcher reflexivity or the use of data from agencies that exist in part to be punitive toward the poor.

I have the impression that sociologists doing research among people stigmatized as underclass are more likely to be on their side while the economists tend to treat them as a dangerous class. Even so, sociologists and economists play only a small causal part in the tragic relationship between the underclass and the rest of America. Indeed, the current research is itself an effect of public appetites for information, scapegoats, and, of course, solutions. These appetites have themselves emerged for such reasons as the increasing fear of crime—and of dark-skinned Americans—the rise of homelessness, the economic insecurity created in many parts of the population by the Reagan economy, and the relentless pressures by the Reagan administration on people who cannot afford the values of mainstream cultures.

My second example might serve as a model not only of what we have done well as sociological researchers but also of the ways in which sociology can be useful, and relatively easily. I think here of the large set of findings that indicate, on the one hand, that informal groups and related social supports have both illness-preventing and healing functions, and, on the other hand, that isolation and loneliness as well as alienation produced by hostile or distant formal institutions can breed and worsen physical and mental illness. The basic idea goes back to nineteenth-century sociology, but since World War II many researchers have shown how the presence or absence of kin, friends, neighbors, and other informal groups and networks affect health (Litwak and Messeri 1989).

For the study of sociology in America, and for the making of health policy, we must examine whether and how such findings are, or could be, providing competition for purely medical models of health and illness. In addition, we need to know whether and how these findings are leading to changes in medical activity, from physician practice to national health policy. Conversely, we must also study why changes did not take place, so that we can try to understand how they could take place. Since informal groups should cost less than doctors and hospitals, social supports would help reduce medical costs and might be welcomed for that reason alone—unless hospitals and doctors decide to turn them into a medical specialty, and charge accordingly.

Whether the study of Sociology in America involves basic, applied, or policy-oriented research, we will, in effect, be studying ourselves. I need not list the dangers of a disciplinary-wide self-study, and in a utopian world, another social science would study us while we study yet a third. However, in this world, *we* have to do the needed studies and *we* have to learn how to deal with the likely conflicts of interest.

An essential ingredient for self-study is the right mixture of deliberate and systematic reflexivity and an equally deliberate and systematic distancing. Appeals for more reflexivity without structural underpinnings and instrumental incentives being the material of sermons, I am reluctant to go further except to hope with Alvin Gouldner that what I have in mind here does not become "just another topic for panels at professional conventions and not just another little stream of technical reports" (Gouldner 1970, 489).

Consequently, as relevant studies are undertaken, we have to begin to think about what we will do with the results. Even before we know more about our contributions, roles, and effects, we must debate how to increase sociology's positive effects and cut back the negative ones. We ought also to confront once more an old, recently forgotten question: what is a good society, and how can sociology help bring it about?

I have no illusions about how much we can agree on the nature of the good society or how much we can do to bring one about, but the discussion of these questions will have beneficial results for the discipline itself. The very innocence of the notion of the good society may be a useful antidote for our too frequent tendency toward excessive abstraction. Moreover, asking fundamental general questions, even the kind that cannot be answered easily or completely, forces us to address issues of widespread interest in America and is, in addition, a way of reaching out to the general public.

SOCIOLOGY AND THE LAY PUBLIC

The second part of my paper is about improving relations with the public and its institutions. I begin again on an empirical note, because at least two further topics badly need study if we are going to act intelligently to improve our relations with both the large general and the smaller well-educated public.

One study seeks to identify *lay sociology,* the generalizations about society and its parts that all people—we included—start learning as children, long before knowing of the existence of professional sociology. True, lay people do not label their knowledge about society *sociology,* but nonetheless it consists of ideas and data in all of the fields we study. Much lay sociology is learned during the process of socialization, yet more is discovered through the applied participant-observation we all do constantly in everyday social life, and some comes from nonprofessional, or so-called *pop sociology:* research done by nonprofessional sociologists who use some of our methods but few of our concepts and theories.

For my purpose, the significant questions center around what happens when people's lay sociology comes into contact with our professional sociology. We have to discover what impacts we have on lay sociology, and whether and how we add to and change it. Perhaps even more to the point, we have to find out if and why we are ignored or rejected. When the generalizations of lay and professional sociology diverge, we generally seek to replace the lay kind, and our students may fail to learn because they are not persuaded that our sociology is more valid than theirs. I wonder, for example, what happens when working-class and poor students, whose lay sociologies are particularly rich in the fields of class and inequality, take a course in social stratification, which sees society solely from a middle-class perspective. Although we assume that professional sociology is always better than the lay version, that assumption also deserves some inquiry.

The other study strikes at the heart of our relations with the educated public because we must know in detail how our sociology is judged by that public. If, when, and where our standing is not as good as it should be, we have to identify the reasons and causes. In addition, we have to find out what the members of this public want from sociology, ours and theirs. There is clearly a great demand for applied organizational research, for the management literature is full of pop sociology on this topic, much of it so poor that every six months yet another new analysis becomes a brief bestseller.

In their nonoccupational reading, however, many members of the educated public seem to specialize in literary and historical works, which is one reason why just about all of the important magazines and publishing houses catering to this public continue to be run by people from literary and historical backgrounds. Why the reading public is so fond of history and why it ignores—and perhaps dislikes—some or much sociology is a research topic of fundamental importance, for until we have a comprehensive answer our work will not get much attention from the journals of cultural and political opinion, the large circulation "class" magazines such as *Time, The New Yorker,* or *The Atlantic,* and "trade book" publishers who publish nontechnical books in the social sciences.

Despite the need for these researches, many suggestions can be made *now* for how to improve our relations with the lay public, but I will limit myself to five I consider particularly significant.

First, I assume the lay public—general and educated—will pay more attention to professional sociology if and when our research addresses salient subjects and issues. Many of these center around the family, the economy, and health—subjects about which we have something to say that can help people's understanding, if we can present our ideas and findings in plain English. Other lay concerns touch on or are set off by current events, and we should figure our how we can do more studies on significant topics of the moment. Many years ago Gladys and Kurt Lang proposed "firehouse research" for such studies, and their proposal is as timely as ever. We can also supply useful comments on topical issues, especially as debunkers and correctors when the early journalistic reports and nonprofessional sociology are wrong. In addition, we can report on trends underlying topical subjects and can often provide more systematic explanation of events and trends than do journalists and pop sociologists.

An already existing lay interest in our sociology has to do with the diversity of American life. Because of that diversity, some members of the lay public want to know how other Americans cope with common problems such as familial and community ones, as well as how they interpret, or substitute for, the conventional rules and norms of American life. It is no coincidence that the best-known sociological works of the last 75 years—*Middletown, The Lonely Crowd,* and *Habits of the Heart*—respond to one or another of these lay inquiries.

These studies also exhibit what I consider one of sociology's distinctive qualities: they are based on research among ordinary Americans. While other social sciences concentrate on elite decision makers, exotic subcultures, or laboratory subjects, sociology has always done much of its work with and among typical Americans. This is one reason why professional sociology, when properly presented, appeals to the lay public. That appeal is widened when we use the research methods that seem most attractive to this public: the depth-interview, in which people have a chance to talk and to explain themselves fully; and fieldwork, in which sociologists are on the scene to hear them on a continuing basis, and inside the social structures in which they act and interact.

The ideal study format may be the community study, not because I have done a few but because it is broad; it allows researchers the opportunity to report on a variety of people across a wide range of institutions and situations. If the communities and people studied are reasonably representative or thoughtfully chosen deviant cases, the sampling is done properly, and the research is focused on significant theoretical and substantive questions, this is the best way to look at America, for both the discipline and the lay public (Keller 1988).

Community studies are hard work; they can take a long time and, like many qualitative studies, do not fit the currently dominant definition of science. As a result, funding agencies have not been supportive—a serious mistake that helps to explain why sociology is not as much in the public eye as it should be.

The *second* of my five suggestions is a corollary of the first: that undergraduate sociology courses should concentrate, whenever possible, on sociological analyses of American institutions and society rather than on sociological principles illustrated with samples from America. There is nothing like an overly concept-filled introductory course to turn many students against sociology forever. Courses that teach sociology through an analysis of American society also require research on topical issues and current events.[3] Unfortunately, even reading a first-class newspaper or weekly newsmagazine with a sociological eye is not normally part of the graduate school training program. If we carried out more analyses of topical issues and current events, sociology could make more original contributions to understanding both. If any sociologists now prepare such analyses for their classes, we should find a place where the best of them can be published for the rest of us.

My *third* proposal is that we must recruit and encourage talented sociologists who are able and eager to report their work so that it is salient to both their colleagues and the educated lay public. Borrowing Russell Jacoby's concept of public intellectuals (Jacoby 1987), they might be called *public sociologists,* and the public sociologist par excellence that comes at once to mind is David Riesman. Public sociologists are *not* popularizers; they are empirical researchers, analysts, or theorists like the rest of us, although often their work is particularly thoughtful, imaginative or original in some respect.[4]

Public sociologists have three further distinctive traits. One is their ability to discuss even sociological concepts and theories in the English of the college-educated reader, probably because they enjoy writing as well as doing research and may even think of themselves as writers. Their second trait is the breadth of their sociological interests, which covers much of society even if their research is restricted to a few fields. That breadth also extends to their conception of sociology, which extends beyond research reporting to commentary and in many cases also to social criticism. To put it another way, their work is intellectual as well as scientific.[5] A third, not unrelated, trait is the ability to avoid the pitfalls of undue professionalism described by earlier ASA presidents (for example, Hughes 1963, 890; Lee 1976, 927–29).

I do not know how one recruits fledgling or mature public sociologists, but I fear that too many young people with an interest in society get Ph.D.'s in English, literature, or history. Consequently, sociology must encourage those it does attract, beginning in graduate school. It also has to assure them that they can be both sociologists and writers and will not be discriminated against for this combination of skills. For example, they must be rewarded for being writers, and their major sociological writing in nonscholarly publications must be treated as equivalent to scholarly writing in promotion and tenure decisions. We should also find outlets for their writing inside sociology so we do not lose all their work to other publications.

I have been around long enough to remember when David Riesman was not considered a sociologist in many parts of the discipline, although even today some colleagues who hold fervently to a natural science conception of sociology reject public sociologists. Worse yet, they may dismiss them as "journalists," a term that we should never use as a pejorative for yet other reasons I will come to shortly. I am told that John Kenneth Galbraith, the dean of public economists, has never been accepted as an economist by many of his colleagues, but then economics is a backward social science in other respects.

The *fourth* suggestion for adding to our impact on the lay public requires revitalizing an old mode of public sociology: social criticism. I oversimplify only slightly to point out that American sociology began in part as social criticism, and while a handful of sociologists have continued this tradition, today's American social criticism is almost entirely in the hands of journalists, essayists, literary critics, and philosophers. Europe is quite different in this respect, because many European sociologists and researchers double as newspaper or magazine columnists, writing regularly the kind of social commentary found here in journals of opinion and cultural criticism.

We are not Europeans, and we should not even imitate America's current social critics. Our task is *sociological* social criticism. Journalist and humanistic critics too often view social ills by what makes them personally unhappy, and they may also misunderstand the causes of these ills or offer solutions that reflect the values of a single group—be it intellectual elite or working class. Partly as a result, conventional criticism is frequently nostalgic or apocalyptic, with good old days being mourned right and left and many institutions thought to be in permanent rapid decline—headed almost always by the family.

The sociological social critic can do much better! The identification of social ills ought to be based both on empirical data about what the public or several parts of it feel to be wrong, *and* on the critic's own concerns. Proposed solutions can likewise transcend the perspective of the critics' own immediate circle, and they should draw on systematic causal analyses of the problems to be solved.

Social criticism is not for every sociologist, but it should become part of the discipline just as social policy research became a part of it in the last twenty years, once we were able to move beyond the primitive conceptions of value-free sociology on which the early disapproval of social policy research was based. Sociological social criticism will never grow as large as social policy research, however, because it cannot, and should not, become a government function.

My *fifth* and last proposal is particularly focused on the general public. Since its major contact with professional sociology comes from the mass media, we should try to get more of the sociological perspective and our own studies into these media. Reaching the general public requires *popularizers,* sociologists and others who can turn the ideas and findings reported in our journals and books that should be of general interest into everyday English.[6]

Concurrently, we should encourage the journalists who also popularize our work: the small number of free-lancers who do it from time to time, as well as the handful who have regular social or behavioral science beats. We should assist journalistic popularizers as much as we can, for good popularization will increase public interest in sociology. At the same time, we may be able to head off some inaccurate or sensationalized popularization.

In addition, we should help nonprofessional researchers who undertake pop sociology, which I described earlier as research based on the concepts and ideas of lay sociology. We can be particularly helpful with advice on methods. After all, the rules of sampling, question construction, fieldwork, and statistical analysis apply equally to professional and pop sociology. True, nonprofessional sociologists often cannot apply these rules as rigorously as we do, for the lay public is not interested in professional subtleties and qualifications, whether in sociology or in physics. Still, our common interests in good methodology can make us useful as long as we understand and are tolerant about the differences between their sociology and ours.

Good nonprofessional sociology is useful to us for the same reasons as good popularization. We have a special interest in reducing bad pop sociology, however, because its low quality can reflect on us directly and quickly since the general public may not distinguish between professional and nonprofessional sociology.

Professional sociologists should keep an eye on pop sociology, if only because it has a much larger audience than we do. They should also distinguish between good and bad pop sociology, but unfortunately too many of our colleagues look down on all of it, as they do on popularizers of our work. This stance can only hurt the discipline, for when some of us appear distant and superior, we may turn off members of the lay public otherwise ready to pay attention to our work. Worse yet, wholesale rejection of sociologies other than ours may end up by biting the public hand that feeds us.

An ideal solution, allowing us to have our cake while eating it, is an ASA-run or supervised magazine of high-quality popularized and pop sociology, but that solution is unrealistic since the current lay constituency for sociology is too small to support such a magazine. Sociology may be inherently less newsworthy than, for example, psychology or economics, since both give advice about everyday life of a kind that we cannot supply—or anthropology and psychiatry, which can tell more dramatic stories than we. Thus, a *Sociology Today* modeled on the monthly *Psychology Today* is not in the cards.[7]

Today's most significant disseminators of our sociology to the general public are magazine and newspaper journalists who incorporate our work in their stories, occasionally because they judge a sociological study to be newsworthy but increasingly often because they want sociological commentary on and in their stories. In these cases they may look for appropriate sociological findings, a sociological perspective to increase the quality of their story, or a quote to provide the story with some sociological legitimation.

These journalists are a crucial resource for us, a veritable disciplinary treasure, and they should be given our full and immediate cooperation (Gans 1988). That we are being called more and more often by reporters, feature writers, and their equivalents in television can only be viewed as a compliment. I hope it is also a sign that the old days, when sociology was good only for a cranky feature exaggerating our shortcomings, are coming to an end.[8] Besides, the more we help journalists with their stories, the more interested they may become in reporting our studies.

We can be helpful further by eliminating the mindless attacks on journalists that are still heard in the discipline. At one level they reflect a disciplinary stereotype that all journalism is superficial, but at another level they may express unhappiness with the competition journalists provide us in the study of society. While journalism *is* often superficial, sociology would be superficial equally often if it had to report to a diverse and often poorly educated lay audience; if it had a two- to six-hour deadline for data collection, analysis, and writing; and if the research report had to be condensed into a few hundred words. Journalism has other faults too, but we must learn to distinguish between good and bad journalism. Indeed, we should not refrain from criticizing bad news stories about our work and ideas, as long as we make clear to the journalists involved how and why their work was inadequate. Conversely, we have every right to expect that journalists will learn to distinguish between good and bad sociology, to give up their stereotypes of us, and to stop thinking of the term *sociological* as a pejorative.

I end this section of the paper with a modest proposal: that the abstracts of our journal articles and the summaries of our academic books be written in nontechnical English.[9] Journalists may then become interested in our work instead of becoming discouraged at the very outset, and while they will probably still have troubles with the technical writing in the body of the text, they may be motivated to get in touch with the author for help in clarifying his or her work. They may also wean us away from writing so many of our article and book texts in "Sociologese."

SOCIOLOGY FOR *AMERICA*

The third of my three topics is the discipline itself and what we can do to help as well as improve ourselves. I again limit myself to the academic side, mainly at the research university level I know best. I will not systematically evaluate that side of the discipline, however, and I cannot even go into some specific problems that badly need discussing: for example, the ways we still often mistreat graduate students and part-time instructors, which is in part a reflection of long-standing inequalities within the discipline. These inequalities are currently worsened by the ever-expanding star system and the treatment of some colleagues as celebrities.

Here I want principally to outline what we need to do for and in the discipline in order to obtain a better reception from the public, particularly the educated public. This goal requires attention to the intellectual level of our work and the imperfections that intellectual observers and other members of the educated public see in that work. I will limit myself to two such imperfections. Both can also be found in the other social sciences, which means that their causes transcend our own discipline. However, the imperfections of the other social sciences do not excuse ours—and besides, we should be the first to overcome them, thus leading the way for the others.

The initial imperfection is *mindlessness,* research that is poorly thought through. Mindlessness cuts across fields and methods. It is the use of proxies or indicators because tangentially appropriate quantitative data are accessible, even though these proxies have only the most tenuous logical or empirical connection to the phenomena under study. Mindlessness is grounding the analysis of a complicated phenomenon on survey questions without any idea of how respondents understood the questions. Mindless fieldwork supplies thick descriptions of what is already common knowledge but fails to provide the thick analyses that are sorely needed. And whatever the research method, there are still occasional sociological analyses that, once translated into ordinary English, turn out to be examples of what we have often been accused of: restating the obvious.

Another kind of mindlessness sacrifices substantive validity to a favored analytic technique of the moment. That kind of mindlessness is part and parcel of our passion for methodology, which is actually longstanding. Jules Poincaré, who was writing at the turn of the century, even then described sociology as "the science with the most methods and the fewest discoveries."[10] Otis Dudley Duncan (1974, 2), whose theme I am here repeating, has put it more pointedly:

> Writing on "methodology" cultivated for its own sake produces a bifurcation of scientific effort that is stultifying. You have on the one hand inept researchers who think they have no responsibility for the methods they use because they can cite the authority of some "methodologist" and on the other hand "methodologists" whose advice is no good because they do not actually know how to do research (otherwise, we must suppose, they would have done some).

The second imperfection, also of long standing, is what I think of as *overquantification*. I have no quarrel with statistical or mathematical analyses per se; they have advantages and disadvantages just as the various qualitative methods do. However, overquantification takes place when the research problem calls for qualitative analyses but quantitative ones are used instead, or when the use of such analyses changes the research problem. Overquantification occurs when elegant statistical analyses are performed on sloppily collected data, or on data forever made unclean by the covert or overt agendas of the collectors. And it takes place when quantitative analysis is not preceded—or driven—by concept and theory formulation, when researchers are literally merely crunching numbers. Needless to say, equivalent sins happen on the qualitative side. There may be no phrase for qualitative data crunching, but it occurs, and fieldwork alone is inappropriate when the research problem calls mainly for frequency distributions.

Some unfortunate effects of overquantification result from its ideological character. One is the inability of overquantifiers to tolerate disagreement, and their resulting stigmatization of and discrimination against qualitative research. Perhaps as a result, some advocates of qualitative method have also become ideologists. Consequently, a *scientific* discipline, in which research problems ought to determine the methods, and in which many problems are best solved by the use of both types of methods, is locked into an ideological dispute over a dubious typology—which is, moreover, actually about the nature of sociology.

A related effect of overquantification is the time and energy academic departments, individuals, and the discipline as a whole waste in endless battling over the two types of methods. Robin Williams called this a sham battle, adding rightly that "energy should be better utilized in applying whatever techniques seem to produce reliable knowledge" (Hirschman 1987, 5). However, by now the crucial battle is less over ideas than over "scarce resources . . . jobs, research funds, editorial policies of our journals, professional recognition and prestige," as Mirra Komarovsky (1987, 562) pointed out. *Such* battles are not sham, and were they to end now, the superior resource position of quantitative sociology would become permanent. Those of us who believe in the virtues of qualitative empirical and other sociological work have to continue the struggle for equality of resources. I consider it scandalous, for example, when funding agencies with public mandates or tax exemptions nonetheless base their grant policies on the power balance inside disciplines.

A final effect of overquantification that needs mentioning is its tropism toward secondary analysis, which makes it possible for sociologists to study society for their entire lives without ever leaving their offices to talk or listen to the people they study.[11] The reliance on secondary analysis also makes us increasingly dependent on officially produced data. Worse yet, the resulting impersonalization of research is thought to make sociology more scientific, whereas in fact intensive interviewing and fieldwork are generally more scientific because the researchers get to know closely the people and social structures they are studying.

The problems I have described are familiar and have been discussed in previous presidential addresses (e.g., Coser 1975). Thus, nothing is gained by further elaboration. What would be useful, however, is more sociological research into why sociology and the other social sciences have been developing what I see as imperfections. If I were doing the study, I would want to look particularly at three sets of current academic arrangements.

The first of these arrangements might be called scholarly insulation and a correlative lack of reality checks, which can disconnect our work from what is generally referred to as the real world. Unlike practitioners, our research does not need to be accountable to nonsociological kinds of validity, so that, for example, we are not open to, and thus do not receive corrections from, the people we have studied. We are accountable to funders to some extent, but many tend to base their judgments on peer reviews and, whatever their other virtues, peer reviewers can be as insulated from the nonsociological world as other researchers.

The absence of reality checks, which is also one cause of intellectual mindlessness, could actually be remedied somewhat by instituting such checks as part of our empirical procedure at the start and just before the end of our research. Basically such checks would involve informal reconnaissances, through the use of informants, informal interviewing, and fieldwork, among the people or institutions under study, as well as the application of independent statistical data, already available or newly collected from a small sample. Even theoretical papers and quantitative secondary analyses can be improved by reality checking.

Another kind of reality checking would identify thoughtful nonsociologists to critique our work and identify errors of omission and commission. Where possible, these must also include the people we study. Reality checks seem to me to be at least as important as literature reviews, and we will be well served if we can make them intrinsic parts of our research procedures.

The other two causes of imperfection are less easy to remedy. One is *scientism,* the modeling of sociological (and social science) research methods on a highly idealized version of the methods of the natural sciences. Although this modeling began even before sociology first became systematically empirical, it continues today when we know full well, in part from research in the sociology of science, that natural scientists do not operate according to the idealized conception of their method. Indeed, the ideal is humanly unworkable; nevertheless we cannot let go of it. We also know that social structures are not molecules and cannot be studied like them, but we cannot seem to let go of that analogy either. Nor have we yet learned to appreciate Donald McCloskey's lesson that "scientific work is rhetorical" and that it is so "even in its stylistic appeal to a rhetoric of not having a rhetoric" (McCloskey 1985, 98).

Idealized natural science is a kind of civil religion in modern America, and there may be a quasi-religious element both in the ideal and the consensus behind it. The ideal also continues to justify the search for sociological "laws"—the nomothetic approach to sociology—but that search may express the latent hope for power—in an ideal society in which these laws—and their formulators—would play a central decision-making role. Such a society is as millenarian as those of the major religions: when salvation has been achieved, the Messiah has come, Mohammed has returned, or the State has withered away.

The search for sociological laws is, furthermore, sufficiently abstract to be "above" cultural or political conflicts of the moment. It is perhaps no accident that nomothetic sociology—like overquantified work—is usually noncontroversial, and unlikely to produce criticism of economic, political, and cultural power holders who are behaving in undemocratic or unjust ways.

The third and last cause of imperfection in sociology I will discuss concerns that strange institution in which academics work and in which all academic scholarship is therefore embedded. Although we are paid for the number of courses we teach, we are promoted by how much we publish, and only sometimes by the quality of our publications as well. In effect, our strange institution operates like a machine shop in which publications are treated like piecework. And like employees in any other kind of machine shop basically concerned with the amount of productivity, we may overspecialize to study one part of the "social machine."

Moreover, again like workers in other machine shops, we are periodically greeted by new technology oriented to improving productivity, such as the computer. The virtues of the computer for both quantitative and qualitative sociology far outnumber the vices, but there are some downsides too. Despite the potentials for high-quality research, the computer facilitates the speedier and thus greater production of piecework. It further encourages secondary analysis and the use of official, rather than self-generated, data. Although creative researchers can make creative use of the computer, the new technology even reduces the need to think and analyze once the right computer program has been found. Like many other industries, we too are becoming less labor-intensive.

These patterns are also symptoms of the continuing bureaucratization of research and, as often happens, the new technology is merely a hand-maiden to the socioeconomic process. In fact, the computer nicely fits the academic shop routine, for it enables academics to do their research during the interstices of a full teaching load, and to publish more work at a faster clip.[12] The computer adds further to the impersonalization of research, and thus fits in with the worship of the idealized natural science method. What comes out of the computer is therefore automatically judged to be scientific, and insufficient attention is frequently paid to what human beings put into it.

The imperfections I have described not only stand in the way of a better sociology but also damage our discipline and its reputation. The public, general and educated, cannot understand, or even see the justification for, much of what we produce, since in too many cases our work appears to have no benefit, direct or indirect, for people's understanding of society or for their lives. The reactions of the lay public *must not* determine social science policy or shape our research, but they cannot be ignored either. Meanwhile, the leaders as well as the foot soldiers of today's dominant sociologies ought to remember that a good deal of the intellectual standing and goodwill our discipline has developed comes from the work of public sociologists. They—and books like *The Lonely Crowd* and *Habits of the Heart*—essentially persuade much of the lay public and its politicians that sociology ought to be cared about and funded![13]

OUR SOCIOLOGICAL IDENTITY

To conclude my highly selective analysis of the discipline and this essay, I want to raise the issue of our identity as sociologists in an era of ever-greater specialization of fields and subfields within the discipline.[14] That identity should concern all of us, to further our own well-being *and* to help us make our case for the desirability of sociological knowledge to the lay public.

Sociology is once again no different from the other social sciences, although the degree of specialization may be greater than it is among our peers because we are the residual social science. We are more diverse to begin with than economics (even though it is now branching out beyond the economy) and political science, which is basically still concerned with politics only in government.

In any case, it is worth looking into the benefits and costs of further sociological specialization. Among the major benefits are the intellectual vitality usually found in new fields and subfields, as well as the intensive personal contact among researchers as long as these fields remain small. Indeed, because of the vitality that accompanies work in the new fields or at the frontiers of research, we ought also to be moving deliberately across the accepted or imagined boundaries of sociology, and in two ways.[15]

For one, we should look more closely at other social science disciplines to see what we can learn from them as well as to discover how we can improve on their work, jointly or by ourselves. To mention just a few: social history, the study of symbols and symbol systems, which we share with anthropology, and empirical research in and of economic institutions can all gain from such a look.[16] Disciplinary boundaries in the social sciences are arbitrary anyway, and they should be crossed freely, preferably for substantive, not imperialistic, reasons. We should act similarly toward boundaries beyond the social sciences and take a greater interest in the humanities. Among other things, the study of the interrelations between culture and social structure can benefit from the concepts and ideas of literary scholars. These can put some of our concepts and ideas to use as well in their work on literature and society—for instance, what we have learned about the roles of audiences in the production of culture.

Increasing specialization inside sociology also carries costs, however. The more sociologists specialize in particular fields, the more are some likely to limit themselves to really tiny specialties within the discipline as a whole. Moreover, when new fields and subfields develop, they quickly breed their own technical languages.

> The end result is that [the discipline] looks like a wheel. People sit on their own spokes and talk less and less to those on the other side. Eventually the wheel may become a doughnut, with a huge intellectual hole in the middle. (Winkler 1986, 7)

The person I quote is geographer Sam Hilliard talking about his own discipline, but his comment is starting to apply to sociology as well, and the challenge is to prevent both the wheel and the intellectual hole. The hole cannot, however, be filled by pining for one approach or theory that will reintegrate sociology, for such reintegration is neither likely nor desirable in a pluralistic discipline.

Instead we should ask ourselves what can or should bring us together as sociologists. One approach may be to identify intellectual cores that are common to many of us. These can be concepts, frames, theories, methods, or other intellectual forms and qualities that we continue to share. A related approach is to look empirically at some major old and new fields and subfields and determine what ideas, concepts, and theories are operationally similar in the significant research and theorizing in them, even if the terminology is different.[17] Such a project might even increase the sharing of terms and reduce the excessive number of terms in the discipline. The more we emphasize elements of sociology that we share in annual meeting sessions, other conferences, and various kinds of publications, the more we will discover to what extent we can remain a single discipline. Even my previously mentioned question, "What is a good society?" can perform this function. Imagine a medical sociologist, an ethnomethodolgist, a specialist in gender and sex roles, a market researcher, and a mathematical sociologist, all with roughly the same values, being asked to come up with a single answer to this question!

Identity is social as well as intellectual; consequently, we should also look at social mechanisms that can contribute to being and feeling a part of a single discipline. ASA does what it can along these lines, but only a bare majority of all sociologists belong, and much too small a number of them are involved in ASA as other than receivers of its services. Also, the organization still relies excessively for its agenda and leadership on academics from the major research universities to be fully representative. The annual meetings bring about three thousand of us together for a hectic few days, although the sessions themselves increasingly are vehicles for specialization. In 1988, for example, 43 percent of the *regular* sessions were run by sections, and many other regular sessions were on subjects for which there are sections.

Publications could bring us together as well, but I wonder if they do because our journals tend to appeal largely to specialists, whatever the editor's hopes. For example, the *American Sociological Review (ASR),* being the flagship journal, is supposed to represent the best in sociology. However, for this reader—and I imagine many others—it is also a journal of lengthy research reports on specialized topics, only some of which are of general interest. In addition, *ASR* is dominated by often elegant quantitative research. In fact, some have suggested that *ASR* is actually a methodological journal for quantitative sociologists not able or willing to work through the yet more technical articles in *Sociological Methodology.* There are exceptions in *ASR*'s emphasis, to be sure, and recent editors have published more exceptions than past ones. On the whole, however, most major articles continue to be research reports of roughly the same format and from basically one kind of sociology. Sometimes one gets the impression that *ASR* is "run" by its contributors, the editors functioning primarily as quality controllers and traffic cops, even if they might personally prefer to publish a different journal. Like the organizations we study, *ASR* has become institutionalized.

Contemporary Sociology (CS) may be the most general of the journals, for it reviews a large proportion of all the books sociologists publish. While the reviews are classified by sets of specialties, *CS* readers can get a kind of overview of sociology by reading all of the reviews. Conversely, anecdotal evidence suggests that many of *ASR's* readers scan the abstracts, read an article or two, and leave it at that. Over the years many have reported in the discipline's grapevine that they have difficulty understanding or getting involved in many of the articles, and there are regular complaints—some published (Wilner 1985)—that *ASR* almost never deals with any of the severe problems or controversial issues abundant in American society.[18]

None of these observations are intended as criticisms of present or past editors of *ASR,* for they work harder and longer at less celebrated tasks than any other active ASA members. Furthermore, I do not think *ASR* should be anything else than what it is now: a journal of research papers, although it should publish more reports of qualitative research and theoretical as well as historical papers.[19]

Instead of making basic changes in *ASR,* we need another sociological journal that publishes what *ASR* cannot: articles of general interest to sociologists. Although such a journal should be published for sociologists and not the lay public and should be of high intellectual quality, it must not be a technical journal. This should also add to its appeal and help make it profitable for an academic publisher. We would not even be pioneers in establishing such a journal, for in 1987 the American Economic Association began to publish *The Journal of Economic Perspectives,* which described itself in its first issue as "a scholarly economics journal for the general audience of economists" (Stiglitz, Shapiro, and Taylor 1987, 3).

The editors of this new journal would have to use their intuition, experience, and values to decide what their sociologist-readers want and need, but I will describe some kinds of articles this reader would like to see:

1. Analyses of general intellectual issues in sociology, including, for example, studies of the roles and effects of sociology in America, the relevance of sociology in postindustrial societies, and the relation between American sociology and the American economy.

2. Extended debates about, and critiques of, current theories or trends in theorizing, as well as fundamental or controversial issues in empirical research, teaching, and practice.

3. Review articles of sociologically relevant work in other disciplines, such as institutional economics, literary criticism, and theories of knowledge.

4. Nontechnical research reports and *Annual Review of Sociology*–style articles about currently significant or controversial trends in American soci-

ety: for example, downward mobility in the middle class, causes of drug use and abuse, convergences of and relations between high culture and popular culture. This category could also include analyses (and corrections) of pop sociology, for example, of the decline of the nuclear family, the rise of greed and materialism in the 1980s, and the cultural and economic power of "yuppies" and "baby boomers" in American society.

5. Sociological analyses of current events that have been or should have been in the headlines, domestic and foreign, economic, political, and cultural.

6. Long reviews, of *New York Review of Books* quality, of important sociological books, well known and unfairly neglected, as well as of books of significance to sociology but written by nonsociologists.

7. Articles of professional relevance not likely to appear in *Footnotes, The American Sociologist,* or the practice journals: for example, analyses of sources of conflicts in academic departments, reviews of graduate sociology programs from the student perspective, and problems of sociological practice in profit-making organizations. These articles would frequently need to be anonymous.

8. Sociological biographies of influential figures in sociology, not necessarily from the past.

9. Provocative pieces that suggest unusual if untested (and even intestable) hypotheses, or offer thoughtful analyses of the discipline by relevant outsiders.

10. Shorter or lighter articles: for example, sociological reviews of art, literature, and films—highbrow, middlebrow, and lowbrow; studies of the depiction of sociologists in American novels, films, and television, and even cartoons of sociological significance or relevance.

A lively journal that speaks to interests we share may help a little to bring us together as specialization moves us ever further apart. Nevertheless, perhaps the best way to add some unity to the diversity takes me back to the major theme of this essay: our being more useful to the public and to its various sectors. Being useful, as teachers, researchers, writers, practitioners, *and* as experts, advisers, and critics, will make us *feel* more useful—and this will strengthen the commonality of purpose among us. Being useful should also add to our pride in the discipline, and pride is itself a potent social cement. But if we have further reasons to be proud of sociology, we will surely grow intellectually and in other ways in the years to come.

ACKNOWLEDGMENTS

I am grateful to many colleagues who made helpful comments on the version of this essay presented in Atlanta, and to those at the Graduate Center of the City University of New York, the State University of New York at Albany, and Fordham University for allowing me to try out early versions of it on them. My thanks also to Anna Karpathakis for library research assistance and to Allan Silver for convincing me to use an allusion to Alexis de Tocqueville's classic work for the title of this paper and the theme of the 1988 Annual Meeting.

NOTES

1. I had, however, made presentations about where I thought sociology was going to seminars at Columbia University in 1980 and 1985, each time before large enough audiences to suggest that there was considerable interest in the topic.

2. Some of what follows was also said by presenters of the Atlanta thematic and special sessions, but I wrote this essay before reading their presentations.

3. Some time ago I received a blurb for an annual review of sociology text for undergraduates and discovered that the vast majority of contributors were not sociologists.

4. I distinguish public sociologists from visible scientists (Goodell 1977) because the visible scientists she describes earned their visibility not only as scientists but also as popularizers and as commentators on social issues far outside their scientific fields.

5. Jacoby's hopes notwithstanding, public sociologists also have to be academics or practitioners, there currently being no free-lance writing market to provide a living for even one sociologist.

6. Actually, a number of sociologists are already working with ASA's Public Information Committee and ASA staff to write popular articles from papers in various sociological journals. Now we need to find ways to get their work into the media, which also requires learning what kinds and subjects of sociology will appeal to the general public, and the editors who supply their newspapers and magazines.

7. *Psychology Today,* which was founded as, and is once again, a commercially owned magazine, was for some years published by the American Psychological Association, which lost several million dollars in the process and proved that even a giant social science organization is not necessarily commercially adept.

8. Such features, which criticize us for the use of jargon, too many numbers, irrelevance, academic restatements of the obvious, as well as for triviality *and* excessive seriousness, still appear from time to time, and we should make sure that we do not act according to this now-aging caricature.

9. Moreover, article abstracts should not be repetitions of the first and sometimes the last paragraphs of the article but should supply readers with a summary of the article's findings.

10. I am indebted to Otis Dudley Duncan for this quotation, which appears in Sills and Merton 1991: 189.

11. David Riesman has pointed out that some survey researchers draft their in-

terview questions, have others obtain the answers and then analyze the data and never leave their offices either (personal communication).

12. Perhaps the current crisis in university library finances, brought about in part by the ever-increasing number of journals that charge ever-increasing subscription rates, will eventually put a damper on the publish-or-perish syndrome.

13. Their reasons for supporting sociology could shrink if cultural anthropologists who can no longer do fieldwork overseas and who learn to cut back on their appetite for exotic U.S. subcultures replace us even further in doing American community studies.

14. Again, I must omit the practice side of sociology, but the discipline's most serious long-term identity problem is our continuing to conceive of identity in academic research terms, as I do here. Thus, we neglect the fact that many practitioners may have little reason to identify with an academic discipline, especially if and when they are pushed or pulled by industry/agency- and job-specific demands for their loyalty.

15. Both of these boundary-crossing themes were considered by the 1988 Program Committee and translated into a number of special sessions at the Atlanta meeting.

16. The intellectual vacuum created by the economists' emphasis on econometric and model building could and should be filled in part by more ethnographic and other institutional studies by sociologists of the giant, and the small but innovative, firms that currently play a significant role in the American economy.

17. Harriet Zuckerman has suggested, in a personal communication, that some sociologists' practice of changing fields and the migration of problems and approaches from one field to another may act as countertendencies to fragmentation.

18. Despite the high reliability and validity of the sociological grapevine, my evidence is anecdotal, and we badly need sophisticated readership studies of the discipline's major journals.

19. In fact, the number of historical papers in *ASR* is now rising and one way to begin to ensure the publication of qualitative research reports and theoretical papers is to submit them in large enough numbers and at such high levels of quality that *ASR* cannot want to do other than to publish them.

References

Becker, Howard S. "Whose Side Are We On?" *Social Problems* 14 (1967): 239–47.

Coser, Lewis A. "Presidential Address: Two Methods in Search of a Substance." *American Sociological Review* 40 (1975): 691–700.

Duncan, Otis D. "Duncan Requests Reconsideration of Award!" *Footnotes* 2, no. 9 (1974): 2.

Gans, Herbert J. "Improving Sociology's Relations with Journalists." *Footnotes* 16, no. 4 (1988): 8.

Goodell, Rae. *The Visible Scientists.* Boston: Little, Brown, 1977.

Gouldner, Alvin. *The Coming Crisis of Western Sociology.* New York: Basic, 1970.

Hirschman, Charles. "Eastern Sociologists." *Eastern Sociological Society News* 2, no. 8 (1987): 3–5.

Hughes, Everett D. "Race Relations and the Sociological Imagination." *American Sociological Review* 28 (1963): 879–90.

Jacoby, Russell. *The Last Intellectuals: American Culture in the Age of Academe.* New York: Basic, 1987.

Keller, Suzanne. "The American Dream of Community: An Unfinished Agenda." *Sociological Forum* 3 (1988): 167–83.

Kohn, Melvin L. "Cross-National Research as an Analytic Strategy." *American Sociological Review* 52 (1987): 713–31.

Komarovsky, Mirra. "Some Persistent Issues of Sociological Polemics." *Sociological Forum* 2 (1987): 556–64.

Lee, Alfred McClung. "Presidential Address: Sociology for Whom?" *American Sociological Review* 4 (1976): 925–36.

Litwak, Eugene, and Peter Messeri, "Organizational Theory, Social Supports and Mortality Rates: A Theoretical Convergence." *American Sociological Review* 54 (1989): 49–66.

McCloskey, Donald N. *The Rhetoric of Economics.* Madison: University of Wisconsin Press, 1986.

Myrdal, Gunnar. *The Challenge to Affluence.* New York: Pantheon, 1963.

Sills, David L. and Robert K. Merton, eds., *Social Sciences Quotations.* New York: Macmillan, 1991.

Stiglitz, Joseph, Carl Shapiro, and Timothy Taylor. "Foreword." *Journal of Economic Perspectives* 1 (1987): 3–5.

Vidich, Arthur J., and Stanford M. Lyman. *American Sociology: Worldly Rejections of Religion and Their Directions.* New Haven, Conn.: Yale University Press, 1985.

Wilner, Patricia. "The Main Drift of Sociology between 1936 and 1984." *History of Sociology* 5 (1985): 1–21.

Wilson, William J. *The Truly Disadvantaged: The Inner City, the Underclass and Public Policy.* Chicago: University of Chicago Press, 1987.

Winkler, Karen J. "New Breed of Scholar Works the Territory That Lies Between History and Geography." *Chronicle of Higher Education* 33, no. 4 (1986): 6–7.

· 13 ·

Best-Sellers by American Sociologists

An Exploratory Study[1]

American sociology's support from the general public, in its taxpayer and other roles, depends in significant part on how informative that public finds sociology, and what uses it can make of the discipline's work. Since one of the many contributions we make to various sectors of the general public is to inform its reading members through our books and nonjournal articles, this study aims to determine what sociology that general public has read and is reading; it also takes a first cut at answering that question by estimating sociology's best-selling books. The study is about sales, not readership, and this article reports 56 titles that have sold over 50,000 copies.[2]

The identification of these titles turned out to be a difficult empirical problem, and discussion of the study must thus begin with a report on methods. What books by sociologists have been read most often by the general public can really only be answered by a readership study among a sample of that public. As a very exploratory effort what I have done instead is to ask a large number of authors and editors at commercial and university presses about the sales of sociological books (other than texts and classics).

The sales figures I obtained in this fashion were probably dominated in most cases by books sold to undergraduates as supplementary readings, but there is no way to find out from editors or authors how many of their books were bought by members of the general public. Furthermore, most undergraduates, future sociologists excepted, *are* members of the general public. Nevertheless, this is also a study of sociological titles adopted by college instructors. While these instructors chose the titles, I assume that some picked their supplementary readings to some extent because they

This chapter originally appeared in *Contemporary Sociology* in March 1997. This updated version was first published in *Required Reading: Sociology's Most Influential Books,* edited by Dan Clawson (Amherst: The University of Massachusetts Press, 1998), © 1998 by the University of Massachusetts Press. Reprinted with permission.

thought these stood a better chance of being read more than research monographs on the same topic.

For the purpose of this study, I defined sociologists as authors with graduate degrees or teaching affiliations in sociology. In addition, I included social scientists from related disciplines, particularly anthropology, whose books have been virtually adopted as sociological because their concepts and methods are so similar to sociology's, and who are therefore often cited or widely read by sociologists and their students. However, I excluded books by journalists, because while some of their works meet some of our conceptual and methodological criteria and increasingly appear on sociological reading lists, they are not the work of trained social scientists. More important, there is no way to determine what proportion of their often immense sales comes from sociologists, students, or other buyers interested in sociology.[3]

The study was conducted via a brief mail questionnaire sent to editors at all the major commercial and university presses that publish sociologists, and from a similar mail questionnaire sent to sociologist authors I considered likely to have written well-selling books.[4] Both authors and editors were asked to exclude textbooks. I further asked editors not to report on the classic authors, so that sales for the discipline's pantheon of Marx, Durkheim, Weber et. al. are also excluded.

I chose both authors and presses carefully from a number of lists, bibliographies, and ASA annual meeting program advertisers, and from nearly fifty years of experience in the discipline, as well from my knowledge of commercial and university presses.[5] My choices of authors were limited to living American (and Canadian) sociologists, which is unfair to, among other people, some foreign authors also read in the United States, as well as to North American colleagues whose work is read mainly overseas.[6]

Altogether, I wrote to 52 presses, of whom 41 responded and 55 authors, of whom 43 responded.[7] Twenty-seven, or 52 percent, of the publishers or editors—or their representatives—who responded supplied sales figures. So did thirty-nine, or 71 percent, of the authors. Three additional authors responded to an appeal included in the original article to send me eligible titles for an updated table, which was later published in the November 1997 *Contemporary Sociology*. Most of the authors and many of the editors estimated or rounded off sales figures; the number who could supply exact figures were in the minority.

As the numbers above suggest, authors were on the whole more helpful than editors.[8] In a surprising number of cases, press records were incomplete, particularly for books issued before computerization arrived in the book industry.[9] However, four of the twelve editors who responded without data indicated that company policy required holding sales figures proprietary.[10]

In any case, the findings of the study also reflect the problems of self-reporting—and these problems of self-reporting are numerous and obvious.[11] Whenever possible, I made extra efforts to get figures from both authors and their editors, and I practiced some caution by privileging editor figures when these were complete.[12] When respondents offered a range, as many did, I automatically accepted the lower number. Still, I had no reliable way of checking, among editors or authors, who had accurate sales figures or not, and who was supplying hopeful rather than realistic estimates.[13] Nor could I obtain data from presses or authors who did not respond to my mail questionnaire, my reminder, and my appeal for titles in the original article.

THE FINDINGS

The basic findings of the study are shown in Table 13.1. Because so many of the numbers I obtained were rounded figures, estimates and even guesstimates, I decided not to report the sales figures I received. Instead, I ranked by numerical intervals—and in order of reported sales—the top sellers for which I obtained data.

I except only two books from my practice of not publishing sales figures. One is the sole title known to have sold over one million copies: David Riesman, Nathan Glazer, and Reuel Denney's *The Lonely Crowd*. That book had already sold one million copies by 1971; by the end of 1995, Nathan Glazer reported (personal communication) that it had sold 1,434,000 copies. The runner-up to *The Lonely Crowd* was Elliot Liebow's *Tally's Corner*, which had sold 701,000 copies through 1995.

Without a readership study of the general public, I can only offer some hypotheses about what kinds of books by sociologists are bought most often—and these are fairly obvious. They are also risky, because not only do many books have several themes worthy of note, but, as every author knows, what authors write is not always what readers read, or even buy to read. Thus, the explicit subject matter of the book is only one factor in understanding the public's interest in sociology.

First, the age distribution of the books on the list reflects the growth in college and sociology enrollments, as well as in the number of sociologists in the last three decades—not to mention the changes in American society. The list includes only one book first published prior to the 1950s—Wiliam F. Whyte's *Street Corner Society*—and three from the 1950s. Four-

Table 13.1. Reported Book Sales, through 1995
Rank-Ordered Within Numerical Intervals★

Over 1 Million
D. Riesman, N. Glazer, R. Denney, *The Lonely Crowd*, Yale, 1950

1 Million to 750,000
None

749,999 to 500,000
E. Liebow, *Tally's Corner*, Little Brown, 1967
P. Slater, *Pursuit of Loneliness*, Beacon, 1970

499,999 to 400,000
R. Sennett, *Fall of Public Man*, Knopf, 1977
W. Ryan, *Blaming the Victim*, Pantheon, 1971
R. Bellah, et. al. *Habits of the Heart*, California, 1985
S. Lipset, *Political Man*, Doubleday, 1960
L. Rubin, *Worlds of Pain*, Basic, 1976

399,999 to 300,000
L. Rubin, *Intimate Strangers*, Harper & Row, 1983
N. Glazer and D. Moynihan, *Beyond the Melting Pot*, M.I.T., 1963
R. Sennett and J. Cobb, *Hidden Injuries of Class*, Knopf, 1972

299,999 to 200,000
W. Domhoff, *Who Rules America?* Prentice Hall, 1967
W. Whyte, *Street Corner Society*, Chicago, 1943
F. Piven and R. Cloward, *Regulating the Poor*, Pantheon, 1971
R. Sennett, *Uses of Disorder*, Knopf, 1970
C. Stack, *All Our Kin*, Basic, 1974
D. Vaughn, *Uncoupling*, Oxford, 1986

199,999 to 150,000
H. Gans, *Urban Villagers*, Free Press, 1962
R. Kanter, *Men and Women of the Corporation*, Basic, 1977★★
I. Horowitz, *War Games*, Ballantine, 1963

149,999 to 100,000
P. Starr, *Social Transformation of American Medicine*, Basic, 1982
H. Becker, *Outsiders*, Free Press, 1963
K. Erikson, *Everything in Its Path*, Simon & Schuster, 1976
D. Bell, *Coming of Post-Industrial Society*, Basic, 1973
A. Hochschild, *Second Shift*, Viking 1989
K. Erickson, *Wayward Puritans*, Macmillan, 1966

99,999 to 75,000
T. Gitlin, *The Sixties*, Bantam, 1987
I. Wallerstein, *Africa: Politics of Independence*, Random House, 1961
D. Bell, *Cultural Contradictions of Capitalism*, Basic, 1976
W. Wilson, *Truly Disadvantaged*, Chicago, 1987
D. Bell, *End of Ideology*, Free Press, 1963
P. Blumstein and P. Schwartz, *American Couples*, Morrow, 1983
I. Horowitz, ed., *Anarchists*, Dell, 1964
J. Loewen, *Lies My Teacher Told Me*, New Press, 1995
L. Rubin, *Just Friends*, Harper & Row, 1985
L. Coser, *Functions of Social Conflict*, Free Press, 1956
G. Sykes, *Society of Captives*, Princeton, 1958
J. McLeod, *Ain't No Making It*, Westview, 1985

74,999 to 60,000

M. Komarovsky, *Blue-Collar Marriage,* Random House, 1962
F. Piven and R. Cloward, *Poor Peoples' Movements,* Pantheon, 1977
W. Domhoff, *Higher Circles,* Random House, 1970
I. Wallerstein, *Modern World Systems,* Vol. 1, Academic, 1974
N. Chodorow, *Reproduction of Mothering,* California, 1978
R. Sidel, *Women and Children Last,* Viking, 1986
W. Domhoff, *Who Rules America Now?* Prentice Hall, 1983
G. Suttles, *Social Order of the Slum,* Chicago, 1968
R. Bellah et. al., *Good Society,* Knopf, 1991
F. Piven and R. Cloward, *New Class War,* Pantheon, 1982
R. Sennett, *Conscience of the Eye,* Knopf, 1990

59,999 to 50,000

W. Domhoff, *Powers That Be,* Random House, 1978
W. Wilson, *Declining Significance of Race,* Chicago, 1979
K. Luker, *Abortion and Politics of Mothering,* California, 1984
R. Sidel, *Women and Child Care in China,* Viking, 1986
S. Lipset, *First New Nation,* Basic, 1963
T. Skocpol, *States and Social Revolutions,* Cambridge, 1979
S. Steinberg, *Ethnic Myth,* Atheneum, 1981

*Citations are limited to original publisher and year of publication
**Sales for paperback edition only

teen were originally published in the 1960s, thirty-five in the 1970s and 1980s, and three in the 1990s.

Second, all or just about all of the books are jargon-free; whatever their other virtues, they are written in a language that at least educated general readers can understand. As a result, a few authors have several books on the list, and may even have constituencies of their own.

Third, at or near the top of the list are several titles that attract readers, and probably particularly students, from other disciplines. For example, *The Lonely Crowd,* books by Richard Sennett, and some others appear on reading lists in the humanities. S. M. Lipset's *Political Man,* like the works of William Domhoff, are among the several books of political sociology that also show up in political science course syllabi.

Fourth, books that try to understand and explain American society as a whole are among the leaders. *The Lonely Crowd* has often been described as portraying the United States of the 1950s. If decades are actually relevant empirical indicators of anything, their sales figures would suggest that Philip Slater's *Pursuit of Loneliness* and Richard Sennett's *The Fall of Public Man* may have served the same function for the 1960s and 1970s, and Robert Bellah, et. al.'s *Habits of the Heart* for the 1980s and 1990s.

That two of sociology's top sellers mention American loneliness in their titles may also be significant. Analogously, that some of the top sellers and a number of other books lower down on the list were at least partly nostalgic for a better American past is probably not accidental either.

Fifth, sociology was among the first disciplines to respond to the country's increased interest in problems of poverty and racial inequality in the 1960s, which surely helps to explain why *Tally's Corner* is second highest on the list, and why William Ryan's *Blaming the Victim* and Lillian Rubin's *World of Pain* are not far behind. Fewer well-selling books on these subjects have appeared since the 1970s, however, and no book on homelessness made the list.

Sixth, books about the family, children, and friends, as well as other works that deal with primary groups, are as popular as are courses sociologists teach on these subjects; surely one reason why Lillian Rubin has several books on the list. True, most of the best sellers are about larger groups and institutions, as well as macrosociological concepts, but by and large they respond to the audience's interest in specific subjects and political or social issues that had become topical in previous years, for example, race, ethnicity, and gender.[14]

Seventh, most of the books on the list are not empirical research reports, but, of those that are, ethnographies outnumber depth interview studies and surveys by a considerable margin. This is not surprising since they are apt to be most readable, to emphasize narrative over abstractions, and to minimize quantitative analyses. Probably the book on the list with the most numbers is William J. Wilson's *Truly Disadvantaged,* but more completely quantitative studies have no chance in this competition; also, most are published as articles, not books.

Eighth, the authors of the two top best-sellers do not hold Ph.D.s in sociology, but a large number of the other authors do—a pleasant contrast, at least from a disciplinary booster's perspective, to the majority of the authors published in *Contemporary Sociology*'s lists of the most influential books.

Ninth, only seventeen of the titles have women as sole or joint authors, several of whom are repeaters with several books on the list, and just two books were written by (the same) black author. However, these and other inequalities—for example, that most authors are associated with elite or other research universities—should not be surprising, even if they are still dismaying.

Tenth, forty-three of the fifty-six books (77 percent) on the list were first published commercially, twelve were issued by university presses—mostly by Chicago and California—and one was published by a nonprofit publisher (the New Press). Ten years from now, the commercial/university ratio is likely to be lower. Commercial publishers, particularly those belonging to conglomerates, are already being pressed to produce higher profit rates and may therefore not be allowed to publish as much sociology in the future.[15] Some university presses will most likely add to their sociology lists as a result.

Finally, that I could find only fifty-six books that have sold over 50,000 since the 1940s suggests that the discipline still has a long way to go before it makes a significant impression on the general public. How it can best do so is a subject for another article, but it should not do so by deliberately attempting to publish best-sellers. Sociologists ought to publish intellectually and otherwise useful work, empirical and theoretical, that adds to our own and to the public's understanding of society, and if possible, to its improvement as well. If sociologists achieve these goals more adequately, and write more clearly too, some books will sell more copies, including books like the high-quality and serious ones that crowd Table 1. Equally important, others will be more seminal or influential than now, even if they are not best-sellers.[16]

Should sociologists be able to produce more relevant findings and influential ideas about society, particularly American society, we may even be able to attract popular writers, including sociologists, who can report our work to the general public better than we can. The natural sciences have recruited an increasing number of scientists who are serving their fields as popularizers. Meanwhile, part of our informational role is being taken over by talented journalists, although too many of them still write on sociological topics with only a limited understanding of society. The journalists' increasing takeover of what should be our role is a far more serious problem than the scarcity of sociological best-sellers, at least for those of us who believe that sociology must increase its usefulness to the general public if it is to survive as a vital discipline.

NOTES

1. This is a slightly revised and updated version of the article that appeared in *Contemporary Sociology* in March 1997. The study reported in it exists only because of the hard work of staff members of commercial and university presses and, of course, authors who reported their book sales, especially those who went through their royalty files to compile exact figures. I am grateful to all of them, and also to the authors whose book sales did not reach 50,000 copies. They represent the vast majority of all sociologist authors, but I could not include their names and book titles in this article.

2. People may buy books that they do not read, and they may also read books that they do not buy, by borrowing from friends and libraries. Used book sales are another kind of highly relevant but unavailable datum.

3. Of course, the same criticism can be applied to books written by anthropolo-

gists, but their sales and readership audience is sufficiently small that they can be included here. Historians, political scientists, economists, and psychologists without any close connection to sociology were not included because they are all members of disciplines much larger than sociology.

4. The questionnaire asked publishers to report up to eight of their top-selling books by sociologists—other than texts or classics. Authors were asked to report the sales of their three to five best-selling works.

5. I also received and used nominations of authors by the editor of this book.

6. I tried to obtain sales figures for no longer living but popular sociological authors of the last half century, such as Erving Goffman and C. Wright Mills, but was able to do so only for the recently deceased Elliot Liebow, thanks entirely to the persistent efforts of his wife Harriet in obtaining the numbers from the publisher. Liebow, although trained in anthropology, was widely read by and worked mainly with sociologists.

7. Everyone who did not respond received one reminder. I should note that I received no responses from the big mass-market paperback presses, such as Penguin, that publish sociologists, or from their authors.

8. Sociology editors whom I knew personally or to whom I could write by name were more helpful than people whom I addressed as sociology editors or social science editors.

9. In addition, some big publishers that bought smaller ones did not get or keep data on the individual book sales of the smaller companies they bought. Moreover, publishers are required by tax laws to retain sales records for only seven years, and some seem to have destroyed them after the required period.

10. Some of the editors who failed to answer probably also did so for proprietary reasons, but I find the policy mystifying, since even the best-selling sociologists are not a major source of income, especially for large presses. Just about all the authors who provided no data indicated that they had not saved their royalty statements or were not sent data on number of books sold and a surprising number of authors did not look at that number in their statements, although I am sure that some did not respond to my questionnaire because they wanted to keep their book sales to themselves.

11. In addition, although all authors and editors were asked to report foreign as well as domestic sales, not all did so, although foreign sales are usually small. However, the books of some sociologists who sell well in the United States, e.g., Daniel Bell, Richard Sennett, and Immanuel Wallerstein, are very popular overseas.

12. In the handful of cases for which I had conflicting sales figures from author and editor, I wrote to both either to try to reconcile the numbers or to determine why they differed.

13. I can only add that I know personally many of the authors I contacted, but I doubt whether that discouraged anyone from hopeful estimating. Likewise, I assume that some editors who lacked complete data also supplied me with hopeful estimates. The immense logistical and other tasks of checking sales figures requires a funded study, perhaps by a graduate student interested in making the general sub-

ject her or his dissertation topic. In that case, however, I hope he or she undertakes a readership study, even if the sample of readers is small.

14. I also expected a correlation with the most frequently taught courses in sociology, but the number of books about family and marriage and even "deviance" is limited, although many of the best-sellers could fit nicely into courses on social problems and social stratification.

15. One commercial press that had published a number of major sociological titles over the years, Basic Books, was closed down by HarperCollins in summer 1997, but was then sold to a venture capital firm that has acquired several publishing houses. As of October 1997, the firm had not yet announced what kinds of books Basic will publish under its aegis, but it has rehired a previous Basic Books publisher and indicated that it will bring out all 150 of the old firm's titles already under contract.

However, there remains a generic "midlist" problem that refers to the future possibility of commercial publication of "serious" nonfiction books, induced both by declining sales and increased profit demands. The problem spans journalism and the social sciences, but even the most successful titles in the latter, including sociology, are typically at the lower end of the midlist in terms of sales.

16. Still, the books listed in Table 13.1 include a number of influential titles, including what has arguably been the most influential one of the last decade or more, in sociology and among the sociology-reading public: William J Wilson's *Truly Disadvantaged*.

· 14 ·

SOCIOLOGICAL AMNESIA

The Shortness of the Discipline's Attention Span

When I was a graduate sociology student many years ago, I visualized "the literature" as an ever-growing mountain of sociological findings that would continue to grow until, someday, the discipline had obtained reasonably complete and perfect knowledge about the workings of society.

Others held more sensible versions of this image, but the hope that scientific research could be cumulative—or mountain building—was forever destroyed by Thomas Kuhn's finding (1962) that the paradigmatic axioms that underlie everyday "normal science" are overthrown and replaced periodically. However, Kuhn did not go far enough. Even the normal science that is conducted while paradigms remain dominant is not cumulative, at least in sociology, for empirical researchers regularly carry out research that repeats findings already reported by earlier sociologists.

Moreover, they do so not to replicate previous findings. Indeed, they often do not know the earlier work, thus redoing what does not need redoing instead of moving ahead to new knowledge. No wonder the discipline is often accused of reporting common sense, i.e., the already known, or not contributing enough to the stock of social knowledge. Only social theory seems to be exempt from this rule, for theoretical writings often build on the ideas of past major theorists.

The hypothesis that normal sociological science is not cumulative is hardly new. Pitirim Sorokin made it the lead theme of his 1956 book, *Fads and Foibles in Modern Sociology and Related Sciences,* and I would imagine that someday archaeologists will dig up a Babylonian tablet making the same point[1] (Sorokin, 1956:3–4).

This chapter was first published as "Sociological Amnesia: The Noncumulation of Normal Social Science," from *Sociological Forum* 7, no. 4 (December 1992). Reprinted with permission.

291

Today, as surely in the past as well, the amnesia hypothesis is regularly discussed, often in personal terms, whenever older sociologists meet, and tell each other that young colleagues are reporting findings they had reported in the past. Professional pride, and perhaps also the fear that they would be stigmatized for their age, has discouraged older sociologists from publicly voicing their dissatisfaction. However, anyone who began to do research in the 1950s and 1960s must by now have seen repetitions of their own findings, almost always uncredited. I have found it happening in the fields in which I have worked, among them the sociology of housing, the suburban community, poverty research, and the media. A colleague who did not know I was working on this paper wrote recently, "I know that this is a damaging sign of advanced age, but I am struck continually that so many 'new' policy ideas are refrains of the 1960s."

Most of the repetitions are not major findings but small parts of the empirical building blocks that began to be added to older ones after World War II, and that could have been enlarged and added to even further in recent decades had energy not been spent in rediscovering them. For example, I have seen several recent papers on suburban neighboring that reported the dominant role of women, repeating a finding that a number of us made in the 1950s—and that incidentally probably repeated similar findings of the 1920s and earlier.[2] Further, I remember a recent review of institutionalization theory and institutional approaches that began with the 1960s, ignoring the earlier work that had been done (including by the founders of sociology) on these topics.

I am reluctant to report further anecdotes since I do not want to fault young colleagues for a common practice. Also, individual anecdotes do not prove hypotheses, but this particular hypothesis is also difficult to test. I suppose one could review the past and present literatures of a sample of major sociological fields and identify the repeated findings—which might be feasible once all journal issues and monographs ever published are analyzed for key words and computerized. One could also survey older sociologists and ask which of their findings have been reported again, and as novel findings, but not all older researchers find out that their work has been repeated.

Meanwhile, Cynthia Fuchs Epstein (1989) described the problem well in an interview she conducted with Mirra Komarovsky:

> Unfortunately, many feminist scholars today are not aware of the great contributions Komarovsky has made to the analysis of gender roles, regarding her work as a classic but neglecting to see how well it incorporates into today's studies. Many scholars, in fact, have rediscovered her

insights, sometimes claiming them as their own, or attributing them to the more recently published works of younger sociologists.

SOCIOLOGY'S ATTENTION SPAN

Looking for a way to support my hypothesis with some broader empirical materials, I ended up investigating a related one, also interesting on its own merits: what could be called sociology's bibliographic attention span. I tabulated the ages of the references that sociologists doing empirical work have cited in their bibliographies, and while this analysis can neither show whether researchers have repeated or ignored relevant past findings, nor test a more general cumulation hypothesis, it can provide some illustrative data on the attention that footnote-creating researchers pay to past research.

My method was simple: I gathered what I considered the better known and highly respected book-length empirical studies in four sociological fields with which I am familiar: ethnicity, race, urban/community, and media, and classified the cited references in ten-year intervals counting back from each book's publication. Thus, for a book published in 1978, I counted all cited references for 1978–1969, 1968–1959, 1958–1949, etc. I included all references, sociological and other, counting each only once, and leaving out only anonymous newspaper articles and self-references.

Although sociological talk among older sociologists has it that the failure to cite older studies is a shortcoming of the younger generations, a quick look at a couple of older books persuaded me to expand the study backward in time. In the end, I chose six books from each field, one from each decade between the 1980s and 1930s or 1920s.

The basic results are reported in Table 14.1. It suggests that the attention span is indeed short, for across the four fields I looked at, 55 percent of all references date from the decade prior to publication, and another 25 percent from the second prior decade.[3] Only about 20 percent of all references are three or more decades in age.[4]

Moreover, whether the research was published recently or six decades ago makes little difference. In every decade from the 1920s on, about 80 percent of references come from the 20 years prior to a book's publication.[5] Indeed, what Derek de Solla Price first described in 1963 as the "immediacy of interest in recent work," or the immediacy effect, exists in all the sciences (Price, 1986: 165).[6]

If there is a disciplinary sort attention span, however, it is not limited to authors, for there is scattered evidence that editors have the same problem. Barry Schwartz reports (personal communication) that the recipient of

Table 14.1. Age of References, by Fields of Studies

References Decade Prior to Year of Publication	Fields				
	Media	Ethnic	Urban/ community	Race	All
First	69.5	54.1	48.1	44.3	54.9
Second	20.4	26.2	29.8	28.0	24.8
Third	4.4	8.9	13.1	15.7	10.3
Fourth	3.5	4.7	6.9	4.0	4.6
Fifth	1.2	2.1	2.5	5.0	2.7
Sixth or prior	0.9	3.8	3.3	3.0	2.7
Percent	100	100	100	100	100
*N*s, References	1087	769	694	1014	3564
*N*s, Studies	6	6	6	6	24

an *American Journal of Sociology* rejection letter in the early 1970s subsequently informed the editors that he had picked a paper published in the journal 15 years earlier and had resubmitted it under his own name. Dean (1989: 183) describes two experiments in which researchers resubmitted slightly revised versions of previously published sociological or psychological articles to the journals in which they had previously appeared, discovering that the editors had forgotten their earlier publication, which in one experiment was only three years earlier.

That some editors are forgetful and that the authors of twenty major sociological works chose from two-fifths to two-thirds of their references from the decade prior to their own publication does not indicate that their authors, or all sociologists, have a brief attention span or have ignored all earlier findings similar to their own. They could have reported recent similar findings but left out earlier ones because they did not know about these.

However, these results supply enough illustrative data to suggest that my hypothesis of the unintended repetition of empirical findings, and the implications for cumulation, deserve systematic testing. More important would be close examinations of a number of such repetitions to figure out why they occurred, and whether and how they could be avoided. I say this in part because what is probably still a minor trickle of repetition today could soon be a flood, as the new generations of young sociologists doing empirical work in the 1990s and the twenty-first century forget the large amount of research published in the 1970s and 1980s, when books and journal articles reached a new high.

Some Possible Explanations

On the assumption that my basic hypothesis will turn out to be accurate, I devote most of the rest of this article to possible explanations. These may be somewhat premature, but they shed some light on the social structures and cultures of sociology—a topic that the discipline has largely avoided.[7] In addition, they suggest my title may be too strong, for the discipline does not suffer from the clinical malady called amnesia so much as from a structurally encouraged case of forgetfulness.

I propose several explanations. First is the tendency of researchers to cite friends, colleagues, as well as others they may want to impress. A second is sociology's evolutionary myth. It assumes that sociological research is always improving, that past findings stem from methodologically more primitive eras and that the older they are, the less likely they are therefore to be accurate or relevant. This myth, which sociology has borrowed from other sciences, has been expertly debunked by Merton (1984).

A third explanation is sociology's fabled ahistorical thrust. The claim that the discipline ignores the past is an old one, although it may be becoming less accurate as historical sociology becomes a major field. However, part of the traditional ahistorical approach reflects sociology's nearly disciplinewide belief that society and its parts are always undergoing change. As a result, old data must be out-of-date, almost by definition.

However, the fact is that some social phenomena change more than others, and some may not change much at all. What several sociologists reported in the late 1970s about how newspaper, magazine, and television news organizations choose the news remains largely accurate today. News staffs and budgets are smaller, but audience and advertiser demands, professional norms, and the need to cover and report a news story in a short time with a small number of words, or only seconds of television time, all create their own structural and other imperatives (see Tuchman 1978; Kaniss 1991). Conversely, many findings on sexual attitudes and practices from the 1970s are not valid today: a variety of family structures, moral beliefs, contraceptives, and sexual maladies have changed considerably.

Fourth, despite lip service about the need for cumulative findings, there is actually not much interest in scientific cumulation per se. In fact, the academic incentive structure in which sociology operates discourages it. For one thing, instructional patterns are not oriented to reviewing old research. The required course reading lists that each student cohort encounters are often dominated by the work of the students' professors, the reference groups of these professors, and perhaps their personal teachers—which may help to explain the two-decade bibliographic attention span.

Presumably, the pressure to be up-to-date is especially strong in university departments that perceive themselves to be on the "frontiers" of research. For example, one of today's well-known young sociologists had never read a classic in his major field published in 1945. It had been so deeply buried in his graduate-school reading lists that he never looked at it.

Sometimes, students put pressure on professors to be up-to-date and to omit what they consider to be ancient references. They are, after all, engaged in a vocational enterprise and want to be trained in the latest materials even when they are not heading for research frontiers. Thus, the ahistorical tendencies of sociology may be further encouraged by vocational pressures—of a kind also found in other social science disciplines. Indeed, bibliographic attention spans in the journals of these disciplines do not appear to be any longer than those in sociology.[8]

The instructional pressures, both from students and faculty, are embedded in a larger academic economy that includes other, similar, incentives. For one thing, faculty and increasingly students as well must cope with an institutional demand for speedy productivity so that there is no time and no justification for exploring the past. As I have noted elsewhere (Gans, 1990: 12), the academy functions like a piecework industry, and the administrators who reward students with jobs, and faculty with promotions, count how many pieces they have produced.

Under such conditions, noncumulation may be occupationally extremely useful. Sociology, like much of the rest of the academic piecework industry, puts a high value on originality; forgetting the past is functional for increasing (artificially to be sure) the number of original findings, and the number of articles and books that can be produced.[9] The ability to ignore the past also allows more time for the production of new pieces of research. It also leads, however, to the ignoring of older scholars who are either retired or no longer writing, even if their ideas and findings are still in use. This too is functional, because it excludes some colleagues from the citation indices, and thus from the occupational competition, however painful this may be for the older victims.

Fifth, there is the already mentioned unconscious borrowing from teachers, peers, and others in which many of us indulge. No incentive or mechanism for avoiding it seems to be available: while conscious borrowing is strictly punished as plagiarism, it remains gauche for a sociologist to remind a colleague that he or she had unintentionally and unwittingly borrowed a finding or idea.

Sixth and last, the practices of empirical sociologists seem to fit the general pattern first reported by Mannheim (1927/1952): that generations seem almost inherently reluctant to acknowledge the utility of past generations. Then why the concurrent, and seemingly unchanging, sociological preoccupation—in a postindustrial society sitting in a global economy— with a "classical" theory that first developed around the issues and problems of nineteenth-century industrial modernization?

The end result of the disciplinary patterns I have described is that sociology is not growing in substance as much as it could be. Although concept formation seems to progress, in quantity and sophistication, and sociological analysis is generally subtler than it was two decades ago, there is too much rediscovery of old findings—many of which have by now become the conventional wisdom to be found in everyday newspaper feature stories. To the extent that sociology is cumulative, then, the process is not linear but circular; we are going around too much in circles, even if the circles are widening over time.

The Possibilities of Collective Memory

My earlier observations indicate that sociology does not have much of a collective memory, and what it has is predominantly theoretical. Indeed, the term itself was only coined in the 1920s, by the now infrequently remembered French sociologist Maurice Halbwachs (1980). The discussion and worship of Durkheim, Marx, Weber, and a handful of other classical and contemporary theorists, seems in fact to be enough to satisfy the discipline's need for collective memory.

There is also the question of whether sociology, or any academic discipline, is, wants to be, or can be collective—or a collectivity. Annual sociology meetings attract about 25 percent of the 12,000 or so members of the discipline (or about 15 percent of the country's estimated 20,000 sociologists), but many come for reasons other than the desire for disciplinewide collectivity. Some journals reach more than 25 percent of the country's sociologists, though it is probably true that the larger their circulation, and the more mainstream they are, the less well they are read. Sociology does not even have common dramas, or even scandals like Watergate (Schudson 1992), that supply collective memories for a nation of almost a quarter billion people.

The future of sociology, as of other disciplines, is in specialization, and the continuing success of the American Sociological Association's sections suggests that social specialization is as much sought as research specialization. Since collective memories can be intellectually and otherwise confining and inhibiting, this is perhaps as it ought to be. In any case, the relative dearth of collective memory in sociology probably also helps to explain the lack of cumulation.

Should Anything Be Done?

Sociology has many more serious problems than the repetition of old findings, but even so, something is to be gained by more stress on cumulation.

Perhaps at least some of the discipline's ahistorical habits, which make us look foolish in the eyes of the historians and other humanists, could be reduced. If the long-standing faith in the virtues of the cross-sectional approach could be complemented with a look at the relevant past, the quantitative work that dominates sociology would have a little wider appeal—and the overall level of quality of the discipline might rise.

Indeed, judging by the continued public popularity of history, and the danger that well-trained journalistic free-lance writers—some without even undergraduate coursework in sociology—may increasingly take over the already small audience for sociological writing about current phenomena, there are good reasons for increasing the quality of sociological research. Actually, if the current interest in historical sociology holds, interest in old findings may increase as well, and if old studies are still nevertheless repeated, they can at least be repeated in a replicatory framework so that researchers can ask what has changed or stayed the same and why.

This, however, requires more interest than seems currently visible in middle-range theorizing about the dynamics of social change. We need to find out what behavior patterns and institutional arrangements stay largely the same and which ones change—and why. For example, why have sexual practices and attitudes apparently changed more drastically since World War II, than, say, new community sociability patterns, or the family structures and school performance problems among the very poor?

The creation of historical databases will be particularly helpful, but even before this happens, more primitively conducted sweeps of the past literature (e.g., Phelan 1990) are useful. Dissertation and publication bibliographies can be reviewed to make sure they go back in time, so that findings now perceived to be original are actually original by a longer timespan than a couple of decades.

Appeals for more historical consciousness do not usually go very far, however, history normally being less concerned with saving the past than serving the present. Nor is sociology likely to express much need for a disciplinewide historical emphasis as long as the flow of research grants, royalties, promotions, and undergraduate enrollments suffices to maintain the faith in ever-continuing methodological progress as well as ever-continuing social change.

But maybe it will not suffice, and we all know that sociology's future in some parts of the academy does not look as rosy as it did even a decade ago. Being more cumulative will not solve our problems, but it ought to be somewhere on the agenda when we get ready, as a discipline, to think more systematically about our future.

NOTES

I am indebted to Mirra Komarovsky and Michael Schudson for discussions that were helpful in writing this article, and to them as well as to Cynthia Fuchs Epstein, Gary Marx, Barry Schwartz, Charles Tilly, and particularly Robert K. Merton for comments on an earlier draft. Helen-Marie Lekas helped with the bibliographic analysis.

1. Robert K. Merton alerted me to Sorokin's book, and to the fact that his first chapter is entitled "Amnesia and New Columbuses." I do not know whether my use of the same title is a matter of independent discovery or unconscious borrowing of another author's work, however.

Merton had found reason to question the cumulative nature of research in his early work in the natural sciences, but he expressed the situation in the social sciences dramatically at the end of *On the Shoulders of Giants,* quoting David Zeman to the effect that "in the social sciences, each generation steps in the face of its predecessors." (Merton, 1965: 267, 267n).

2. What I have not yet seen are enough studies of suburban neighboring that look at whether gender roles change when both spouses work, and in communities of varying socioeconomic levels.

3. The reference to decades is obviously an effect of my categories, and an analysis of the references by year of publication might have shown that a majority of citations are from less than a decade prior to a book's publication, or coincident with major publishing spurts in the book's field.

4. Charles Tilly was intrigued by, and suggested more analyses of, the variations across fields, but while it is possible that fields have different bibliographic attention spans, my samples were too small to justify testing such a hypothesis. For the same reason if no other, this analysis should not be treated as a norm-setting exercise by colleagues who want to be citationally correct.

5. The high was reached in the 1950s and 1960s, with a figure of 91 percent and 88 percent respectively. Curious about my own bibliographic attention span, I also analyzed the citations in my three fieldwork studies, and found that 73 percent of all citations dated from the first prior decade and another 27 percent from the second.

6. MacRae (1969: 633) found this effect to be somewhat less immediate for sociology, using 1965 data.

7. Some are not so premature, for they have been well known for a long time. For more value-laden and angry explanations, see Sorokin (1956: 17–20).

8. By now, a good deal of anecdotal evidence exists to indicate that when journals run into budgetary difficulties, footnotes and references are cut first, and at times the older references go first. These economic realities will have to be taken into consideration in citation research.

9. The potential for high productivity of original pieces is enhanced further by the fact that each social science discipline can operate largely in total ignorance of the rest, so that its members are able to make the same discoveries, new or old, independently. This is immediately visible by some cross-disciplinary reading in sociology and social, especially urban, anthropology, and in political sociology and behavioral political science.

References

Dean, Dwight G. "Structural Constraints and the Publications Dilemma: A Review and Some Proposals." *American Sociologist* 20 (1989): 181–87.

Epstein, Cynthia Fuchs. "Eastern Sociologist." *ESS News* (Spring 1989): 6–8.

Gans, Herbert J. "Sociology in America: The Discipline and the Public." *American Sociological Review* 54 (1990): 1–16.

Halbwachs, Maurice. *The Collective Memory.* New York: Harper & Row, 1980.

Kaniss, Phyllis. *Making Local News.* Chicago: University of Chicago Press, 1991.

Kuhn, Thomas. *The Structure of Scientific Revolutions.* Chicago: University of Chicago Press, 1962.

MacRae, Duncan Jr. "Growth and Decay Curves in Scientific Citations." *American Sociological Review* 34 (1969): 631–35.

Mannheim, Karl. "The Problem of Generations." *Essays on the Sociology of Knowledge,* edited by Paul Keeskemeti, 276–323. New York: Oxford University Press, 1952.

Merton, Robert K. *On the Shoulders of Giants: A Shandean Postscript.* New York: Harcourt, Brace, Jovanovich, 1965.

———. "The Fallacy of the Latest Word: The Case of 'Pietism and Science.'" *American Journal of Sociology* 89 (1984): 1091–1121.

Phelan, James. "From the Attic of the American Journal of Sociology: Unusual Contributions to American Sociology, 1895–1935." *Sociological Forum* 4: (1989): 71–86.

Price, Derek de Solla. *Little Science, Big Science and Beyond.* New York: Columbia University Press, 1986.

Schudson, Michael. *Watergate in American Memory: How We Remember, Forget and Reconstruct the Past.* New York: Basic Books, 1992.

Sorokin, Pitirim A. *Fads and Foibles in Modern Sociology and Related Sciences.* Chicago: Henry Regnery, 1956.

Tuchman, Gaye. *Making News: A Study in the Construction of Reality.* New York: Free Press, 1978.

· Part Five ·

OTHER WAYS OF DOING SOCIOLOGY

Part Five illustrates some of the less conventional uses of sociology, and I include them in this collection to demonstrate the relevance of sociology outside the academic format. There are many nonacademic formats, of course, for some sociologists write poetry and novels, and a few have written plays, television scripts, and screenplays that draw on their sociological knowledge. (Conversely, many poets, novelists, playwrights, as well as writers for TV and the movies have produced first-rate sociology—many without ever taking any sociology courses, which only proves that writing good sociology can be learned in many ways.)

I begin with two satires. As I noted before, I turn to them when I despair about the usefulness of analyzing urgent social problems; I also enjoy writing them. Some are straight satire, like the first example; others mix satire and ethnography, or in the case of the "Workfare Presidency," satire and fictional history. Only a few of my satires have been published, probably because they are not examples of great writing. However, there is also not much room for humor in serious general magazines, a failing found both on the political left and right—or for that matter, in the academy. Satire is not only what closes on Broadway on Saturday night, as the old show biz saying has it, but it never appears in an academic journal.

I am particularly fond of "The Hard Core Experiment," because it and some pieces I wrote even earlier, initiated a line of analysis that resulted, among other things, in a lengthy and entirely unsatirical study of the underclass as the latest term with which to harass the poor. (It can be found in my 1995 book, *The War Against the Poor*.)

I have included two of the op-ed pieces that appeared in the *New York Times* although I have written many more for the *Times* and other newspapers that were rejected. The first of the two included here was, as far as I know, the earliest analysis of class bias in historic landmarking and preservation, and helped to bring about a change in that enterprise. The second op-ed piece is an early call for the municipal ownership of local professional sports teams. These have often exploited the citizenry's search for community pride by exacting huge public subsidies for the teams' private owners, and the sums they are currently demanding are astronomical compared to those of the mid-1980s when I wrote my piece.

I also include the op-eds because they are marvelous vehicles for sociologists to show off their and their discipline's analytic stuff. In addition, they provide expert training for clear writing, there being no room in these short pieces for anything else. Some of my best writing teachers have been unsung op-ed page copy editors who taught me over the telephone how to turn my somewhat-muddy 850 words into 700 clear ones.

I end this section with two reviews. The first is one of the twenty-five film reviews I wrote as film critic for *Social Policy* in the 1970s. Frank Riessman, its founding editor, gave me this job, and a column called "Gans on Film" when I became a father and discovered that only a writing deadline would force me to make time to see some films. Later, I turned the column into a bimonthly analysis of American popular culture by reviewing the big popular films of the day, and the review of "Jaws" included here is an example. I gave up the column when I discovered that I had caught the columnist's incurable occupational disease—becoming repetitious.

The final piece is my favorite among the many book reviews I have written over the years. It applied sociology—and my knowledge of urban renewal—to a children's book and allowed me to see how social issues were romanticized, infantilized, and depoliticized for children at that time. Children's books have improved dramatically in the nearly forty years since I wrote this review, and perhaps more so overall than the sum of books written for adults.

TWO SATIRES

THE HARD-CORE EXPERIMENT

Scientists working at a research laboratory financed by several major United States corporations recently extracted a small cyst-like growth from the foreheads of several monkeys in an operation that "may help to abolish unemployment and crime," according to N. A. Morton, head of the laboratory. Before the operation, these monkeys had been apathetic and hostile loners; afterward they showed remarkable improvement in energy level, emotional state, and group participation.

"The relevance of this experiment to unemployment and crime may not be immediately obvious," Morton explained at a press conference, "but a brief history of the research will make it clear. For the last several years, both government and private enterprise have been vitally concerned with the hardcore unemployed, but so far neither job placement, manpower training, nor other methods have been entirely successful. Evidently, some other causal factors must also be dealt with."

"In searching for these causes, science was once again inspired by common sense. One day, I was thinking about the problem of the hard-core unemployed and began to speculate about the meaning of this popular term. Curious about what unemployed persons had to do with hard cores, I wondered whether they had within them some sort of hard core that distinguished them from employed workers. It seemed a pretty fantastic idea; after all, apples have cores, but human beings do not—until I recalled that habitual criminals are often described as hardened. Consequently, I initiated studies to identify what we called the hardness factor. We looked first for a psychological syndrome, but found a sample of unemployed men to be less tough-minded than the employed. Then we proceeded to physiological surveys, comparing the two samples for hardness of heads, hearts, noses, and even for rates of sexual frustration. These surveys being inconclusive, we finally resorted to experimental operations on laboratory animals,

---

This essay was first published in *Society* 6 (1969). Reprinted by permission of Transaction Publishers, © 1969.

searching around the brain for a substance that might resemble the hard core. We are not yet entirely certain that we have found it, but this latest set of operations is certainly suggestive. The cysts we extracted form a kind of core around a portion of the frontal lobe, and what is even more interesting, they were found only among male monkeys, and among darker-skinned monkeys more often than lighter-skinned animals. This may, of course, be only a coincidence."

"Still, we are now applying our finding to the study of human beings, and at this very moment, members of my staff are touring the unemployment offices and prisons, examining chronically unemployed males and habitual prisoners for a similar growth. If this survey is positive, and we can obtain permission to carry out some operations, we may be on the verge of a breakthrough. And since the operation is simple, almost painless, and much less expensive than the conventional social and economic programs for abolishing unemployment and crime, the federal government is, of course, very much interested."

"But our findings may have additional payoffs, for my staff is now examining the adjectives by which the mass media describe black militants, draft evaders, student protesters, and welfare clients for clues to further experiments. For example, since radicals are often called fiery, we shall undertake studies of their gastric chemistry. I don't want to be overly optimistic, but it may be that physiological and chemical factors are responsible for many of America's ills."

Most members of the scientific community around the country reserved comment on Dr. Morton's findings until they could examine the full report on the experiment. But several physiologists were skeptical, and one Nobel prize-winning animal biologist was outspoken in his criticism. "All that talk about hard-core cysts is rubbish. We have some animals with bumps on their foreheads too, but if Dr. Morton had any common sense, he would first have visited the cages in which his animals are kept. Whenever my assistant forgets to feed the monkeys or clean their cages, they start banging their heads on the cage walls. I can't say I blame them, and the only thing Dr. Morton has isolated in his experiment is what we here call militant mammalian protest."

The Workfare Presidency

Historians compiling the record of the twenty-first century now think that they have solved the puzzle of the workfare presidency, that two-term period early in the century in which a politician on workfare occupied the Oval Office.

The story began, the historians report, with two twentieth century social changes and one record snowstorm. The first change was, of course, workfare itself, the policy of turning welfare recipients into subminimally paid workers in many public agencies and private firms, eventually including even the biggest multinationals. Workfare was initially used by a New York City mayor seeking to lay off city workers in order to cut the municipal budget, but it soon became the latest national policy for persecuting the poor—and covering up the drastic shortage of decent jobs for them.

The second change was the national recognition that the SATs, LSATs, GREs, and all the other computerized tests that universities relied on to reach admission decisions had very little to do with school or subsequent career performance. The most-often retold example is still Martin Luther King Jr.'s below-average score on the verbal portion of his graduate school test.

The disaster was a weeklong Northeast snowstorm that prevented teachers in the poorest schools of several major American cities from getting to work because they lived so far away. A number of "workfarers" assigned to clean the schools took over their classes, and several produced early student performance miracles in the lowest-tracked classes. The new teachers explained that teaching their own and their neighbors' children was easier than mopping floors, but sociologists added that the poor are often smarter than professionals from the pampered classes, for how else could they survive the hazards of poverty?

To be sure, even the new teaching stars could not keep up their success without proper training, but after low-income parents stormed school boards in several cities, the workfarers received training. Before long,

311

workfarers were teaching successfully in a number of urban neighborhoods all over the country, and even in a few suburbs.

Once the news media had spread this success story, other public agencies and private companies hired the ablest workfarers on a massive scale. In fact, some economists now argue that they gave the United States a special advantage in the global economy, allowing it to compete successfully with many third-world countries and ending the drainage of American jobs overseas.

Since the workfarers had to wear special identifying uniforms, they were highly visible and easily organized, and, as their numbers grew, they set up their own union. Forbidden by the courts to use the term union, they called themselves the Workfarers Guild (WG).

The workfarers also became increasingly attractive to the major political parties, and a few politically ambitious ones were able to get themselves elected. At first, workfarers ran well only in the poorer cities, but as more people had to go on workfare and workfarers became almost respectable, workfarer candidates were victorious all over the country.

Even conservative voters sometimes endorsed the workfarer platform, which stressed self-reliance, hard work, and mistrust of the government, while less affluent conservatives surprised everyone by supporting the workfarers' plan to restore the welfare state and the progressive income tax. But polls showed that the workfarers did best among voters who looked forward to a low-cost, low-tax government, staffed by elected and appointed officials earning only welfare benefits.

As the WG's political power grew, workfare benefits were increased, and eventually, they rose above the poverty line, so that poverty was abolished. For a while, every raise in the benefits also drove up wages and salaries, and the American economy, faced with a record-setting consumer demand from the once-poor, grew like never before.

The workfarers took political credit for it all. In 2016, they gained control of the Democratic party, and four years later, their first presidential candidate, Frances D. Ruina, won the election. In her initial term, FDR the Second, as she is now sometimes called, eliminated workfare, welfare, and corporate welfare, and in her second term, she won passage of the "Living Wage Job or Income" Amendment to the Constitution, which guaranteed economic security to all Americans.

Not long after the end of her second term, however, the workfarers and the Democrats were in political trouble. Economic growth had begun to evaporate, and a new political party sponsored by the country's biggest multinationals persuaded enough taxpaying voters that their fortunes would rise if old-style workfare and welfare were reinstated.

At the same time, several workfarer candidates were found to have resorted to the same questionable campaign practices employed by most other overambitious or underfinanced politicians. Before long, the Republicans, advised by a firm of high-priced lawyers descended from the original workfarers, were able to close down the Workfarers Guild.

By the middle of the century, the WG was virtually forgotten. Its surviving members were not dismayed, however, for as one of them put it:

> We workfarers showed that when they treated poor people just like other Americans, we were exactly as good, and bad, citizens as everyone else. And the amendment guaranteeing all Americans economic security remains in the Constitution.

Two Op-Ed Pieces

PRESERVING EVERYONE'S NEW YORK

Every time the Landmarks Preservation Commission designates another building as a landmark, the outside of which must be retained in its present state, the commission rewrites New York City's architectural history. Since it tends to designate the stately mansions of the rich and buildings designed by famous architects, the commission mainly preserves the élite portion of the architectural past. It allows popular architecture to disappear, notably the homes of ordinary New Yorkers, and structures designed by anonymous builders without architectural training.

This landmark policy distorts the real past, exaggerates affluence and grandeur, and denigrates the present. When only the most prominent old buildings are protected, the new must look worse than the old. The policy is undemocratic, for it implies that the only city history worth protecting is that of the élite. It ignores the contributions ordinary people have made to the city.

To be sure, the commission's practice only follows the élitism of most public cultural policy, which routinely discriminates against the popular; it is also similar to typical museum practices, which save and exhibit mainly the art of the rich and famous.

In a democratic society, landmarks policy should serve a more representative purpose. The commission should be protecting some typical and atypical buildings erected by and for all the city's people. It should designate a sampling of popular residential architecture, for example, the incredible variety of small rowhouse designs to be found especially in Brooklyn, and of office buildings and factories. It should also preserve some of the nineteenth-century tenements that still stand in lower Manhattan and elsewhere.

These should not only become landmarks; some should be restored to

This essay first appeared in *The New York Times,* 28 January 1975. © 1975 by the New York Times Co. Reprinted with permission.

317

their original condition, and others should be preserved as they are today, in their dilapidated, stinking state.

Aside from their historical value, these slums provide those of us lucky enough not to have to live in them visible evidence of how many people still have to call them home in 1975—which might help to get rid of such buildings.

Finally, the commission should designate some of the special buildings that served ordinary New Yorkers: a nineteenth-century vaudeville theater, a public bathhouse, and some taverns, for example. Indeed, these should be made into museums, to leave a permanent record of how most New Yorkers lived, worked, and played in the past. The Museum of the City of New York has made such a record of the city's Dutch ancestors, albeit mainly the rich ones, but its collection virtually stops with the eighteenth century. And if the Metropolitan Museum can erect an Egyptian temple on its grounds, should it not also put up a Lower East Side synagogue and an old New York church?

My proposal may be questioned on several grounds. Why, for example, make landmarks of buildings that are still plentiful? A good point, except that bit by bit, the popular architecture of the past is being demolished. Then, aren't most New Yorkers more interested in looking at old élite architecture than at its popular equivalent? No one knows, but they have never been given a choice, or even consulted on landmarks policy.

But wouldn't the designation of popular architecture encourage the preservation of the ordinary and the ugly? I believe that history should always include both the ordinary and the extraordinary, and whether buildings are beautiful or ugly is a personal judgment that should not be left solely to professional estheticians.

Once good economic times return, public funds should be used to help landmark owners whose buildings cannot be altered inside for contemporary uses, or which cannot be sold once they are designated. The popular museums I have proposed are entitled to the same public funds as museums that collected the élite past, for fairness alone demands that ordinary people, who pay most of the taxes, should be able to protect their past the same way.

STOP LETTING GEORGE DO IT

New York City ought to take over the New York Yankees. Professional athletic teams are supposed to represent and symbolize the communities in whose names they play, but George Steinbrenner's Yankees have failed this city on both counts—and the fault lies almost entirely with Steinbrenner.

Although he is occupying a publicly owned stadium, he seems to run the Yankees mostly as an ego trip. His incessant hassling of the whole team and individual players during slumps, his frequent demands for lineup changes, and his regular dismissals of managers began to demoralize the team several years ago, with predictable effects on its performance and, above all, its ability to function effectively as a team.

Steinbrenner's belief that bullying professional athletes will make them win pennants has instead led to the departure of Reggie Jackson, Tommy John, Goose Gossage, and Graig Nettles—all of whom the Yankees need desperately.

Now Steinbrenner is threatening and humiliating manager Yogi Berra by "consulting" with Billy Martin, who apparently is eager for yet another temporary turn as manager—it would be his fourth. An already depression-filled season shows no sign of improvement, and most forecasters relegate the Yankees to fourth or fifth place.

All of this is turning New York City into a national laughingstock.

The Bronx Bombers of old, while excessively arrogant, at least created a fairly accurate image: New York was top dog then and did not mind being considered elitist. Today's Yankees suggest, wrongly, that New York is a community of unhappy losers and a municipality that tolerates destructive executive behavior and a plantation-master's approach to labor relations.

Eventually, Steinbrenner may give major league baseball such a bad name that his fellow owners will force him to sell out, but Yankee fans and

---

New York City should not wait that long. Perhaps a local individual or syndicate could buy the franchise, but there is no indication that Steinbrenner is willing to sell. Maybe he would have to sell if an outpouring of New Yorkers in the hundreds of thousands bought stock in a new Yankee corporation organized to oust him.

But the most effective solution is for the city to buy the Yankees, using its power of eminent domain, which allows it to purchase private facilities for "public use" in order to enhance the general welfare.

Although eminent domain is normally invoked to assemble land for highways and public buildings, Oakland, Calif., is using it in a court case to try to purchase the former Oakland Raiders and get them back from Los Angeles. And this spring, Baltimore went to court seeking to buy the Colts in order to reclaim that football team from Indianapolis. The outlook for both cases was enhanced last week when the United States Supreme Court, in upholding a Hawaiian land-reform program, strongly supported legislators who invoke "public use" to obtain private facilities. Thus, precedents for buying the Yankees under eminent domain are available. In addition, public ownership would ensure that neither Steinbrenner nor anyone else could ever move the team out of town.

What kind of city agency the Yankees should become is a matter for experts in public administration, but it goes without saying that the team must be run by professional baseball executives, managers, and coaches.

Even so, under municipal ownership the Yankees could be asked to work harder to recruit and train good young local players, persuade more team members to live here, and encourage them to participate in the community during the off-season.

Public ownership would undoubtedly involve the Yankees in politics. Politicians and citizens alike would add the team and its fortunes to ongoing political debates, which could even be healthy for political participation—unless more urgent but less popular issues were ignored as a result.

One can imagine campaigning politicians using the Yankees to make headlines and win votes, young men asking their City Council members to help get them a trial with the team, and a losing manager or declining player lobbying for political support to stay with the team. Thus, players and team officials would have to be insulated from politics as much as possible, and from bureaucratic rules as well.

Public ownership is no cure-all, and it could turn out to be a bad idea. Then, after due public debate, the Yankees could be returned to private ownership. But if public ownership worked, New York would once more be celebrated as a pioneer in governmental innovation. Meanwhile, a municipal takeover looks like the fastest way of getting rid of Steinbrenner.

Two Reviews

JAWS

Urban Hero Saves Small Town

Since I generally try to choose the most popular film of the moment, I devote *Social Policy*'s first film review of 1976 to *Jaws,* the biggest box-office success of 1975. *Jaws* has also become the biggest moneymaker of all time (replacing *The Godfather*), but *Gone with the Wind* probably still holds the record for the largest total audience—even before its rereleases—since the huge receipts of recent films stem in part from ever-higher ticket prices.

Jaws is basically an exciting disaster film, describing people's ability to overcome a major catastrophe. A giant shark kills an unsuspecting swimmer in Amity, a Long Island summer resort. When Police Chief Brody tries to close the beaches to prevent further deaths, he is overruled by Mayor Vaughn and the business community, who fear the closing will keep away the summer visitors that provide the only source of income for Amity's year-round residents. After the shark claims several more victims, the beaches are finally closed, and Quint, a local fisherman, is hired to kill the shark. The last half of the film describes the long and finally victorious pursuit of the shark by Quint, Brody, and Hooper, a Woods Hole ichthyologist called in by the police chief.

Jaws differs from the disaster films I reviewed in the January/February 1975 issue in that its disaster is strictly natural, neither caused nor aggravated by modern technology; and this time, the heroes are not converted sinners. Most important, however, *Jaws* deals with an economic catastrophe, and is thus more topical than the earlier disaster films, although the film makes no direct reference to America's economic crisis and even plays down the economic crisis generated by the shark. Brody fights to close the beaches because he believes that saving individual lives takes priority over preserv-

This essay first appeared in *Social Policy* 6, no. 4 (1976). © 1976, Social Policy Corporation, New York N.Y. Reprinted with permission.

ing Amity's economy—and that the individual is more important than the community. The businesspeople who want the beaches kept open are depicted as callous; none is allowed to offer a reasonable justification for protecting the local economy; and *Jaws* actually seems to sneer at the way Amity earns its income.

Neither Peter Benchley, who wrote the novel and the first draft of the screenplay, Carl Gottlieb, who wrote the final version, nor Steven Spielberg, who directed the film, was especially interested in America's or Amity's economic problems; they were making a film about the struggle between a supernaturally monstrous animal and heroic people. Still, their title character is a handy symbol for the national crisis. The shark is an instinct-driven "eating machine," which can represent impersonal and relentless economic forces, but also an animal powered by greed, which can stand for the business community—and the way in which it gradually disables Quint's boat could supposedly symbolize the spiraling disintegration of the American economy. No wonder, then, that political cartoonists have used *Jaws* to represent various participants in the economic crisis. Only President Gerald Ford seems to have escaped being drawn as a shark, even though he and the shark share a stubborn determination to act blindly, endangering an economy in the process.

As a film about the economy, *Jaws*'s most interesting point, surely unintentional, is to laud slow, old-fashioned and individualistic ways of dealing with the crisis. Any halfway modern community faced with the immediate destruction of its livelihood would have called on the Coast Guard to make short shrift of the shark, but Amity's powerful rely instead on a fisherman with an ancient boat and primitive tools, who cannot even guarantee that he will kill the big fish. The film thus implies that Amity's leaders are readier to trust a local entrepreneur than the federal government.

Needless to say, a film in which the shark is quickly dispatched by the Coast Guard would not have been very entertaining—or profitable—but *Jaws* demonstrates once again the extent to which the moviemakers, like President Ford, defend individualistic but dubious solutions to pressing problems. The film's box-office success suggests that the moviegoers are still inclined to see such solutions, but they are seeking diversion. Besides, the federal government has been less effective in dealing with economic disaster than Brody, Quint, and Hooper.

Jaws is also noteworthy because the novel has undergone several sociologically interesting changes in becoming a film. As is the case with most novels, the film version of *Jaws* has cooled down the sexual scenes, eliminated some subplots, and simplified the main plot in order to condense the action into two hours. In addition, however, the novel's class conflict has been replaced by urban-small town conflict, and the characters have been modified accordingly. In the book, Amity is a very fancy town of luxurious summer homes, marked by cultural and other strains between the working-class natives and the rich summer people—Quint and Brody represent the former and Hooper, who summered in Amity as a teenager, the latter. The conflict erupts most vividly around Mrs. Brody, a one-time summer visitor who married a native, but now wants to rejoin the social circles of the rich, and seduces Hooper partly for this reason. Brody suspects Hooper of having made love to his wife and fights with him while they are on the boat. But Hooper is subsequently killed by the shark, and back in Amity Mrs. Brody decides that life is really better among the working-class natives. Furthermore, Mayor Vaughn is a turncoat working-class native who joined the summer people's social set after he became a rich builder. In short, the novel sides with the working-class natives, criticizes upward mobility, and treats capitalist speculation as criminal.

In the film, Amity is a seaside honky-tonk, inhabited by owners of small businesses who depend on large crowds to fill the beaches. Brody is a former New York City policeman who took the Amity job just a year earlier to escape the violence of the Big Apple. Not only is he still uncomfortable with the islanders, as they call themselves, and they with him, but his fight to close the beaches would save the lives of city dwellers who came to Amity to cool off. Brody is also far more middle class than in the novel, and lives in a large oceanfront house. Hooper is still rich but is not from Amity, and Quint alone remains a working-class character. He and Hooper fight briefly on the boat about their difference in socioeconomic status, but their real quarrel is over technology—Quint being the self-taught fisherman with simple tools and Hooper the possessor of the latest gadgets for killing sharks. Their conflict ends when they discover their common love for the sea and their similar earlier experiences with sharks that traumatized them both. They tease Brody, the city slicker, who had to bring dramamine on the boat with him and was initially reluctant to tangle with the shark.

Even so, in the film, Brody replaces the fisherman as the hero. After the shark kills Quint (who in the book had mortally wounded the fish before dying), Brody manages to feed it an oxygen tank and then shoots a bullet into the tank, causing the shark to explode. Thus, while Amity is saved by quick thinking and individual heroics in both versions, in the novel the savior is a misogynous small-town craftsman, but in the film he is a conscientious, middle-class, ex-urban policeman.

Although I had visions of the moviemakers deliberately altering the novel to argue the heroism of urban man, the changes actually resulted from nonideological, technical decisions taken mainly to meet the needs of the film medium. According to Carl Gottlieb, with whom I talked after reading his fascinating *Jaws Log* (Dell 1975), Spielberg asked that Benchley's rather venal characters be made more sympathetic so as to simplify the plot of what he conceived as an "action film" starring a shark—and to increase the film's box-office appeal. Once the actors were chosen, the characters were then further altered to resemble the actors physically and socially, in order to make them easier to play. Brody became a New Yorker solely because he was to be played by Roy Scheider, a New York actor; and he became the shark killer because, as Gottlieb put it, "an action film needs a hero who starts out weak and ends up strong by undertaking a positive action."

Yet even technical decisions have sociological attributes and explanations. Although Spielberg cast Scheider because he is a good actor, he could presumably have found an equally good one with "islander" qualities; but Spielberg, like Gottlieb, is of urban origin, which may have unconsciously affected his preference for Scheider, and even for an urban hero. The trouble with this explanation is that Benchley also grew up in the city—in Manhattan, in fact—and besides, place of birth has only minor effects on attitudes. The novelist and the moviemakers also differ in class and ethnicity, however, and these differences offer a more plausible sociological explanation for the film's changes. I did not talk to Benchley to find out why he chose to write about small-town characters, but he is a WASP, and his novel restates the celebration of the small town, which has been part of WASP ideology since the nineteenth century. Conversely, Gottlieb and Spielberg are of middle-class Jewish background and as such had no particular reason to celebrate the small town.

Nevertheless, *Jaws* is ultimately a film about a shark, which argues, above all, that nature continues to be society's major source of danger, and that the nation has a continuing need for heroes. This only reminds me once more of my favorite Brechtian epigram, in *Galileo,* that fortunate is the country that needs no hero. But I was also pleased that, even as New York City was being eaten up by a variety of fiscal sharks, the biggest moneymaking film of all time was telling its audience that the man who saves small-town America is a New Yorker.

URBAN RENEWAL POLICY FOR CHILDREN

MAKE WAY FOR THE THRUWAY, by Caroline Emerson. New York: Golden Press, 1961.

Much has been written recently about the financial and emotional costs imposed on people whose homes are taken by urban renewal projects, but less attention has been paid to a population that suffers even more, those in the path of new highways. They must move on short notice, and they are not even given the meager moving allowances paid by urban renewal. But such planning problems exist only in the world of adults. In the world that adults construct for children, they are solved with ease.

This "Little Golden" book tells what happens when three bulldozer operators building a new thruway find their path blocked by a house belonging to a rose-growing little old lady. There has evidently been no advance planning, and when the little old lady refuses to move, the operators are stymied, and they call the Big Boss. The little old lady does not want money; she argues that people need not hurry as much as they do and that the preservation of her rosebushes is more important to society than the highway. By no coincidence, the mothers of the three bulldozer men also grow roses. When the Big Boss is unable to decide what to do, and calls for the Bigger Boss, the operators get an idea. "The road could run a little to the right," says one. "People driving by would like to see the roses," says another. They work all night and when the Bigger Boss arrives in the morning, the highway has gone right past the little old lady's house. And later, when it is opened to traffic, the little old lady is proven right, for people do slow down to look at her roses. "Hm," she says to her cat, "they're not in such a hurry after all."

What is one to make of such a book? Old socialists might rejoice in the depiction of society as one in which a kindly and humane working

This essay first appeared in *The Journal of the American Institute of Planners* 29, no. 1 (February 1963). Reprinted with permission.

class is in charge of highway construction and outwits the bosses to boot; pastoralists, in the fact that their values are compatible with modern transportation needs. Conservatives should be pleased that change does not do away with the status quo, or hurt those who embrace the remnants of an agrarian way of life. Planners do not fare so well, however; they are left out of the book altogether, and the processes by which highways are built are fearfully distorted.

Adult reactions to children's books are not decisive, of course, and what matters is how children themselves receive the books. Until we allow children to review their books, we adults can only speculate. Perhaps children should be taught to believe that all problems can be solved without conflict, that planning is not necessary, and that the only techniques needed are kindness—and mother love. But I suspect that even children—who are, after all, masters in the use of power politics to get what they want from their parents—know that kindness is not enough. I wonder whether they are persuaded to the contrary by the books that adults write for them. One can only hope that, somewhere along the way, they are given the materials for a moral and ethical code that allows them to deal realistically but still kindly with the world as it exists.

· *Part Six* ·

APPENDIXES

Part Six consists of two appendixes. The first is an autobiography that I wrote in the late 1980s for a collection of sociologists' autobiographies. Although just about all of the twenty sociologists whose life stories appeared in the book believed that one could not understand anyone's research without knowing something about the researcher, many of us were nonetheless uncomfortable about our assignment, having never before been asked to write more than a one- or two-paragraph "bio" about ourselves. Like many of my coauthors, I approached my assignment hesitantly and earnestly professional, and as a result, I tried to write a sociological self-study. Our disciplinary earnestness not only made us appear more pompous than we actually are, but it was not even appreciated by the reviewers, some of whom were disappointed that we failed to report on our sex lives.

Self-studies include a degree of self-censorship and self-deception, but I tried hard to minimize both, because I was also aiming for self-understanding. Although I enjoyed writing about myself, I now wish I could have written a more informal memoir. Still, the autobiography should serve the purpose for which I include it here, to give readers of my work some background about the person who wrote it.

Books of essays assembled when authors are past middle age normally end up with their selected bibliographies—and even though the age at which senior citizenship begins is constantly moving forward, I am now past middle age. I do not plan to stop writing or publishing, however. I follow bibliographic tradition here by including a complete list of books and monographs but only a portion (actually about half) of the more than 160 articles or chapters I have so far published in academic journals and books, general magazines, federal reports, and the like. Not all are major works, but sometimes short pieces make a bigger stir than long ones. The list as a whole is also meant once more to illustrate the varieties of sociology I have written to date, and to inspire others to move beyond the journal article or monograph, and even to invent new sociological varieties.

· *Appendix A* ·

An Autobiographical Account

Introduction

This essay, written for a book of "intellectual biographies" by mainly senior American sociologists, began as a full-fledged attempt at autobiography. However, finding it difficult at first to write about myself, I turned the assignment into a research project about myself. Also, to stay within the editor's page limits, I chose to limit the self-study mainly to my first twenty-three years, and to focus it primarily on my work in popular culture, which had begun with a paper written for David Riesman's graduate seminar in popular culture at the University of Chicago about the time I celebrated my twenty-third birthday. The paper, which I expanded later into my 1974 book *Popular Culture and High Culture,* also dealt with issues of relativism and equality, which gave me an excuse to stretch the boundaries of the self-study somewhat beyond work done by age twenty-three.

I began my self-study with two hypotheses, which I will discuss further at the end of the essay. One is that having been born in Germany, my interest in American popular culture may have been in part a function of my own acculturation as a first-generation ethnic of Jewish origin; the other is that my espousal of cultural relativism and equality—as well as my interest in using social science research for developing policy—was connected to changes and inconsistencies in class and status that came with my being an immigrant. I used these hypotheses mostly to help me structure my recall and to put boundaries on my self-study. This procedure can be questioned on methodological grounds, but autobiography cannot be science. I should add two other initial hypotheses: one, that more basic marginalities unre-

This essay was first published in *Authors of Their Own Lives: Intellectual Autobiographies by Twenty American Sociologists,* edited by Bennett M. Bergen. © 1990 The Regents of the University of California. Reprinted with permission. The essay was originally titled "Relativism, Equality, and Popular Culture," and the introduction above was written especially for this volume, and replaces the first five paragraphs of the original essay.

lated to ethnicity or class encouraged me to become an observer of society and a sociologist, and two, that being better at writing than talking about my ideas helped make me a writer of sociological studies. The latter two hypotheses are probably virtual axioms that are true for many sociologists, especially those who do qualitative analysis.

1927–1944

I was born in 1927 as the first child of a bourgeois Jewish family in Cologne, Germany. We were comfortable but not rich. My father ran a small family business that had been founded by his father, who had moved to the city from Herlinghausen, a Westphalian village, and from a centuries-old family cattle dealership. My mother came from a family of affluent small-town merchants and bankers in the Hanover area, though her father had been an eye doctor. Both my parents were *Gymnasium* graduates, and my mother had a year of junior college; my father had hoped to attend the university in Cologne but had to join the family firm instead. My mother's ancestors had broken with Orthodoxy earlier than my father's, but both my parents were nonreligious, acculturated, and unconnected to the formal and informal Jewish communities in Cologne.

My parents' social life was limited to a handful of relatives and family friends, and my own therefore almost entirely to their children. Athletically inept and shy, I soon found myself more comfortable with books than with these children or school friends. When I was old enough to read books, I spent a lot of spare time in my parents' library and now remember most vividly that I enjoyed reading both fiction and adventure (including James Fenimore Cooper, in German translation) and nonfiction (for example, books by archaeologists excavating in Egypt and especially the books of Sven Hedin, the first Westerner to explore Tibet). I think that by age nine or ten I wanted to be an explorer. I was too young for, and my parents were not much interested in, German high culture, and German popular culture was sparse. The creative output of the Weimar era was banned in 1933, and when German filmmakers began to make mostly Nazi propaganda films, we no longer went to the movies. Beyond that, I recall only the brothers Grimm and the "Max and Moritz" cartoons, which described how the minor mischiefs of young boys and girls inevitably ended in death, loss of limbs, or other forms of mutilation. Tibet was both less dangerous and more interesting.

By 1937 my parents had decided to leave Germany and applied for an American visa, but the number of applicants was huge and the quota small.

Early in 1939 we therefore went to England, where my uncle and his mother had moved in the mid-1930s. Because one of my mother's aunts was a close friend of a high-ranking Sears Roebuck executive in Chicago, the latter gave us an affidavit, a crucial prerequisite to the visa, which enabled us to enter the United States, still visaless but under a special wartime exemption from the immigration law.[1] In September 1940 we arrived in Chicago, moving into a rooming house in Woodlawn, then a predominantly Irish low-rent area.

America was still in the throes of the Depression, and although our life in Nazi Germany and wartime England had already been austere, it now became even more so; my father worked as a Fuller Brush salesman, my mother as a domestic. Our downward mobility was surely harder on them than on me, although we were so happy to have escaped from Germany— even before we knew of the Holocaust—that our economic problems were bearable. Besides, the drive to regain bourgeois status began at once. I am not even sure that I even felt a decline in fortune. Compared to my mostly working-class fellow students, I was so well educated in English and already sufficiently interested in writing that a few weeks after I was enrolled in the eighth grade of the neighborhood school, I was made editor of the school newspaper.

My parents wanted nothing more to do with Germany or things German, and we spoke English at home. I knew precious little German culture anyway, but now I also discovered American popular culture. I still remember spending a lot of time in the basement of our rooming house reading a year's worth of Sunday *Chicago Tribune* comics in newspapers that had been stored there by a frugal landlady.

I must have been starved for adventurous and humorous popular culture because I also became a fan of radio serials like "Captain Midnight" and "Jack Armstrong" and of comedians like Jack Benny. When I had the money, I spent Saturdays at the local triple-feature movie theater, where I caught up on American Westerns. In addition, I became a sports fan and especially admired athletes whose prowess was said to be based on brains, such as Chicago Bears quarterback Sid Luckman, and Ted Lyons, the aging knuckleball pitcher of the Chicago White Sox.

My unqualified enthusiasm for popular culture seems not to have lasted very long, because in 1942, as a sophomore at Hyde Park High School, I was writing long essays, some of which were critical of the mass media. Later I submitted short features on the same theme to the high school newspaper. I also wrote a couple of pretentious pieces urging my fellow students to enjoy the good music I was learning about in music appreciation class, by Tchaikovsky and Rimsky-Korsakov, in particular. I was also still a sports fan, became sports editor of the high school newspaper in my junior year, and contributed to a *Chicago Daily News* readers' column on the sports pages.

Meanwhile, both my parents had obtained easier, better-paying, and more secure jobs as their spoken English and the Chicago economy improved. We moved into our own apartment, first in a basement that flooded with every storm, and then into a much better one in Southmoor, a small buffer area between poor Woodlawn and middle-class South Shore. And I gave up an afternoon newspaper route for a better job as a bookrunner in the University of Chicago library stacks.

Although I was as shy as ever, I was now on the margins of a clique, mostly the ambitious children of Jewish shopkeepers in the area. I paid little attention to my poor fellow students unless they were varsity athletes but was conscious of the affluent Jewish youngsters from Hyde Park and South Shore who dominated student life. While my clique wrote the school publications, the affluent students were active in fraternities and sororities, organizing Saturday-night dances for which they were able to hire nationally known bands. I imagine some of my cultural criticism was directed against them, although I do not remember any strong feelings of resentment.

In 1944, my senior year, I edited the high school newspaper and began to think seriously about becoming a journalist, although my father thought I should play it safe and learn business skills and my mother was sure I would become a teacher. Lloyd Lewis, a *Daily News* editor, persuaded me to study liberal arts instead of journalism. Unable to afford Oberlin, then an "in" college for Chicagoans with writing ambitions, I applied to the University of Chicago. With the help of a half scholarship, I had enough money the first year, which, having begun in January, I had to finish in record time because in August 1945 I was drafted. After fourteen months in the United States Army, first as a typist, then as an editor of an army base newspaper, I returned to the university in the fall of 1946. Thanks to the GI bill, some scholarship aid, and part-time work, I was able to stay until I received my M.A. in June 1950.

My socialization in the German and American class structures was accompanied by a very different set of experiences in the Jewish community. My parents had not wanted me to go to a Jewish school, but in 1933, when I started school, Nazi law required it, and I spent my first years in a secular Jewish public school. In 1937 my parents sent me to a strictly Orthodox *Gymnasium* because it taught English. This it did superbly, but I bitterly disliked the religious classes and teachers. However, in England I suddenly turned to prayer for a while, perhaps as a way of coping with *that* immigration. By the fall of 1939, World War II had begun, and all German-Jewish men, including my father, were interned by the British, who suspected that the Nazis had hidden spies among the refugees. Moreover, my fellow students could not distinguish between German Jews and Nazis, beating me up a couple of times. My religiosity ended after we arrived in the United States, but I was also back in a predominantly Jewish milieu, for Hyde Park High School was in effect another secular Jewish school.

In the summer of 1943, needing to earn some money, I went to a Jewish summer work camp, which provided wartime "stoop labor" to Chicago-area truck farmers. There I met a young and immensely charismatic Jewish youth worker, Samuel Kaminker, who believed in reading Hebrew and American poetry rather than prayers at Sabbath services. I was sufficiently interested in his essentially nontheistic conception of Judaism, radical at the time, to take some courses later at the College of Jewish Studies, searching for what I described in my 1947 autobiographical paper as "a rational Jewish religion for myself."

Kaminker was also an admirer of the Israeli kibbutz, ran the camp on a modified kibbutz basis, and started me thinking about spending my life in an egalitarian community of farm workers in which no one had to struggle to make a living. That vision stayed with me for the rest of my student days, and just before I received my M.A., I joined a small group of budding sociologists who planned to go to Israel and carry out participant-observation research at a kibbutz—as a way, I think, of trying to see whether we wanted to become permanent members of a collective. Even so, my interest in equality extended beyond the kibbutz because, after reading R. H. Tawney in social science courses and hearing him lecture at Chicago in 1948, I seriously considered studying with him at the London School of Economics. However, I never made it to Israel as a researcher or to London as a student.

1945–1950

My arrival at the University of Chicago in January 1945 produced a new set of marginalities, which had little to do with class, ethnicity, or religion but were more traumatic. One was the normal undergraduate experience of discovering my naïveté. Although I had been a top student at a top Chicago high school, where I had hung out with a quasi-intellectual clique, I was an utter provincial. My new fellow students were smarter and more sophisticated; many were combat veterans, four to five years older than I and many more years wiser in the ways of the world. I thought they were wiser in all respects, proper students with their own apartments, whereas I was socially immature, had to live at home and commute, and worked on the side to help pay the rent. Whatever inferiority feelings I had in high school were now magnified.

A second trauma was intellectual. In the 1940s the high school curriculum did not include any social sciences or humanities, and even social studies had not yet been invented. There was only civics and American history, which was just more civics but about the past. All course materials at the university, except in the natural sciences, were brand new to me, and I had never even heard of Aristotle, Plato, Kant, Hume, or Karl Marx. Old assumptions and certainties were therefore shattered quickly and often.

A third and related trauma was political. Once the war veterans arrived, the campus was rife with political discussion and action, involving groups of ideas of which I had never heard. I was wooed by Socialists, Stalinists, Trotskyites, and others who stimulated my interest in politics but also overwhelmed me, so I joined nothing. By the 1948 presidential election, I had begun to make up my mind, however, for I said no to the Progressive party and worked for Socialist party candidates Norman Thomas and Maynard Krueger.

The one early source of certainty at Chicago was my field of studies. Having spent the first college year in survey courses in the natural sciences, the humanities, philosophy, and the social sciences and having taken a graduate social science course in my second year, I knew where I wanted to spend the three years of study toward the M.A. In my 1947 autobiographical term paper, written in the first semester of graduate school, I reported that I was majoring in social science "but confused by too many interests: writing, sociological research, teaching, educational administration, social work (youth groups) and . . . Jewish religion and community life."[2]

Sociology was already my favorite subject because it seemed closest to some of what I had already been writing about America and to the kind of feature journalism that interested me. It was also sometimes less abstract than the other social sciences. Although I did my share of reading—and even tried to write—abstract theory, I was always more comfortable with what later became known as grounded and middle-range theory, one reason to gravitate toward fieldwork. However, I also read some John Dewey and believed in the unity of the social sciences. In addition, I did not like some of the required first courses in sociology and therefore entered the divisional master's program in the social sciences, headed by Earl Johnson, a sociologist who advocated many of Dewey's values. Johnson's program gave me the chance to take graduate work in all the social sciences, which provided a fine background for my electives, almost all of which were in sociology.

Earl Johnson also taught that the social sciences existed to help improve society, and thus he supported and strengthened my predispositions toward what is today called social policy.[3] Still, those feelings were not strong enough to get in the way of what I was learning elsewhere about the virtues of detached research and how to do it. In any case, the relative ease with which I settled on my fields of interest reduced my earlier intellectual flounderings. Another source of reduced uncertainty was my discovery of cultural relativism. Because all beginning students in the social sciences were required to take two survey courses (which covered sociology, anthropology, social psychology, and "human development"), I heard lectures from all the Chicago social anthropologists and read the other major American and British ones. More important, I discovered Karl Mannheim's *Ideology and Utopia,* and was very excited by his concept of relationism as well as his emphasis on the idea that all knowledge was a function of the knower's perspective. Most of my papers that year were Mannheimian in one or another way, and his relationism provided a criterion by which to compare diverse ideas—or cultures—without having to choose between them. Later, when I began to do fieldwork in Park Forest, Illinois, Mannheim's notion of perspective proved useful, although I was surprised by how many perspectives toward the same event were possible even in a small, fairly homogeneous community. However, I also learned that for some issues, including high culture and popular culture, it is not always necessary to elevate one perspective above all others.

Two other authors helped me to develop my relationist position. One was W. Lloyd Warner, also one of my teachers, whose lectures and Yankee City books made the notion of class more meaningful to me at the time than readings in Marx, Weber, and even the Lynds. Warner also started me thinking about class and the mass media, and then about class culture, because of his lectures on what he called symbol systems. Since he taught that different classes looked at society from different perspectives, a culturally relativist approach to class made sense to me, although Warner himself clearly preferred the higher classes. The other author was Robert K. Merton, whose essay "Manifest and Latent Functions," which I first read in early 1950, made an enormous impression because, among other things, it enabled me to see that cultural patterns disliked by one group can be functional for another.[4]

My preoccupation with cultural relativism and relationism also helped, I now suspect, to nurture what I earlier called my antiexpert position. Although I was trying to become an expert myself and was spending most of my time listening to or reading experts, I had always disliked those whose expertise manifested itself in the exercise of absolute and autocratic authority. My early rebelliousness against Orthodox Jewish teachers in the Cologne *Gymnasium* was followed by similar reactions in Chicago to a number of rabbis I met during my activities in the organized Jewish community. As the editor of the school newspaper at Hyde Park High School, I had bitter but unsuccessful struggles with the supervising teacher and the principal, who censored every criticism of the school and the school system. Later I waged a less vocal campaign against Aristotle and Plato, who were the much-assigned experts in every college course at Chicago while Robert Maynard Hutchins was chancellor.[5]

In graduate courses at Chicago from 1947 to 1949, I studied other subjects as well. I learned to become a novice fieldworker in Everett Hughes's course, and took Louis Wirth's course on the sociology of knowledge only to discover that by then he was much less interested in teaching relationism than in improving race relations. I learned economic history—and I think a good deal of what is now called social history too—from Sylvia Thrupp, and was taught content analysis and communication theory by Barney Berelson and Douglas Waples. In fact, I took as many communications courses as possible in the social sciences because, whenever possible, I was trying to connect sociology with communications and the mass media. In Avery Leiserson's course on public opinion and in other political science courses, I tried to figure out how the governed communicate with the governors, a subject that continues to fascinate me today but then helped lead to my M.A. thesis on political participation and to an interest in audience-feedback processes in mass-media organizations.[6] For Sylvia Thrupp I wrote a paper on the merchant writers of early seventeenth-century England, part of a larger and convoluted attempt to determine the functions of writers and symbol systems in social change. At one point I even studied the invention of the typewriter, and one of my early topics for the master's thesis was acculturation in the Yiddish theater.[7]

At that time I was not formally interested in popular culture—I am not sure I even knew the term. I tried to keep up with movies, best-selling books, and "Hit Parade" songs, but my interest was not scholarly, and, besides, my own tastes were changing. I had been persuaded somehow that a successful graduate student had to be able to play tennis, which I could never master, and to appreciate chamber music, especially the Beethoven quartets, which was far easier for me and much more enjoyable. I also shifted from Hollywood movies to foreign "art" films and went to some of the Broadway plays that toured in Chicago.

If my interest in popular culture was latent, it quickly turned manifest in 1949, for two reasons. One was the appearance of an article in the February 1949 issue of *Harper's Magazine* by Russell Lynes, entitled "Highbrow, Lowbrow, Middlebrow," a light but comprehensive survey of four "brow levels" and their cultural preferences and peccadilloes. Lynes described these levels with an implicit class terminology, although he was concurrently arguing that stratification by taste was replacing that based on wealth and education.[8] Lynes's analysis was often acute, but he was more interested in expressing his low opinion of all brow levels. However, the article crystallized a lot of disconnected thinking I had done about culture, class, and symbol systems, and I had no difficulty in jettisoning Lynes's tone and values and adapting the brow levels to Warnerian class culture.[9]

The other reason for thinking about popular culture was David Riesman's return to campus from Yale University, where he had been working on *The Lonely Crowd*. I had already corresponded with him about my plans for studying political participation for my M.A. thesis, and in the process he sent draft chapters of the book to me for comment, chapters that were filled with observations about popular culture. Dave was then, as now, one of the few professors I have ever met who treats students with intellectual respect, and once he arrived in Chicago, we engaged in frequent discussions about popular culture. Partly because he lacked time and, I think, inclination to keep up systematically with the mass media himself, he often interviewed his students about popular novels, movies, radio programs, and popular culture in general, and I learned an immense amount by keeping Dave *au courant*. His other important contribution was his insistence that studying popular culture was not only a legitimate but also a highly desirable scholarly endeavor. In those days American sociology was still close to its Germanic and American-Protestant origins, even at the University of Chicago, and popular culture was simply not a fit topic for study before Riesman returned from Yale.

One of Riesman's first graduate courses at Chicago was his seminar on popular culture. I took it in the spring of 1950, writing a paper called "The Metaphysics of Popular Culture." Of metaphysics there was nary a word, but in it I began to translate Lynes's approach into a more sociological one, developing the notion of leisure cultures and discussing how to assign people to them. I was apparently a total relativist then, for I suggested that the several cultures were functional for the creators and audiences in each and proposed the "complete equality [of cultures] from the point of view of social science research."

I also commented critically and at length about the different value judgments of some seminar members, who used the study of popular culture as a way of scorning disliked or less prestigious cultures and people. Above all, I came out against an anonymous member of an unspecified elite I called the literary critic, who represented past aristocracies and the present humanities in advocating high culture and attacking popular culture. Although I observed that high culture was equivalent to the German *Kultur,* the literary critics I had in mind were writers like José Ortega y Gasset, Russell Kirk, and socialist Dwight Macdonald. I was then already bothered that some socialists were culturally as elitist as the conservatives—and later I said so in the second paper I ever published on popular culture.[10] My literary-critic figure was the autocratic expert who defended universal standards that fed particularist self-interests, resembling in some ways the high school officials, rabbis, and student Stalinists I had encountered in earlier years.

1950–1989

The study design for my research on political participation called for a community with clearly visible boundaries, and Riesman suggested I speak with Martin Meyerson, a member of the University of Chicago's planning faculty, who was also involved, with his wife Margy, in community research related to the *Lonely Crowd* study. Meyerson told me about Park Forest, a new town south of Chicago, which proved a fine site for my thesis fieldwork. He also got me interested in urban sociology and city-planning issues. Although I still wanted to write, I had by then decided that I preferred writing as a sociologist to writing as a journalist. At that point I had neither the money nor the inclination to study for a Ph.D., however, and after I received my M.A. in June 1950, I worked first for Margy Meyerson and then for Martin, obtaining a marvelous basic education in city planning from them in the process.

By 1953 Martin Meyerson was teaching at the University of Pennsylvania, and he invited me to work on a study applying social science ideas and analyses in planning and at the same time enroll for a Ph.D. in city planning.[11] Because of my interest in popular culture, my part of the research was a study of leisure behavior and recreation planning, which became my dissertation and in the process enabled me to keep my intellectual fingers involved in popular culture. In 1957, the summer after I finished my Ph.D. and before I took a job on the project studying the West End of Boston, I researched the popularity of American movies in Britain. This study turned into an opportunity to test empirically my ideas about popular culture and class. I discovered that British movies were then made by Oxbridge graduates mainly for the upper middle-class audience, and that the other 80 percent of the country's inhabitants, who were still working class, went to imported American movies, which seemed virtually classless to them and, in effect, upheld many working-class values.[12]

In 1959 I began to develop the paper I had written for the Riesman seminar, and in the several longer versions that culminated in the 1974 book, I began with a fuller historical critique in which the original literary critic was replaced by names both on the right and the left.[13] I also elaborated the idea of leisure cultures, later called taste cultures, and attempted to describe the cultural preferences and aesthetic standards shared by each culture. Moreover, I began to move from value judgments and general policy ideas to more concrete policy proposals, which I labeled subcultural programming and which essentially involved government aid to cultures that could not make it on their own in the marketplace, particularly those of the poor, folk, and ethnic and racial groups, but also high culture.

In the first longer version, written as I was studying the Levittowners and working on the first draft of *The Urban Villagers,* I drew on my fieldwork among working-class Italian-Americans to qualify my original relativism. Although I defended people's right to choose the culture they thought good, I also began to realize that being richer and better educated, upper middle-class people had a better life—and surely more cultural choice—than poor and working-class people. Consequently, I wrote diffidently that "it seems likely that the so-called 'higher [leisure] cultures are, in the long run, more satisfying and desirable for their publics than the 'lower' ones for theirs."[14] I added emphatically, however, that the first step in readying people for the higher cultures had to be more income and education. My paper for the Riesman seminar had been apolitical, like its writer, but my stay in the West End had politicized me, first about urban renewal but then about other issues too.

By 1972, when I was writing *Popular Culture and High Culture,* I had played some minor roles in the War on Poverty, had written a good deal about poverty and antipoverty planning, and had just prepared for publication a collection of my essays about equality. As a result of the events of the 1960s and my own writing, I began to suggest that economic and political equality were far more important than culture, arguing that "a good life can be lived at all levels of taste and that overall taste level of a society is not as significant a criterion for the goodness of that society as the welfare of its members."[15] I was still being indirect and overly polite, but then as now, I think policies to reduce unemployment and poverty are absolutely essential, and until effective ones have been implemented, cultural policies are of minor importance.

Just as ideas and observations from my Boston and Levittown studies crept into the book on popular culture, themes from that work have also appeared in my other books. The literary experts whose judgments feathered their own nests I encountered again among the planners who decided that low-rent neighborhoods were harmful slums that needed to be torn down and replaced by middle-class housing, and among "poverticians" who decided that the poor suffered from a malady called the culture of poverty, which required behavioral therapies administered by other poverticians rather than jobs and income grants for the poor themselves.[16] I found another breed of the selfsame experts in my study of Levittown, for the critics who accused the Levittowners and other lower middle-class suburbanites of conformity, homogeneity, and various other alleged pathologies were blaming them for failing to support the higher taste cultures that were then exclusively urban.[17] The suburban critique also condemned the residential and other communal preferences of the lower taste cultures, once more using quasi-medical terms to legitimize the cultural attack. A somewhat later version of the same critique was employed against television entertainment, particularly violent programming, and although serious moral objections can be raised about television violence, I am not yet convinced by the now voluminous research literature that it is a significant cause of violence in the real world, even among children.[18]

Taste culture also plays a role in how people use the news media and what kind of news media and news they select as well as prefer, just as their position in American society influences the extent to which they find national news necessary or useful. I did not pursue this analysis in my book on the national news media because it was mainly a study of news organizations and because I could not find the audience data to back up my hunches. Even so, having retained my old interest in how the governed communicate with the governors, I devoted a chapter of the book to how national news organizations deal with audience feedback.[19]

The mostly indirect relationship of journalists to the news audience, and my fieldwork at the national news organizations, later made me start to think about how Americans connect themselves to their national society. That question then turned into a study of American individualism and society, on which I worked for several years until its completion in 1987 and publication in 1988. The study also tried to make explicit some populist ideas I had first begun to think about in graduate school, and to figure out whether a populist sociology is desirable and possible.[20] In my research I encountered latter-day versions of my 1950 literary critic because some current writers about individualism, for example, those who charge young people with being a me-generation or diagnose them as suffering from narcissism, are offering new versions of some of the old charges of the high-culture critics.[21] These writers are unhappy with the "lower orders" for seeking the material comforts and self-realization that affluent income groups and the higher-taste cultures with which the critics are affiliated have already achieved. Once again, people are being attacked with medical terminology for not living like the critics or following their cultural prescriptions.

ANALYSIS

In summary, I want to suggest which background and other factors seem to have influenced my work on popular culture and my advocacy of cultural relativism and equality. I began with two hypotheses, one relating to ethnicity and religion, the other to class, but both are limited in what they explain.

That I was born in Germany and am technically a first-generation ethnic undergoing acculturation and assimilation may help to explain why almost all my empirical work has been involved in trying to figure out what has been happening in America, and why I have done virtually no research in or about other societies. Perhaps being an immigrant encouraged my specific interest in American popular culture, but so did the sparsity and harshness of German popular culture for children, made sparser yet by my growing up under the Nazis. In fact, I did not arrive in the United States with much of an old-country culture. German culture had no prescriptions or leads for being an adolescent, and there were few German or German-Jewish cultural patterns that my parents wanted me to retain. They did not always understand or like the American teenage ways I developed, but given our poverty, wartime conditions, and my shyness, I did not develop many. Further, we did not belong to an ethnic community that sought to uphold old-country ways; the small German-Jewish refugee community in Chicago interested neither my parents nor me. I think the only host society to which I ever wanted to acculturate and into which I wanted to assimilate was neither society nor host, but sociology—that is, what we still call *the discipline*. (This I think I have done, although only to the Everett Hughes–David Riesman branch of "Chicago Sociology." I continue to be a participant-observer and essayist in a discipline whose dominant research tradition is highly quantitative. Once more I am a member of a minority, albeit by choice.)

The critique of *Kultur* that was part of my earliest writing on popular culture was not a rejection of my German origins, for, as I noted earlier, the major targets of the critique were WASPs. Moreover, many of the leading figures in German high culture were themselves Jews, almost all of whom also became American immigrants.[22] Perhaps my unhappiness with autocratic authority and later with self-interested expertise was a reaction against Germany and my conventionally strict German upbringing. However, my identification of the literary critic as the enemy in my 1950 term paper may have been connected to the fact that, when I was a graduate student, the kind of sociological analysis in which I was most interested was being done by essayists, novelists, and scholars from literature and the humanities. They still dominated American intellectual life, saw no need for sociology, and did not want to lose their virtual monopoly on writing about America, particularly for the general reader. They also dominated the serious general magazines for which I most wanted to write. Coming from the humanities, they were expected to express feelings and judgments about society—and no one cared if these also served their own interests.

If ethnicity is a major variable in my background, religion is surely more important, for being a Jew and a Jewish refugee from Nazi Germany had to shape my ideas even if I was fortunate not to suffer personally in significant ways at the hands of the Nazis. Most of the relatives I lost in the Holocaust were old people I had never met or had met once as a small child, and by the time the full scope of the Holocaust began to be revealed, in the late 1940s, I was so American that I reacted no differently from most other American Jews at the time. My brief period of religiosity when I was about twelve years old may not have had an effect, but something kept me tied to, and in conflict with, the Jewish religious community all through my adolescence. I do not remember now what I was looking for in my rational Judaism, but perhaps it was a forerunner of my later interest in social policy and equality. For a while, and from a distance, the kibbutz may have been the manifestation of my rational religion, but I soon realized that what made me want to be a sociologist and writer would probably make me a poor *kibbutznik*. Further, I was too much of an American and too little a Zionist to want to live in Israel.

My involvement with Judaism as a religion was eventually sublimated and ended by research, for I think now that I undertook a study of the Jews of Park Forest in 1949 partly to demonstrate the obtuseness and shortsightedness of the Jewish experts who did not want to understand the Jews who moved to the suburbs, and who thought that sermons against acculturation and heavier doses of traditional Jewish education would bring back their own good old days.[23] However, the ingenious ways in which the young Jewish couples I studied in Park Forest, and later in Levittown, organized their communities *sans* experts were also fascinating to watch—and since the arguments about what was to be done were always held in public, fieldwork in the Jewish community was always far more lively than elsewhere.[24]

The roles that class and status changes and inconsistencies played in my early life and work are the most difficult to untangle. I would have to begin, of course, with my family's indirect tie to a high Sears Roebuck executive, without which there would have been no affidavit and no chance to come to the United States. I cannot imagine that I could have been an academic sociologist in England even if I had been pulled in the same career directions there. I suppose that coming to America without any money but with a good education, and arriving at a time when my own and my family's desire was to be upwardly mobile and pursue an American version of our past bourgeois life, evoked my interest in studying class, although I think Lloyd Warner's analyses of and anecdotes about Newburyport were also persuasive.

If my encounters with the American class and status hierarchies of the 1940s encouraged my endorsement of cultural relativism and my interest in equality, I cannot now picture the process by which that happened. Other advocates of cultural relativism and equality have been upwardly mobile, of course, but upwardly mobile people have also looked down on and oppressed poor people who were not mobile. My early interest in the kibbutz as a place where job security was guaranteed and materialism appeared to be absent may have been a response to my parents' initial occupational hardships and a just-reviving consumer culture in America that seemed strange to a European and wrong in wartime.

I do not remember feeling any kinship with, and sympathy for, the underdog in those early years, either among the poor whites of Woodlawn who were our neighbors or among the much poorer blacks my father's employer was exploiting. Nor did the social science I learned at Chicago encourage such empathy, for it was largely apolitical and often indirectly supportive of the status quo. The realities of poverty and racial segregation really only hit home in the fall of 1957, when I began to live in the West End of Boston, met some of the poor residents of that working-class area, and saw how urban renewal would force additional West Enders into poverty or deprive them in other ways. I am still surprised, however, how unaware I remained earlier of the poor whites with whom I lived in Chicago's Woodlawn neighborhood, even as I was reading and admiring the egalitarian writings of R. H. Tawney and advocates of the kibbutz.

I imagine that my interest in equality and relativism was also a way of coming to terms with the feelings of marginality and inferiority that I experienced in high school and college and with the shyness that had already placed me on the social margins in Cologne. Surely yet other factors are relevant that a psychoanalyst can best fathom. I must add one more consideration: my two marriages have both been to women who were more emphatically and actively egalitarian than I. Since 1967 I have been married to Louise Gruner, a Legal Services lawyer who was helping poor people directly while I was lecturing and writing.[25]

Ultimately the personal needs and inclinations with which one enters a scholarly discipline are impulses that must be brought out and developed by the intellectual training one receives. Thus I must implicate and credit the people with whom I studied, especially at the Universities of Chicago and Pennsylvania. The teachers (and authors) who are most responsible are mentioned by name in the text and notes of this essay, but many others are not named, some of them fellow students rather than faculty.[26] Then there are those people whom I did not even know but who helped to shape the intellectually and otherwise stimulating period from 1945 to 1950 at the University of Chicago. Surely I am also explained as a product of those particular 1940s.

NOTES

1. Sears Roebuck had been built up by Julius Rosenwald, himself a German-Jewish immigrant in the nineteenth century, and the store was then still run mostly by Jews. Many years later we discovered that one of my mother's ancestors was a cousin of Rosenwald's.

2. The paper was written for an education course that some of my fellow sociology students and I took because it would make us eligible for high school teaching later. I suspect that my interest in educational administration may have been included to impress the instructor, but I did not go back for the other required education courses. I suppose I would have liked to be a sociology professor even then, but such jobs were scarce, and I was not even in the department. I still do not understand my failure to make any practical occupational plans while in graduate school, but I do not recall any major anxiety about how I would earn a living after the M.A. However, the late 1940s were the start of the affluent society, even if it did not arrive for sociologists until much later.

3. Earl S. Johnson, *The Humanistic Teachings of Earl S. Johnson,* ed. John D. Hass (Boulder, Colo.: Westview Press, 1983). In addition, I was enrolled in an introductory graduate survey course entitled "The Scope and Methods of Social Sciences," which focused on "how the problem of a united, free, peaceful, prosperous world may be attacked by social science" ("Syllabus, The Scope and Methods of the Social Sciences," Division of the Social Sciences, University of Chicago, 1st ed. [October 1946], 11). My section of the course was led by Bert Hoselitz, but many other social scientists at the university lectured in the course.

4. I still remember virtually sneaking into the campus bookstore for my copy of Merton's *Social Theory and Social Structure* because the rivalry between the Co-

lumbia and Chicago sociology departments discouraged undue interest in Columbia authors.

5. During my undergraduate days, I was on the staff of the college humor magazine and wrote a number of satirical pieces in which Plato and Aristotle were the villains. The only one I published reported the desertion of the university by its students after the chancellor banned bridge playing (of which I seem also to have disapproved) until researchers discovered that the game had been invented by a close friend of Aristotle; then the chancellor reversed his decision. "Hearts Were Trump When Aristotle Smiled," *Pulse Magazine,* April 1947, 17.

6. My interest in audience feedback mechanisms resulted in one of my first published papers, "The Creator-Audience Relationship in the Mass Media: An Analysis of Movie-Making," in *Mass Culture: The Popular Arts in America,* ed. Bernard Rosenberg and David M. White (Glencoe, Ill.: Free Press, 1957), 315–24.

7. I had to drop this topic because I did not read or speak Yiddish and thus could not content-analyze the plays, but I later made and published studies of acculturation in the work of two popular American-Jewish comedians, Mickey Katz and Allan Sherman. My interest in sociological research in the Jewish community was stimulated by a brilliant course that Erich Rosenthal, who later taught for three decades at Queens College in New York, gave at the College of Jewish Studies in 1947, using mainly novels because of the lack of sociological studies. In those days sociology was close to heresy at the college, and Rosenthal was able to give the course only once.

8. Lynes later reprinted the article as chapter 13 of *The Tastemakers* (New York: Harper, 1955).

9. In fact, I did so virtually at once, in a term paper comparing the concepts of culture and *Kultur,* which I wrote in the spring of 1949 for Kurt Riezler, a visiting professor from the New School for Social Research.

10. Moreover, that paper was published in a socialist magazine and consisted largely of a critique of Harold Rosenberg, the art critic who was one of its major contributors. "Popular Culture and Its High Culture Critics," *Dissent* 5 (1958): 185–87.

11. I also had an invitation from Robert K. Merton to study for my Ph.D. in sociology at Columbia University and a job offer from the Bureau of Applied Social Research, but it involved assisting Fred Inklé in a study to help plan the evacuation of American cities in World War III. Partly because I had lived through the London blitz in 1940, it was not a subject I wanted to study.

12. I wrote a book-length monograph, which also dealt with the topics I had covered in my 1950 seminar paper, and later published an article, "Hollywood Films on British Screens: An Analysis of the Functions of Popular Culture Abroad," *Social Problems* 9 (1962): 324–28.

13. Herbert J. Gans, "The Social Structure of Popular Culture," unpublished paper, February 1959, 29. Later versions of the paper were "Pluralist Esthetics and Subcultural Programming: A Proposal for Cultural Democracy in the Mass Media," *Studies in Public Communication,* no. 3 (Summer 1961): 27–35; and "Popular Culture

in America: Social Problem or Social Asset in a Pluralist Society," in *Social Problems: A Modern Approach,* ed. Howard S. Becker (New York: Wiley, 1966), 549–620. A revised version, written for an abortive second edition of Howard Becker's text, is in *Literary Taste, Culture and Mass Communication,* ed. W. Phillips Davison, Rolf Meyersohn and Edward Shils (Teaneck, N.J.: Somerset House, 1972). An updated version of my book *Popular Culture and High Culture,* entitled "American Popular Culture and High Culture in a Changing Class Structure," appears in *Art, Ideology and Politics,* ed. Judith H. Balfe and Margaret Wyszomirski (New York: Praeger, 1985).

14. Gans, "Social Structure of Popular Culture," 29.

15. Gans, *Popular Culture and High Culture,* 130.

16. Herbert J. Gans, *The Urban Villagers,* updated and expanded ed. (New York: Free Press, 1982), 283–88.

17. Here my conclusions agreed with those of the editor of this anthology. See Bennett M. Berger, *Working-Class Suburb* (Berkeley and Los Angeles: University of California Press, 1960).

18. This argument appears in my essay "The Audience for Television—and in Television Research," in *Television and Social Behavior,* ed. Stephen B. Withey and Ronald P. Abeles (Hillsdale, N.J.: Erlbaum, 1980), 55–81.

19. Herbert J. Gans, *Deciding What's News: A Study of CBS Evening News, NBC Nightly News, Newsweek, and Time,* chap. 7 (New York: Pantheon Books, 1979).

20. The book is *Middle American Individualism: The Future of Liberal Democracy* (New York: Free Press, 1988). By the 1980s populism had become a conservative term, and, for this reason and others, I went back to a concept I had learned from Martin Meyerson in the 1950s. It looked at people as users—of goods, services, ideas, policies, and the like, and I spent some pages of the book on the possibility of more user-oriented sociology.

21. One of those writers is Christopher Lasch, whose analysis I discuss in "Culture, Community, and Equality," *democracy* 2 (April 1982): 81–87.

22. Many of those immigrants were hostile to American popular culture, however, partly for class reasons but also because they felt that German popular culture had helped bring the Nazis to power and feared that the United States could become a fascist dictatorship.

23. That study also owed a considerable debt to W. Lloyd Warner and Leo Srole, *The Social Systems of American Ethnic Groups* (New York: Yale University Press, 1945). It is reported most fully in my "The Origin and Growth of a Jewish Community in the Suburbs: A Study of the Jews of Park Forest," in *The Jews: Social Patterns of an American Ethnic Group,* ed. Marshall Sklare (Glencoe, Ill.: Free Press, 1958), 205–48.

24. My search for a rational religion ended more than thirty years ago, but occasionally the urge to do more empirical research in the Jewish community and to see whether the experts are still offering the same solutions has to be suppressed. For some observations of American Jewry not based on systematic research, see my "Symbolic Ethnicity: The Future of Ethnic Groups and Cultures," in *On the Mak-*

ing of Americans: Essays in Honor of David Riesman, ed. Herbert J. Gans, Nathan Glazer, Joseph R. Gusfield, and Christopher Jencks (Philadelphia: University of Pennsylvania Press, 1979), 193–220.

25. In 1987 my wife was elected to a judgeship in New York's Civil Court. During the latter half of the 1950s, I was married to Iris Lezak, an artist who had taken a vow of poverty.

26. Some other sociologists at the University of Chicago to whom I am indebted are two then-junior professors: Reinhard Bendix, the first of my sociology teachers when I was an undergraduate, and Morris Janowitz, for whom I conducted some initial research as he was beginning his community newspaper study. I also benefited from teaching assistants and researchers associated with the Department of Sociology—and the names I now remember are Margaret Fallers, S. C. Gilfillan, Robert Johnson, and Harvey L. Smith—as well as from many professors in sociology and in other departments who are too numerous to mention.

· *Appendix B* ·

Selected Works by Herbert J. Gans

Books and Monographs

Accelerated Urban Growth in a Metropolitan Fringe Area. Summary report, mimeographed. Philadelphia: Institute for Urban Studies, University of Pennsylvania, 1953.

American Films and Television Programs on British Screens: A Study of the Functions of American Popular Culture Abroad. Mimeographed. Philadelphia: Institute for Urban Studies, University of Pennsylvania, June 1959.

The Urban Villagers: Group and Class in the Life of Italian-Americans. New York: Free Press of Glencoe, 1962; paperback, 1965; Updated and exp. ed., 1982; London: Collier Macmillan Publishers, 1982.

The Levittowners: Ways of Life and Politics in a New Suburban Community. New York: Pantheon Books, 1967; New York: Vintage (paperback), 1967; London: Allen Lane, The Penguin Press, 1967; Paperback, 1969; Berlin: Bertelsmann Fachverlag, 1969; Florence, Italy: Saggiatore, 1971; Morningside edition. New York: Columbia University Press, 1982.

People and Plans: Essays on Urban Problems and Solutions. New York: Basic Books, 1968; paperback, 1971; London: Penguin (paperback), 1972.

The Uses of Television and Their Educational Implications. New York: Center for Urban Education, June 1968.

More Equality. New York: Pantheon Books, 1973; New York: Vintage (paperback), 1974.

Popular Culture and High Culture: An Analysis and Evaluation of Taste. New York: Basic Books, 1974; Harper Colophon (paperback), 1977.

Deciding What's News: A Study of CBS Evening News, NBC Nightly News, Newsweek and Time. New York: Pantheon Books, 1979; New York: Vintage (paperback), 1980; London: Constable Books, 1980.

On the Making of Americans: Essays in Honor of David Riesman, edited with

Nathan Glazer, Joseph R. Gusfield, and Christopher Jencks. Philadelphia: University of Pennsylvania, 1979.

Middle American Individualism: The Future of Liberal Democracy. New York: Free Press, 1988. (New preface and subtitle: *Political Participation and Liberal Democracy.*) Oxford (paperback), 1991.

Sociology in America. Newbury Park, Calif.: Sage Publications, 1990 (editor).

People, Plans, and Policies: Essays on Poverty, Racism, and Other National Urban Problems. New York: Columbia University Press and Russell Sage Foundation, 1991. New Preface (paperback), 1994.

The War Against the Poor: The Underclass and Antipoverty Policy. New York: Basic Books, 1995; paperback, 1996.

ARTICLES: SCHOLARLY AND GENERAL

"Park Forest: Birth of a Jewish Community." *Commentary* 11 (April 1951): 330–39.

"Planning and Political Participation: A Study of Political Participation in a Planned New Town." *Journal of the American Institute of Planners* 19 (1953): 3–9.

"The 'Yinglish' Music of Mickey Katz: A Study in American-Jewish Popular Culture." *American Quarterly* 5 (1953): 213–18.

"The Sociology of New Towns." *Sociology and Social Research* 40 (1956): 231–39.

"Planning, Institutional Policy and User Behavior: The Public Library, A Case Study." Chicago: Institute of Social Research, University of Chicago, 1956.

"American Jewry: Present and Future." *Commentary* 21 (May 1956): 422–30.

"The Future of American Jewry." *Commentary* 21 (June 1956): 555–63.

"The Creator-Audience Relationship in the Mass Media: An Analysis of Movie Making." In *Mass Culture: The Popular Arts in America,* edited by B. Rosenberg and D. White, 315–24. New York: Free Press, 1957.

"The Progress of a Suburban Jewish Community." *Commentary* 22 (February 1957): 113–22.

"The Goal-Oriented Approach to Planning." Mimeograph, Puerto Rico Planning Society and Puerto Economic Association, February 1958. Published in *People and Plans,* New York: Basic Books, 1968.

"The Origin and Growth of a Jewish Community in the Suburbs: A Study of the Jews of Park Forest." In *The Jews: Social Patterns of an American Group,* edited by Marshall Sklare, 205–48. New York: Free Press, 1958.

"The Human Implications of Current Redevelopment and Relocation Planning." *Journal of the American Institute of Planners* 25 (1959): 15–25.

"Planning and Social Life: An Evaluation of Friendship and Neighbor Relations in Suburban Communities." *Journal of the American Institute of Planners* 27 (May 1961): 134–40.

"The Balanced Community: An Evaluation of Homogeneity and Heterogeneity in Residential Areas." *Journal of the American Institute of Planners* 27 (August 1961): 176–84.

"Pluralist Esthetics and Subcultural Programming: A Proposal for Cultural Democracy in the Mass Media." *Studies in Public Communications* 3 (Summer 1961): 27–35.

"Urban Vitality and the Fallacy of Physical Determinism." *Commentary* 33 (February 1962): 170–75.

"Urbanism and Suburbanism as Ways of Life: A Re-evaluation of Definitions." In *Human Behavior and Social Processes,* edited by Arnold Rose, 625–48. Boston: Houghton-Mifflin, 1962.

"Hollywood Films on British Screens: An Analysis of the Functions of American Popular Culture Abroad." *Social Problems* 9 (1962): 324–28.

"Outdoor Recreation and Mental Health." In *Trends in American Living and Outdoor Recreation,* Outdoor Recreation Resources Review Commission Study Report no. 22, 234–42. Washington, D. C.: U.S. Government Printing Office, 1962.

"Social and Physical Planning for the Elimination of Urban Poverty." *Washington University Law Quarterly* (February 1963): 2–18.

"Jewish Parody as American Popular Culture." In "Allan Sherman's Sociologist Presents." *The Reconstructionist* 29 (1963): 25–31.

"Effects of the Move from City to Suburb." (Published as *The Urban Condition*), 184–98, edited by Leonard J. Duhl. New York: Basic Books, 1963.

"Some Proposals for Government Policy in an Automating Society." *The Correspondent* 30 (January–February 1964): 74–82.

"The Rise of the Problem Film: An Analysis of Changes in Hollywood Movies and the American Audience." *Social Problems* 11 (Spring 1964): 327–36.

"Planning for the Everyday Life and Problems of the Average Suburban and New Town Resident." Mimeograph, Planning Work Group, The Rouse Company. Columbia, Maryland, February 1964. Published in *People and Plans,* New York: Basic Books, 1968.

"Redefining the Settlement's Function for the War on Poverty." *Social Work* 9 (October 1964): 3–12.

"Sex, Vitality and Skepticism: America's New Image of Britain" (published as "America's New Sexual Idols"). *Twentieth Century* (England) 173 (Autumn 1964): 86–92.

"Planning—and City Planning—for Mental Health." In *Planning* 1964, 165–84. Chicago: American Society of Planning Officials, 1964.

"The Failure of Urban Renewal: A Critique and Some Proposals." *Commentary* 39 (April 1965): 29–37.

"Controversy: Urban Renewal." *Commentary* 39 (July 1965): 77–80.

"The Negro Family: Reflections on the 'Moynihan Report'." *Commonweal* 83 (15 October 1965): 47–51.

"Some Changes in American Taste and Their Implications for the Future of Television." In *The Future of Commercial Television, 1965–1975,* edited by Stanley Donner, 35–50. Stanford, Calif.: Stanford University, Dept. of Communication, 1965.

"The New Radicalism: Sect or Political Action Movement." *Studies on the Left* (Summer 1965): 126–31.

"A Rational Approach to Radicalism." *Studies on the Left* 6 (January–February 1966): 37–46.

"Popular Culture in America: Social Problems or Social Asset in a Pluralist Society." In *Social Problems: A Modern Approach,* edited by Howard S. Becker, 549–620. New York: Wiley, 1966.

"The Federal Role in Solving America's Urban Problems." In *The Federal Role in Urban Affairs,* Hearings before the Subcommittee on Executive Reorganization ("Ribicoff Committee on the Crisis of the Cities"), Committee on Government Operations, U.S. Senate, 89th Cong., Part II, December 8, 1966, 2400–17.

"The Mass Media as an Educational Institution." *Urban Review* 2 (February 1967): 5–14. Rev. in *American Education in the Electronic Age,* edited by Peter Klinger, 58–77. Englewood Cliffs, N.J.: Educational Technology Publications, 1974.

"Urban Poverty and Social Planning." In *Uses of Sociology,* edited by P. Lazarsfeld, W. Sewell, and H. Wilensky, 437–76. New York: Basic Books, 1967.

"Social Accounting for a Democratic Society." In *Full Opportunity and Social Accounting Act of 1967*, Hearings before the Subcommittee on Government Research, U.S. Senate, 89th Cong., Part II, July 1967, 181–89.

"The Future of the Suburbs" (published as "The White Exodus to Suburbia Steps Up"). *New York Times Magazine*, 7 January 1968, 25, 85–97.

"City Planning in America: A Sociological Analysis" (Published as "Planning: Social"). *International Encyclopedia of the Social Sciences*, New York: Macmillan, 1968. Vol. 12: 129–37.

"Comparing the Immigrant and Negro Experience." Chapter 9 in *Report of the National Advisory Commission on Civil Disorders*. Washington, D.C.: Government Printing Office, March 1968.

"The Equality Revolution." *New York Times Magazine*, 3 November 1968, 36–37, 66–76.

"The Participant Observer as a Human Being: Observations on the Personal Aspects of Field Work." In *Institutions and the Person: Essays Presented to Everett C. Hughes*, edited by H. S. Becker, et. al., 300–17. Chicago: Aldine Pub. Co., 1968.

"Culture and Class in the Study of Poverty: An Approach to Anti-Poverty Research." In *On Understanding Poverty*, edited by Daniel P. Moynihan, 201–28. New York: Basic Books, 1969.

"Negro-Jewish Conflict in New York City: A Sociological Evaluation." *Midstream* 15 (March 1969): 3–15.

"The Urban Crisis as the Failure of American Democracy," (published as "We Won't End The Urban Crisis Until We End Majority Rule"). *New York Times Magazine*, 3 August 1969, 10–15, 20–28.

"Planning for People, Not Buildings." *Environment and Planning* (England) 1 (1969): 33–46.

"The Politics of Culture in America: A Sociological Analysis." *Communications* (France) 14 (1969): 162–71.

"TV News Selection Practices and the Depiction of American Society" (published as "How Well Does TV Present the News?"). *New York Times Magazine*, 11 January 1970, 30–45.

"Broadcaster and Audience Values in the Mass Media: The Image of Man in American Television News." In *Transactions of the 6th World Congress of Sociology* 4: 1–14. Milan: International Sociological Association, 1970.

"The Welfare Problem as the Failure of the American Economy" (published as "Three Ways to Solve the Welfare Problem"). *New York Times Magazine,* 7 March 1971, 26–27, 94–100.

"Social Science for Social Policy." In *The Use and Abuse of Social Science,* edited by Irving L. Horowitz, 13–33. New Brunswick, N.J.: Transaction Books, 1971.

"The Famine in American Mass Communications Research." *American Journal of Sociology* 77 (January 1972): 697–705.

"The American Malaise." *New York Times Magazine,* 6 February 1972, 16–17, 24–34.

"The Positive Functions of Poverty." *American Journal of Sociology* 78 (September 1972): 275–89. (An earlier version appeared as "The Uses of Poverty." *Social Policy* 2 [July–August 1971]: 20–24.)

"The Journalistic Sociology of Vance Packard" (published as "Vance Packard Misperceives the Way Most Americans Live"). *Psychology Today* 6 (September 1972): 20–28.

"The Possibilities of Class and Racial Integration in American New Towns: A Policy-Oriented Analysis." In *New Towns: Why and For Whom,* edited by H. I. Perloff and N. C. Sandberg, 137-59. New York: Praeger, 1973.

"The Integration of Social Policy, Social Planning, and Community Organization in Social Work: An Outsider's Perspective." In *Dilemmas of Social Work Leadership,* edited by C. Grosser and G. Goldberg, 19–38. New York: Council on Social Work Education, 1974.

"The Housing Allowance, Housing Policy and Urban Poverty," (published as "A Poor Man's Home is His Poorhouse"). *New York Times Magazine.* 31 March 1974, 20, 49–54, 58.

"The Role of Education in the Escape from Poverty," In *Education, Inequality and National Policy,* edited by N. F. Ashline, T. R. Pezzullo, and C. I. Norris, 61–72. Lexington, Mass.: Lexington Books, 1976.

"Jobs and Services: Toward a Labor-Intensive Economy." *Challenge* 20 (July/August 1977): 41–45.

"Democracy and the Arts: Adversary or Ally." In *Arts in a Democratic Society,* edited by Dennis A. Mann, 98–117. Bowling Green, Ohio: Popular Press, 1977.

"Toward a Human Architecture: A Sociologist's View of the Profession." *Journal of Architectural Education* 31, no. 2 (1978): 26–31. Rev. in *Professionals and Urban Form,* edited by J. R. Blau, M. LaGory, and J. S. Pipkin, 303–19. Albany, N.Y.: SUNY Press, 1983.

"Symbolic Ethnicity: The Future of Ethnic Groups and Cultures in

America." *Ethnic and Racial Studies* 2 (January 1979): 1–20. Exp. in *On the Making of Americans: Essays in Honor of David Riesman,* edited by H. Gans, N. Glazer, J. Gusfield, and C. Jencks, 193–220. Philadelphia: Univ. of Pennsylvania Press, 1979.

"The Audience for Television—and in Television Research." In *Television and Social Behavior,* edited by S. B. Withey and R. P. Abeles, 55–81. Hillsdale, N.J.: L. Erlbaum Associates, 1980.

"The Future of Poverty: The Possibilities of Egalitarian Social Policy in the 1980s." *Dissent* (Winter 1980): 40–46. Exp. in "Social Justice Revisited." *Politics* (Australia) 16 (May 1981): 46–56.

"Design and the Consumer: The Sociology and Culture of 'Good Design'." In *Design Since 1945,* edited by K. B. Hiesinger and G. H. Marcus, 31–36. Philadelphia: Philadelphia Museum of Art, 1983.

"American Urban Theories and Urban Areas: Some Observations on Contemporary Ecological and Marxist Paradigms." In *Cities in Recession,* edited by Ivan Szelenyi, 278–308. Beverly Hills, Calif.: Sage Publications, 1984.

"Toward the Thirty-Two Hour Work-Week." *Social Policy* 15 (Winter 1984–85): 58–61.

"American Popular Culture and High Culture in a Changing Class Structure." In *Art, Ideology and Politics,* edited by J. Balfe and M. Wyszomiriski, 40–57. New York: Praeger, 1985. Exp. in *Prospects* 10 (1985) 17–37.

"Are U.S. Journalists Dangerously Liberal?" *Columbia Journalism Review* 24 (November–December 1985): 29–33.

"Sociology in America: The Discipline and the Public." (American Sociological Association: The 1988 Presidential Address.) *American Sociological Review* 54 (February 1989): 1–16.

"Bystanders as Opinion Makers: A Bottoms Up Perspective." *Gannett Center Journal* 3 (Spring 1989): 97–104.

"Relativism, Equality and Popular Culture." In *Authors of Their Own Lives: Intellectual Autobiographies by Twenty American Sociologists,* edited by Bennett M. Berger, 432–51. Berkeley: University of California Press, 1990.

"Deconstructing the Underclass: The Term's Dangers as a Planning Concept." *Journal of the American Planning Association* 55 (Summer 1990): 271–77.

"Planning for Worksharing: Toward Egalitarian Worktime Reduction." In

The Nature of Work, edited by K. Erikson and S. P. Vallas, 258–76. New Haven, Conn.: Yale University Press, 1990.

"Second-Generation Decline: Scenarios for the Economic and Ethnic Futures of the Post–1965 American Immigrants." *Ethnic and Racial Studies* (April 1992): 173–92.

"Ethnic Invention and Acculturation: A Bumpy-Line Approach." *Journal of American Ethnic History* 12 (Fall 1992): 42–52.

"The High Rise Fallacy." *Design Quarterly* 157 (Fall 1992): 24–29.

"The Positive Functions of the Undeserving Poor: The Uses of the Underclass in America." *Koelner Zeitschrift fuer Soziologie und Sozialpsychologie,* Sonderheft 32 (1992): 48–62. Rev. in *Politics and Society* 22 (September 1994): 269–83.

"Sociological Amnesia: The Non-Cumulation of Normal Social Science." *Sociological Forum* 7 (December 1992): 701–10.

"Varieties of American Ideological Spectra." *Social Research* 60 (Fall 1993): 513–29.

"Reopening the Black Box: Towards a Limited-Effects Theory of the Mass Media." *Journal of Communication* 43 (Autumn 1993): 29–35.

"Time for an Employees' Lobby." *Social Policy* 24 (Winter 1993): 35–38.

"Symbolic Ethnicity and Symbolic Religiosity: Toward a Comparison of Ethnic and Religious Acculturation." *Ethnic and Racial Studies* 17 (October 1994): 577–92.

"Epilogue to 'Symbolic Ethnicity (1979)'." In *Theories of Ethnicity: A Classical Reader,* edited by Werner Sollors, 452–59. London: Macmillan, 1996.

"Best-Sellers by Sociologists: An Exploratory Study." *Contemporary Sociology* 26 (March 1997): 131–35. Rev. in *Required Reading,* edited by Daniel Clawson. Amherst, MA: University of Massachusetts Press, 1998.

"What Can Journalists Actually Do for American Democracy?" *Harvard International Journal of Press/Politics* 3 (Fall 1998): 6–13.

"Toward a Reconsideration of 'Assimilation' and 'Pluralism'; The Interplay of Acculturation and Ethnic Retention." *International Migration Review* 31, (Winter 1997): 875–92. Rev. and exp. in *Becoming American,* edited by C. Hirschman, J. DeWind, and P. Kasinitz. New York: Russell Sage Foundation, 1999.

"The Possibility of a New Racial Hierarchy in the 21st Century United States." In *Cultural Territories of Race,* edited by Michelle Lamont. Chicago: University of Chicago Press and New York: Russell Sage Foundation, 1999.

About the Author

Herbert J. Gans was born in Germany and came to the United States in 1940. Educated at the University of Chicago and the University of Pennsylvania, he was trained both as a sociologist and a planner. After working in and teaching planning for some years, he became a professor in Columbia University's sociology department, where he had been since 1971. He is the author of nine other books, his first being *Urban Villagers,* written in 1962, and of over 160 academic and general articles. He has served as president both of the Eastern Sociological Society and the American Sociological Association.